Behavioral Assessment
and Rehabilitation of the
Traumatically Brain-Damaged

APPLIED CLINICAL PSYCHOLOGY

Series Editors: Alan S. Bellack, *Medical College of Pennsylvania at EPPI,*
Philadelphia, Pennsylvania, and Michel Hersen, *University of Pittsburgh, Pittsburgh,*
Pennsylvania

A Continuation Order Plan is available for this series. A continuation order will bring delivery of
each new volume immediately upon publication. Volumes are billed only upon actual shipment.
For further information please contact the publisher.

Behavioral Assessment and Rehabilitation of the Traumatically Brain-Damaged

Edited by

Barry A. Edelstein

West Virginia University
Morgantown, West Virginia

and

Eugene T. Couture

Camarillo State Hospital
Camarillo, California

Plenum Press • New York and London

Library of Congress Cataloging in Publication Data

Main entry under title:

Behavioral assessment and rehabilitation of the traumatically brain-damaged.

   (Applied clinical psychology)
   Bibliography: p.
   Includes index.
   I. Brain damage—Patients—Rehabilitation—Addresses, essays, lectures. 2.
Behavioral assessment—Addresses, essays, lectures. 3. Neuropsychology—Addresses,
essays, lectures. I. Edelstein, Barry A., 1945–   . II. Couture, Eugene T., 1947–
III. Series. [DNLM: 1. Brain injuries—In adulthood. 2. Brain injuries—Rehabilitation.
WL 354 B419]
RC387.5.B44   1983   617′.481   83-22973
ISBN 0-306-41295-0

© 1984 Plenum Press, New York
A Division of Plenum Publishing Corporation
233 Spring Street, New York, N.Y. 10013

Printed in the United States of America

I dedicate this book to my wife and son, whose forbearance allowed me to complete this volume and my dissertation at the same time.

E. C.

I dedicate this book to the memory of Jack (Big John) Germas, a wonderful friend and dedicated psychologist.

B. E.

Contributors

Sara Averbuch • Loewenstein Rehabilitation Hospital, Ra'anana, Israel, and University of Tel Aviv, Sackler School of Medicine, Tel Aviv, Israel

Betty Elazar • Loewenstein Rehabilitation Hospital, Ra'anana, Israel, and University of Tel Aviv, Sackler School of Medicine, Tel Aviv, Israel

Charles Golden • Nebraska Psychiatric Institute, The University of Nebraska Medical Center, Omaha, Nebraska

Gerald Goldstein • Veterans Administration Medical Center, Highland Drive, Pittsburgh, Pennsylvania, and Department of Psychiatry, University of Pittsburgh, Pittsburgh, Pennsylvania

Jordan Grafman • Vietnam Head Injury Study, Department of Clinical Investigation, Walter Reed Army Medical Center, Washington, D.C.

William J. Haffey • Neuropsychology Service, Casa Colina Hospital for Rehabilitative Medicine, Pomona, California

Louise Kent-Udolf • Education Service Center, Region II, Corpus Christi, Texas

William J. Lynch • Brain Injury Rehabilitation Unit, Veterans Administration Medical Center, Palo Alto, California

James Malec • Psychiatric and Behavioral Medicine, Mount Sinai Medical Center, Milwaukee, Wisconsin

Craig A. Muir • Neuropsychology Service, Casa Colina Hospital for Rehabilitative Medicine, Pomona, California

Theodore Najenson • Loewenstein Rehabilitation Hospital, Ra'anana, Israel, and University of Tel Aviv, Sackler School of Medicine, Tel Aviv, Israel

Levy Rahmani • Loewenstein Rehabilitation Hospital, Ra'anana, Israel, and University of Tel Aviv, Sackler School of Medicine, Tel Aviv, Israel

Mitchell Rosenthal • Department of Rehabilitation Medicine, Tufts University School of Medicine, Boston, Massachusetts

Erica M. Sufrin • Department of Psychiatry, Albany Medical College, Albany, New York, and Department of Psychology, Russell Sage College, Troy, New York

Preface

This book developed out of the editors' longstanding interest in the retraining of traumatically brain-damaged adults and the management of their behavior by family members. A search for relevant experimental evidence to support the clinical use of behavioral principles for retraining, which began in 1977, turned up little empirical support. Moreover, the literature on retraining was dispersed among a variety of journals published in various countries. Nowhere was there a compendium of literature that addressed issues of assessment and retraining. There was no place to turn if one wanted to move from a standard neuropsychological evaluation to the retraining of skill deficits revealed in the evaluation. We have attempted to edit a book that represents what we had hoped to find in the literature and could be used by professionals in clinical psychology, clinical neuropsychology, rehabilitation medicine, physical therapy, speech therapy, and other disciplines that address rehabilitation of brain-damaged adults—a book that addresses assessment and rehabilitation issues and is sufficiently detailed to offer the reader a starting point in developing behavioral assessment and rehabilitation programs. The book contains conceptual foundations, reviews of research, descriptions of successful rehabilitation programs, and relatively detailed approaches to the retraining of specific skills.

A shift from an assessment-based practice to one encompassing both prescriptive assessment and treatment has become a recognized transition in the neuropsychological literature and was best articulated in an article by Gerald Goldstein in March of 1979. Goldstein's chapter describes some of the problems and the promise of the relationship between behavior therapists and neuropsychologists. He outlines some of the philosophical differences in both professionals' approach to brain damage and suggests areas of integration and possible gain for both. He goes on to note the beginnings of a behavioral technology for cognitive, perceptual, and motor retraining for brain-damaged individuals. He also notes that the behavior modification techniques that have been so successfully applied in the habilitation of the congenitally brain-damaged have yet to be shown to be effective in the rehabilitation of the traumatically brain damaged. It seems appropriate to begin this book with Goldstein's chapter and to follow it with the beginnings of the demonstration of effectiveness that he so appropriately sought.

Louise Kent-Udolf's chapter presents a comprehensive introduction to functional language in brain-injured persons. Functional language is defined as the "degree to which the patient is able to get his messages across to others, and how well she/he is able to understand the messages directed to them by others" in the natural environment. She first presents the specific speech disorders in some detail, discussing prognoses, and points out that while speech may be impaired or precluded, functional communication may continue, especially if appropriately timed and structured therapy is provided. Various methods of assessment and general evaluation strategies are then presented; the tests of functional language are highlighted. This discussion leads to the presentation of treatment strategies, including methods of recording and data collection and specific strategies for teaching functional language. Throughout the chapter, Kent-Udolf presents sufficient detail to clarify the matter at hand; she then directs the readers to specific references for further study.

One of the newest, and in some ways more controversial, of the assessment and rehabilitation tools in neuropsychology is the Luria-Nebraska Neuropsychological Battery (LNB), which is presented here by Charles Golden. He discusses the theoretical basis for the battery and briefly reviews the supporting theoretical work of Luria, referring the reader to other works for further detail. The development and rationale for the LNB is then outlined, including some of the most recent reliability and validity research. Golden next discusses how to interpret the battery and how rehabilitation goals and approaches may be suggested by the neuropsychological information. Specific case materials are used to illustrate rehabilitation planning using the LNB.

James Malec's chapter is predicated on the idea that many of the functional deficits seen in brain-injured adults are the result of impaired and therefore inadequate self-regulatory skills. If the brain-damaged person is unable to self-monitor the antecedents and consequences of a sequence of behavior, then the person will be unable to regulate the sequence, and it will probably become dysfunctional. If an appropriate educational program can be developed to circumvent these disruptions in self-regulation, the disrupted self-management skills may be learned or relearned by the brain-damaged individual. Malec goes on to present a neuropsychological rationale for this position derived from the works of Luria and others. He then demonstrates, in several case studies, the techniques and procedures used in a self-management approach to the rehabilitation of brain-damaged adults.

In a related vein, Jordon Grafman's chapter describes, in theory and practice, a cognitive-behavioral approach to the assessment and remediation of memory deficits in amnesic brain damaged patients. First, a review of the pertinent literature in human information processing is presented. The author goes on to suggest an integrated neuropsychological and information-processing model of memory to guide research and treatment. He then presents, in some detail, a data-based memory retraining program, flowing from his earlier synthesis, that is now in operation. Finally, he comments on proposed revisions in that program and suggests guidelines for future research in the area.

Erica Sufrin reviews the all-too-brief literature on the use of behavioral principles with the elderly, especially as they relate to physical rehabilitation of the brain-damaged. She presents an overview of the sensorimotor changes that can be expected in the average elderly population (e.g., decreased auditory and visual acuity, etc.) and notes useful techniques for treatment personnel to use in overcoming these limitations. Some of the evidence suggesting that behavioral techniques could be useful with the brain-damaged elderly is then presented. Finally, Sufrin reviews her own successful research into the area of behavioral engineering in rehabilitation programming for the brain-damaged elderly.

Mitchell Rosenthal's chapter describes strategies for intervention with families of brain-injured patients, a topic that has received little attention in the literature. Rosenthal discusses the relationship between specific deficits of the brain-injured patients and the family, describes certain families that are in greatest need for family intervention, and finally discusses various types of family intervention techniques. Case illustrations are provided for each intervention approach.

An integration of the systems approach to trauma and a behavioral-neuropsychological approach to brain damage is presented in the chapter by Craig Muir and William Haffey. They draw on their experiences at the Case Colina Hospital for Rehabilitative Medicine, systems theorists, the works of Luria and other neuropsychologists, and the literature on death and the mourning process to explain the unique impact of traumatic brain damage on the individual and the family system. They have developed the concept of mobile mourning—that is, the mourning of a loss that remains in a state of flux as the extent of the brain damage and the success of the rehabilitation process gradually become known. Techniques are then suggested that recognize and make use of the family system in the different phases of the mobile mourning process, integrating neuropsychological information, and building a behavioral retraining program for the brain-damaged individual. Muir and Haffey illustrate their approach with case material relevant to each theoretical point.

The chapter written by William Lynch reviews the operation of the Brain Injury Rehabilitation Unit (BIRU) located at the Palo Alto Veterans Administration Hospital. He describes the measurement systems selected for use at the BIRU at intake, discharge, and follow-up as well as the methods used to organize the resulting data into a coherent problem list. He then goes on to present the unit's treatment strategies, including the involvement of the patient's family, and presents some data to illustrate the success rate of the BIRU. Finally, Lynch discusses the opportunities that, in his opinion, are likely to open up in the future in the treatment of the brain-damaged elderly.

Theodore Najenson and his colleagues present a second program for brain-damaged veterans located at the Loewenstein Rehabilitation Hospital, Ra'anana, Israel. The authors have developed a program in the occupational therapy department that involves both cognitive and perceptual-motor retraining. They describe their assessment battery and discuss the factors that have emerged over many cases from their data. Some of their treatment techniques, with illustrative case histories, are presented.

Contents

Chapter 3

Rehabilitation and the Luria-Nebraska Neuropsychological
Battery: Introduction to Theory and Practice 83
Charles Golden

Chapter 4

Training the Brain-Injured Client in Behavioral Self-Management
Skills 121
James Malec

Chapter 7

Strategies for Intervention with Families of Brain-Injured
Patients.. 227
Mitchell Rosenthal

1

Methodological and Theoretical Issues in Neuropsychological Assessment

GERALD GOLDSTEIN

1. Introduction

Parsons and Prigatano (1978) have written an article entitled "Methodological Considerations in Clinical Neuropsychological Research," and the reader is referred to it for an excellent review of many of the problems of design and data analysis in clinical neuropsychology. We will attempt to deal with other issues here. Neuropsychological assessment is the attempt to relate behavioral deficits to underlying brain dysfunction, generally through the use of psychometric and other examinational procedures known as neuropsychological tests. Some investigators would view neuropsychological testing as an extension of the neurological examination, with an emphasis on the so-called higher functions of the nervous system. Clinical neuropsychologists, as opposed to human neuropsychologists in general, are particularly interested in the application of scientific findings in the area of brain–behavior relations to diagnosis and evaluation of patients. This application occurs in three major areas: diagnostic evaluation, assessment of impaired and preserved functions, and rehabilitation planning.

GERALD GOLDSTEIN • Veterans Administration Medical Center, Highland Drive, Pittsburgh, Pennsylvania 15206 and Department of Psychiatry, University of Pittsburgh, Pittsburgh, Pennsylvania, 15213.

In other words, the procedures are commonly used to determine whether or not an individual has a brain lesion, to delineate what the defects and preserved abilities associated with the lesion are, and to plan a program of treatment or rehabilitation based on the obtained pattern of deficits and assets.

Clinical neuropsychology may be viewed as a field at odds with certain aspects of behaviorism in general and with the behaviorist influence on clinical psychology in particular. While one might question the value of putting forth a proposed reconciliation between two schools of thought, particularly since the reconciliation between behaviorism and psychoanalysis attempted during the 1940s and 1950s (Dollard & Miller, 1950) did not appear to lead to much, we will nevertheless make a similar attempt here. The only excuse we have for doing so is that there have already been several productive alliances between behavior therapists and clinical neuropsychologists, so it is possible that any general reconciliation made may have significant practical as well as theoretical value.

2. Relationships between Behaviorism and Neuropsychology

The emphasis of behaviorist theory on observable stimulus–response relationships and on the rejection of the need to seek underlying mechanisms at the psychodynamic or physiological levels is well known. At one time it was quite an extreme view, as represented in Boring's assertion, "Science does not consider private data" (1945). This point of view within psychology was often taken to mean that psychologists should work at a purely behavioral level and ignore "variables operating beneath the skin." We heard a great deal about the "black box" into which it was not deemed necessary to look. As Skinner succinctly put it, "The study of human behavior need not be described in physiological terms" (1950). Psychologists were viewed from the behaviorist side as students of behavior and not of physiology, biochemistry, or neurology. Furthermore, they were also scientists and so were compelled to work with what was objective and observable. Private events and subjective states tended to be rejected as uninvestigable scientifically. The issues involved here are thoroughly reviewed in a chapter by Hefferline (1962).

Neuropsychologists have tended to follow a position perhaps most strongly stated by Hebb (1958), who has been sharply critical of the antiphysiological bias of behaviorism. We need say no more than the following quotation:

> For their part, psychologists too often fail to keep themselves informed about
> what goes on in the neurological field, and in defense of such ignorance, too
> often deny that it has any relevance for their work—a position so pre-
> posterous and indefensible that it is hard to attack. (Hebb, 1958, p. 451)

In Hebb's tradition, other psychologists such as Hans-Lukas Teuber, Brenda Milner, Ward Halstead, and Ralph Reitan, all in their own ways, have made major efforts to relate behavior to brain function, primarily through research with brain-damaged patients. The lines would appear to be sharply drawn. However, the issue between behaviorism and neuropsychology is not centered around objectivism vs. subjectivism. It is not about the issues dividing the "hard-nosed" as against the "soft-headed." Rather, it has more to do with whether neuropsychological theories of behavior are of more heuristic value than behavioral theories, granted that both approaches are impeccable in regard to scientific methodology.

It is to be hoped that we now live in an era of science in which it is no longer fashionable to provide gratuitous advice concerning what course will lead to the most significant and rigorous theory. Psychology has apparently gone through an age of polemics in which various "schools" took issue with one another on a rather broad front. In the case of neuropsychology and behaviorism, it is now apparent that some psychologists continue to seek relationships between the brain and behavior, while others are content to pursue their interests in further discovery concerning the laws and principles of behavior itself. There has, in fact, been a great deal of mellowing, as a result of which attempts have been made to build bridges between behavioral theory and neuropsychological concepts (e.g., Wickelgren, 1979). Human neuropsychologists have also used methods developed within the framework of behaviorist learning theory to investigate certain functions in brain-damaged patients (e.g., Butters & Cermak, 1976). If one may interpret this historical development, it is possible that extensive investigation of brain function over many years turned the brain into less of the mysterious "black box" than it appeared as in earlier times. On the other hand, students of human brain function became dissatisfied with the subjectivism and lack of rigor characteristic of their clinical investigations and looked toward behavior theory as a guide to methodological improvement of neuropsychology as a science. Thus one aspect of the reconciliation may have been in the possibility of objective study of brain function.

Another problem has to do with the data and theory languages of behaviorism and neuropsychology. Behaviorists use terms like "frequency," "number of reinforced trails," "delay of reinforcement," "re-

sponse latency," and the like to describe their data. While neuropsychologists may use the same terms, their theoretical constructs are of
a different nature. While some forms of behaviorism profess to be completely atheoretical, those who use theories employ intervening variables or concepts that relate sets of independent and dependent variables. Thus habit $(_sH_r)$ would be an intervening variable in Hull's system
used to relate response parameters to number of reinforced trials, length
of deprivation, and other independent variables. In neuropsychology,
the focus is on the brain with regard to independent and intervening
variables. Thus the experimental neuropsychologist might ablate a portion of an animal's brain and attempt to relate this procedure to alterations in behavior. Clinical neuropsychologists depend on accidents of
nature for this purpose and typically contrast patients with localized
brain lesions instead of animals with surgically generated lesions. While
the intervening variables of behavior theory may or may not have "exis-
tential referents" (Koch, 1954), neuropsychological theories in general
always tend to use such referents. Thus their intervening variables tend
to be hypothetical constructs, utilizing the distinction originally made by
MacCorquodale and Meehl (1948). The language of these constructs is
generally physiological or chemical in nature. Hebb (1955, 1958) takes
the position that the constructs of neuropsychology should be basically
psychological; that is, they should be aimed at explaining complex behavior. However, he encourages "physiologizing," suggesting that
physiological psychology represents an attempt to form physiological
hypotheses about the intervening variables of psychology in general. He
uses his own concept, the "phase-sequence," as an example of a psychological conception somewhat consistent with physiological and anatomical data. Perhaps "inhibition" and "memory trace" are some of the
more commonly used constructs in neuropsychology. In recent times,
one of the more original and powerful theoretical constructs was proposed by Pribram (1971, 1979), who suggests that neural representations
in the brain have the characteristics of holograms or physical processes
based on optical interference effects. They are thought to be of the type
seen in physical holograms, which allow for reconstructions having all
the visual properties of the original object. It would therefore appear
that while behaviorists and neuropsychologists may use the same dependent variables (e.g., response latency), they use quite different independent variables and theoretical constructs. These differences in regard
to the domains from which variables are derived almost necessarily lead
to explanations of behavior that may be quite diverse. Thus, for example, neuropsychologists may explain agression on the basis of stimulation or ablation of some central nervous system structure, while behav-

ior theorists may use the reinforcement history as an explanatory variable. Both of these views may be completely supportable on the basis of empirical data, and both explanations may be in some sense true. The question becomes one of preferred level of explanation. It would appear that the reconciliation regarding this matter must be on a practical rather than a theoretical level. Obviously, there will continue to be behaviorally oriented and neurologically oriented psychological theory formation. The problem becomes one of determining which type of theory is more useful in particular situations. One situation in which the two approaches would clearly converge is in the clinical assessment and management of brain-damaged patients. In the case of such patients, it is generally abundantly clear that a neurological variable has great relevance to alterations seen in behavior, but, on the other hand, purely behavioral methods may provide highly effective assessment and treatment methods.

There is still a remaining issue, perhaps more subtle in nature than the others. There has traditionally been a strong association between behavior theory and learning or environmentalism. The early behavior theorists such as Hull, Thorndike, Skinner, and Tolman were also known as learning theorists. For advocates of behaviorism, the terms "learning theory" and "behavior theory" seemed to be almost interchangeable. Thus a great deal of the experimental research had to do with demonstrations of altering behavior under various conditions. On the other hand, neuropsychologists and clinical neuropsychologists in particular took quite a different course. Traditionally, what they did was study patients with brain lesions in known locations in order to describe the behaviors associated with those lesions. For example, perhaps the first finding of modern clinical neuropsychology is Broca's discovery that a lesion in the area of the third convolution of the left frontal lobe is associated with impairment of the ability to speak (Broca, 1861). Many neuropsychologists continue to focus their research on this issue of the relationship between site of structural damage and consequent alterations of behavior rather than on the role of experience in determining behavior. More broadly speaking, some neuropsychologists have attempted to develop comprehensive behavior theories based on studies of brain function (Goldstein, 1939; Halstead, 1947; Luria, 1973; Pribram, 1971), while behaviorally oriented psychologists have attempted to develop equally comprehensive theories based primarily on experiments in learning. It is not being maintained here that neuropsychologists are not interested in learning and do not do learning related research. However, they tend to be largely interested in the neural basis for learning as well as for other behaviors such as perception and attention. Thus they do not give learning the primacy characteristically associated with behavior theory. It would appear that the major issue here relates to the dual issue of the primacy of learning and the desirability of basing a comprehensive behavior theory on learning related concepts.

Reconciliation in this area must again be a pragmatic one. Behavioral science theory will continue to have its neuropsychological advocates such as Luria (1973) and Pribram (1971) as well as its behavioral advocates, perhaps best represented in contemporary times by Skinner (1953). The pertinent point would seem to be that, in any particular case, neurological or purely behavioral considerations may be most salient. For example, in the famous case of H. M. (Milner, 1966), it is quite clear that the bilateral surgical removal of the hippocampi was the major issue with regard to producing the patient's memory disorder. On the other hand, there are doubtless numerous cases of memory difficulties in which environmental–learning factors are the major considerations. The practical resolution here is essentially a clinical one in which caution must be exercised in not allowing one's biases to unduly influence decision making. Thus, to use an extreme example, it would be unproductive to conceptualize H. M.'s difficulty in terms of history of reinforcement, while it would be equally unproductive to attribute recondite neurological deficit to an ostensibly neurologically normal individual whose behavioral deviations can be reasonably attributed to environmental considerations. In principle, one could argue that all behavior must have a biological substrate and, conversely, that no behavior is totally determined by biological conditions alone. However, such arguments tend to lose their potency in individual cases in which either biological or environmental factors are clearly more salient.

In summary, it has been indicated that neuropsychological and behavioral theories differ from each other in three respects: (1) Behaviorally oriented psychologists may be at least in part characterized by their programs to build theories at a purely behavioral level, while neuropsychologists have attempted to build brain models for the purpose of relating brain function to behavior. (2) Behaviorists generally use environmental manipulation as their source of independent variables, while neuropsychologists directly manipulate brain function or use accidents of nature to achieve such manipulation. Thus surgical or chemical alteration of the brain in animal studies or naturally occurring brain lesions in human studies are the major independent variable sources. (3) Behaviorists tend to stress the significance of learning and experience in their theories of behavior. While neuropsychologists are often quite interested in learning and experience, they tend not to give it the same degree of primacy either in theory construction or in research content.

It was suggested that newly developed objective methods of studying brain function, selecting independent variables on the basis of the particular application at hand and judicious determination as to whether experience or brain-related considerations are more pertinent to explaining the behavior observed, may contribute to some degree of reconciliation between behavior theory and neuropsychology, particularly in regard to clinical and educational applications. The issues involved in this discussion are well summarized in the following passage written by Pribram (1971):

> Over the past half century subjective experience has rarely been admitted as a legitimate field for scientific inquiry. Instead, the focus of study has been instrumental or verbal behavior *per se*. This approach has been generally successful in quantitatively delineating environmental variables that influence behavior, but somewhat less than successful when variables within the organism codetermine what happens. In such circumstances the data make considerably more sense when physiological as well as environmental variables are monitored. It is important to emphasize that the behavioral approach cannot, however, be dispensed with: many clinical neurologists and brain physiologists have neglected specification of relevant environmental circumstance, uncritically asserting an identity between what they observe physiologically and some psychological function. (pp. 99–100)

3. Clinical Aspects

3.1. Recovery of Function

Both neuropsychology and behavioral theory have established an area of application within clinical psychology. Thus we have the fields of clinical neuropsychology and behavioral assessment/therapy. In recent years these two subspecialities have interacted, the focus generally being the brain-damaged individual. This interaction has led to accumulation of evidence to support the proposition that brain-damaged individuals may frequently be effectively treated with some of the same classes of behavior-therapeutic procedures shown to be effective with other clinical groups. However, before defending this assertion, it is necessary to clarify the meaning of terms like "effective treatment," "recovery," "cure," and other treatment outcome descriptors in the case of individuals with brain damage. As is well known, central nervous system tissue does not regenerate and thus there is no replacement of dead neurons. However, recovery of functions mediated by such neurons prior to destruction is commonly noted. Such recovery was observed in animals many years ago by Lashley (1933), who found that subjects with surgically destroyed areas striata recovered a brightness discrimination habit following several days of training. In reviewing this and related studies, he raised two questions that are still incompletely answered: "by what neural changes is such recovery brought about and what are the limits of recovery for any function?" (Lashley, 1933). Subsequent studies up to recent times (Stein, Rosen, & Butters, 1974) have coped with this issue and more is known now than was known during Lashley's time. However, the mechanisms and limits of recovery of function following brain damage remain incompletely understood. It is particularly interesting to note in the present context that Lashley concluded on the basis of his own and others' research that recovery occurs only after training. It would now appear on the basis of many years of research and clinical observation that there is substantial recovery of function following brain damage, particularly if the damage is traumatic in nature. Unfortunately, what Lashley did not point out is that his findings are based almost entirely on the type of traumatic brain damage produced by surgery. However, there are other forms of brain damage that are progressive in nature, and in these cases little is seen in the way of recovery of function. Such diseases as multiple sclerosis and Huntington's chorea are of this progressive type. Thus expectations concerning recovery of function generally obtain only in the case of nonprogressive brain damage.

It now seems clear at the human level that while destroyed brain cells do not regenerate, the functions in which these cells were originally involved may return to a greater or lesser extent. Such recovery may not occur or may only occur to a less than optimal extent if training is not given. Thus one important task of clinical neuropsychological assessment is that of identifying the area or areas of deficit and recommending retraining programs. An extensive presentation of how this task may be accomplished has been made by Golden (1978) and Luria (1963). In this area in particular, it becomes clear that one cannot operate at a purely behavioral level. An appreciation of the distinction between progressive and nonprogressive brain disorders is obviously crucial to rational rehabilitation planning. In one case the therapist is working with a relatively stable organism while in the other any efforts made must be programmed to cope with an inexorable decline in function. Indeed, one of the classic errors in medicine and psychology is that of providing exclusively behavioral treatment to an individual with an undetected progressive neurological condition. It is particularly tragic when the condition would have been medically treatable at an earlier state in its development.

In practical terms, recovery from brain damage does not generally connote complete restoration of function. More often than not there is a permanent reduction in the capacity of the individual to function at his or her premorbid level. A common clinical problem is that in some cases the level of aspiration does not change with the decline in function and the recovering patient may verbalize the intention or actually make the attempt to return to premorbid activities. Thus an important task of neuropsychological assessment is that of evaluating the degree of discrepancy between the patient's aspiration level and objective capacity. One of the tests used by Luria (Christensen, 1975a, b, c) is a modification of a simple memory task in which the subject is asked for free recall of a word list. However, on each trial after the first one, the subject is told how many items he remembered correctly and is then asked how many he thinks he will get right on the next trial. The degree of discrepancy between the guess and actual performance may be of great clinical significance.

The limitations of recovery from brain damage call for a relatively high degree of selectivity in the training given. Such selectivity is generally determined on a practical basis having to do with attempting to restore those abilities that are impaired and that play a major role in the patient's general adaptation. An obvious example is speech. Speech clearly plays a major role in human existence, and impaired speech produced by brain damage can have a devastating effect on adaptation. Thus the speech-impaired, or aphasic, patient often receives speech therapy in an effort to restore an optimal capacity to communicate. Such restoration often does not consist of a return to normal speech but rather of either some degree of improvement in normal speech or mastery of some system designed to communicate with others in the absence of normal speech.

Another clear example is related to the problem of memory. Certain types of brain damage produce major deficits in the ability to remember. More often than not, recent memory is more impaired than remote memory, but sometimes there is a global amnesia. The capacity of retraining methods to restore memory defects associated with brain damage is a little-explored area, but some attempts have been made. The attempt is generally accomplished through the use of mnemonic devices, as in the study of Lewinsohn, Danaher, and Kikel (1977) in which visual imagery was used to aid in restoring memory. In general, the aim of these procedures is that of teaching the patient to recall limited sets of factual material important for daily living rather than to achieve complete restoration of memory. The sudden and complete restoration of memory sometimes portrayed in fiction does not occur in the case of the brain-damaged amnesic patient. In these examples of speech and memory, it is clear that the issue of cure or recovery from the consequences of brain damage is necessarily limited, and is often aimed at practical solutions to fundamental problems of daily living.

The role of neuropsychological assessment in the rehabilitation process is that of specifying the behaviors that may serve as appropriate targets for treatment. In the following section the advantages of neuropsychological assessment as opposed to behavioral or clinical assessment will be discussed. Here, we will only note that the symptoms and syndromes associated with the large number of conditions that come under the general heading of brain damage are often quite specific and complex.

3.2. Types of Assessment

The history of assessment in psychology is characterized by controversy and rapid change. It may now be seen as having gone full cycle from clinical examination and the interview through refined quantitative and qualitative evaluation, and back to the more clinical methods. It may be instructive to think in terms of overlapping historical eras in organizing this history. The era of exclusively clinical evaluation merged into the era of psychometrics or mental testing. Concurrent with developments in psychoanalysis, the projective tests emerged, but dissatisfaction with various features of these techniques rekindled an interest in objective tests and some manifestations of a return to psychometrics. A number of developments in clinical psychology then led to an "antitesting" era during which the whole process of formal assessment was criticized in some quarters. Soon, however, it became apparent that this movement represented something of an overreaction, and that some form of assessment is needed, but the perception of this need did not lead to a widespread return to the projective techniques or objective tests. Rather, it appears to have led to a number of new developments, some revolving around the structured interview, some around what is now known as behavioral assessment and some around single-subject research (Bellack & Hersen, 1978). It is clear that these new developments, while in some way resembling the old clinical interview and case history methodology, really have little similarity to the older methods. The interview and other assessment techniques have benefited significantly from numerous developments in the behavioral sciences, and have achieved a high degree of quantification and objectivity.

This cursory history is offered primarily for the purpose of contrasting it with developments in neuropsychological assessment. While significant changes have occurred in this area, they are of a different nature from what happened in the case of general psychological assessment. The upshot of these developments is that, in contrast to assessment in general, many clinical neuropsychologists continue to maintain a psychometric orientation. Put simply, they still give tests, and these tests are generally expected to have the traditional psychometric virtues of validity, reliability, and adequate standardization. In general, clinical neuropsychologists never developed significant research interests in the interview or in the projective tests. Even such strong advocates of individualized clinical assessments as Luria (1973) are increasingly having their work "psychometrized" (Christensen, 1975a, b, c; Golden, Hammeke, & Purisch, 1978). If one were to make a prediction, it would be that clinical neuropsychology will become increasingly objective and psychometrically oriented. Some neuropsychologists might object to characterizing what they do as "psychometric testing" (Luria & Majovski, 1977), but we are using the term in its broadest sense, including a number of methodological approaches that may be described on a continuum ranging from "clinical investigation" to "laboratory procedure." The essential point is that neuropsychologists have not found the interview, no matter how tightly structured, or behavior observation, no matter how systematically accomplished, to be adequate and complete assessment methods. It is interesting to note that many clinicians who have tended to eschew the use of psychological tests in general, continue to use "tests for brain damage." It is our view that there is a rational basis for this phenomenon, which we will present briefly in what follows.

Neuropsychological assessment is, in essence, the assessment of cognitive, perceptual, and motor (CPM) abilities. This association did not develop because clinical neuropsychologists lack interest in matters such as affect, motivation, interpersonal relations, and social behavior. It emerged because most of the consequences of brain damage appear to lie in the CPM realm. Thus the best diagnostic tests for the presence of brain damage have historically been CPM tests. Attempts at diagnosing brain damage with personality tests have tended to be unsuccessful, while attempts with CPM tests have often been quite successful. Even the attempts to diagnose brain damage with the Rorschach test (Piotrowski, 1936; Reitan, 1955) leaned heavily on the cognitive aspects of Rorschach performance, such as organizational ability (e.g., Beck's Z) (Beck, 1944). If, as seems to be the case, CPM abilities are the most salient factors to look at in the case of the behavioral assessment of brain-damaged patients, then the question becomes one of determining the best method for evaluating such abilities. In answering this question there is a parting of the ways among neuropsychologists. There are

numerous test batteries and procedures each having their own advocates and each having their critics as well. Some of the more basic divi-
sions are discussed by Luria and Majovski (1977) in terms of differences
between American and Soviet approaches to clinical neuropsychology.
However, all clinical neuropsychologists face common methodological
and theoretical problems, and it is this common set of problems that will
be discussed here.

The first problem has to do with the complexity of the relationships
between altered brain structure or function and behavior. This complexity was convincingly illustrated in a study by Teuber (1959), who was
able to demonstrate an improvement on a test of general intelligence
(AGCT) following the sustaining of brain injury by a group of war veterans. He makes the following remark concerning this clearly puzzling
finding:

> Such results suggest either (1) a remarkable resiliency of intelligence after
> brain injury, or (2) a lack of sensitivity of psychometric tests to the presence
> of residual alterations in behavior. That the second interpretation is correct
> was shown by the outcome of numerous special tasks, presented to the same
> subjects.

Teuber's remarks get to the essence of neuropsychology: the point that
brain–behavior relationships may be exceedingly complex and not readily detectable by "talking to the patient" or utilizing standard psychological tests in a manner that lacks some rationale.

Perhaps a case example may illustrate the same point in a different
manner. A patient was observed to walk in a peculiar manner in which
he would always stay in close proximity to the right wall of the corridor
or room in which he was walking. The behavior was puzzling to the
staff, who tended to interpret it as having some significance associated
with personal meanings the patient attached to walking in unprotected
space. Neuropsychological examination of this patient revealed a condition known as a right homonymous hemianopia, half-field blindness
associated with damage to the left hemisphere of the brain. Therefore,
the patient was protecting his blind side in an adaptive manner rather
than engaging in some form of neurotic behavior. Often patients with
this condition also have speech difficulties, so they cannot report having
it, and observation of the patient in ordinary settings may not reveal the
defect. The most efficient and definitive way to detect it is through
examination of the visual fields using methods developed by neurological and neuropsychological research.

The second problem is that the neuropsychologist has a dual alle-
giance with regard to interdisciplinary relationships. Unlike clinical psychologists, who generally work primarily with psychiatrists and other

mental health specialists, neuropsychologists work with both mental health specialists and specialists in the neurological disciplines, including neurologists, neurosurgeons, and electroencephalographers. They are therefore often concerned with problems of physical health, sometimes involving seriously and critically ill patients. In these cases, diagnosis is often a crucial issue and the establishment of a neurological diagnosis frequently involves an interdisciplinary cooperative effort. Neuropsychologists are often called on to assist in localization of brain lesions or to offer a general opinion concerning the condition of the patient's brain. Typically, such assessments are done in a laboratory setting or at bedside. Thus a great deal of the literature in clinical neuropsychology is based on the study of seriously ill patients, and a great many of the methods of neuropsychology have been developed in a manner appropriate to assessment of such patients. The realities of the situation as well as empirical research findings suggest that particular tests sensitive to the condition of the brain are the best procedures we currently have for behavioral evaluations of the type of patient described here. Indeed, a neuropsychological test may be defined as a test sensitive to the condition of the brain. In effect, neuropsychological assessment may become a component of a more comprehensive neurological evaluation that might include a physical examination, an electroencephalogram, computer-augmented tomography, and other neurodiagnostic procedures. This clinical alliance between neurology and psychology should put to rest the view that the psychologist should work only at a behavioral level regardless of the context. The question of contingencies operating in the environment would appear not to be the primary consideration in the case of the seriously ill patient with brain disease.

In view of these factors, it would appear that psychometric–laboratory methodologies are currently the best approaches available for diagnosis of brain damage using behavioral methods. The complexities of brain–behavior relationships in combination with the limitations of time and space often associated with evaluations of brain-damaged patients seem to point to testing as the most practical productive approach. This position is supported by the fact that empirical research has generally attested to the validity of predictions made on the basis of neuropsychological tests in such areas as diagnosis (Klove, 1974; Russell, Neuringer, & Goldstein, 1970) and prediction of outcome (Meier, 1974). It seems clear that theoretical constructs based on underlying neurological mechanisms are crucial to prediction of the behavior of brain-damaged patients and are practical necessities in view of the interdisciplinary relationships among neuropsychologists and their medical colleagues. As we will go on to illustrate in the next section, we are not asserting that behavioral treatment is of no value with brain-damaged patients. Quite the contrary. It is being suggested that behavioral treatment based on a thorough assessment of brain function may be more productive than treatment administered without such an assessment.

4. Rehabilitation as the Interface

There is an aura of pessimism concerning brain damage. It is viewed by many as an incurable condition worthy of study but not of vigorous treatment efforts. Often the treatment of the significantly brain-damaged patient is in the nature of nursing care and reduction of demand. In discussions of rehabilitation, it is always necessary to keep in awareness the unfortunate fact that there is no cure in the medical sense for the majority of the brain disorders. However, while some brain disorders are progressive and ultimately fatal, others are nonprogressive and leave the individual with varying degrees of residual but relatively stable deficit. As indicated above, it is crucial to distinguish between these two types of disorders in order to develop a rational treatment plan. The point of making such a distinction is not that of ruling out active treatment for the patient with a progressive illness. Rather, it is for the purpose of taking into consideration the expected course of the illness in formulating the treatment plan.

In recent years, the aura of pessimism has been partially lifted, primarily through the work of three groups of investigators: A. R. Luria and his group in the Soviet Union, Leonard Diller and his associates at New York University, and a group led by Howard Gudeman at the University of Hawaii. These groups, while varying in approach, have produced concrete methods of retraining brain-damaged patients, and empirical data indicating that such training is often effective. Two books have been written in the area of neuropsychologically oriented rehabilitation of brain-damaged patients, one by Golden (1978) and the other by Luria (1948; translation published in 1963). The New York University group has written a number of articles, with their basic philosophy of rehabilitation presented in a report by Diller (1976). Despite the diversity in approach among these groups, they share an attitude of optimism in regard to hope for recovery from some of the consequences of brain damage through active, specific treatment.

The point of view that we would like to propose is that neuropsychological assessment can form a productive alliance with behavior therapy in regard to the planning, implementation, and evaluation of individual rehabilitation programs. The usual first step in this process is that of evaluating the patient with one of the several neuropsychological test batteries currently available. Such an evaluation should eventuate in a list of target defective behaviors that may be remediable. The difference between this listing and the standard neuropsychological report is that the emphasis is on rehabilitation rather than on diagnosis. Thus, while a speech discrimination defect may suggest the presence of a lesion in the left temporal lobe, it also suggests that the patient may have a potentially remediable defect in the area of speech discrimination. The question then becomes one of how to treat it. Here the behavior therapist may become involved in the process of seeking an appropriate reinforcer and reinforcement schedule. Often the framework for the treatment may be in the form of a single-subject design study. When the reinforcer and reinforcement schedule are selected, the program is implemented and its effectiveness can be evaluated within the context of the experiment. Thus a return to baseline or multiple-baseline design may be employed to determine whether or not the treatment worked.

The beginnings of an educational technology for cognitive, perceptual, and motor retraining of brain-damaged patients has emerged. There is a chapter on rehabilitation techniques in Golden's book (1978), and the NYU group has written a number of articles devoted to this matter (Diller, Buxbaum, & Chiotelis, 1972; Ben-Yishay, Diller, Mandleberg, Gordon, & Gerstman, 1971; Ben-Yishay, Diller, & Mandleberg, 1970; Ben-Yishay, Gerstman, Diller, & Haas, 1970). Such retraining deals with such contents as visual–spatial relationships, motor skills, deployment of attention, memory, and academic skills such as reading and calculation. Research evaluations of these retraining efforts have been generally positive and suggest, contrary to traditional beliefs, that relearning is possible at least in patients with relatively nonprogressive brain damage. It is our belief that even greater effectiveness can be achieved when a firmer alliance develops between neuropsychologists and behavior therapists. The question of whether or not the behavior modification techniques that have been so effective in psychiatric and educational applications will work with brain-damaged patients remains basically unanswered. This question is a major theoretical one for neuropsychology, because if behavior therapy does in fact work it will become necessary to rethink some of our basic assumptions involving brain–behavior relationships. If it is found that, under the proper conditions of reinforcement and training, behaviors thought to be permanently impaired because of damage to certain structures in the brain recover, there is clearly more plasticity in the system than was originally imagined. One could view this speculation as over-optimistic except for the fact that evidence is accumulating that retraining programs for the brain-damaged are effective. Even if this training simply provides prostheses that help the patient get around the deficit, such efforts would clearly still be worthwhile, and furthermore would still challenge the more static views concerning relations between brain and behavior. If, for example, it is assumed that patients with significant degrees of brain damage are incapable of new learning, one might wonder about how they learn to use prostheses.

The matter of reinforcement is also of concern. Some brain-damaged patients are quite aware of their defects and need little in the way of external reinforcement to sustain the desired behavior. However, particularly in the case of more impaired individuals with lesions that have particular implications for motivation (such as limbic system lesions), some external reinforcer may often be desirable. One difficulty with regard to rehabilitation of brain-damaged patients has been selection of appropriate reinforcers. Types of reinforcement that are effective with children, the mentally retarded, or psychiatric patients may not be effective with or appropriate for brain-damaged patients. The issues this problem raises are complex and can be discussed only briefly here. There are basically three problems. First, severely brain-damaged patients are often too intellectually impaired to deal with secondary reinforcers. Thus such devices as tokens may have no meaning to them. Second, neural structures and systems that mediate reinforcement may be impaired or destroyed. Finally, a number of situational factors may affect the viability of various reinforcers. For example, it is often not possible to arrange the conditions of deprivation that foster the effectiveness of token economy programs (Hersen, 1976) as they are typically applied to psychiatric patients. Health reasons may discourage the use of tobacco and certain foods as reinforcers. The general availability of money to the client may weight against its use as a reinforcer. It would thus appear that if an external reinforcer is to be used in rehabilitating a brain-damaged patient it must be an individualized matter in which matters of cognitive, physiological, health, and psychosocial natures need to be considered.

The treatment of the patient with progressive brain damage requires special comment. Once it is determined that the patient has multiple sclerosis, Alzheimer's disease, Huntington's chorea, or one of the other progressive disorders, a program of treatment should be initiated that has a number of goals: (1) to minimize the many psychiatric and general medical complications that can accompany these disorders, (2) to relieve treatable symptoms of the disorder, and (3) to create an environment in which the individual can live as long, productive, and comfortable a life as possible. Clearly, such programs require multidisciplinary efforts, but the neuropsychologist and behavior therapist may play crucial roles in initial assessment, program planning, and evaluation of treatment. One way of looking at treatment of these individuals is that, while one cannot alter the course of the patient's disease process, one can alter the environment in which he or she lives. One can also alter the person's physiology with various medications such that some of the symptoms of the disorder can be controlled. The patient with Huntington's chorea provides a good example of these considerations. The jerky, spasmodic movements characteristic of Huntington's chorea can be diminished to a greater or lesser extent with various types of medication. These medications do not alter the disease procss; they simply help to alleviate the symptom of abnormal movements. Patients with Huntington's chorea can live long lives, during many years of which the characteristic cognitive and motor symptoms may be present. Behavioral assessment of adaptive, affective, and social behaviors can be used to plan interventions that may be of definite therapeutic benefit. While cognitive–perceptual retraining might not be the treatment of choice in these cases, contingency management aimed at maximizing potential and minimizing discomfort through the course of the illness would appear to be a worthwhile endeavor.

5. Specification of Target Behaviors

A remaining task for clinical neuropsychology is that of further definition of behaviors that might serve as targets for rehabilitation. It may be best to first illustrate this point with an example. Let us take the task of copying designs, such as is done when the Bender-Gestalt test is taken (Bender, 1938). If an individual fails to perform this test normally, there are three explanations from a neuropsychological standpoint: (1) the figures were incorrectly perceived, (2) there is a defect in the motor ability needed to execute figures, or (3) there is a defect in the ability to coordinate visual input with movement. While the diagnostician may not be overly concerned with this matter, since regardless of the specific cause, the abnormal end product may be viewed as suggestive of brain damage, the distinction is a crucial one to the rehabilitation planner. What is to be rehabilitated: a visual disorder, a movement disorder, or a coordination disorder? Many neuropsychological tests share the lack of specificity of the Bender-Gestalt test. From a diagnostic standpoint this lack may be an advantage since it provides a broad net for detection of deficits. However, from the point of view of rehabilitation planning, the more specific the test, the more helpful in formulating a program.

Diller (1976) has suggested that the factors that may be varied in retraining may be divided into stimulus and response variations. For example, one could vary stimuli with regard to orientation or speed of presentation. Response variations could include such parameters as type of error, rate, and duration. Many neuropsychologists are interested in the question of modality specificity and attempt to determine whether perceptual defects are specifically visual, auditory, tactile, or present in all modalities. There is also a great deal of interest in whether the task is verbal or nonverbal. Great care has been taken to construct tasks that are as purely verbal or nonverbal as possible (Milner & Teuber, 1968). Luria, in his testing methods, has attempted to identify as precisely as possible the specific disabilities present. These numerous variations in stimulus and response factors are crucial to rehabilitation programming. Such matters as the speed at which stimuli are presented, modality of presentation, and error type in responding can be highly significant matters. Brain-damaged patients often vary from normal in regard to stimulus or response considerations, and rehabilitation efforts often involve establishing some channel of effective communication on the stimulus side or improving such dimensions as speed or accuracy on the response side. Slowing down stimulus presentation, for example, may improve the patient's comprehension, while increasing speed of some motor activity may be a major goal of a retraining program. If one could make a conclusion such as "The patient has a specific defect in auditory comprehension of verbal stimuli," the goals of the rehabilitation program become immediately apparent. Unfortunately, not all assessment methods can generate such specific conclusions, and not all brain-damaged patients have such specific deficits. Nevertheless, with improved assessment methods it should be possible to increase the precision with which patients' preserved abilities and deficits are delineated. In this regard, neuropsychologists tend to be critical of such broad, encompassing concepts as "dementia" or "organic brain syndrome," unless such concepts are defined in regard to specific behavioral patterns.

The great complexities of neuropsychological deficit clearly call for the type of analysis being described here. There are several classic examples of such complexities, a few of which will be briefly mentioned. There are patients who can read but not write. These patients cannot read what they themselves have just written. There are patients who cannot recognize objects by touch but can do so visually, and there are other patients who demonstrate the opposite. These patients do not have primary impairment of vision or sense of touch; the disturbances can be documented to be at the level of recognition. There are patients who can read normally but cannot recognize faces. These and numerous other phenomena, some of which are quite subtle, point first to the importance of neuropsychological assessment and second to the need for neuropsychological assessment to become increasingly sensitive to disorders that may be quite specific.

6. Conclusions

We have attempted to show that despite marked differences in theoretical framework, neuropsychological assessment and behavioral assessment may have a common focus of interest in the brain-damaged patient. It is quite possible that the successes of behavior therapy with various clinical populations may be repeated in treatment of brain-damaged patients. We have pointed out, however, that such treatment should ideally be based on the exceedingly complex relationships that exist between brain damage and behavior. Such relationships are probably best discerned through the use of neuropsychological tests, and are probably not readily discernible by interview or the more global types of systematic behavior observation. When neuropsychological tests are administered, the neuropsychologist and behavior therapist can form a productive partnership aimed at the formulation of rehabilitation programs that incorporate information concerning the specific target behaviors with the various techniques and strategies that have developed within behavior therapy.

7. References

Beck, S. J. *Rorschach's test*. Vol. I: *Basic processes*. New York: Grune & Stratton, 1944.

Bellack, A. S., & Hersen, M. Assessment and single-case research. In M. Hersen & A. S. Bellack (Eds.), *Behavior therapy in the psychiatric setting*. Baltimore: Williams & Wilkins, 1978.

Bender, L. A visual motor gestalt test and its clinical use. *Research Monographs of the American Orthopsychiatric Association*, 1938, 3.

Ben-Yishay, Y., Diller, L., & Mandleberg, I. The ability to profit from cues as a function of initial competence in normal and brain-injured adults: A replication of previous findings. *Journal of Abnormal Psychology*, 1970, 76, 378–379.

Ben-Yishay, Y., Diller, L., Mandleberg, I., Gordon, W., & Gerstman, L. J. Similarities and differences in block design performance between older normal and brain-injured persons. *Journal of Abnormal Psychology,* 1971, *78,* 17–25.

Ben-Yishay, Y., Gerstman, L., Diller, L., & Haas, A. Prediction of rehabilitation outcomes from psychometric parameters in left hemiplegics. *Journal of Consulting and Clinical Psychology,* 1970, *34,* 436–441.

Boring, E. G. The use of operational definitions in science. *Psychological Review,* 1945, *52,* 243–245.

Broca, P. (New observation of aphemia produced by a lesion of the posterior half of the second and third frontal convolutions.) *Société Anatomique de Paris,* 1861, *36,* 398–407.

Butters, N., & Cermak, L. S. Neuropsychological studies of alcoholic Korsakoff patients. In G. Goldstein & C. Neuringer (Eds.), *Empirical Studies of Alcoholism.* Cambridge, Mass.: Ballinger, 1976.

Christensen, A. L. *Luria's neuropsychological investigation.* New York: Spectrum, 1975. (a)

Christensen, A. L. *Luria's neuropsychological investigation: Manual.* New York: Spectrum, 1975. (b)

Christensen, A. L. *Luria's neuropsychological investigation: Test cards.* New York: Spectrum, 1975. (c)

Diller, L. A model for cognitive retraining in rehabilitation. *The Clinical Psychologist,* 1976, *29,* 13–15.

Diller, L., Buxbaum, J., & Chiotelis, S. Relearning motor skills in hemiplegia: Error analysis. *Genetic Psychology Monographs,* 1972, *85,* 249–286.

Dollard, J., & Miller, N. E. *Personality and psychotherapy.* New York: McGraw-Hill, 1950.

Golden, C. J. *Diagnosis and rehabilitation in clinical neuropsychology.* Springfield, Ill.: C. C Thomas, 1978.

Golden, C. J., Hammeke, T. A., & Purisch, A. D. Diagnostic validity of a standardized neuropsychological battery derived from Luria's neuropsychological tests. *Journal of Consulting and Clinical Psychology,* 1978, *46,* 1258–1265.

Goldstein, K. *The organism.* New York: American Book Co., 1939.

Halstead, W. C. *Brain and intelligence.* Chicago: University of Chicago Press, 1947.

Hebb, D. O. Drives and the C. N. S. (conceptual nervous system). *Psychological Review,* 1955, *62,* 243–254.

Hebb, D. O. Alice in Wonderland or psychology among the biological sciences. In H. F. Harlow & C. N. Woolsey (Eds.), *Biological and biochemical bases of behavior.* Madison: University of Wisconsin Press, 1958.

Hefferline, R. F. Learning theory and clinical psychology—an eventual symbiosis. In A. J. Bachrach (Ed.), *Experimental foundations of clinical psychology.* New York: Basic Books, 1962.

Hersen, M. Token economies in institutional settings. Historical, political, deprivation, ethical and generalization issues. *The Journal of Nervous and Mental Disease,* 1976, *162,* 206–211.

Klove, H. Validation studies in adult clinical neuropsychology. In R. M. Reitan & L. H. Davison (Eds.), *Clinical neuropsychology: Current status and applications.* New York: Winston-Wiley, 1974.

Koch, S. Clark L. Hull. In W. K. Estes, S. Koch, K. MacCorquodale, P. E. Meehl, C. G. Mueller, W. N. Schoenfeld, and W. S. Verplanck, *Modern learning theory.* New York: Appleton-Century-Crofts, 1954.

Lashley, K. S. Integrative functions of the cerebral cortex. *Physiological Review,* 1933, *13,* 1–42.

Lewinsohn, P. M., Danaher, B. G., & Kikel, S. Visual imagery as a mnemonic aid for brain-injured persons. *Journal of Consulting and Clinical Psychology,* 1977, *45,* 717–723.

Luria, A. R. *Restoration of function after brain injury.* New York: Macmillan, 1963 (original in Russian published in 1948).

Luria, A. R. *The working brain.* New York: Basic Books, 1973.

Luria, A. R., & Majovski, L. C. Basic approaches used in American and Soviet clinical neuropsychology. *American Psychologist,* 1977, *32,* 959–968.

MacCorquodale, K., & Meehl, P. E. On a distinction between hypothetical constructs and intervening variables. *Psychological Review,* 1948, *55,* 95–107.

Meier, M. J. Some challenges for clinical neuropsychology. In R. M. Reitan & L. A. Davison (Eds.), *Clinical neuropsychology: Current status and applications.* New York: Wiley, 1974.

Milner, B. Amnesia following operation on the temporal lobes. In C. W. M. Witty & O. L. Zangwill (Eds.), *Amnesia.* Woburn, Mass.: Butterworth, 1966.

Milner, B., & Teuber, H.-L. Alteration of perception and memory in man: Reflections on methods. In L. Weiskrantz (Ed.), *Analysis of behavior change.* New York: Harper & Row, 1968.

Parsons, O. A. & Prigatano, G. P. Methodological considerations in clinical neuropsychological research. *Journal of Consulting and Clinical Psychology,* 1978, *46,* 608–619.

Piotrowski, Z. Personality studies of cases with lesions of the frontal lobes: II. Rorschach study of a Pick's Disease case. *Rorschach Research Exchange,* 1936–1937, *1,* 65–77.

Pribram, K. H. *Languages of the brain: Experimental paradoxes and principles in neuropsychology,* Englewood Cliffs, N.J.: Prentice-Hall, 1971.

Pribram, K. H. Holographic memory. *Psychology Today,* 1979, *12,* 71–84.

Reitan, R. M. Validity of the Rorschach Test as measure of psychological effects of brain damage. *AMA Archives of Neurology and Psychology,* 1955, *73,* 445–451.

Russell, A., Neuringer, C., & Goldstein, G. *Assessment of brain damage: A neuropsychological key approach.* New York: Wiley-Interscience, 1970.

Skinner, B. F. Are theories of learning necessary? *Psychological Bulletin,* 1950, *57,* 193–216.

Skinner, B. F. *Science and human behavior.* New York: Macmillan, 1953.

Stein, D., Rosen, J., & Butters, N. (Eds.) *Plasticity and recovery of function in the central nervous system.* New York: Academic Press, 1974.

Teuber, H.-L. Some alterations in behavior after cerebral lesions in man. *Evolution of nervous control.* Washington, D.C.: American Association for the Advancement of Science, 1959.

Wickelgren, W. A. Chunking and consolidation: A theoretical synthesis of semantic networks, configuring in conditioning, S-R versus cognitive learning, normal forgetting, the amnesic syndrome, and the hippocampal arousal system. *Psychological Review,* 1979, *86,* 44–60.

2

Functional Appraisal and Therapy for Communication Disorders of Traumatically Brain-Injured Persons

Louise Kent-Udolf

1. Introduction

1.1. Functional Communication and Its Appraisal

Functional communication means the ability to participate effectively in the everyday give-and-take of communicating with family and friends, colleagues at work, and outright strangers. It implies a degree of reciprocal enjoyment and good humor as well as the ability to negotiate meaning through communicative exchanges.

The appraisal of functional communication has as its focus the degree to which the patient is able to get his messages across to others and how well he is able to understand the messages directed to him. It considers the patient's ability to work within and around the constraints of his production problems, whatever they may be, and his ability to cause others to assist him in communicating and in understanding. It does not focus on localization of injury or on diagnostic label. Although positively correlated with performance on tests of general language ability such as the Boston Diagnostic Aphasia Examination (Goodglass &

Louise Kent-Udolf • Education Service Center, Region II, Corpus Christi, Texas 78401.

Kaplan, 1972), the Minnesota Test for Differential Diagnosis of Aphasia (Schuell, 1972), or the Porch Index of Communicative Ability (Porch, 1967, 1971), the patient's performance on a test of functional communication might be expected to reflect the discrepancy, often only anecdotally documented, between results on tests of general language ability and just how well the patient actually manages communicatively in his everyday environment.

Although a functional description of the patient's communicative status may not provide a sufficient basis for the most appropriate choice of speech/language treatment strategies for him, such a description is useful for several reasons. First, it allows the clinician to appraise the patient's communicative status in the patient's own sphere of activities. Second, it allows the clinician to see how well the patient's functional impairment correlates with his performance on tests of general language ability. And third, it may prompt the clinician to give first treatment priority to domains of high functional value for the patient and to choose content relevant to the patient's pretrauma status. When it is clear that the patient is communicating effectively and in reasonably good humor and good taste, has acquired a repertoire of functional communication schemes and uses them, has addressed and somehow resolved the mundane problems of daily living, and has renegotiated his family relationships, the clinician and the patient are in a winning position to achieve something more. The first stage of therapy forges their partnership; demonstrates the possibility of finding alternative ways to achieve old ends; restores the patient's confidence in his ability to meet the challenge, albeit with help; and establishes a pattern of patient initiative. With functional status secure, clinician and patient can strive for greater elegance, possibly allowing the patient to resume his former style of work and living more fully.

1.2. Suggested References for Review

Although in some conspicuous ways the brain-injured patient is different from the patient whose communication problems are the result of neurogenic problems arising from stroke, hemorrhage, tumor, or infectious disease, there are also many parallels; it would be a mistake for those interested in the traumatically brain-injured patient to ignore the substantial literature regarding neurogenic speech and language disorders arising from other etiologies. One can access and gain an appreciation of the literature in neurogenic communication disorders through a study of the writings of Goldstein (1942, 1948), Granich (1947), Head (1926), Mills (1904), Nielsen (1947), Weisenburg and McBride (1935),

Wepman (1951), and Wilson (1926). These works contain rich details of the sequelae of traumatic brain injury and are still of interest and instructional value. Sources such as these have shaped current thinking to a large degree, especially with regard to therapy. Recent trends in neurogenic communication disorders can be sampled by a careful reading of several significant works and by an exploration of references to topics of special interest contained within them. This approach will yield the basic information needed to understand most of the current literature and the issues that are likely to be addressed. Suggested works include Brookshire (1978); Darley (1979; see also, 1977); Darley, Aronson, and Brown (1975); Holland (1980); Johns (1978); Luria (1966, 1970); and Schuell, Jenkins, and Jimenez-Pabon (1964).

The Brookshire work is an excellent comprehensive text in aphasia. It contains a concise, though thorough, presentation of the neurophysiological bases of speech and language. Terms are clearly defined, and the author makes excellent use of examples. Darley (1979) has recently edited a collection of critical evaluations of current appraisal techniques, including a large number of tests in current usage and frequently cited in the literature on neurogenic communicative disorders. Suggested also is a short article by Darley (1977) entitled "A Retrospective View: Aphasia." *Motor Speech Disorders*, a text by Darley *et. al.* (1975), is a new classic and is important for a thorough understanding of current thinking, critical appraisal, and intervention. Holland (1980) has recently published her measure of functional communication adequacy entitled Communication Assessment for Daily Living (CADL); this instrument not only offers a new norm-referenced appraisal tool but also makes a fresh statement about the patients it is designed to test. This work will affect intervention strategies every bit as much as the appraisal of linguistic adequacy. The Johns book *Clinical Management of Neurogenic Communicative Disorders* (1978) is again a new classic and required reading in this field. The book is a collection of chapters that are exceptionally lucid, current, to the point, integrated, and scholarly. The Schuell *et al.* (1964) text seems to fit better among the current works than among the earlier ones cited, since much of what is current is argumentatively entangled with Schuell's conceptualization of aphasia, her appraisal approaches, and her rehabilitative strategies. The Luria works are incredibly fascinating; they are better understood when there is already some familiarity with the literature as a whole.

1.3. Neurogenic Disorders of Communication

The neurogenic disorders of communication resulting from traumatic brain injury are referred to as "the language of confusion," "aphasia," "apraxia of speech," and "the dysarthrias." These terms label syndromes or clusters of behaviors associated with brain damage or injury. The disorders associated with these labels vary vastly in degree, and the disorders themselves and even specific components of them can occur in isolation or in seemingly almost any combination along with other nonlanguage but language-related cognitive problems. Accordingly, the diagnostic dilemma are multiple and not always satisfactorily resolved.

Clear indication for the need to involve a speech/language pathologist, if one is not involved from the outset, is the presence of any of the following behaviors when they appear as sequelae of traumatic brain injury:

1. Patient is alert but seems unable to speak.
2. Patient is alert but does not try to speak.
3. Patient effortfully gropes for words, makes repetitive attempts to speak.
4. Patient speaks but voice is weak, nasal, breathy; utterances are of short length and seem limited due to insufficient breath support.
5. Patient speaks but speech is slurred and slow.
6. Patient exhibits stereotyped utterances involving meaningful or nonmeaningful words or phrases; patient perseveres in the use of a limited repertoire of utterances that may include jargon and neologisms.
7. Patient speaks but intelligibility is poor; errors may or may not be consistent; patient may or may not be aware of errors, attempt to self-correct, or respond appropriately to cueing.
8. Patient occasionally utters swear words or phrases or other seemingly automatized utterances with excellent fluency and intelligibility; patient seems unable to inhibit these responses.
9. Patient may stutter or display dysfluent speech, with negative pretrauma history of stuttering.
10. Patient talks but speech lacks variability in pitch, loudness, rate, and the use of pause time.
11. Patient talks but content is often irrelevant; nonsensical, absurd conversations, confabulation-filled, are easily occasioned.
12. Patient talks but seems to have extreme difficulty thinking of particular words and complains of same; vocabulary is very restricted; patient is unable easily to supply words on request.
13. Patient talks but frequently substitutes one word for another

with errors often semantically based; also may substitute sounds and syllables for other sounds and syllables in words.
14. Patient is alert and gives evidence of hearing but seems unable to understand speech addressed to him.
15. Patient seems to need excessive time in order to understand; exhibits long latencies before following commands and may not initiate response at all.
16. Patient seems to understand commands better when length of utterance is short; when content is simple as opposed to complex; when vocabulary is limited to common, frequently used words; when speech is slower, louder, and contains more pauses than ordinary adult–adult speech.
17. Patient complains that others do not speak clearly.
18. Patient has difficulty in writing from dictation and composing letters to a degree that is inconsistent with history.
19. Patient is unable to read or reads with impaired comprehension, again, when inconsistent with history.

This is a conglomeration of symptoms, unsorted and incomplete; it gives some notion of the scope of neurogenic communicative disorders. Although in any particular case there always seem to be pieces of evidence or symptoms that are inconsistent with the ultimate diagnosis, the symptoms generally can be ordered with respect to syndromes with which certain sets of them are usually associated. It is true, however, that the same symptom can be associated with more than one disorder or syndrome, and all patients with the same disorder or given the same diagnostic label do not exhibit the same symptoms. These disorders, then, are not mutually exclusive; while one may appear primary, it can be complicated by other coexisting disorders. For example, Wertz, Rosenbek, and Deal (1970) have reported that apraxia of speech and aphasia often occur together and that the presence of one may mask the presence of the other. Furthermore, while the focus here is on the communicative disorders associated with trauma, the reader must remain aware that these problems occur in concert with the more general behavioral manifestations of brain injury. Although the brain-injured person often presents with the language of confusion, he is obviously at risk for other neurogenic communicative disorders, depending upon the specific nature of his trauma experience. Therefore, it seems appropriate here to characterize the range of neurogenic communicative disorders and to consider their prognostic significance.

1.3.1. The Dysarthrias

The dysarthrias are speech disorders resulting from disturbances in muscular control, including paralysis, weakness, abnormal tone, or incoordination of the muscles used in speech. Respiration, phonation, resonance, and articulation are all affected and result, overall, in reduced intelligibility. Speech is characterized by breathy voice quality, shortened utterance length, low vocal intensity, hypernasality, abnormal phonation, slow movement of the articulators, and imprecise and slurred articulation. There is generally a restricted range of pitch patterns, loudness, timing, and rate; but there also may be abnormal variability in these features of prosody resulting from involuntary movements of muscles for which there has been some loss of control. All of these features combine to affect the intelligibility of the spoken message negatively and are the result of the disturbance and impairment of the speech system as a whole. For example, the loss of efficiency in velopharyngeal valving can result in shorter utterances, reduced loudness, nasality, inappropriate nasal emission of air, a hoarse voice quality, and articulation errors, all of which take their toll on intelligibility. In a "pure" dysarthria, language, cognition, and orientation are unimpaired, as is the ability to "program" articulatory postures and movements for the deliberate production and sequencing of speech sounds into words and phrases. The dysarthric speaker is unable to compensate completely for his motoric impairment.

According to the findings of Gilchrist and Wilkinson (1979), the dysarthrias represent the greatest number of speech and language disorders among persons under the age of 40 with severe head injuries. Darley et al. (1975) provide a comprehensive analysis of the dysarthrias, including detailed descriptions of the various types.

1.3.2. Apraxia of Speech

Apraxia of speech presents as an articulatory disorder resulting from disturbance or impairment in the ability consistently and deliberately to produce and combine speech sounds into sequences to form words and phrases. According to Rosenbek (1978a), the nemesis of apractic patients is the five-syllable, rare word, whose accent falls toward the end and whose syllables are made of fricatives grouped in clusters and unrelieved by plosives. Speaking is the problem; and speech is much poorer than reading, writing, or the understanding of speech–language. In its "pure" form, apraxia of speech is not associated with significant weakness, slowness, or motor incoordination; other forms of apraxia; confusion; disorientation; memory problems; general intellectual deficit; hearing loss; sensory discrimination deficits; word-finding problems; abnormal resonance; or aphasic difficulties in understanding.

Apractic speech may be characterized by its articulation errors, lack of fluency, repetitive attempts to self-correct, groping for correct articulatory postures, slowness, insertion of inappropriate intra- and inter-syllabic pauses, inappropriately even stress pattern, and struggle. None of these problems may be evident, however, when the patient engages in automatized, nondeliberate utterances. Patients with severe apraxia of speech may be totally unable to speak, exhibit extreme difficulty initiating deliberate phonation, or present with a limited repertoire of overworked utterances. Further, there is the possibility of oral apraxia and limb apraxia, disorders that refer to deficits in the ability to make deliberate nonspeech oral movements or movements in response to commands such as "Lick your lips" or "Pull the string."

In spite of all of these difficulties, "purely" apractic patients know what they want to say and can communicate their messages by gesture and writing if not by speech. Disturbances in prosody are viewed as manifestations of the patient's effort to speak. Language problems, if present, are likely due to coexisting aphasia.

Apraxis of speech and the dysarthrias are both characterized by articulatory disorders, and there is a considerable amount of information available regarding differential diagnosis of these disorders on the basis of careful articulatory appraisal (see Wertz, 1978; Rosenbek, 1978b; Johns & Darley, 1970). As Wertz (1978) points out, however, the task of differential diagnosis is made more difficult when the two disorders coexist or when apraxia of speech is associated with a negligible amount of analyzable speech.

1.3.3. Aphasia

Aphasia is a central integrative language disorder that manifests itself across all language modalities including the formulation of spoken and written messages by the patient as well as the understanding of spoken and written messages directed to the patient. The severity of impairment in one mode is usually predictive of the severity in the others; however, some modes may be less impaired than others. If only one very specific deficit is identified, this is not a "true" aphasia and is usually referred to by a label that specifies the exact nature of the language problem, for example, "anomia." In aphasia, the language disorder is disproportionately severe relative to other intellectual deficits and is not attributable to dementia, hearing loss, loss of sensory discrimination, or motor dysfunction.

The speech/language of the aphasic patient is characterized by reduced vocabulary, simplification of syntax, presence of paraphasias (substitution of semantically related words and phrases such as bird/bee as well as substitution of phonologically related sounds and syllables for others); presence of stereotypic utterances, neologisms, jargon; and circumlocutions secondary to word finding difficulties. The patient's understanding of speech/language is highly dependent on the quality of the input; that is, understanding is facilitated by input characterized by slow rate, short utterance length, use of common vocabulary, simple syntax, increased pause time within utterances, increased loudness, exaggerated prosody, and facial expressions/gestures congruent with the message. The patient typically has difficulty switching focus from one source of input to another or from one topic to another. The degree of reading comprehension impairment varies but often is not as severe as the patient's impairments in the formulation of written communication.

In a series of 50 patients with closed head injuries, Levin, Grossman, and Kelly (1976), found that nearly half of the patients exhibited word-finding difficulties and one-third experienced impaired comprehension of spoken language. These results were obtained under controlled test conditions and were contrasted with results obtained from medical patients not suffering from any sort of neurogenic disorder or injury. These investigators consider aphasia to be an important sequel of closed head injury.

Recently it has been shown that when a normal amount of linguistic and situational contexts are provided, aphasic persons comprehend messages surprisingly well (Stachowiak, Huber, Poeck, & Kerschensteiner, 1977; Wilcox, Davis, & Leonard, 1978). Further, Holland (1977) asserts that aphasic persons retain their expressive communicative competencies, as evidenced by their use of conversational rules and their expression of a variety of speech acts.

1.3.4. Language of Generalized Intellectual Impairment (Dementia)

The language of generalized intellectual impairment presents as an intellectual deficit, verbal and nonverbal, associated with a variety of diseases and conditions of the brain but rarely with trauma. Confusion and disorientation for person, time, and place may be present, along with impaired memory and problems in all communicative modes. The severity of the language impairment in dementias is consistent with depressed abilities in other areas of intellect.

Speech and language of generalized intellectual impairment is characterized by its paucity. Utterances are short, often stereotyped, perseverative, and concrete. There is reduced efficiency across the language modes: speaking, understanding speech, reading, writing, and gesturing. Deterioration of performance is most evident in language tasks that make heavy demands on memory, concentration, abstracting, and the production and processing of linguistic complexity. Wertz (1978) has provided a comprehensive current review of the language of generalized intellectual impairment and its differential diagnosis. In this review he makes the point that given a history of trauma, the examiner must be satisfied that the patient's syntax and word-finding abilities are sufficiently adequate to be inconsistent with a diagnosis of aphasia and that the patient's disorientation, confabulation, and irrelevancy cannot be explained by an intellectual impairment.

1.3.5. Language of Confusion

The language of confusion is the neurogenic communicative disorder most often occurring, if one does occur, subsequent to traumatic brain injury. The problem first presents as a feature of the recovery process. Since the patient is disoriented, his memory not recovered, and he is unable to maintain an attentional set, it is not surprising that his speech/language is confused, often irrelevant, and riddled with confabulations. Functional communication suffers unless the sender and receiver are similarly, and more or less correctly, oriented and able to maintain sufficient attentional set to remember what has just been said and to stay on topic. As the recovery process proceeds, difficulties may be manifest in tasks requiring confrontation naming and controlled word association; it may also emerge that the patient has difficulty demonstrating retention of newly "learned" material. Although any brain injury may result in a patient's failure to regain full pretrauma intellectual status, deficits in intelligence are not part of the symptom complex in the language of confusion. Nevertheless, patients may perform poorly on both verbal and nonverbal tests of intelligence because of their difficulty in maintaining attentional set generally (see Mandleberg & Brooks, 1975).

The following symptoms characterize the communicative features of the language of confusion:

1. Patient displays word-finding difficulties, particularly on confrontation naming tasks; performance worsens as level of abstraction increases.

2. Patient displays poor performance on controlled word-association tasks, often referred to as "fluency" tasks. (Patient is asked
to utter as many words as he can in one minute that begin with a
specific letter of the alphabet, repeated for three letters; score is
the total number of words. Some examiners do not accept proper
nouns.)

3. Patient often responds to open-ended conversational situations
with irrelevance, confabulation; often responds appropriately to
closed questions requiring only a one-word response or yes/no.

4. Patient exhibits poor performance following nonredundant instructions; performance worsens as length and complexity of
commands increases.

5. Patient appears frequently to be unable to initiate deliberate acts,
verbal or nonverbal, or response is very delayed.

6. Patient seems unable to inhibit specific automatized responses.

7. Patient displays deficits in listening, speaking, reading, and writing. Often ability to compose written material or to write from
dictation is especially impaired, and there are marked deficits in
remembering newly "learned" material. All of these problems
may be secondary to inability to maintain attentional set, usually
described as high distractibility.

With the exception of confabulation, which typically disappears,
the patients seem to be at risk for residual impairments that differ only
in degree from those present early on. Inhibition of initiation of deliberate speech, inability to inhibit that which is automatized, difficulties in
word finding, and the inability to maintain attentional set seem to characterize the long-term disturbance. Presumably the attentional problem
is central to problems in remembering newly "learned" material, following nonredundant instructions, and writing.

According to the findings of Halpern, Darley, and Brown (1973), the
primary distinction between confused patients and those with generalized intellectual impairment is relevance. On open-ended language
tasks, confused patients may respond with surprising and sometimes
humorously irrelevant and confabulatory responses, responses that
readily reveal their disorientation, unclear thinking, memory difficulties, and lack of awareness of their errors. Both confused and demented
patients may display difficulty in reading comprehension, auditory comprehension, and arithmetic, but the demented patients are less often
irrelevant and tend to do better than confused patients on writing from
dictation. Darley (1964) has offered four questions that are helpful in
differentiating between the language of confusion and aphasia: (1) Is the

patient oriented in terms of space and time? (2) Does the patient stay in contact with the examiner? (3) Is the patient aware of his inappropriate responses? (4) Does the patient demonstrate vocabulary and syntax problems? According to Darley, if the answers to all of these questions are no, the results are more consistent with confusion than with aphasia.

References of particular interest here, not previously cited, include Critchley (1970), Geschwind (1974), Chédru and Geschwind (1972), and Isaacs and Walkey (1964).

1.4. The Problem of Prognosis

The early postonset communicative status of the traumatically brain-injured patient ranges from essentially zero to normal pretrauma status. The severity and type of communicative sequelae are probably most importantly functions of the location, extent, and type of initial brain injury or injuries and secondary brain damage resulting from complications (for example, cerebral hypoxia and the need for surgical decompression). Prognosis for full recovery of pretrauma communicative status is usually made on the basis of the presence of and duration of coma and subsequent amnesia. Duration of coma is generally accepted as the best single prognostic indicator. These are well-known generalities that are usually stated before the exceptions that are often the rule. Clinically, when the patient is stabilized and is beginning to display behavior more appropriate than inappropriate in his interactions with people and in his approach to the basics of daily living, it is possible to conduct an initial appraisal of his communicative status and to begin treating him in ways that are likely to influence his recovery of speech and language function favorably.

The patient's response to treatment appears to depend on a host of interacting variables. The most frequently reported prognostic variables are listed below in the approximate order in which one might expect to have information pertinent to them.

1. Sex
2. Age at time of trauma
3. Presence and duration of coma (coma defined as an uncommunicative state of the patient in which he fails to display vocal response or deliberate motor activity following spoken or somatic stimulation by the examiner)
4. Primary cause of injury, that is, penetrating head wound or closed head injury

5. Presence of other injuries
6. General preonset health, physical condition
7. Presence of alcoholism
8. Location of lesion or affected area of the brain
9. Size or extent of lesion or affected area
10. Presence and degree of cerebral edema or hypoxia
11. Preonset personality variables
12. Cerebral dominance inferred from pretrauma handedness preference
13. Time elapsed between onset of symptoms of communicative disorder and commencement of treatment for same
14. Severity of communicative disorder
15. Absence of nonverbal oral apraxia
16. Marked improvement in speech resulting from positioning or palatal lift
17. Patient's ability to profit from feedback, ability to follow instructions resulting in immediate improvement of performance
18. Patient's ability to self-correct
19. Skill of the speech/language pathologist responsible for therapy
20 Intensity of treatment (amount of time spent with patient in therapy per day)
21. Duration of treatment
22. Appropriateness of treatment

From a probabilistic point of view, these are all valid predictors of patient response to treatment. In the individual case, however, statements of prognosis can best be made on the basis of comprehensive appraisal, including a thorough knowledge of the patient's pretrauma status.

The problem of prognosis with respect to communicative disorders associated with traumatic brain injury is that the disorders are so varied as they present in the individual case: varied in kind, degree, complexity, and associated nonverbal behavioral sequelae. What follows here is a summary of the recovery process for a hypothetical patient with a traumatic closed head injury uncomplicated by aphasia, apraxia of speech, dysarthrias, or dementia. Next, the residual communicative impairments that might typically follow such an injury are considered. And last, the prognoses of the neurogenic disorders of communication in their "pure" forms are reviewed. The reader can then reflect upon the ways in which the presence of various neurogenic disorders of communication might alter and complicate the process of recovery from traumatic brain injury.

Early in recovery, the trauma patient responds to attempts to communicate with him in much the same way as he does to other types of invading stimuli. At first he is completely unresponsive; later he follows simple commands in an inconsistent, delayed manner. When he responds vocally, the response is meaningless or stereotypic. He is somewhat more likely to respond to family and friends than to staff. During the confused/agitated period that follows, the patient displays most dramatically the language of confusion. His ability to process information is severely diminished. He is disoriented with respect to persons, time, and place. He is unable to maintain any impressive attentional set. When he speaks, he makes no consistent sense; relevance ranges from relevant to confabulatory.

As the recovery process continues and agitation abates, the patient responds fairly consistently to simple commands. As commands become longer or more complex, the patient is unable to process the complexity or is unable to maintain sufficient attentional set to permit him to process the complexity. In any event, increased length and complexity of command pose risks of disorganized failure. The patient converses socially for short periods of time. Some responses are appropriate, but confabulation is occasioned easily. Memory and orientation remain severely impaired, and the patient seems unable to retain new information.

Gradually, inappropriate behaviors lessen. The patient consistently follows simple directions and begins to show improved memory for new content. Memory deficits interfere with specific responses, and responses are delayed. However, responses are typically appropriate to the situation. The patient still has difficulty processing information. His behavior is more appropriate than inappropriate; although orientation to space and time may remain impaired, he recognizes some staff members. Selective attending is adequate for self-care activities. Prior to this time the patient has had difficulty orienting to his own body with respect to left–right and to acting on himself as necessary in order to dress or shave. At this point in the recovery process, it is possible to begin to work with the patient on structured tasks for up to 30 minutes at a time. It is at this time that speech/language therapy should begin, if it has not already been initiated. If the patient is already being seen by a speech/language pathologist, the treatment approach shifts now from a generally supportive one for both the family and the patient to a much more aggressive attack on the patient's orientation problems and specific communication deficits.

As the recovery process proceeds, the patient becomes better oriented in his environment and behaves appropriately, although flat affect and some confusion remain. His recall of immediate past events is still limited. He is beginning to be aware of his condition. Memory for newly "learned" materials continues to improve. The patient still needs structure in order to be able to initiate. He is more interested now than earlier in social or recreational activities, and he is now more likely to cooperate with therapy.

At the next stage the patient becomes fully oriented and able to recall and integrate past and recent events. He resumes his life. The rate of recovery is at times rapid and sometimes unmeasurable for several weeks at a time. The recovery process continues active for up to 3 years, but the greatest amount of recovery occurs during the first 6 months after coma. (In children, the recovery process may remain active up to five years—longer, at any rate, than for adults.)

In general, the language of confusion associated with closed head trauma is not expected to last indefinitely. The patient is expected to recover in a more or less predictable manner or to present with symptoms of other of the neurogenic disorders of communication, some combination, or perhaps a specific language deficit. Variables frequently mentioned as having specific prognostic value for such patients include the patient's ability to initiate without delay deliberate responses, his ability to inhibit automatized verbal responses, his good performance on confrontation naming and word fluency tasks, and his ability to retain newly learned material. The presence of these abilities is prognostically favorable; their absence reflects the presence of the most frequently reported residual communicative deficits.

It is important to point out here that patients initially diagnosed with language of confusion may be judged fully recovered when they are not and when they might still benefit from therapy. Although functional in society, the patient may continue to show deficits—relative to pretrauma status—in abstract reasoning, tolerance for stress, judgment in emergencies or unusual circumstances, and in the areas described above. The deficits that remain for any particular patient may be residual language sequelae closely related to the postconcussion syndrome or subtle specific language deficits. Residual deficits may be present more often than is recognized.

The literature on children tells us that severe academic problems are ahead for many "discharged as recovered" traumatically brain-injured children (Shaffer, Bijur, Chadwick, & Rutter, 1980). If these children have so much trouble in school, we can only assume that adults also have difficulties when confronted with situations in which efficient new learning is essential. The residual problems of children are described as continuing manifestations of the postconcussion syndrome, impaired intelligence, speech and language deficits, and persistant reading and writing problems. The topic of long-term residual sequelae of traumatically brain injured persons deserves a major current research effort. For those interested in sampling the children's literature on this topic, it can be approached through recent contributions of Klonoff, Low, and Clark (1977); Gilchrist and Wilkinson (1979); Stover and Ziegler (1976); and Alajouanine and Lhermitte (1965).

Before making a survey of prognostic indicators for other of the neurogenic communicative disorders, the question "Prognosis for what?" deserves mention. Usually, the speech/language pathologist would reply "Prognosis for full recovery of pre-onset levels of speech and language performance across all domains of language including speech, the understanding of speech, gesturing, reading, and writing." And the term "full recovery" would imply a return to pretrauma levels of abilities to learn, remember, and integrate new material as well as to form and maintain interpersonal relationships. As we shall see, this idealized notion of recovery is not equally appropriate for all of the neurogenic speech/language disorders.

1.4.1. Dysarthrias

Prognosis is specific for each of the dysarthrias. In general, however, prognosis depends on the severity of impairment of intelligibility and whether improvement in intelligibility results from positioning, the use of a palatal lift, a voice amplifier, masking, delayed auditory feedback, or the ability to follow instructions. If any of these strategies improves intelligibility significantly, prognosis is better than if they have negligible effects. If the patient's intelligibility can be demonstrably improved and the patient is willing to submit to training and, in some instances, medical management, the prognosis for intelligible speech is good.

If the patient is unable to achieve satisfactory intelligibility by any of these means, intelligibility may still improve with appropriate speech therapy. Regardless of his speech, prognosis for communication is good if the patient is able and willing to write or type or to learn to use a typewriter or alternative communicative modes such as Amerind, an alphabet board, or a speech synthesizer. The modes are available depending upon the patient's motor skills, financial resources, and willingness to use them.

In summary, then, the prognostic concern with the dysarthrias is primarily for intelligibility of speech. In the absence of intelligible speech, prognosis for communication is good but depends on the patient's use of alternative communication modes. The presence of dys-

arthrias can clearly complicate the recovery of traumatically brain injured persons.

1.4.2. Aphasia

When traumatic brain injury resolves to aphasia, prognosis depends generally on the severity of deficits across all language modes and
the presence of other neurogenic disorders of communication. Significant among multiple other comingling variables are the patient's ability
to profit from feedback, to self-correct, and to formulate and risk alternative solutions following communicative failure.

Depending on the severity of the aphasia, the prognostic concern
may be for full recovery of speech/language functioning in all pretrauma
spheres. When aphasia is very severe, however, the prognostic focus
shifts to functional communication. For severely impaired persons, rehabilitative efforts that are social and functional in thrust may be rewarded with functional communication (Sarno, Silverman, & Sands,
1970); when speech does not seem feasible, the use of alternative communicative modes such as Amerind and picture-pointing-type devices
may extend communication and facilitate the patient's use of his residual abilities. Of special interest here is that aphasia resulting from
nonpenetrating trauma has a better prognosis generally than aphasia
resulting from penetrating trauma, infection, or vascular or neoplastic
disorders; aphasia localized to the temporoparietal region in the left
hemisphere is considered to have a poorer prognosis than aphasia associated with lesions located in other parts of the left or dominant
hemisphere.

The timing of the commencement of therapy for aphasia is considered to be extremely important to the result. Schuell *et al.* (1964) claim
that "dramatic cures result from priming a mechanism when physiological readiness is present." Speech/language pathologists do not always
have the opportunity to work with the aphasic patient at the "prime"
time. I hope that this is less true now than it was in 1969, when Holland
wrote that "aphasic patients are usually referred to language services
only when the critical period for maximum therapeutic effectiveness—
the spontaneous recovery period—is over." When this is the case, Holland says that a vicious cycle is likely to ensue such that even the speech
pathologist's most creative and skillful work is blunted. This is probably
as true for other neurogenic disorders of communication as for aphasia.

Some of the tests used to appraise neurogenic language disorders
generate predictions of a patient's recovery from aphasia. Schuell's Minnesota Test for Differential Diagnosis of Aphasia (MTDDA) (1965) can be

used as a basis for predictions ranging from excellent recovery of all language skills to a poor prognosis for language that becomes functional in any mode. Porch, Wertz, and Collins (1974) describe a preliminary effort to predict specific recovery levels based on patient performance on the Porch Index of Communicative Ability (PICA) (1967, 1971). Scores at 3, 6, and 12 months postonset were predicted on the basis of the scores obtained a month after onset. Correlations between predicted and obtained scores in the initial samples were impressive; the procedure is now widely used to make 6-month predictions. There is an alternative procedure than can be used for patients who are already more than one month postonset.

It is Porch's impression that aphasia resulting from nonpenetrating trauma shows a stair-step recovery pattern during the first 6 months after onset, continuing up to 18 months after onset. Others have suggested that the recovery process in such patients is much longer, extending up to 3 years. At any rate, there is some evidence and considerable testimony to support continued speech/language services for such patients through the 18th month postonset regardless of the pattern of month-to-month improvement during this time (Gilchrist & Wilkinson, 1979; Wilkinson, 1969). The predictive validity of the MTDDA and the PICA is discussed in their respective reviews in Darley (1979).

1.4.3. Apraxia of Speech

For apraxia of speech in its "pure" form, prognosis for full recovery of pretrauma communicative status is associated with all of the same variables described for aphasia. In addition, the absence of aphasia is viewed as a favorable prognostic sign; the absence of oral apraxia is considered to be especially favorable. Rosenbek (1978b) views rapid recovery (within the first few days) as a more important prognostic indicator than the initial severity of oral apraxia or apraxia of speech. Deficits that resolve quickly are assumed to be the result of inhibition resulting from edema or damage that will mend during the course of physiologic recovery.

Patients who show mild residual apraxia of speech may recover a large measure of their pretrauma communicative status to the extent that they learn effective strategies for "reprogramming" or reintegrating their speech. If the patient is severely apractic, prognosis for *speech* is poor; but with the use of a variety of strategies that may facilitate speech and alternative communication modes, prognosis for *communication* is good. As is true for patients with dysarthrias, prognosis for resuming full control of their pretrauma lives is good to the extent that residual speech problems are resolved or do not interfere with success on the job or with family relations.

1.4.4. Language of Generalized Intellectual Impairment (Dementia)

When dementia complicates the recovery process for a traumatically brain-injured individual, prognosis for the elimination of the symptoms of the dementia depends on its cause. Some of the causes can now be controlled or eliminated through medical management; for example, causes such as benign intracranial tumors, neurosyphilis, and vitamin B_{12} deficiency are now treatable (Espir & Rose, 1970). Wertz (1978) offers a succinct review of the prognoses of dementias associated with various medical causes, reminding us, particularly, that senile dementia (dementia commencing at or after age 65) carries the extra negative influence of advanced age regardless of cause.

2. Appraisal

2.1. Introductory Comments

From the foregoing descriptions of disorders of communication that might be associated with traumatic brain injury, it should be evident that the trauma patient needs comprehensive appraisal. Such appraisal is needed in order to establish with reasonable certainty the absence of communicative deficits as well as to make and confirm diagnoses and develop appropriate treatment plans. The appraisal process consists of all initial testing and evaluating that is done and its documentation, subsequent testing done to follow leads revealed by initial testing, and all reevaluations done to assess progress. It includes the compilation and study of the patient's life history and an attempt to relate his present status to the former. It includes observations, structured and unstructured, and may include trial therapy to ascertain the patient's tendency to respond to a particular therapeutic approach.

Since no treatment program can be expected to address all of the patient's deficits, there is need for periodic reevaluation to determine whether progress is being made in areas not directly addressed in therapy and whether a shift in the focus of therapy is indicated. We hope and we program for generalization. Periodically, we need to probe for it. There is also need to reevaluate for purposes of accountability alone. The clinician is responsible for routinely evaluating and documenting the presence or lack of progress. There are no rigid rules for when a patient should be reevaluated, but in long-term care once every 60 days in prudent.

The purposes of speech/language appraisal include the formulation of statements regarding localization and extent of brain damage to support medical diagnoses, the diagnosis of speech/language disorders and description of their severity and prognoses, the collection of baseline measures of performance against which changes can be measured, and the compilation of behavioral data that can support individualized plans for therapy. Some speech/language pathologists such as Rosenbek (1978b) consider diagnosis to be essential; others such as Brookshire (1978) are not so sure that labeling is essential to good clinical management. Presumably, the behavioral neuropsychologist leans toward Brookshire's point of view, more concerned with behavioral description than with labeling *per se*. It may be, however, that behavioral descriptions of multiple-patient series will yield patterns or clusters of common features consistently enough to support the use of syndrome labels followed by descriptions of how they are characterized in individual patients. The focus here is on the appraisal of functional communication; however, the appraisal of all aspects of the patient's speech/language and language-related attentional and cognitive functioning deserves careful attention in the appraisal process.

Understanding of the patient's medical history and current status can be gained through the study of his medical record and through conferences with his physician or physicians. Neurological data that are consistent with a diagnosis of language of confusion include rapid onset associated with traumatic cause; multifocal or diffuse, focal, or bilateral brain damage; and an EEG reflecting general or bilateral dysrhythmia. When possible, it is helpful for the speech/language pathologist and physician to conduct jointly some aspects of their examinations, sharing observations and learning from each other about their patients. This procedure applies equally well for other pairs of professional team members, such as psychologist and speech/language pathologist. Indeed, speech/language assessment batteries may in many ways resemble neuropsychological batteries. For example, both should include evaluation of appearance, mood and behavior, orientation, concern toward illness, level of general intellectual functioning, fluency, spoken verbal repetition, oral reading, spatial relationships, memory, and so on.

Of special importance to speech/language appraisal is accurate information concerning the patient's immediate pretrauma use of aids related to communication, such as corrective lenses—either eyeglasses or contact lenses—hearing aid, dentures, obturator, or electrolarynx. When the patient has been accustomed to the use of any of these aids, restoration should be made as quickly as possible. Because their restoration may facilitate orientation, speech intelligibility, the understanding of speech, and self-esteem, the administration of tests of intellectual and language functioning should be deferred until the aids have been replaced or checked for appropriate fit. When this is not possible, their absence should be considered in the assessment. This assumes, of course, that the patient accepts their restoration; this is not always the case. In any event, knowledge of their prior use is essential to a valid appraisal.

Although hearing and vision are rarely affected by trauma to the extent that disorders of speech/language can be attributed to them, knowledge of the patient's posttrauma vision and hearing function is needed for a comprehensive appraisal and for valid interpretation of medical and behavioral test results and observations. When indicated, patients should be fitted with appropriate aids regardless of pretrauma history. In the event that a patient has a history that includes deafness and the use of manual communication, it will be necessary for the examiner either to be or to request assistance from an interpreter for the deaf.

Because of the likelihood of confabulation and memory disturbances, accurate pretrauma biographical data are extremely important to the appraisal and therapeutic process for the traumatically brain-injured person. Such data include details of personal history, educational achievements, the accident itself, and the patient's medical status, pre- and posttrauma. Biographical information can be obtained through interviews with family, friends, and coworkers; the study of school records and other documents; and by conferences with team professionals. The point to be made here is that the effort made to research the patient's history is of value to the patient. The clinician simply must be confident of the facts if he is to deal most effectively with a confused patient or to assist the patient optimally in learning to access his memory.

The patient's history can also importantly influence the clinician's choice of therapeutic strategies and the patient's response to therapy. Depending upon the pretrauma history, certain treatment strategies may be prepotent over others; and response to therapy is undoubtedly affected by pretrauma intellectual and linguistic characteristics. Accurate biographical information can reveal unique attributes of the patient with respect to pretrauma language habits, mannerisms, areas of expertise, social and emotional patterns, cognitive style, reinforcers, response patterns and sources of stimulus control. We expect patients to display first and most frequently patterns of behavior and problem-solving strategies that were used most often pretrauma. We expect them to make use of their knowledge and experience to the extent that it is, or can be made, available to them. And, we expect pretrauma emotional patterns to be reflected and magnified during the recovery process. It is for all of these reasons that information about the patient's history can be so helpful to the speech/language pathologist in planning for and working with the patient.

Some therapeutic decisions can best be made by observing the patient's response to a particular management procedure or technique or type of therapy. These would include decisions relating to positioning, the use of a palatal lift, possible pharyngeal flap surgery, and the use of manual communication or a variety of other nonvocal communication systems. Some of these techniques can be tried and evaluated quickly; for example, the effects of a palatal lift on the intelligibility of the speech of a dysarthric patient may be immediate and dramatically positive. On the other hand, it may take several weeks to assess the effects of Amerind on the functional communication status of a severely aphasic patient.

Behavioral information is obtained from tests of general language ability, specialized tests, and observations. The results of batteries of standardized, formal assessment tools can support diagnoses and prognoses; they can also help indirectly in making clinical management decisions. For example, a diagnosis of dysarthria of a particular type should prompt preliminary therapeutic decisions different from those prompted by diagnoses of aphasia, apraxia of speech, or the language of confusion.

Although most of the tests of general language ability for adults are designed to measure aphasia, each contains subtests appropriate for appraising other of the neurogenic speech/language disorders. Since trauma resulting from accident, stroke, or other cause is not planned, however, there is usually no precise way to measure the magnitude of the difference between post- and pretrauma status. Posttrauma behaviors seen as deficient or abnormal may or may not be the result of the trauma. This is especially the case with respect to behaviors associated with socioacademic experiences such as reading, writing, grammar, diction, and arithmetic and with personality variables. Because of the lack of pretrauma assessment data, assessment tools for aphasia are constructed so that average persons, not known to have been subjected to experiences associated with neurogenic speech/language disorders, perform the test tasks with relative ease. Accordingly, such tools may fail to detect residual trauma related deficits that can significantly affect subsequent learning and resocialization. Indeed, the risk of failing to detect subtle language or language-related deficits may be particularly high for the traumatically brain-injured person. For this reason, all professional team members should be alert to the signs of trauma-related deficits and should know how to refer the patient for special testing.

Not to be overlooked in the appraisal process is the direct approach wherein the examiner simply asks the patient to describe the sorts of difficulties, if any, he is experiencing with respect to understanding words, thinking of words, reading, writing, saying what he means to say, remembering, numbering, calculating, and so on. The patient may readily volunteer critical information that might otherwise not be disclosed.

Decisions regarding appropriate content and contexts for therapy may be based in part on information acquired from pretrauma biographies, observations of the patient's communicative exchanges with those about him, and the structured appraisal of functional communication. The appraisal of functional communication has as its focus the degree to which the patient succeeds in communicative exchanges in everyday situations. It considers the patient's ability to work within and around the constraints of his production problems, whatever they may be, and his abilities to occasion others to assist him in communicating and in understanding. A functional description of the patient's communicative status is useful in that it assists the clinician in initiating speech/language therapy that is of high functional value and relevance to the patient. After functional communicative losses have been redressed, the option of working for recovery beyond the functional sphere remains viable; *without* recovery of functional communication, the recovery of other language skills has little impact on the patient's ability to resume his former style of work or living.

The clinician who wants to focus first on functional communication may wish to administer tests of general language abilities and functional measures of communication. In this way, she can measure progress on both types of measures after administration of treatment plans that are initially primarily functional in focus. The clinician who focuses therapy on deficits tapped only by tests of general and special language abilities may be less interested in the patient's functional communication performance. Both clinicians, however, will be interested in obtaining baseline data against which progress can later be measured.

While there are numerous appraisal instruments and procedures that satisfy most of the purposes of appraisal, there are few that focus on functional communication. What follows here is a potpourri of appraisal gleaned from aphasia literature with particular attention given to the appraisal of functional communication.

2.2. "Testing"

There can be no standard battery of tests that serves each patient equally well. To be most efficient and effective, appraisal must be tailored to the patient. The patient's responses to a basic battery of tests initially administered will suggest to the experienced examiner other tests to be given and observations to be made. These specialized tests and procedures may highlight the presence of particular disorders and suggest the viability of particular therapeutic strategies. Both Wertz (1978) and Brookshire (1978) provide extensive coverage on the nature of comprehensive speech/language evaluations for the traumatically brain-injured person. Always, the professional is expected to be able to state clearly the rationale for each test administered. The patient is not expected to endure or to pay for testing that has no pertinence to his future. Testing done solely for the purpose of predicting the locus of lesion is appropriate when surgery is being contemplated. Testing done to establish baseline is appropriate when results are used to measure progress or the lack of it, to guide clinical decisions, and to advise and counsel the patient.

It is important to emphasize at some point that trauma patients fatigue very easily and that the effects of fatigue can invalidate the results of even the most excellent test instruments. The examiner, then, must be sensitive to patient fatigue and must resist the possible urgings of others to proceed with the appraisal process until the patient is rested. Common signs of fatigue include an increase in the tendency to perseverate either verbally or nonverbally, a decrease in tolerance for frustration, an increase in agitation or general irritability, and drowsiness.

2.2.1. Tests of General Language Ability

As indicated above, tests of general language ability designed to measure aphasia in adults contain subtests appropriate for appraising other neurogenic speech/language disorders; and they are used, when possible, by most speech/language pathologists to appraise trauma patients initially. Many of the most frequently used tests of general language ability are expertly reviewed in Darley's recent *Evaluation of Appraisal Techniques in Speech and Language Pathology* (1979). Brookshire (1978) also provides descriptive and critical reviews of many of the same tests. Tests that are often referred to as tests of general language ability are listed in Table 1. Of the four, the Porch Index of Communicative

Ability (PICA) and the Minnesota Test for Differential Diagnosis of Aphasia (MTDDA) are favored by Darley's reviewers on their test construction attributes and their overall usefulness. Brookshire (1978, pp. 63–64) provides an extremely clear and helpful discussion regarding the relative merits of these four instruments. This discussion plus the reviews in Darley (1979) and Eisenson (1973) and comments throughout the Johns (1978) volume provide an overview of the measures themselves and the ways in which they are regarded by various reviewers. They are all long, relatively comprehensive tests of general language ability including, each to a greater or lesser degree, subtests dealing with speech, com-

Table 1. Tests of General Language Ability

Boston Diagnostic Aphasia Examination (Goodglass & Kaplan, 1972)	From 1 to 4 hours administration, 30 minutes scoring time. Allows for discrimination among types of aphasia and for inferences about localization of lesion. Yields no prognostic information.
Minnesota Test for Differential Diagnosis of Aphasia (Schuell, 1972)	From 1½ to 2½ hours administration and scoring time combined. Allows for prognostication of recovery of language function and for discrimination among aphasic patients based on severity of language impairment and specific effects of associated visual, auditory, or sensorimotor impairment. Minimal sensitivity to mild impairments.
Neurosensory Center Comprehensive Examination for Aphasia (Spreen & Benton, 1977)	About 1 hour administration, 20 minutes scoring time. Additional possible testing and scoring add about 30 minutes overall. Interpretation depends heavily on experience of examiner. Minimal sensitivity to mild impairments.
Porch Index of Communicative Ability (Porch, 1971)	About 1 hour administration, 20 minutes scoring time. Allows for prognostication of recovery of language function, discrimination among language disorders. Acclaimed for multidimensional scoring system and sensitivity to aphasia. Appraisal of auditory modality is limited. Special training in administration/scoring/interpretation is essential.

prehension of speech, reading, writing, and gesturing abilities. Some of their features are described in the last column in Table 1.

With the intent of reducing time of administration, shorter tests of general language ability have been developed, from the Boston Diagnostic Aphasia Examination (BDAE), the MTDDA, and the PICA. For example, the Western Aphasia Battery (WAB) (Kertesz & Poole, 1974; Shewan & Kertesz, 1980) is a modification of the BDAE; and the Mayo Clinic Procedures for Language Evaluation is an adaptation of Schuell's (1957) Short Examination of Aphasia, which is a shortened version of the MTDDA. Recently DiSimoni, Keith, and Darley (1980) reported the development and investigation of two short versions of the *PICA*. According to the authors, these short versions (SPICAs) predict overall scores by standard administration at acceptable confidence levels.

2.2.2. Special Tests

As indicated earlier, it is sometimes difficult to detect language and language-related cognitive and attentional deficits resulting from trauma. Even patients who seem to be engaging in normal conversation may be experiencing word-finding difficulties and fluency problems. Accordingly, it is extremely important that linguistic examinations be sufficiently comprehensive to reveal these deficits, and there are special tests that help. Most often cited in this regard are the Token Test (DeRenzi & Vignolo, 1962; see also DeRenzi & Fablioni, 1978; and DiSimoni, 1978) and tests of verbal fluency (see Borkowski, Benton, & Spreen, 1967, and review by Wertz, 1979). The Token Test is a sensitive measure of auditory comprehension, while tests of verbal fluency pose open-ended verbal situations that may occasion behaviors associated with a variety of neurogenic language syndromes. Typically, the confused patient reveals his irrelevance and tendency to confabulate on tests of verbal fluency.

The Token Test detects mild auditory comprehension deficits by manipulating the length and complexity of auditory stimuli in nonredundant commands involving the arrangement of tokens varying in color, shape, and size. Currently, it is probably the most widely used test for measuring the auditory abilities of aphasic patients. Several versions of the Token Test exist—so many, in fact, that examiners are advised to include in their reports operational descriptions of test administration and scoring procedures used. When appropriate, the test can be made more difficult by imposing 10- to 20-second delays between delivery of the test commands and exposure of the tokens for the patient's response.

Fluency tests are used to detect brain damage and word-finding difficulties. They are variously referred to as verbal fluency tests, controlled word-association tests, tests of verbal associative fluency, and so on. There are again several variations; all are discussed in the Wertz review (1979b). The patient is asked to state all the words he can think of beginning with a particular letter in 1 minute. The patient repeats the task for three letters specified by the examiner; the score is the total number of different words given by the patient that satisfy the restrictions. In addition to the usual fluency assessment procedure, it is sometimes helpful to probe in a similar manner for the patient's ability to supply names of members of categories—such as fruits, games, or holidays—or to ask him to describe pictures that occasion attempts to retrieve abstract terms such as names of occupations—for example, pharmacist, plumber, and so on.

The Brookshire (1978) text contains reviews of a variety of other special tests especially helpful and needed in the appraisal of head-injured patients. For example, there is an extensive section pertaining to tests of memory. Comprehensive appraisal procedures and rationales for their use with traumatically brain-injured patients can also be found in Wertz (1978) and Rosenbek (1978b).

Areas of appraisal that suggest special comment here include general intelligence, orientation, motor speech, prosody, and stuttering. Intelligence is appraised in order to determine whether patients perform at levels consistent with pretrauma history and to expose possible trauma-related discrepancies between intelligence and the quality of language. The relationship between intelligence and language disturbance subsequent to traumatic brain injury is not clear (see Mandelberg & Brooks, 1975, and Shaffer et al., 1980). Because of this and the possibility of the presence of neurogenic language disorders, nonverbal intelligence tests are preferable to verbal for assessing intellectual functioning. Even when nonverbal tests are used, however, the examiner must be aware that the patient is not likely to perform at his best until his attentional set can be reliably maintained and switched from one stimulus or task to another. Further, the examiner must be alert to the possibility of errors resulting from the intrusion of unrecognized verbal content into the stimulus materials and test administration procedures. For more specific information, refer to Wertz (1978).

Orientation and general information are routinely appraised for trauma patients because orientation problems, though common, are sometimes subtle and general information tasks are apt to occasion irrelevancy and confabulation from the confused patient. Since orientation problems are sometimes persistent, it is especially important to do a thorough job here, assessing orientation to persons, time, and place/space in considerable depth.

Because of the likelihood of motor involvement, motor speech evaluations are sometimes indicated for trauma patients (Gilchrist & Wilkinson, 1979). Rosenbek (1978b) suggests that the test designed by Moore, Rosenbek, and LaPointe (1976) may be particularly helpful in this regard. Motor speech evaluations highlight the contributions of disorders of respiration, phonation, articulation, resonance, and prosody to the presenting speech/language problems. Such tests may reveal the presence of apraxia of speech, one of the dysarthrias, or coexisting disorders. Excellent discussions of the appraisal of motoric aspects of speech are contained in Wertz (1978) and Rosenbek (1978b). The speech/language pathologist is also alert to dysfunctions of prosody, the patient's ability to vary in conventional ways loudness, pitch, articulation rate, pause time, and stress in his connected or conversational speech. Dysfunctions of prosody associated with trauma may suggest, again, the presence of one of the motor speech problems or a combination.

The current literature (Rosenbek, 1978a; Helm, Butler, & Benson, 1978), as well as occasionally the less current, mentions stuttering as an aspect of speech behavior following brain injury. This topic is poorly understood and clearly requires further study. It is mentioned here only to alert the examiner to the possibility and to the literature.

Even with all these tests, the examiner's observations remain very important in appraisal. Test results alone may support conclusions of no impairment or complete recovery while the experienced examiner's observations may occasion quite different interpretations of the same test results.

2.2.3. *Appraisal of Functional Communication/Speech/Language*

Last we address the most neglected area in appraisal: functional speech/language/communication. The clinician interested in addressing functional therapeutic content can extract helpful information regarding content and context from tests of general language ability and the special tests already described; however, additional very valuable information can be obtained from frankly functional appraisal instruments.

Patients with neurogenic language disorders often seem to perform better in "real life" situations than on formal tests such as the Token Test or the PICA. Basing their view on interesting experimental findings, Wilcox *et al.* (1978) suggest that this is so because aphasic patients retain the ability to interpret extralinguistic contextual cues correctly in natural (i.e., somewhat redundant) settings. Holland (1980, p. 1) also states that except for the most severely brain-injured, aphasic patients probably retain considerable communicative competency. Holland elaborates on her reference to communicative competency: "understanding of how language functions, its social conventions, who is worth listening to, when to speak, and when to listen." Further, she includes in communicative competency the abilities to discriminate between verbal affection and verbal abuse, between an order and a request, and between a statement and a question. Out of Holland's 40 aphasic subjects, who were each observed for 2 hours distributed over 4 hours in 5-minute segments, only one was credited with more unsuccessful than successful communicative interactions, a successful interaction being defined as one in which the patient is able to get his message across regardless of the means used to convey it. For these reasons and because of the face validity of its relevance to both appraisal and therapy, we now consider the appraisal of functional communication.

The earliest and for a long time the only instrument designed to assess functional language ability was Sarno's Functional Communication Profile (FCP) (1969; see review by Swisher, 1979). This tool provides a systematic way for an experienced examiner to rate communication after a 10- to 20-minute conversation with the patient. Forty-five behaviors, divided into five categories (movement or gestural communication, speaking, spoken and gestural understanding, reading, and a miscellaneous category that includes temporal orientation, writing, and calculation) are rated on a nine-point scale ranging from "no ability" to "normal," with "normal" referring to the examiner's judgment of the patient's premorbid abilities. The ratings reflect the patient's ability to compensate for his deficits—his speed, accuracy, and consistency of performance. As Swisher points out in her review, "No other evaluation tool permits as rapid an overall assessment of a patient's general pattern of impairment in an informal setting."

Holland's recent *Communication Abilities in Daily Living* (CADL) (1980), goes several steps beyond the FCP. Although administration time is slightly longer (generally about 35 to 40 minutes), the CADL offers a far more comprehensive assessment of functional communication than the FCP. Most importantly, the CADL provides information for identifying relevant treatment objectives.

What the CADL actually purports to measure is how a patient gets along communicatively, using residual skills in everyday encounters. This test does not attempt to replace tests of general language abilities; rather, it is a supplementary instrument that can reveal basic communication deficits and point the way to fruitful therapeutic approaches for them. The test has been impressively normed, validated, and checked for reliability; all supporting data are available in the book that accompanies the test. Scoring of its 68 items on a 0, 1, 2 point system (incorrect, adequate, correct) takes from 5 to 20 minutes. The score is determined by cumulating the points earned, the maximum number being 136.

The CADL simulates daily life activities. Only functional communication activities are measured, that is, those that are common in the daily lives of "most" Americans. Gesturing, speaking, writing, reading, and understanding are tested in simulated activities including going to the doctor's office, riding in a car, shopping, using the telephone, and being interviewed by a stranger. The test items are spread across 10 categories described and exemplified below:

1.   Reading, writing, and using numbers to estimate, calculate, and judge time. Example: Role playing a visit to a doctor's office with the patient, the examiner says, "And here is the building directory. What floor is Dr. Clark's office on?"

2.   Speech acts, defined as pragmatic interchanges in which speech, gesture, or writing are used to convey both information and intent. Speech acts sampled include explaining, correcting misinformation, informing, requesting, negotiating, advising, and reporting. Example: The examiner in the role of the doctor's receptionist is trying to arrange an appointment with the patient and says, "What time is good?" This item is classified as a speech act of "negotiation."

3.   Utilizing verbal and nonverbal context. Example: On one item, the stimulus material, a picture of a "No Smoking" sign, is presented in the context of a person smoking, and the examiner says, "What's happening in this picture?"

4.   Role playing. Some CADL items are done in a role-playing mode; for example, the patient "pretends" to be visiting the doctor's office while the tester assumes the roles of receptionist and doctor. Example: Role playing a shopping trip with the patient, the examiner says, "You need shoelaces. You can't find them. A clerk says, 'May I help you?' What do you say?"

5.   Sequenced and relationship-dependent communicative behavior. Some CADL items require either the ability to perform sequences of behavior, such as dialing a phone number or untangling, communicatively, a set of cause–effect relationships. Example: Shown a picture of a vending machine and given 85 cents in change, the patient is told, "Here is a vending machine and some change. Show me how you would get a drink."

6.   Social conventions. Although greeting, accepting apologies,

leave-taking, and so on could properly be included as speech acts (Category 2), they have been separately categorized here because they appear to be somewhat more primitive and overlearned than the other CADL speech act items. Example: Role playing an episode at the doctor's office, the examiner assumes the role of the receptionist and says to the patient, "May I help you?" The patient is scored on the basis of his response.

7. Divergencies. This category includes items that allow the patient to demonstrate his ability to generate logical possibilities and a ready flow of ideas as well as his readiness to change the direction of his responses. Example: "Show me the drawing that goes with the saying: 'He hit the ceiling.'" Another example: "You have 85 cents to spend (give patient 85 cents). Which can you buy?" Question is in the context of a fan, a cord, and a child.

8. Nonverbal symbolic communication. This category is concerned with nonverbal communication and symbols, such as recognizing a playing card or associating facial expression with emotion. Example: "Look at these cards. Find the four of clubs."

9. Deixis. Deixis is operationalized here as movement-related or dependent communicative behaviors. Example: At the beginning of the test interview, the examiner says to the patient, indicating "where" by pointing, "Would you go over there, please?"

10. Humor, absurdity, metaphor. Example: At the end of the visit to the doctor's office, the examiner in the role of the doctor says to the patient, "Okay, Mr./Mrs. _____, before our next visit, I want you to smoke three packs of cigarettes and drink a bottle of gin a day. Okay?"

The patient who performs well on the CADL does not need functional communication training *per se*. Such a patient may be ready to address some of his fine-grain language or language-related cognitive and attentional deficits. The CADL is a test of functional communication. It allows us to probe for this communicative base in a way that has not been possible before, and it does so in a way suggesting that training activities can effectively be couched in a functional context that supports social reintegration and involves such features as humor and divergent thinking in addition to whatever refinement of speech/language is the primary target.

3. Therapeutic Strategies

Some of the strategies reviewed here have broad clinical applicability, while others have a narrow focus. Among them, the two prevailing trends are toward strategies that place high priority on functional communication and accountability. For a comprehensive review of intervention strategies, the reader is directed to previously cited works of Johns (1978), Brookshire (1978), Wepman (1951), and Schuell *et al.* (1964).

3.1. Speech/Language Pathologists

A few words about speech/language pathologists seem in order. Speech/language pathologists certified as clinically competent (CCC-S means that the owner holds a Certificate of Clinical Competency in Speech) by the American Speech-Language-Hearing Association, vary enormously in skills, kind and amount of training, and experience in neurogenic communication disorders. Some with master's degrees are exceedingly competent and experienced in this highly specialized field, while some with doctorates have only the most superficial acquaintance. When a certified speech/language pathologist who is especially trained and experienced in neurogenic communicative disorders is available, regardless of level of academic attainment, the traumatically brain-injured patient and family are well served by her presence, full acceptance, and involvement on the rehabilitation team responsible for the clinical management of the patient.

3.2. Goals of Functional Communication/Speech/Language Therapy

The goals of functional therapeutic intervention for persons with neurogenic communication disorders can be collapsed into six:

- To make it easier for the patient to maintain attentional set
- To make it easier for the patient to understand the message
- To make it easier for the patient to remember the message
- To make it easier for the patient to make his message understood
- To foster in the patient reasonable good humor, good taste, and self-esteem
- To prevent withdrawal or the acquisition or strengthening of inappropriate compensatory behaviors stemming from communicative failure

Ideally, clinician, patient, and family work together toward these goals. For example, in order to make it easier for the patient to remember messages, the therapist uses a teaching register that highlights the message. The therapist provides explicit rehearsal of the message to be remembered, arranges the environment so that reminders are intrusive, and instructs the patient in memory strategies. During the course of therapy, the patient is expected to learn to rehearse independently, write and post notes for himself, keep a calendar, set his own alarm clock to occasion his attending to this schedule and notes to himself, keep readily accessible communication devices and materials such as paper and pencil, and utilize deliberately other memory strategies that might be helpful including asking others to remind him of something. The family is expected to participate in therapy, follow through with the patient on homework assignments, and learn to prompt the patient to practice the strategies that are emphasized in therapy.

In order to make it easier for the patient to understand incoming messages from others, the therapist uses a teaching register and may combine congruent gestures and/or written messages with speech. The patient learns to ask speakers to heighten the quality of their input to him. For example, he might ask the speaker to slow down, repeat the message, write it down, speak louder, or demonstrate the message. The family is expected to assist the patient by adjusting to his needs and to serve as catalysts for him in social situations. For example, it is OK for the patient to ask a family member to help him with a particular word in the midst of a conversation with someone else. Such assists can be performed with grace and are expected of the sensitive family member.

The clinician uses a variety of approaches to make it easier for the patient to make himself understood by his audience. These may include supplying the patient with a palatal lift, a voice amplifier, a delayed auditory feedback device, or an artificial larynx; teaching the patient to use an alternative communicative mode such as Amerind, a speech synthesizer, or an alphabet board to supplement his speech; and encouraging him to take advantage of other compensatory strategies at his disposal. In the course of therapy, the patient is expected to learn to use without prompts the devices, alternate modes, and strategies that are most helpful to him.

3.3. Special Instructions and Precautions

The speech/language pathologist/clinician is assailed by myriad special instructions and precautions regarding the therapeutic management of patients with neurogenic speech/language disorders. A distillation of common clinical tips and precautions is presented in Table 2 and may provide a needed context for the descriptions of the therapy approaches that follow.

3.4. Treatment Specific to the Language of Confusion

The role of the speech/language pathologist in the treatment of patients demonstrating the language of confusion may involve reality-

Table 2.   Tips and Precautions on Therapeutic Intervention for Patients with Neurogenic Communication Disorders

1. Use a meaningful functional context.
2. Use the teaching register to facilitate understanding: increase stimulus exposure time, insert pauses between word groups, surround important words with pauses, reduce overall rate of speaking, exaggerate stress and intonational pattern, reduce length and linguistic complexity of utterance, increase contextual redundancy, use high-frequency words, use words of low abstraction value.
3. Be sure the patient responds in some way to each training stimulus provided; if he is unable to respond in speech, he may be able to respond in gesture or in another mode. For every target response, have a backup response that you can count on.
4. Carefully manage the patient's success density on training tasks and experiences. Maintain success density at better than 50%.
5. Begin session with items low in error risk.
6. Be critical of how you prompt the patient; try to increase your use of intrastimulus prompts.
7. Work with the patient frequently for short sessions: two or three times a day for 15 to 20 minutes per session.
8. Schedule therapy at times when the patient is least likely to be fatigued: early in the morning, after naps.
9. Give patient what may seem like an excessive amount of time to respond before prompting.
10. Probe frequently for generalization and for the facilitating effects that therapy may have on nontargeted objectives.
11. Use multimodal input. Since this approach may not be best for all patients, be ready to change tactics depending on patient response.
12. Make use of assignments, even in the hospital.
13. Provide a setting for successful practice.
14. Provide the patient access to verbal input: talking books, tapes from family and friends, tapes from you, records, radio, television.
15. Treat the entire family when possible: involve them in therapy, give them assignments, let them know that you need and expect their involvement and help.
16. Include orientation content in conversational exchanges: who you are, what you are doing, where you are, what day it is, what time it is, and so on. Do this often.
17. Provide changes in environmental background for therapy.
18. Provide variety of sensory stimulation: taste, smell, heat, cold, and pressure as well as kinesthetic, tactile, auditory, and visual stimuli.
19. Provide things for patient to do alone, for pleasure only, that never become the content of therapy tasks—for example, listening to talking books.
20. Introduce new materials and procedures as extensions of familiar ones in order to minimize disruptive effects.
21. Provide patient with accurate feedback of his performance; teach him to evaluate his own performance; share progress notes with patient. The best reinforcer is likely to be accurate, positive feedback from the clinician or the natural environment. By calling attention to improvement, you may strengthen the patient's inclination to attend, practice, and risk successful communication.

orientation therapy, therapy designed to ameliorate memory and attentioal deficits, and language therapy to improve specific communication deficits.

Reality-orientation therapy has been described by Phillips (1973) and Wertz (1978). In an organized and comprehensive manner, patients are continuously reminded of relevant names of persons, names of places, relationships to persons, significance of places, relative spatial arrangement of places, time, temporal relationships, sequence of events, and facts pertaining to themselves and their present condition. The therapy is accomplished through the involvement of all staff and through individual and group therapy for the patients. The patient's schedule is rigidly adhered to, with as few changes in personnel as possible. Ideally, the environment is calm; there is a set routine; consistent, clear responses are given to the patient's questions or requests for directions; physical guidance is provided to the extent needed; orientation information is present continuously; and confabulation or rambling is interrupted. Much of the language therapy for the confused patient is structured around individualized orientation data. For example, the patient may be asked a series of questions regarding biographical information; when needed, he is encouraged to refer to his personalized orientation reference material to supply the information requested. When irrelevancy or confabulation occur, the patient is stopped and questioned and appropriate information is supplied as necessary in a calm consistent manner.

Memory strategies are basically of two kinds. Some are designed to teach the patient to utilize strategies that aid him in storing information in an easily retrievable form. Others are designed to teach the patient to set up and then to use external assists. In other words, the patient is taught to make lists, set alarms, post notes to himself in strategic places, write almost literally everything down, use a tape recorder, and ask others to remind him of things and remember things for him. Once having set up external assists, he is expected to use them in managing his daily affairs. The strategies that concentrate on storage and retrieval may include semantic associations, visual associations, vocal rehearsal, and explicit self-instruction to remember. It is important for the therapist to be aware of the patient's memory problems and to work with and around them. For example, at first it may be better to supply accurate orientation information to the patient frequently than to confront him with questions. Later, memory tasks can be included in therapy; these may appropriately be retrieval tasks or tasks that teach the patient to set up and consult cues, such as his log book, to find the answers to questions. Gianutsos (1980) describes the use of mnemonics and a new professional, the cognitive rehabilitation specialist.

When the patient displays difficulties in focusing, maintaining focus, and discriminating among stimuli, these problems also affect the patient's response to speech/language therapy and accordingly must be recognized and dealt with by the clinician. The teaching strategies described later in this section (3.6) are relevant here, especially highlighting, because they blend so easily with the patient's need for structure. When maintenance of attentional set is a problem, therapy tasks should be highly structured, gradually becoming less so as the patient's tendency toward irrelevance and confabulation decreases. In addition, a special effort is made to promote the patient's practice of self-regulatory strategies that may ultimately help to overcome attentional deficits.

3.5. The Accountability Strategies

The strategies described here have broad clinical applicability and approach the problem of accountability from quite different perspectives. Undoubtedly other such strategies will emerge; for now, however, these serve as models.

3.5.1. The Problem Oriented Medical Record (POMR)

The Problem Oriented Medical Record has been widely adopted in the rehabilitation setting because it affords clarity to the documentation of service to the patient. In addition, it is widely acclaimed as a clinical tool because it organizes patient data, facilitates communication among team members, and is thought to add significantly to a high overall quality of service to the patient. Speech/language pathology discovered POMR in the medical/physical rehabilitation setting and is now adopting it in other areas of service (Bouchard & Shane, 1977; Balick, Greene, Kaplan, Press, & Demopoulos, 1978; Kent & Chabon, 1980).

To the individual therapist, regardless of discipline, POMR means that the patient's record will contain a problem list that is current and documented in a data base; it also means that the therapist contributes to the problem statements and to the data base. Further, the therapist contributes to the development of objectives and plans designed to resolve the problems. The therapist records data in each therapy session and collapses it regularly into the record. And the therapist contributes to the progress-notes section of the record. The progress notes are the meat of the record, a continuous chronology of events that describe the patient's course in the clinical setting. For example, on any one day there may be separate but continuous progress-note entries signed by a physician, a physical therapist, a chaplain, a nurse, a social worker, and a psychologist. Each clinician is able to review the current status of the patient quickly through the progress-note entries of others before seeing the patient and adding her own progress note. When entries are of special interest, the clinician is often able to access flowchart data with the record that support the progress note; if questions remain unanswered, the clinician is able to request clarification from the person who wrote the note. When used appropriately, POMR affords excellent accountability and a tight feedback loop that may benefit the patient and further educate the members of the clinical team. The use of POMR in medical/physical rehabilitation can be surveyed by a review of the following references: Dinsdale, Gent, Kline, and Milner (1975); Dinsdale, Mossman, Gullickson, and Anderson (1970); Grabois (1977); Granger and Delabarre (1974); Milhouse (1972); Reinstein (1977); Reinstein, Stass, and Marquette (1975).

3.5.2. La Pointe's Base-10 Response Form

La Pointe (1977, 1979) has made a singular contribution to accountability in clinical speech/language pathology through the introduction of his *Base-10 Response Form* and the description of its use. The concept lends itself best to highly structured types of speech/language therapy; for example, it is ideally suited to drill on orientation information. A sample form ready for use is shown in Figure 1. Note that the form allows space for describing the general nature of the task (e.g., Orientation—personal data) and for specifying the criterion and scoring method. Under "postbaseline therapy" there is space to describe the therapy procedure telegraphically; the nature of 10 different stimulus items along with baseline performance for 3 days and acquisition for 10 are recorded under "stimuli" and "session." At the end of each training session, the clinician computes the mean score on the 10 items in the task and plots the percent correct on a display that accommodates baseline and 10 training sessions. In any one session, a separate response form is completed for each task undertaken.

The system lends itself well to the use of a 0, 1, 2 scoring system, as in the CADL, and a multidimensional scoring system, as in the PICA (see McNeil, 1979). Because these scoring procedures are more sensitive than + − systems to changes in patient performance, their use makes a further contribution to accountability. The *Base-10 Response Form* helps the clinician to document the effects of treatment over time, and it may indirectly contribute to therapeutic effectiveness. A variety of samples of the use of the forms are available in La Pointe (1977, 1978).

3.5.3. Brookshire's Clinical Interaction Analysis System

The third accountability model is Brookshire's (1978) method of observing and recording events in treatment sessions. The system provides a fine-grain analysis of clinician–patient interaction by means of observation of clinician and patient responses such as the type of materials used, the form of feedback given to the patient, the complexity of requests made to the patient, requests for information made by the patient, and responses attempted by the patient. Thirty-nine event categories are used to analyze videotaped sessions and 26 are used in an on-line system. Good reliability has been demonstrated after 24 hours of training on the long system and 15 on the short. The results provide feedback to the clinician regarding the effectiveness and efficiency of therapy. Further, the system lends itself to the assessment of differences among therapy approaches. The system is not simple and requires training; nevertheless, it is simultaneously a clinical training tool, a research tool, and a means of accountability. For these reasons, it is recommended for consideration.

3.6. The Teaching Strategies

Therapy can precipitate counterproductive emotional stress for the patient unless it provides a comfortable level of success. The following strategies are adaptable to the Base-10 format of therapy, to multidimensional scoring, and to the design of homework assignments. They are most adaptable to tasks that focus on motor programming, memory, and word retrieval. Only the first group of these procedures was designed specifically for adult aphasic patients; however, all of the strategies described are adaptable to clinical practice for selected patients. Their primary merit is in their potential for guiding the therapist in the design of training activities that focus the patient's attention, support his attentional set through task completion, and maintain a high response rate and success density. Three basic strategies are involved: (1) highlighting the critical dimensions of the training stimuli, (2) providing the opportunity for practice on behaviors of low strength, and (3) maintaining a high density of success throughout the activity.

3.6.1. Programmed Strategies

Rosenbek, Lemme, Ahern, Harris, and Wertz (1973) report a speech production shaping procedure that is highly structured and effective in teaching selected utterances to some apractic patients (Deal & Florance, 1978). Examples of statements that might be taught are "I want water," "I want coffee," "I want milk." The procedure is referred to as the eight-step continuum for treatment of apraxia; the eight steps are as follows:

BASE-10 RESPONSE FORM

by Leonard L. LaPointe, Ph.D.

The **Base-10 Response Form**© allows space for specification of the task, definition and listing of acceptable performance score on each item during every session. Finally, the **Base-10 Response Form** permits a subject's performance levels to be converted to a graphic display of progress (or lack of it) in percentage over 10 sessions.

The **Base-10 Response Form** does not dictate what to work on or how to reinforce; but once these decisions are made, it organizes stimulus presentation and provides a medium from which clear judgments of session-by-session progress can be made.

Selection of Tasks

A critical decision in using the **Base-10 Response Form** in therapy is task selection. The rationale for selecting therapeutic tasks, of course, is based on evaluation and testing of the individual person.

A number of tasks may be appropriate in a session. A different response form for each task is used so that progress on each can be plotted. For sessions of 30 to 45 minutes, three or four different tasks may be used, e.g., sentence completion, naming objects, auditory retention of directions, etc.

Criterion

For the space marked "criterion," a decision must be made about the acceptable level of performance for that task. The decision is guided by the severity of the client's disorder and by the base rate for the task and can be stated as percentage of correct responses for a specified number of sessions.

Stimulus Items

The next decision is to select 10 functional stimulus items for each task and specify them clearly on the **Base-10 Response Form,** which has adequate space for words, phrases, or sentences. Occasionally the stimuli selected are too lengthy for the space provided; then a simple code that refers to more extensive word or sentence lists can be written in the item spaces.

Scoring

Each stimulus item is presented to the subject and can be scored in one of several ways. Many tasks lend themselves to plus or minus scoring; after each one is scored, the total score for the session is computed and entered on the percentage graph. However, for many tasks a multidimensional scoring system, such as that used with *PICA*, has been found to be sensitive to small changes in patient performance. The mean of the *PICA*-type scores achieved on each of the 10 stimuli is computed and then divided by 15 (on the PICA a 15 represents an accurate, undelayed, complete, and efficiently produced response); this conversion to percentage is then entered on the graph.

Baseline Measurement and Postbaseline Therapy

Establishing baseline performance on a task can be done in several ways, including measuring performance during successive sessions before initiating any drill or therapy on error items. Baseline may be measured by scoring the 10 items several times during one day or several times within a session with subsequent plotting of the mean performance as a base rate. Space is provided on the **Base-10 Response Form** for recording three baseline measurements (B_1, B_2, B_3). The number of baseline measurements necessary is guided by the stability of these measurements. Demonstration of treatment effectiveness requires departure from a baseline that is only modestly variable. If baseline performance varies widely from measurement to measurement, this usually suggests modification of task difficulty.

It is important to emphasize that the measurement, or merely scoring performance on 10 stimulus items, does not constitute the therapy. After baseline performance is established, it is time to introduce the therapeutic variable, which is the particular strategy selected for improving the subject's performance on the 10 stimulus items. Usually error items are separated, and attention is focused on each one in an attempt to modify the deviant response. This is the point at which all the stimulation and facilitation strategies designed to elicit the best possible response are used. Such techniques as integral stimulation ("Watch me." "Listen to me."), additional cuing, cue fading, alternating rhythm or tempo, temporal gapping, association, synthesis of stimulus components, explanation and model presentation, and repetition are all effective means of modifying deviant responses. These strategies of therapeutic intervention on the error items are specified and recorded on the **Base-10 Response Form** under the section labeled "postbaseline therapy." The continuing measurement of session-by-session performance on the task can be used to judge effectiveness of therapeutic intervention.

Figure 1. Base-10 Response Form ready for use. (Copyright 1979 by C. C. Publications. Reprinted by permission).

BASE-10 RESPONSE FORM

PROGRAMMED SPEECH-LANGUAGE STIMULATION

TASK _____

_____

CRITERION _____ SCORING _____

Post Baseline Therapy

_____	

PERCENTAGE

100
90
80
70
60
50
40
30
20
10
0

B   1   2   3   4   5   6   7   8   9   10

DATE / / / / / / / / / /

STIMULI	B₁	B₂	B₃	1	2	3	4	5	6	7	8	9	10
1													
2													
3													
4													
5													
6													
7													
8													
9													
10													

SESSION

MEANS _____
Baseline

1. Clinician and patient say the statement simultaneously.
2. After the clinician says the statement alone, the patient says it while the clinician "mouths" it.
3. Clinician says the statement, after which the patient imitates it.
4. Same as (3) except that the patient repeats the statement several times with no intervening assists from the therapist.
5. The patient reads the statement from a card.
6. Same as (5) except that the patient responds after the card has been removed.
7. Patient responds with the statement when asked a relevant question by the therapist.
8. Patient responds with the statement appropriately in a role-playing situation with the therapist.

Correct responses are initially reinforced continuously, but the schedule of reinforcement is switched to a variable ratio after the patient begins to experience some success. Criterion performance required for moving to the next step is defined as 80% correct in 20 consecutive trials, but a more stringent criterion may sometimes be indicated (Deal & Florance, 1978). The procedure is simple, lends itself to fuctional content, and can easily be adapted to homework assignments for the patient. The success of this procedure suggests that it could serve as a model for the development of a variety of other training sequences.

Other programmed strategies of special interest that lend themselves to a Base-10 format approach include Kushner and Winitz's (1977) extended comprehension practice and Helm's (1978) visual action therapy. In the Kushner–Winitz procedure, systematic and extended comprehension practice is followed by probes for confrontation naming. Visual action therapy uses visual and gestural communicative modes along with a set of objects and drawings of the objects. The earliest of the program's 12 steps teaches the matching of the actual objects first with life-size and then smaller drawings of them. The second set of steps train manipulation of all of the objects using action pictures and ultimately the pretended use of an object randomly selected from the set. The next three steps teach recognition and production of gestures associated with the objects. The final steps train the patient to gesture–label a missing object. Two objects are shown, both are then hidden, and one is brought back into view; the patient is required to label the missing one. There are two additional levels that involve the use of action cards and small pictures. At the program's end, the patient labels concealed small line drawings with gestures.

3.6.2. The Alternation Procedure

The alternation procedure provides the patient with practice and a guaranteed success density of at least 50%. Training items are alternated with low-error risk items: items that the patient responds to correctly, easily, and quickly without prompts. All correct responses are socially reinforced in a manner appropriate to the patient. When the patient makes an error, the therapist, without comment, re-presents the item and simultaneously prompts a correct response. Next, the therapist introduces a low-error-risk item. Data are not recorded for the low-error-risk items; however, the therapist notes that the alternation procedure is being used and describes the nature of the low-error-risk items.

The alternation procedure yields a high density of success independent of the patient's performance on the training tasks. The procedure helps maintain the patient's attending and supports his positive affect throughout the task. In addition, it may facilitate performance and learning (Neef, Iwata, & Page, 1977, 1980). The low-error-risk items need not be verbal or in any sense linguistic in order to be effective. For example, a photo-matching task or setting a clock to match the time shown in a picture might be alternated with items that request personal orientation information. The only fixed requirement for a low-error-risk task is that it *be* a low-error-risk task for the patient and that it take about the same amount of time to execute as the high-error-risk task with which it is alternated.

Since the purpose of this strategy is to maintain the patient's attending and positive affect during training, the therapist must be careful not to abort its effectiveness by inadvertently alternating one high-error-risk task with another. The best low-error-risk items seem to be those that are reinforcing to the patient but not necessarily functional or related to the training task.

3.6.3. The Encore Procedure

When the patient responds correctly, without a prompt, on an item that has been a high-error-risk item, he can sometimes be prompted to follow this performance with several more correct productions. (Note similarity to Brookshire's step 4.) For example, when the patient labels "coffee" in a confrontation naming task, the therapist provides appropriate social reinforcement and then requests five repetitions: "Tell me again, please, five times." This is called the "encore procedure." It is a simple way to strengthen correct responses. It is easy to use because the therapist and the patient are already primed for the repetition of the response. The encore procedure provides practice on high-risk items within the context of success and inflates the proportion of correct to incorrect responses.

3.6.4. The Rehearsal Strategy

The rehearsal strategy reduces errors that are due to forgetting resulting from poor storage strategies and it may facilitate retention of new material. Further, it maintains attentional set, seems to compete with impulsive responding, and facilitates self-regulation. At first, the therapist rehearses *for* the patient by repeating what the patient is to remember until the patient makes a designated response. For example, the therapist might say "Find the key. . . key . . . key . . . key" while the patient searches for a key among a group of sundry objects. Next the therapist invites the patient to join her in rehearsal. (Rehearsal can be executed vocally or manually or simultaneously.) Once the patient begins to rehearse with the therapist, the therapist fades out her participation. This procedure is repeated as needed. Sometimes patients begin to use the strategy spontaneously on training tasks and in novel situations. Regardless of whether generalization occurs, rehearsal is helpful when it can be prompted; it has good potential as a self-cueing device.

When impulsive responding is a problem (i.e., the patient tends to initiate a response before the therapist has finished requesting it or otherwise to respond prematurely), the patient is required to repeat the object name in speech or sign several times before he is allowed to begin his search. By applying this strategy to various requests and by systematically lengthening the time delay between the request and the opportunity to follow through on it, the therapist can help the patient to begin to maintain his attentional set during the delays and to inhibit the impulsive or premature response.

3.6.5. Highlighting

"Highlighting" refers to a strategy that prompts correct discrimination by exaggerating the perceptual salience of some critical feature of the training stimulus. The prompt is incorporated within the training stimulus and is progressively faded once the patient is consistently making correct discriminations. In two clinical populations, autistic and mentally retarded children, highlighting followed by a progressive fading procedure has been shown to be markedly superior to prompting strategies that add qualitatively different cues, such as the therapist's pointing to the correct choice (Schreibman, 1975; Wolfe & Cuvo, 1978).

Pointing is called an "extrastimulus prompt" because the prompt is external to the stimulus. A within-stimulus prompt attracts attention to the training stimulus by exaggerating or intensifying one of the critical features or dimensions of the stimulus. Highlighting attracts the patient's attention to the critical feature without pointing or verbal instruction. The therapist can sometimes highlight or accent critical visual features of stimuli by widening, darkening, or adding texture to them. In this regard, it is important to note that only the critical feature is highlighted, not the entire stimulus. There are also a variety of ways in which the therapist can highlight vocal stimuli. For example, the therapist can exaggerate loudness, stress, or intonational pattern. She can slow down her rate and surround the stimulus with pauses—for example, "Show me the . . . tall . . . man." She can avoid complex grammatical transformations when possible; for example, instead of asking "What did you say you did?" she might ask "You did what?" All of these behaviors combined make it easier for the patient to understand the input signal and are referred to, collectively, as the teaching register.

In the fading process, highlighting is gradually eliminated and the patient is taught to disregard irrelevant stimulus dimensions, maintaining a prescribed density of success. Fading is accomplished with a sawtoothed approach: fade, slight increase in error rate, error rate reduced to 5 to 10%, another fading step, slight increase in error rate, error rate again reduced, another fading step, slight increase in error rate, error rate is not reduced, highlighting is increased, error rate reduced, another fading step, and so on. Once the patient is consistently responding correctly to the training stimulus without highlighting, the therapist begins systematically to vary *irrelevant* stimulus dimensions. For example, if the discrimination to be learned is a complex visual form discrimination such as the recognition of a printed word, the size of the print, the color of the print, and the color of the background would all be irrelevant to the form. These irrelevant dimensions are varied systematically while a high density of success on the form discrimination is maintained. When the introduction of irrelevant features is associated with an increase in errors, highlighting is reintroduced at a low level and then faded or augmented depending upon the course of the error rate.

3.6.6. The Delay Procedure

The delay procedure has to do with the timing of prompts. When a patient makes an error, the therapist immediately re-presents the item and prompts a correct response. For example, when the therapist says "What is this? Say 'key,'" there is no time delay between "What is this?" and the prompt "Say 'key'"; there is no opportunity for error, assuming that the patient is attending, does not respond impulsively, and is able to approximate an imitative response. On the next trial on the same item, the therapist delays the prompt for about 4 seconds. If the patient responds correctly within 4 seconds, no prompt is given—only reinforcement. If the patient does not respond within 4 seconds, a correct response is prompted and reinforced. If the patient makes an error within the 4 seconds, the therapist re-presents the item, delivering a prompt with no delay. Gradually, the patient learns to respond correctly within 4 seconds or to wait for a prompt. (See Touchette, 1971, and Johnson, 1977.)

Sometimes patients persistently respond incorrectly before the prompt is given (Snell, 1979). When this is a problem, several identical items are placed on the table in front of the patient. The therapist touches one of the items and simultaneously says "Touch the. . . ." For example, "Touch the key." The patient is reinforced when he touches the *same* key that the therapist touches. This procedure is repeated with randomly selected choices among the identical items. After all items have been selected at least once on a random basis, the therapist says "Touch the key" and then waits briefly before touching one. When the patient waits for the prompt and then touches the key that the therapist touches, he is reinforced. The same procedure is continued, randomizing the position of the "correct" key and gradually increasing the amount of delay up to 4 seconds as long as there are no errors. When the patient touches an item before the therapist does, the therapist drops back to a shorter delay. Once the patient learns to wait for 4 seconds, the delay procedure can be used effectively.

The delay procedure can be used to help teach a variety of tasks. It is easy to use and does not require the preparation of highly sophisticated teaching materials. It is compatible with the alternation and the encore procedures. Delay should be considered whenever there is a need to prompt. It is an excellent alternative to highlighting when highlighting is not feasible.

3.6.7. Physical Guidance and Fading

This is an "errorless" strategy used to teach motor imitation and the performance of actions inherent in functional skills. Initially, the therapist gives a verbal command and then models the behavior; as necessary, she guides the patient through the response in a hands-on fashion. Guidance is withdrawn or faded as the patient's performance permits. Withdrawal of guidance typically proceeds from the end of the response to the beginning. That is, guidance to initiate the response is the last step in withdrawal; this last step is faded very gradually, usually from the hand, up the arm, and off at the level of the shoulder.

Once the patient consistently motor-imitates without physical guidance, the therapist attempts to bring the response under verbal stimulus control using the delay procedure. When the patient fails to respond in 4 seconds, the therapist provides first a full imitative model and later only a partial one. When a full imitative model is not sufficient, the therapist backs up to physical guidance and fading.

3.6.8. Total Communication and Amerind

Total communication (TC) is simultaneous communication in more than one mode and is also a highlighting strategy. It involves the selective blending of all communicative modes including speech, sign, touch, gesture, song, movement, exaggerated facial expressions and intonational patterns, language boards, alphabet boards, mime, finger spelling, writing, pictures, and drawing. Initially, TC seems to capture the patient's attention, maintain it, and facilitate communication. As attentional skills and comprehension increase, the redundant features of TC are faded. For adults, the signing system most often used with TC is Amerind (Skelly, Schinsky, & Smith, 1974; Skelly, 1979).

At present we can only speculate about why TC, in particular the signing aspect of it, facilitates the restoration of functional communication and sometimes speech. There are visible similarities between the Amerind signs and their referents. This similarity of shape or movement between a sign and its referent may clarify and highlight the referent, thereby conveying more information to the patient than speech alone. The combined use of sign and speech may make it easier for the patient to understand, and understanding may be viewed here as a reinforcer for attending. Sign permits the therapist to maintain the presence of the referent in a way that speech does not: the therapist's hands can repeat the movement of a sign and hold still its beginning or ending. The sign can be made slowly without distorting it. The therapist can mold and manipulate the patient's hands to match his example. The patient can see and manipulate the configuration and movement of his own hands and visually compare the result with that of the therapist. The making of a sign, the sight or feel of it, may function as a reminder for the spoken word. Accordingly, word retrieval may be facilitated by signing; the therapist may be able to prompt a spoken response with a sign. In these ways, signing may provide a bridge between seeing or thinking of the stimulus object and saying the object's name. Ultimately, the patient may prompt himself to say something by first signing it; hence, Amerind may offer an avenue to self-cueing.

When the patient is motorically handicapped such that his productive use of speech or sign seems out of the question, the use of other expressive modes such as alphabet boards or a language board can be explored. Beukelman and Yorkston (1977) describe a system developed for persons with severe dysarthria but essentially intact language and intellectual capabilities. The patient uses an alphabet board to indicate the first letter of each word he speaks. The patient tends to speak more slowly with than without the board and also cues his listener. If necessary, the patient continues to spell the word until the listener understands. This simple adaptation of alphabet board use has the advantage of improving the patient's speech intelligibility by slowing the rate of speech and increasing speed in communicating by reducing the need to spell each word in its entirety. Some alphabet or language boards are electronic, can be activated by very unusual input channels, and provide printed or synthetic speech output. For descriptions of these types of devices and for information regarding the use of alternative communication modes in general, excellent sources include Vanderheiden and Grilley's *Non-Vocal Communication Techniques and Aids for the Severely Handicapped* (1977); Silverman (1980); Harper, Wrens, and Metarazzo (1978); and the Trace Research and Development Center for the Severely Communicatively Handicapped, 1500 Highland Avenue, Madison, WI 53706. The Trace Center provides current information on all types of communication systems and devices for the motorically handicapped. There are available now a growing variety of alternative expressive modes, including speech synthesizers; the use of these alternative systems can greatly enrich the life experience of many patients and their families.

3.6.9. The Whitney Strategies

Suggested by the work of Berman and Peele (1967) and Marshall (1976), the Whitney strategies (Whitney, 1975) teach the patient to maximize his use of effective compensatory communicative strategies. These strategies are based on the careful observation of the strategies used successfully by the patient and by others with similar problems. By observing the strategies used successfully by the patient, the therapist decides which strategies to emphasize in therapy. The therapy situation, then, becomes a time to practice successful communication supported by compensatory strategies.

Patient-initiated strategies may be comprehension-, production-, or memory-oriented. The comprehension strategies make the message easier for the patient to understand; the patient prompts the speaker to repeat the message, say it again louder, say it again more slowly, or demonstrate the meaning of the message through nonspeech means. In some instances, the patient may ask the speaker to write his message, or he may just offer the speaker paper and pencil, gesturing that the speaker write. Production strategies make it easier for the patient to get his message across to others in spite of production deficits. Some of the patient-initiated production strategies accomplish their goal indirectly by depending on the listener or a third party to communicate for the patient. The strategies used directly by the patient may be nonspeech (such as writing or gesturing), or they may be spoken.

Production strategies that depend on the assistance of others include the patient's requesting a third party to help him communicate to a second: "You tell him who they are." With another indirect strategy, the patient circumlocutes, fishing for a particular word, describing it variously, and then says, "You know. . ." with an engaging inflection. When the listener supplies the correct word, the patient says "Right!" and continues with his side of the conversation in such a gracious way that the listener may be quite unaware of his special role. Similarly, the patient may cause the "listener" to supply words for him based on his gestures. In the process, the "listener" glosses the patient's gestures with speech, after which the patient confirms, denies, or expands upon the listener's interpretation. "Outside? You want to go outside? OK." "Over there? You want to sit by the pool? No? You want me to leave you alone for awhile? OK. I'll be back in 10 minutes." "You want your daughter to go with you? No? You want me to go with you. OK. But, your daughter, too? OK. You want both of us to go with you." It is amazing just how much business can be transacted in this way. The patient may never speak, but his determination to communicate, initiate, deal, negotiate, and persist until he is understood makes him a successful communicator.

The patient may communicate directly by means of gesture or pantomime:

1. The patient may point to his referent.
2. The patient may use nonspeech oral noises, facial expressions, or body postures.
3. The patient may search for the actual object he is referring to and then show it to his "listener."
4. The patient may write his message on a pad of paper and then show it to his "listener."
5. He may point to and show his "listener" something in a picture or in printed form.
6. He may draw and show a picture of his referent.
7. He may pause to think of a word, gesturing to his listener not to interrupt.

The patient may also employ direct strategies to make his speech more intelligible, make it easier for him to retrieve elusive words, and correct mistakes that he recognizes. He may spell the word aloud. He may prompt himself with high-association words—for example, "It's not a cake, it's strudel." He may try for a literal description of the word: "It has three syllables and starts with a 'g.'" He may substitute "empty" words such as "thing" or "something," "doomigadget" or "thingama-jig" for words he cannot retrieve. Similarly, the patient may cue himself or his listener by circumlocutions involving a mixture of associational strategies. For example, "It's a really big city. It's in California . . . hills, cable cars, San Francisco! That's it. San Francisco." The patient may cue himself from word lists that he has constructed for himself, or he may consult other kinds of printed matter that have been prepared for him or that are generally available, such as a *TV Guide*. When the patient de-tects his own error or when he is unsuccessful in retrieving a word, he may deliberately stop and start over, successfully revising his first at-tempt. Holland's observations of the communicative behaviors of 40 aphasic adults reveal that, as a group, nonspeech strategies are more successful than those involving speech (Holland, 1980). Only 10 of her subjects had failures on spontaneous self-initiated nonspeech strategies while 36 experienced failures on strategies that involved talking.

The Whitney strategies involve the systematic application of suc-cessful patient-initiated strategies. The patient is taught to prompt him-self and his listener. He is encouraged to keep trying to communicate one way or another. He is taught to take his time, to self-monitor, and to self-correct. Measures of progress in this kind of therapy might include the number of communicative interactions initiated by the patient, the number of successful interactions initiated by the patient, the number of appropriate topic changes initiated by the patient, and the number of faulty patient productions spontaneously self-corrected.

Whitney suggests five basic steps in implementing her strategies:

1. *Observe.* Identify spontaneously occurring patient behaviors that facilitate comprehension or production. The observations of patient-ini-tiated strategies can be facilitated by the use of a checklist or tape record-er, by scheduling observations during communicatively active times of the day for the patient, and by enlisting the help of family and other team members. A sample checklist is shown in Figure 2. Comprehen-sion strategies generally prompt the speaker to make his message easier for the patient to understand and are judged successful on the basis of whether they actually achieve this. Production strategies are successful if they prompt either the patient or his listener to say the sought-after word or phrase. The identification of successful therapist-initiated strat-

egies should be evident from the documentation of therapy sessions.

2. *Direct.* Direct the patient to use a particular strategy, for example, "Listen carefully. Ask me to repeat when you need to." To facilitate comprehension, then, the therapist directs the patient to request help:

Ask me to repeat.
Ask me to write it down.
Ask me to slow down.
Ask me to speak louder.
Ask me to show you.

To facilitate production, the patient may be told to try any of the following:

Tell me to wait. Tell me you need more time.
Show me what you mean. Act it out.
Draw me a picture.
Give me a word or two.
Tell me something about it.
Tell me what you use it for.
Tell me what it goes with.
Tell me another word for it.
Try to write it.
Try to spell it.

Encouragement to respond, to do something, seems to facilitate word finding or a more complete response.

3. *Give feedback.* When a patient uses a strategy successfully, call attention to the strategy and to the success; for example, "You used your hands to make me understand and it worked. That's good. When you can't think of the word, remember to use your hands." "You asked me to repeat and it helped you to understand. Ask me to repeat whenever you need it."

4. *Facilitate self-monitoring.* Encourage the patient to use a slow, deliberate rate, to listen to himself, and to stop when he hears an error. Initially the patient may be unable to self-monitor. The therapist may pace the patient's rate by tapping on the table and signaling him to stop when he makes an error. To facilitate monitoring, stop the patient when he makes an error and ask "Was that the right word?" or "How was that?"

5. *Facilitate self-correction.* When the patient recognizes his production error or failure to get his message across, prompt him to self-correct. For example,

(Patient ID)

Date _____
Duration of observation _____
Observer(s) _____

Strategy	Frequency Counts, Comments, Verbatim Transcriptions
Asks speaker to repeat	_____
Asks speaker to speak slower	_____
Asks speaker to speak louder	_____
Asks speaker to write message	_____
Asks speaker to demonstrate	_____
Hand gestures	_____
Pointing	_____
Facial expressions	_____
Body postures	_____
Shows real object	_____
Nonspeech oral noises	_____
Head movements, yes-no	_____
Requests more time	_____
You know . . . Right!	_____
You tell	_____
Circumlocutions	_____
"Thing" words	_____
Spells aloud	_____
Consults written reminders	_____
Literal word description	_____
Other: _____	_____

Figure 2. Observation checklist for patient-initiated communication strategies.

THERAPIST: How was that?
PATIENT: Not right.
THERAPIST: What do you need to do? (*Full cue to self-correct*)
PATIENT: Slow down.
THERAPIST: Good. You need to slow down. Try it again.

At first the therapist provides a full cue, as above. The cueing progresses from a therapist-initiated full cue to a patient-initiated signal. When the patient monitors his own production, detects his own errors or difficulties, stops, signals his detection, and makes a successful adjustmental response to his own signal, the patient has demonstrated his ability to self-regulate—a major goal of therapy.

3.6.10. PACE

Whitney has suggested that her strategies be used in group therapy and with group sessions with family members; Wilcox and Davis (see

Bedwinek, 1983) have put forward a format for doing this. They call the system PACE, which is an acronym for Promoting Aphasics' Communicative Effectiveness. PACE is a game that teaches the patient to use Whitney-type compensatory strategies to communicate successfully and efficiently with the therapist; it can be adapted easily for group therapy and for therapy with family members. Patient and therapist take turns choosing a card from a set of stimulus cards and prompting the other, in as few attempts as possible, to guess what picture or message is on the card. A player is charged one point for every cue given to occasion the other player's correct guess. Low score wins. The clinician's correct guess is assumed to be a positively reinforcing consequence for the patient's communicative effort. When it is the clinician's turn to prompt the patient to guess what is on a card, the clinician models a compensatory strategy he wants the patient to use when it is the patient's turn. The general game plan can be varied by changing the number of cards used and the type of stimulus material pictured or printed on the cards. For example, the stimuli may be pictures of objects, actions, absurdities, or printed directions to be given to one's opponent.

The communication skills required to play PACE appear to be generalizable to everyday situations, to provide natural feedback, and to facilitate flexibility. What is more, PACE is actually fun. It provides a setting for alternating practice on comprehension and production tasks, with the therapist modeling strategies thought most appropriate for the patient at the time. In some instances, the therapist may progressively work through an hierarchy of strategies, beginning with nonspeech and progressing to successful word retrieval via self-regulated delay. PACE provides an excellent opportunity to probe for generalization of skills trained with the Whitney strategies. The patient is free to cue a correct guess in any way he can but it is clear that he will be penalized by inefficient strategies such as 'thing' talk. The give and take of PACE forces therapy into a functional format quite unlike traditional therapy that depends on the therapist's direction and the patient's compliance. The clinician can help the patient communicate by prompting production attempts generally; but, since she does not know what is on the card, the therapist cannot be specific. For example, the therapist can say, "Show me how you use it" but she is not in a position to say, "Tell me that you can use it to sweep the floor." The system blends turn-taking, modeling, and the alternation of high and low error risk items in a context that puts the focus on communication rather than on speech or word retrieval per se.

Implied in the strategy are two goals: (1) Get the patient to sample the reinforcer of successful communication using any communicative

modes at his disposal; and (2) once the patient is communicating, shape
the communicative mode in the direction of speech without any concomitant loss in efficiency. What seems to be most important is to
achieve a high stable rate of successful communicative interactions and
to maintain this rate without loss in efficiency regardless of whether
speech can be facilitated.

3.6.11. Melodic Intonation Therapy (MIT)

MIT occupies a unique niche among therapeutic strategies for neurogenic speech/language-disordered persons. The therapy itself is unlike any other and is an application of neurophysiological theory and
basic research (Berlin, 1976). It was designed for aphasic adults whose
verbal output is severely limited while their auditory comprehension is
only mildly to moderately impaired. More to the point, the therapy may
be specific for patients with conduction aphasia, a communication disorder resulting from a lesion that disconnects Wernicke's area from Broca's
while leaving the two intact. It has also been used to improve slurred
articulation and to reduce the frequency of phonemic errors (Sarno et al.,
1970; Sparks, Helm, & Albert, 1974).

The therapy has been definitively described by Sparks and Holland
(1976). Utilizing a series of intoned sentences and phrases, the patient is
taken through a series of levels and steps in which the speech units
increase in length while dependency on the clinician's support and on
the intonational feature is systematically reduced. The patient learns to
say, literally, the sentences of the program. Having achieved this, the
patient is ready for a transition phase leading to his participation in
other styles of therapy. Samples of content reported by Sparks and
Holland includes the following functional phrases and sentences:

> Twelve o'clock
> Time for lunch
> Bowl of soup
> Read the newspaper
> Turn on the TV
> Go for a walk

3.6.12. Potpourri

Completion of this survey of strategies requires mention of several
additional specialized methods. Their brief mention should not be con-
strued as an indication that they are somehow less important or of less

value than others. They are mentioned here together because their application is limited to very select populations. Nevertheless, any one of them might make the crucial difference to the optimal restoration of communicative status for a particular patient.

Delayed auditory feedback (DAF) appears to be a strategy of high potential for patients whose rapid rate of speaking contributes to their poor intelligibility (Rosenbek, 1978b; Hanson & Metter, 1980). For example, Hanson and Metter have described the use of a small solid-state battery-operated DAF device as a permanent speech prosthesis for a patient with progressive supranuclear palsy and hypokinetic dysarthria. The systematic use of DAF in therapy to teach the patient to regulate his rate has not been fully explored (Boller & Marcie, 1978; Lozano & Dreyer, 1978); and a model that might be adapted for this purpose is offered by Shames and Florance (1980).

Helm (1979) describes the use of a pacing board for controlling rate, in particular in palilalia, a speech disorder sometimes associated with Parkinson's syndrome and pseudobulbar palsy. The board is approximately 36.5 cm long and 5 cm wide and is divided into eight colored segments separated by raised wooden dividers. As the patient utters each syllable, he taps a segment with his finger, moving from left to right on the board. Helm discusses the possibility that the patient might eventually be able to pace his speech without the actual activity of tapping the board. Again, the possibility for training focused on monitoring and self-regulation appears to warrant exploration.

The use of biofeedback techniques to assist the patient in learning to monitor and to self-regulate has been described by Netsell and Cleeland (1973) with respect to the management of chronic upper lip hypertonia in a patient with Parkinsonism. Another provocative description of the use of biofeedback to induce relaxation resulting in improved speech production is found in McNeil, Prescott, and Lemme (1976). The clear advantages of biofeedback over feedback provided by the therapist alone lie in its ability to provide the patient consistently with immediate, unequivocal information about his performance. The creative use of this approach has probably not yet been fully exploited.

When dysarthria is associated with hypernasality resulting from velopharyngeal incompetency, intelligibility may be improved through the use of a palatal lift, a speech prothesis that fits into the patient's mouth and assists him in correcting the insufficiency. When results are good with a palatal lift, pharyngeal flap surgery is sometimes a viable alternative. The application of these strategies is detailed and discussed in Johns and Salyer (1978; see also Gonzales & Aronson, 1970). When the patient is unable to produce voice or is able to do so only weakly, the use of an artificial larynx or a voice amplifier may result in functional speech not otherwise possible.

Seron, Deloche, Moulard, and Rousselle (1980) have described an errorless computer-based procedure for training patients with writing disorders. The patient types from dictation. Each letter typed correctly is displayed on a screen while errors are not displayed. The results reported show a significant reduction in errors over time and some potential for generalization to handwriting. This strategy may be especially significant for patients with trauma histories, inasmuch as having difficulty writing from dictation is a commonly noted residual disorder; to the extent that writing from dictation is related to written composition, the technique may have high functional training potential.

4. Conclusion

This chapter's content need not be summarized, but its purpose might need clarification. This chapter is intended to introduce the neurobehaviorally oriented psychologist to some of the developments in speech pathology as they pertain to the study and treatment of disorders associated with head trauma and to provide him with some leads that he might follow for further study.

5. References

Alajouanine, T. & Lhermitte, F. Acquired aphasia in children. *Brain*, 1965, *88*, 653–662.

Balick, S., Greene, G., Kaplan, J., Press, D., & Demopoulos, J. T. The problem-oriented medical record applied to communication disorders. *Archives of Physical Medicine and Rehabilitation*, 1978, *59*, 288–289.

Bedwinek, A. P. The use of PACE to facilitate gestural and verbal communication in a language-impaired child. *Language, Speech, and Hearing Services in Schools*, 1983, *14*, 1–6.

Berlin, C. I. On: Melodic intonation therapy for aphasia by R. W. Sparks and A. L. Holland. *Journal of Speech and Hearing Disorders*, 1976, *41*, 298–300.

Berman, M., & Peele, L. Self-generated cues: A method for aiding aphasic and apractic patients. *Journal of Speech and Hearing Disorders*, 1967, *32*, 372–376.

Beukelman, D. R., & Yorkston, K. A communication system. *Journal of Speech and Hearing Disorders*, 1977, *42*, 265–270.

Boller, F., & Marcie, P. Possible role of abnormal auditory feedback in conduction aphasia. *Neuropsychologia*, 1978, *16*, 521–524.

Borkowski, J. G., Benton, A. L., & Spreen, O. Word fluency and brain damage. *Neuropsychologia*, 1967 5, 135–140.

Bouchard, M. M. & Shane, H. C. Use of the problem-oriented medical record in thee speech and hearing profession. *American Speech and Hearing Association Journal*, 1977, *19*, 157–159.

Brookshire, R. H. *An introduction to aphasia.* Minneapolis: BRK Publishers, 1978.

Brookshire, R. H., Nicholas, L. S., Krueger, K. M., & Redmond, K. J. The clinical interaction analysis system: A system for observational recording of aphasia treatment. *Journal of Speech and Hearing Disorders,* 1978, *43,* 437–447.

Chédru, F., & Geschwind, N. Disorders of higher cortical functions in acute confusional states. *Cortex,* 1972, *8,* 395–411.

Critchley, M. *Aphasiology and other aspects of language.* London: Edward Arnold, 1970.

Darley, F. L. *Diagnosis and appraisal of communication disorders.* Englewood Cliffs, N.J.: Prentice-Hall, 1964.

Darley, F. L. A retrospective view: Aphasia. *Journal of Speech and Hearing Disorders,* 1977, *42,* 161–169.

Darley, F. L. (Ed.) *Evaluation of appraisal techniques in speech and language pathology.* Reading, Mass.: Addison-Wesley, 1979.

Darley, F. L., Aronson, A. E., & Brown, J. R. *Motor speech disorders.* Philadelphia: Saunders, 1975.

Deal, J. L., & Florance, C. L. Modification of the eight-step continuum for treatment of apraxia of speech in adults. *Journal of Speech and Hearing Disorders,* 1978, *42,* 89–95.

DeRenzi, E., & Fablioni, P. Normative data and screening power of a shortened version of the token test. *Cortex,* 1978, *14,* 41–48.

DeRenzi, E., & Vignolo, L. A. The token test: A sensitive test to detect receptive disturbances in aphasia. *Brain,* 1962, *85,* 665–678. See also McNeil, M. R., and Prescott, T. E. *Revised token test.* Baltimore: University Park Press, 1978; and Wertz, R. T. The token test (TT). In F. L. Darley (Ed.) *Evaluation of appraisal techniques in speech and language pathology.* Reading, Mass.: Addison-Wesley, 1979.

Dinsdale, S. M., Mossman, P. L., Gullickson, G., Jr., & Anderson T. P. The problem-oriented medical record in rehabilitation. *Archives of Physical and Medical Rehabilitation,* 1970, *51,* 488–492.

Dinsdale, S. M., Gent, M., Kline, G., & Milner, R. Problem oriented medical records: Their impact on staff communication, attitudes and decision making. Archives of Physical and Medical Rehabilitation, 1975, *56,* 269–274.

DiSimoni, F. *The Token Test for Children.* Hingham, Mass.: Teaching Resources Corp., 1978.

DiSimoni, F. G., Keith, R. L., & Darley, F. L. Prediction of PICA overall score by short versions of the test. *Journal of Speech and Hearing Research,* 1980, *23,* 511–516.

Eisenson, J. *Adult aphasia: Assessment and treatment.* New York: Appleton Century Crofts, 1973.

Espir, M. L. E., & Rose, F. C. *The basic neurology of speech.* Philadelphia: Davis, 1970.

Geschwind, N. Writing disturbances in acute confusional states. In R. S. Kohen, & M. W. Wartofsky (Eds.), *N. Geschwind selected papers on language in the brain.* Boston: Reidel, 1974.

Gianutsos, R. What is cognitive rehabilitation? *Journal of Rehabilitation,* 1980, 36–40.

Gilchrist, E., & Wilkinson, M. Some factors determining prognosis in young people with severe head injury. *Archives of Neurology,* 1979, *36,* 355–359.

Goldstein, K. *After effects of brain injuries in war.* New York: Grune & Stratton, 1942.

Goldstein, K. *Language and language disturbances.* New York: Grune & Stratton, 1948.

Gonzales, J., & Aronson, A. Palatal lift prosthesis for treatment of anatomic and neurologic palato-pharyngeal insufficiency. *Cleft Palate Journal,* 1970, *7,* 90–104.

Goodglass, H., & Kaplan, E. *Boston diagnostic aphasia examination* (BDAE). Philadelphia: Lea & Febiger, 1972.

Grabois, M. The problem-oriented medical record: Modification and simplification for rehabilitation medicine. *Southern Medical Journal,* 1977, *70,* 1383–1385.

Granger, C. V., & Delabarre, E. M., Jr. Programmed examination formats: Use in rehabilitation medicine. *Archives of Physical Medicine and Rehabilitation*, 1974, 55, 235–239.

Granich, L. *Aphasia: A guide to retraining.* New York: Grune & Stratton, 1947.

Halpern, H., Darley, F. L., & Brown, J. R. Differential language and neurological characteristics in cerebral involvement. *Journal of Speech and Hearing Disorders*, 1973, 38, 162–173.

Hanson, W. R., & Metter, E. J. DAF as instrumental treatment for dysarthria in progressive supranuclear palsy: A case report. *Journal of Speech and Hearing Disorders*, 1980, 45, 268–276.

Harper, R. G., Wrens, A. N., & Metarazzo, J. D. *Non-verbal communication: The state of the art.* New York: Wiley, 1978.

Head, H. *Aphasia and kindred disorders of speech.* New York: Macmillan, 1926. (Reprinted by Hafner, New York, 1963.)

Helm, N. A. Visual action therapy for global aphasic patients. Paper presented to the Academy of Aphasia, Chicago, 1978.

Helm, N. A. Management of palilalia with a pacing board. *Journal of Speech and Hearing Disorders*, 1979, 44, 350–353.

Helm, N., Butler, R., & Benson, D. Acquired stuttering. *Neurology*, 1978, 28, 1159–1165.

Holland, A. Some current trends in aphasia rehabilitation. *American Speech and Hearing Association*, 1969, 11, 3–7.

Holland, A. *Communication abilities in daily living (CADL).* Baltimore: University Park Press, 1980.

Holland, A. L. Some practical considerations in aphasia rehabilitation. In M. Sullivan, & M. S. Kommers (Eds.) *Rationale for adult aphasia therapy.* Omaha: University Nebraska Medical Center, 1977.

Holland, A. L. Observing functional communication of aphasic adults. *Journal of Speech and Hearing Disorders*, 1982, 47, 50–56.

Holland, A. L. Personal communication, 1978–1980.

Isaacs, B., & Walkey, F. A. The measurement of mental impairment in geriatric practice. *Gerontology Clinics*, 1964, 6, 114–123.

Johns, D. F. (Ed.) *Clinical management of neurogenic communicative disorders.* Boston: Little, Brown, 1978.

Johns, D. F., & Darley, F. L. Phonemic variability in apraxia of speech. *Journal of Speech and Hearing Research*, 1970, 13, 556–583.

Johns, D. F., & Salyer, K. E. Surgical and prosthetic management of neurogenic speech disorders. In D. F. Johns (Ed.), *Clinical management of neurogenic communicative disorders.* Boston: Little, Brown, 1978.

Johnson, C. Errorless learning in a multihandicapped adolescent. *Education and Treatment of Children*, 1977, 1, 25–33.

Kent, L. R., & Chabon, S. S. Problem-oriented record in a university speech and hearing clinic. *American Speech and Hearing Association*, 1980, 22, 151–158.

Kertesz, A., & Poole, E. The aphasia quotient: The taxonomic approach to measurement of aphasic disability. *Canadian Journal of Neurological Science*, 1974, 1, 7–16.

Klonoff, H., Low, M. D., & Clark, C. Head injuries in children: A prospective five year follow-up. *Journal of Neurology, Neurosurgery, and Psychiatry*, 1977, 40, 1211–1219.

Kushner, D., & Winitz, H. Extended comprehension practice applied to an aphasic patient. *Journal of Speech and Hearing Disorders*, 1977, 42, 296–306.

La Pointe, L. L. Base-10 programmed stimulation: Task specification, scoring and plotting performance in aphasia therapy. *Journal of Speech and Hearing Disorders*, 1977, 42, 90–105.

La Pointe, L. L. Aphasia therapy: Some principles and strategies for treatment. In D. F. Johns (Ed.), *Clinical management of neurogenic communicative disorders*. Boston: Little, Brown, 1978.

La Pointe, L. L. *Base-10 response form*. Tigard, Ore.: C. C. Publications, Inc., 1979.

Levin, H. S., Grossman, R. G., & Kelly, P. G. Aphasic disorder in patients with closed head injury. *Journal of Neurology, Neurosurgery, and Psychiatry*, 1976, *39*, 1062–1070.

Lozano, R., & Dreyer, D. Some effects of delayed auditory feedback on dyspraxia of speech. *Journal of Communication Disorders*, 1978, *11*, 407–415.

Luria, A. R. *Higher cortical functions in man*. New York: Basic Books, 1966.

Luria, A. R. *Traumatic aphasia: Its syndromes, psychology and treatment*. The Hague: Mouton, 1970.

Mandleberg, I. A., & Brooks, D. N. Cognitive recovery after severe head injury. *Journal of Neurology, Neurosurgery, and Psychiatry*, 1975, *38*, 1121–1126.

Marshall, R. C. Word retrieval of aphasic adults. *Journal of Speech and Hearing Disorders*, 1976, *41*, 444–451.

McNeil, M. R. Porch Index of Communicative Ability. In F. L. Darley (Ed.), *Evaluation of appraisal techniques in speech and language pathology*. Reading, Mass.: Addison-Wesley, 1979.

McNeil, M., Prescott, T., & Lemme, M. An application of electromyographic biofeedback of aphasia/apraxia treatment. In R. H. Brookshire (Ed.), *Clinical aphasiology: Conference proceedings*. Minneapolis: BRK Publishers, 1976.

Milhous, R. L. The problem-oriented medical record in rehabilitation management and training. *Archives of Physical and Medical Rehabilitation*, 1972, *53*, 182–185.

Mills, C. K. Treatment of aphasia by training. *Journal of the American Medical Association*, 1904, *43*, 1940–1949.

Moore, W. M., Rosenbek, J. C., & La Pointe, L. L. Assessment of oral apraxia in brain-injured adults. In R. H. Brookshire (Ed.), *Clinical aphasiology: Conference proceedings*. Minneapolis: BRK Publishers, 1976.

Neef, N. A., Iwata, B. A., & Page, T. J. The effects of known item interspersal on acquisition and retention of spelling and sight-reading words. *Journal of Applied Behavior Analysis*, 1977, *10*, 738.

Neef, N. A., Iwata, B. A., & Page, T. J. The effects of interspersal training versus high-density reinforcement on spelling acquisition and retention. *Journal of Applied Behavior Analysis*, 1980, *13*, 153–158.

Netsell, R., & Cleeland, C. S. Modification of lip hypertonia in dysarthria using EMG feedback. *Journal of Speech and Hearing Disorders*, 1973, *38*, 131–140.

Nielsen, J. M. *Agnosia, apraxia, aphasia: Their value in cerebral localization*. New York: Hoeber, 1947.

Phillips, D. F. Long term care: Reality orientation. *Hospitals, Journal of the American Hospital Association*, 1973, *47*, 46–49.

Porch, B. E. *Porch index of communicative ability*. Palo Alto, Calif.: Consulting Psychologists Press, 1967, 1971.

Porch, B. E., Wertz, R. T., & Collins, M. J. A statistical procedure for predicting recovery from aphasia. In B. E. Porch (Ed.), *Proceedings of the conference on clinical aphasiology*. New Orleans, La.: Veterans Administration Hospital, 1974.

Reinstein, L. Problem-oriented medical record: Experience in 238 rehabilitation institutions. *Archives of Physical and Medical Rehabilitation*, 1977, *58*, 398–401.

Reinstein, L., Staas, W. E., Jr., & Marquette, C. H. A rehabilitation evaluation system which complements the problem-oriented medical record. *Archives of Physical and Medical Rehabilitation*, 1975, *56*, 396–399.

Rosenbek, J. C. Stuttering following brain damage. *Brain and Language*, 1978, *6*, 82–96. (a)

Rosenbek, J. C. Treating apraxia of speech. In D. F. Johns (Ed.), *Clinical management of neurogenic communicative disorders*. Boston: Little, Brown, 1978. (b)

Rosenbek, J. C., Lemme, M. L., Ahern, M. B., Harris, E. H., & Wertz, R. T. A treatment for apraxia of speech in adults. *Journal of Speech and Hearing Disorders*, 1973, *38*, 462–472.

Rosenbek, J. C., Collins, M. J., & Wertz, R. T. Intersystemic reorganization for apraxia of speech. In R. Brookshire (Ed.), *Clinical aphasiology: Conference proceedings*. Minneapolis, Minn.: BRK Publishers, 1976.

Sarno, M. T. *Functional communication profile (FCP)*. New York: Institute of Rehabilitation Medicine, New York University Medical Center, 1969.

Sarno, M., Silverman, M., & Sands, E. Speech therapy and language recovery in severe aphasia. *Journal of Speech and Hearing Research*, 1970, *13*, 607–623.

Schreibman, L. Effects of within-stimulus and extra-stimulus prompting on discrimination learning in autistic children. *Journal of Applied Behavior Analysis*, 1975, *8*, 91–112.

Schuell, H. A short examination for aphasia. *Neurology*, 1957, *7*, 625–635.

Schuell, H. *The Minnesota test for differential diagnosis of aphasia (MTDDA)*. Minneapolis: University of Minnesota Press, 1965, 1972.

Schuell, H., Jenkins, J. J., & Jimenez-Pabon, E. *Aphasia in adults: Diagnosis, prognosis, and treatment*. New York: Harper & Row, 1964.

Seron, X., Deloche, G., Moulard, G., & Rousselle, M. A computer-based therapy for the treatment of aphasic subjects with writing disorders. *Journal of Speech and Hearing Disorders*, 1980, *45*, 45–58.

Shaffer, D., Bijur, P., Chadwick, O. F. D., & Rutter, M. L. Head injury and later reading disability. *Journal of the American Academy of Child Psychiatry*, 1980, *19*, 592–610.

Shames, G. H., & Florance, C. L. *Stutter-free speech: A goal for therapy*. Columbus, Ohio: Merrill, 1980.

Shewan, C. M., & Kertesz, A. Reliability and validity characteristics of the Western aphasia battery (WAB). *Journal of Speech and Hearing Disorders*, 1980, *45*, 308–324.

Silverman, F. H. *Communication for the speechless*. Englewood Cliffs, N.J.: Prentice-Hall, 1980.

Skelly, M. *Amer-Ind gestural code*. New York: Elsevier, 1979.

Skelly, M., Shinsky, L., Smith, R. W., & Fust, R. S. American Indian sign (Amerind) as a facilitator of verbalization for the oral verbal apraxic. *Journal of Speech and Hearing Disorders*, 1974, *39*, 445–456.

Snell, M. Personal communication, 1979.

Sparks, R., Helm, N., & Albert, M. Aphasia rehabilitation resulting from melodic intonation therapy. *Cortex*, 1974, *10*, 303–316.

Sparks, R. W., & Holland, A. L. Method: Melodic intonation therapy for aphasia. *Journal of Speech and Hearing Disorders*, 1976, *41*, 287–297.

Spreen, O., & Benton, A. L. *Neurosensory center comprehensive examination for aphasia (NC-CEA)*. Victoria, B.C.: University Victoria Neuropsychology Laboratory, 1969, 1977.

Stachowiak, F. J., Huber, W., Poeck, K., & Kerschensteiner, M. Text comprehension in aphasia. *Brain and Language*, 1977, *4*, 177–195.

Stover, S., & Ziegler, H. Head injury in children and teenagers: Functional recovery correlated with duration of coma. *Archives of Physical Medicine and Rehabilitation*, 1976, *57*, 201–205.

Swisher, L. Functional communication profile. In F. L. Darley (Ed.) *Evaluation of appraisal techniques in speech and language pathology*. Reading, Mass.: Addison-Wesley, 1979.

Touchette, P. Transfer of stimulus control: Measuring the moment of transfer. *Journal of the Experimental Analysis of Behavior*, 1971, *15*, 347–354.

Vanderheiden, G. C., & Grilley, K. *Non-vocal communication techniques and aids for the severely physically handicapped*. Baltimore: University Park Press, 1977.

Weisenburg, T., & McBride, K. *Aphasia*. New York: Commonwealth Fund, Division of Publications, 1935.

Wepman, J. M. *Recovery from aphasia*. New York: Ronald Press, 1951.

Wertz, R. T. Neuropathologies of speech and language: An introduction to patient management. In D. F. Johns (Ed.), *Clinical management of neurogenic communicative disorders*. Boston: Little, Brown, 1978.

Wertz, R. T. The token test. In F. L. Darley (Ed.) *Evaluation of appraisal techniques in speech and language pathology*. Reading, Mass.: Addison-Wesley, 1979. (a)

Wertz, R. T. Word fluency measure. In F. L. Darley (Ed.) *Evaluation of appraisal techniques in speech and language pathology*. Reading, Mass.: Addison-Wesley, 1979. (b)

Wertz, R. T., Rosenbek, J. C., and Deal, J. L. A review of 228 cases of apraxia of speech: Classification, etiology, and localization. Presented to the American Speech and Hearing Association, New York, N.Y., 1970.

Whitney, J. Developing aphasics' use of compensatory strategies. Paper presented to the American Speech and Hearing Association, Washington, D.C., 1975.

Wilcox, M., Davis, A., & Leonard, L. Aphasics' comprehension of contextually conveyed meaning. *Brain and Language*, 1978, *6*, 362–377.

Wilkinson, M. The prognosis of severe head injuries in young adults. *Proceedings of the Royal Society of Medicine*, 1969, *62*, 541–542.

Wilson, S. A. K. *Aphasia*. London: Trubner, 1926.

Wolfe, V. F., & Cuvo, A. J. Effects of within-stimulus and extra-stimulus prompting on letter discrimination by mentally retarded persons. *American Journal of Mental Deficiency*, 1978, *83*, 297–303.

Rehabilitation and the Luria-Nebraska Neuropsychological Battery

INTRODUCTION TO THEORY AND PRACTICE

CHARLES J. GOLDEN

1. Introduction

In recent years there has been increased interest in the application of neuropsychological test results to rehabilitation planning. In general, rehabilitation psychologists who have worked with brain-injured patients have developed their own batteries by combining a variety of individual tests, chosen on the basis of their own idiosyncratic preferences. Recently, attempts have been made to adapt more standardized batteries (such as the Halstead-Reitan Neuropsychological Battery) to this process. However, all of these tests have been limited in that they were developed with no clear theory of rehabilitation in mind. Their purpose was most often diagnostic rather than prescriptive.

An alternative system to neuropsychological assessment and diagnosis has been suggested in the works of A. R. Luria (1963, 1970, 1973, 1980). This approach has the advantage of being based on a distinctive theory of brain function as well as a well-educated theory of rehabilitation. The Luria-Nebraska Neuropsychological Battery is based on this

CHARLES J. GOLDEN • Nebraska Psychiatric Institute, The University of Nebraska Medical Center, Omaha, Nebraska 68105.

theoretical system and thus can lead to direct rehabilitation recommendations. However, to understand both these recommendations and the battery itself, it is necessary to look at the theory advocated by Luria.

2. Theoretical Basis

The most basic and fundamental idea in Luria's system is the notion of *functional systems*. Luria says that no one area of the brain is responsible for any observable behavior. All human behavior is the result of interactions between diverse areas of the brain, each representing a specific psychological skill. Thus, we do not talk about behavior as a unitary, indivisible unit but rather regard it as a result of the interaction of different basic skills. Only when all of these discrete skills are present can behavior be emitted. The interrelationship of skills required to produce any given behavior is the result of the interaction of the brain areas responsible for each of those specific skills. Behavior can be thought of as a chain, with individual skills interacting in series until the desired end behavior is produced. The more complex the behavior to be produced, the more complex the chain of interacting skills necessary to produce that behavior. The conjoint operation of the brain areas responsible for these interacting skills is referred to as the *functional system* for that behavior.

Luria's theory of functional systems has several implications for rehabilitation theories. First, any behavior can be damaged or eliminated by any injury that interrupts any part of its functional system. Thus, the chain can be broken by interrupting any link. Any behavior, such as speech or reading skills, can be interrupted by a number of different lesions in the brain, all of which produce the end result of speech problems and/or reading deficits.

Within this conceptual system, the role of rehabilitation is to fix the break in the chain at the point at which it has been broken. It is inefficient simply to try to reteach the entire process of reading to the brain-injured patient. More effective rehabilitation involves reteaching the specific skills that have been destroyed by the brain lesion. An attempt to fix the chain at any point at which it has not been broken would not be generally helpful for the patient, even though "progress" might apparently be made serendipitously.

Reading provides an example of this. On a simple level, reading requires the ability to focus on a page; see a word; be able, spatially, to scan across a line and switch to other lines without spatial disorientation; visually encode what is seen into letters; match the letter to its auditory counterpart; put together the auditory phonemes, produce words; put words together to produce sentences; and interpret the meaning of these sentences (which in turn requires a number of brain skills, depending upon the actual concepts involved). The process of reading or reading comprehension can be interrupted in any of these places. When reading deficits are observed, the problem may be visual, auditory, visual/spatial, motoric, sequential, analytical, and so on.

In order to understand a patient's reading problem, one must isolate the specific deficits responsible for that reading problem. In order to be most effective, rehabilitation must then focus on the specific skill deficit area(s) rather than more generally attempting to get at the entire skill implied by the term "reading."

The concept of the functional system also leads to several other important observations. First, there are no limitations on the number of functional systems responsible for reading. An injury that interrupts only one of those functional systems may not result in a reading deficit, since a substitute functional system could still produce the behavior. The concept of alternate functional systems for specific behaviors is also useful in rehabilitation planning. If the patient's functional system has been disrupted, the patient may simply be taught an alternate functional system, using intact parts of the brain, that will allow the patient to produce the same behavior.

Planning ways in which patients can elaborate such alternate functional systems requires that the rehabilitation psychologist be aware of the demands of the task, be able to imagine ways in which the task may be alternately attempted, and be keenly aware of the exact nature of the deficits and strengths possessed by the patient to be rehabilitated. An alternate functional system that uses areas of the brain which have been damaged will be no more useful than the original, damaged functional system. Thus, the exact nature of training using this concept would differ considerably from individual to individual, depending upon the exact pattern of deficits.

An understanding of functional systems depends upon an understanding of the specific skills that are mediated by the brain. By understanding these specific skills and the symptoms that arise from their disruption, we can better understand the behaviors of the patient. A full understanding of the specific skills mediated by the brain allows us to specify the types of skills and skill combinations that need to be measured by a comprehensive neuropsychological examination.

Additional aspects of Luria's theories enable us to delineate the basic skills that are mediated by brain function. Luria divides the brain into three major sections labeled as the first brain unit, second brain unit, and third brain unit. Each of these units of the brain has specific functions that need to be measured in any comprehensive neuropsychological battery. The following is a short summary of the information found in Luria (1980, 1973) and Golden (1981b).

2.1. Unit I

The first brain unit is responsible for arousal and attentional processes. This unit can be divided into the ascending reticular system, which involves the core structures running from the brainstem through the diencephalon and limbic system to the cortex, and the descending reticular system, which begins in the frontal cortex and goes to the brainstem. These two systems have primary responsibility for maintaining an optimal cortical tone, which results in appropriate arousal and attentional states. They are also involved in emotional reactions. Disruptions in this unit may result in abnormal states of consciousness, akinesis, emotional indifference, or anxiety reactions coupled with autonomic responses, disorientation to time and place, memory disturbances, confabulation, and micrographia.

Memory disorders can result from damage to the hippocampus. Injury of the hippocampus within the left hemisphere may lead to some loss of verbal memory, while injury to the hippocampus in the right hemisphere may lead to some loss of nonverbal memory (Milner, 1972). Most striking, however, are the memory losses that occur when bilateral destruction of the hippocampi occurs. In these cases, the patient basically retains most old memories but is unable to establish new long-term memories. Such patients have intact short-term memories but lose the information as soon as it is pushed out of short-term memory by new information or by distraction. Individuals with bilateral hipocampal injuries will be able to describe their past before the injury but not events occurring afterwards. However, many patients with lesions in the anterior zones of the first unit or the right anterior zones are unable to give accurate biographical details, frequently resorting to confabulating stories.

2.2. Unit II

The second unit of the brain consists of the temporal, occipital, and parietal lobes of each of the two cerebral hemispheres. The second unit can be subdivided into three specific types of areas: primary reception areas, secondary integration areas, and tertiary integration areas. The primary areas of the secondary unit are responsible for sensory input. The primary reception areas are almost exclusively involved with only one sensory modality (e.g., hearing, vision, or touch). These areas have a topographical organization, with a one-to-one correspondence between the external world and the structure of the cortex. The secondary integration areas are also modality-specific, but they encode information, have interhemispheric connections, and involve specialized functions for the two hemispheres. The tertiary are not modality-specific and involve even more encoding, hemispheric specialization, and interhemispheric connections.

2.2.1. Primary Area

In the temporal lobes of the two hemispheres, the primary areas receive acoustic information, with the primary area in the left temporal lobe receiving about 80% of its input from the right ear and approximately 20% of its input from the left ear. Conversely, the reception area in the right temporal lobe receives about 80% of its input from the left ear and 20% of its input from the right ear. It is the responsibility of the primary auditory area initially to organize the sounds being heard in the outside world. However, the primary area is not responsible for interpretations of these sounds.

The primary visual areas are located in the occipital lobe. Information from the left half of both eyes is fed back to the primary area in the right occipital lobe, while information from the right half of both eyes is fed back to the primary reception area in the left occipital lobe.

Finally, primary areas for tactile/sensory input are in the left parietal lobe, just posterior to the central sulcus. About 80% to 90% of the information from the left side of the body is fed to the right parietal lobe, while the remaining information goes to the left parietal lobe. Conversely, most of the information from the right side of the body is fed to the left parietal lobe, with the remaining information fed to the right parietal lobe.

Injury to a primary area does not cause impairment in cognitive skills *per se*. In general, an injury to either of the auditory primary areas simply results in the failure of that lobe to receive certain frequencies of sound. Since this information is also fed from the other ear, unilateral injuries to the primary area often cause little dysfunction. Complete destruction of either primary acoustic area results in an increase in the threshold of sounds necessary to be detected by that area. Bilateral injury that destroys the auditory primary areas completely results in the condition known as cortical deafness.

Partial injuries to either of the visual areas results in what is called a scotoma, an area of the visual fields in which the individual is not able to see. However, because of eye movements, the brain is able to fill in the necessary information by using alternative parts of the eye. Complete loss of the primary visual area in the right hemisphere will result in complete loss of vision in the left half of both eyes, while complete loss of the visual area in the left hemisphere will result in the complete loss of vision in the right half of both eyes. These conditions are known as left and right hemianopsia.

Injuries to the left tactile primary will result in a loss of somatosensory feedback from the right side of the body, while injuries to the right parietal primary area will result in a loss of somatosensory feedback from the left side of the body. Depending on exactly what part of the primary area is destroyed, sensation may be specific to certain areas of the body such as the trunk, legs, hand, or face. In an isolated injury, these individuals will not have real motor deficits, although they will appear to have some extreme motor problems because of the lack of muscle and joint feedback.

2.2.2. Secondary Areas

The secondary areas for each modality are adjacent to the primary areas in the temporal, occipital, and parietal lobes in each hemisphere. While the primary areas are responsible for reception of information from the outside world, the secondary areas are responsible for integration of this information into meaningful groups. Thus, the auditory areas are responsible for taking the sounds heard and identifying speech phonemes, pitch, rhythm, tone, and so on. The visual areas are responsible for identifying objects, backgrounds, foregrounds, distance, movement, color, and other properties of the visual field. The secondary tactile areas are responsible for locating where one is touched, the strength of a touch, the nature of a touch, the location of limbs on the body, the identification of objects, the shape of objects held in the hands or otherwise touching the body, the movement of muscles and limbs, and changes in bodily posture.

The actions of the secondary areas differ between the two hemispheres. The secondary areas of the left hemisphere are more heavily responsible for verbal tasks, while the secondary areas of the right hemisphere are more responsible for nonverbal tasks. It should be emphasized that this is only relative: both the right and left hemisphere secondary areas are involved in nonverbal and verbal tasks to some degree.

Injuries to the secondary auditory area can cause a complete loss of phonemic hearing—that is, the ability to discriminate between the basic speech sounds. Less severe injuries may cause a partial loss of phonemic discrimination skills, where the individual has difficulty discriminating between phonemes that have similar sounds such as "b" and "p." In other injuries to the left secondary auditory areas, the patient may be able to discriminate phonemes but only one phoneme at a time, thus losing the ability to do a successive analysis of incoming speech. The individual may also retain the ability to do two or three phonemic discriminations at a time while finding more complex discriminations impossible. Differences in functioning depend upon the extent and exact location of the injury. Damage to the secondary auditory area of the right hemisphere may also result in the inability to analyze tone or pitch. Severe injury to the right temporal secondary area can result in a complete loss of appreciation of music.

Injuries to the secondary visual areas in the left hemisphere may result in the inability to recognize letters. There may also be a loss of the ability to perceive two objects or two sensory attributes of the object at the same time. In serious injuries, a patient may simply be unable to combine visual input into any type of pattern at all. The individual may be able to appreciate one part of a complex figure or picture but not the other parts at the same time. Injury to the secondary visual area may also lead to disorders of the motor movements of the eye because of the importance of visual feedback in determining eye movements. Disorders of the left visual secondary area may also result in the inability to retain verbal material presented visually.

Lesions of the right occipital secondary areas are more likely to cause disorders of spatial relationship. Since objects can be appreciated only one at a time, perception of the spatial relationship between them is lost. Deficits in this area may also cause an inability to recognize faces—an inability to appreciate complex visual patterns—or semi-inattention. The phenomenon of inattention may cause a patient to ignore the left side of the visual field, including the left side of printed pages. The patient may also show deficits in the recognition of color hues. Another major deficit seen in these patients is the inability to remember or analyze facial expressions. Since facial expressions are extremely important in the nonverbal analysis of emotions, such patients are impaired in their ability to determine the emotional status of other individuals. In severe forms, patients with injuries to the right occipital secondary area may be unable to recognize the faces even of close friends or may feel that a person resembles a particular individual but somehow is a substitute or fake. In some cases, we have seen patients with this disorder end up in the psychiatric hospital with a diagnosis of paranoid schizophrenia.

The secondary area of the left parietal lobe is closely involved with speech and writing because of the importance to these tasks of kinesthetic and proprioceptive feedback from the hands, tongue, and mouth. Thus, lesions of the secondary area of the parietal lobe may affect smoothness of speaking and cause difficulties when the patient must shift between sounds made by similar movements of the speech musculature. Disorders of writing may arise when letters that use similar oral motor movements, such as "h" and "k," are made. Disorders of the secondary tactile area may result in the inability to localize touch along the body; this is seen in finger agnosia, in which the patient is unable to tell which finger has been touched. Disorders of the right parietal secondary area may produce similar deficits except that speech and writing processes are much less likely to be impaired. Disorders in the left parietal areas are much more likely to produce bilateral deficits.

2.2.3. Tertiary Integration Areas

The final areas of the second brain unit are the tertiary integration areas. Unlike the secondary integration areas, which integrate information within a given modality, the tertiary integration areas are responsible for integration between the modalities. Within the parietal lobe, there are two major subdivisions of the tertiary area, the parietal–temporal–occipital area and the parietal–occipital area. The parietal–occipital area is responsible for the integration of visual and somatosensory information. Since a combination of these inputs is normally used to locate one's body in space, damage to this area can cause a disturbance of body schema. The patient is unaware of the location of his body and the relationship of one body part to another. Disorders of spelling may also accompany problems in this area. Such individuals are able to give the correct letters to spell a given word but will often get the letters in the wrong order. This area is also responsible for construction dyspraxia—the inability to put together objects (e.g., inability to complete jigsaw puzzles). Lesions of this area may make it difficult for a person to show how to use an object such as a key or to manipulate arithmetic symbols and processes. Deficits in the parietal–occipital area in the left hemisphere may make a person unable to understand the meaning of arithmetic symbols, although the deficit may not interfere with the ability to do well-practiced arithmetic problems requiring only memory. Finally, this area is responsible for the understanding of words denoting spatial relationships, such as "below" or "beside." Injuries to this area may also cause the inability to relate spatial and verbal concepts, which would make it difficult for the patient to do such things as tell the time from a numberless clock dial simply by the spatial positions of the hand.

The tertiary parietal–occipital–temporary area in the left hemisphere plays an important role in many speech processes. This area is responsible for integrating information from all the sensory modalities and thus for the coordination of skills such as reading, writing, and the association of names with objects. Patients with disorders in this area may show memory deficits specific to verbal material, due to an inability to categorize this material rather than a primary inability to retain the memory trace. These patients may also show disorders of linguistic organization and make wide varieties of grammatical and semantic errors. Finally, patients with disorders in this area may be unable to *name* colors while still being able to *recognize* them.

The tertiary areas of the right parietal lobe are responsible for the awareness of the left side of one's body or environment. Patients with disorders of the tertiary area may show many of the symptoms of semi-inattention described above. The right parietal area is also responsible for the recognition of faces and the sense of familiarity of objects as well as the classification of nonverbal material. The tertiary right parietal plays a major role in such basic abilities as determining perception of slope and directionality of lines, assembling objects, or drawing things. It is also involved in arithmetic operations in which numbers must be spatially aligned. Difficulty with multiplication problems (because of frequent carrying operations) are particularly common with disorders of this area. However, disorders of the right parietal lobe do not affect the performance of arithmetic operations in the same way as left parietal tertiary injuries do. For example, the patient with an injury to the right hemisphere might add 29 and 43 as follows:

$$
\begin{array}{r}
29 \\
+43 \\
\hline
612
\end{array}
$$

The patient with an injured left hemisphere, on the other hand, will be entirely unable to do the problem.

2.3. Unit III

The third unit of the brain is located in the frontal lobes anterior to the central sulcus. Like the secondary area, the third unit may be subdivided into primary, secondary, and tertiary areas. The primary area of the third unit is responsible for the output of motor impulses rather than the reception of sensory impulses. The primary motor area is located just anterior to the central sulcus and is adjacent to the primary area of the parietal lobe. Like the primary area of the parietal lobe, the primary motor area contains specific areas devoted to each part of the body (e.g., legs, arms, mouth, tongue, etc.). In fact, the motor area for a given part of the body corresponds, in general, directly with the tactile/somatosensory area for the same part of the body which lies just behind the central sulcus.

Luria (1966, 1973) notes that there are heavy interconnections between the primary somatosensory area in the parietal lobe and the primary motor area in the frontal lobe. He states that this is because there is a heavy dependence of motor skills on continual sensory information and of sensory skills on motor movement. This is further illustrated, Luria states, by the fact that 20% of the cells in the primary tactile area are, in fact, motor output cells. He has suggested that—rather than being considered as two areas—they can be regarded as a single motor–sensory unit that links together the second and third brain units. In general, impulses from the left primary motor area are sent to the right side of the body, although some of these impulses may also be directed to the left side of the body. Conversely, output from the right primary motor area generally goes to the left side of the body but may also be directed partially to the right. Injuries to the primary motor areas will result in hemiplegia or motor paralysis, but this may not be total and can respond to treatment, especially if one set of connections is intact.

The secondary areas in the frontal lobes lie just anterior to the primary motor area and are often referred to as "premotor" areas. The secondary frontal areas are responsible for smoothing out individual movements in the continuous chain of interchanging impulses necessary for major motor activities. In essence, these areas organize behavior in detail, while the primary motor area sends the "orders" to the body. The tasks demands ever-changing reactions to adjust for past movements and environmental demands. The premotor areas, using the feedback they receive from the sensory areas of the cerebral hemisphere, provide these adjustments. Consequently, they are extremely important for smooth, skilled behavior. As with the motor areas, the left hemisphere's premotor area is primarily responsible for the movements of the right side of the body, while the right premotor area is primarily responsible for the movements of the left side of the body.

Lesions of the secondary frontal areas result in jerky, disturbed movements in the opposite limbs. More severe disorders of the secondary areas may lead to perseveration; the patient is unable to inhibit a movement once begun and repeats it over and over again. The opposite problem may develop as well. In this case the patient is unable to switch from one behavior to another and thus is able to perform only one motor movement at a time. This can be seen clearly in the speech of some patients who are able to say a single syllable but unable to go beyond that without a pause between syllables.

Left frontal secondary area lesions may result in expressive verbal symptoms, with lesions of the right secondary frontal areas less frequently affecting expressive verbal skills. However, lesions of the right secondary frontal areas can lead to an expressive amusia in which the individual, while able to talk, is unable to sing. Motor disorders are generally not as serious in the patient with right secondary premotor injuries, since the left hemisphere appears to be more effective in taking over the motor functions of the nondominant hemisphere (Luria, 1980).

The tertiary areas of the frontal lobes, also called the prefrontal cortex, lie in the most anterior part of the brain. When severe, lesions of the tertiary prefrontal areas can be particularly striking, although small lesions may have no apparent effect. The tertiary area is responsible for planning, structuring, and evaluating voluntary behavior. It is especially important in the development of new voluntary behavior, although it may play a minor role in already learned behavior. Severe destruction or impairment, however, can result in the complete disintegration of behavior. The patient may be echolalic, perseverative, inflexible, mute, and nonreacting to environmental cues or instructions obtained from the self or from others. In general, these severe deficits have more often been seen in bilateral than unilateral involvements of the prefrontal tertiary area. In less serious lesions, simple movements may be preserved, as may complex movements that have previously been overlearned; however, the patient is unable to perform complex activities requiring successive changes, especially when they demand new learning.

Patients with tertiary frontal lobe problems may have difficulty focusing attention. They can be distracted by small noises or events that others are able to ignore easily. As a result, the patient's performance may actually be much worse than it would be if effective levels of attention and concentration could be maintained. These patients may also be very inflexible and resistant to changing activities or doing things in an alternate manner.

Lesions of the left tertiary frontal area may result in a complete loss of voluntary speech. Patients may do poorly on tasks involving word fluency. For example, the patient may be unable to produce more than a few words beginning with a given letter. The regulating role of speech may also be lost. The patient may be able to state what he or she wants to do but be unable to change the verbal intentions into actual motor behavior. Deficits in judgment are seen in patients with prefrontal damage. Such patients may fail to scan the environment and therefore may not be aware of all that is occurring. As a result, they may reach decisions without gathering sufficient data, symptoms that make such patients look impulsive or uncaring. Such individuals may also show extreme memory deficits, especially for verbal materials (Luria, 1980).

Patients with disorders of the right tertiary frontal areas are impaired on spatial tests, especially those that are complex and demand intellectual analysis. Deficits in visual/spatial integration have been reported, as have deficits in maze learning and nonverbal visual memory. The speech deficits frequently seen in left tertiary motor injuries are rare. We have seen several cases in which large right tertiary frontal lesions have existed without any apparent symptoms.

It should be noted that the disorders discussed above are associated with the destruction of the lateral surface of the tertiary areas of the frontal lobes (Unit III). Lesions of the medial and orbital surface of the frontal lobe do not produce similar results but rather result in symptoms associated with Unit I brain damage, because this area is intimately associated with the limbic and reticular activating systems. Thus, with injuries to these areas, there may be changes in cortical tone, with the patient becoming either hyperactive or apathetic. Emotional changes may be seen as well. The patient may be impulsive, show a lack of inhibition, use obscene language, confabulate, or be emotionally flat. The patient may lose spontaneity and become apathetic, showing little motivation to act. Behavior disorders resulting from lesions in the medial orbital areas are more pronounced with bilateral lesions. The frontal lobe acts as a strong controlling agent on the first brain unit, possessing the capacity to inhibit or augment stimuli passing through the first unit. Consequently, dysfunction of the frontal lobe may lead to dysfunction of the first unit. Conversely, because the frontal lobe is so intricately tied with the activating system and the rest of the first unit, disorders of the first unit may affect the functioning of the tertiary areas of the frontal lobes, causing the patient to act as if there were a frontal lesion.

In summary, it should be emphasized that none of the behaviors discussed in the preceeding section are absolutely localized, only that these units play certain roles in behavior when combined with the remaining two units. All behavior is the result of functional systems that reflect continual interchange and interaction among the three basic units of the brain. In general, Unit I contributes tone, arousal, and emotional reactions; Unit II provides sensory input and integration; and Unit III provides executive and motor functions. Acting together, the three units produce all behavior. Only by exhaustive analysis of the pattern of results from each patient can the exact area of dysfunction be inferred. This makes Luria's theories more difficult to work with than many more traditional approaches; however, it is this difficulty which, we believe, also makes it more accurate in its general outline.

3. Development of the Standardized Battery

Luria's approach to evaluation was not standardized but consisted of a loose set of procedures, some of which were given to each patient as Luria saw appropriate. Each of these procedures attempted—as closely as possible—to focus on one discrete, specific brain-based skill. This, of course, is actually impossible to do, as all behaviors reflect an integration of basic skills. Thus, there is a need for a series of items involving each skill combined with a variety of other skills. If all the items that contain a given skill are impaired, this implies impairment of the specific skill (provided that the items are properly chosen). Using such an approach, Luria might have asked the patient to complete task X. If behavior X is composed of the functional system ABCDE and the patient is unable to complete the task, Luria would not have known what essential, basic skill had been impaired. However, if the patient was unable to complete a variety of tasks in which skill B was a part of the functional system, he could more confidently feel that the cortical area mediating skill B has been damaged. The particular items that a given patient was given depended upon Luria's clinical assessment of the patient.

The structure of the standardized battery was based on similar reasoning by Golden, Hammeke, and Purisch (1980). However, instead of using clinical intuition to guess at deficits, items were chosen to evaluate all major deficit areas systematically. This was fairly easy to do, as the major deficit areas had already been described by Luria in 1970, discussed in his 1980 book, and laid out in detail along with suggested test items by Christensen (1975). Working from Christensen (1975), items were chosen to represent each major deficit area so that detailed analysis of specific skills could be made. Skills were assessed in a variety of ways so as to test how the various units of the brain interact in an individual. Both standardized administration procedures and standardized scoring instructions were developed for each item. In contrast to some of Luria's procedures, scoring generally focuses on a single dimension of performance, such as accuracy. The same item may be scored along several dimensions. This acts to simplify the scoring of single items. A final version of the test was developed using 269 items which covered the 11 major behavioral areas as identified by Luria. In addition, three derived scales (pathognomonic, right hemisphere, and left hemisphere) are included (Golden, Hammeke, & Purisch, 1980).

Within each section and across sections of the battery, there is a qualitative analysis of the function, with cross checks to allow identification of specific functional deficits. For example, phonemic discrimination is evaluated in a large number of ways, including repeating, writing, and a manual conditioning item. Similarly, we look at the individual's ability not only to hear rhythmic patterns but also to reproduce them by either imitation or on verbal command. It is this type of breakdown of skills that makes the battery particularly appropriate for rehabilitation planning. By analyzing skills into their various components and recombining them in a wide variety of ways, one can get at the essence of a patient's specific deficits.

In using the standardized Luria-Nebraska Battery, the main goal of the rehabilitation psychologist is to identify the items missed and the skills that those items have in common. Then, by comparing the performance on these items to other items in the battery containing the same skill, one may ascertain which skills are still intact as indicated by good performance on other items. Eventually, the psychologist can determine which specific skills have been impaired and which remain intact. When the psychologist is aware of which skills have been impaired, tasks aimed at replacing these skills or retraining them as necessary can be designed. Golden, Hammeke, Purisch, Berg, Moses, Newlin, Wilkening, and Puente (1982) provide a summary of the types of items covered by the Luria-Nebraska Battery.

4. Reliability

Reliability studies have never enjoyed a major place in clinical neuropsychology, which instead has emphasized validity studies. However, several reliability studies have been run on the Luria-Nebraska. Golden, Hammeke, and Purisch (1978) reported a series of five subjects scored simultaneously by two examiners to provide a measure of interrater reliability. Of 1,425 comparisons, there was agreement in over 95% of the cases.

Golden, Fross, and Graber (1981) examined the split-half reliability of Luria-Nebraska. The patients in the study represented a wide range of diagnostic types: 74 normal controls, 83 psychiatric patients, and 181 patients with neurological disorders. Split half correlates ranged from .89 (memory) to .95 (reading), all highly significant.

The final reliability study at present was run by Golden, Berg, and Graber (1982), who examined the test–retest reliability of the Luria-Nebraska scales using 27 patients. The average time between test and retest was 167 days (SD = 133.8 days) with a range from 10 to 469 days. The lowest test–retest reliabilities were on the tactile (.78) and right hemisphere (.77) scales, while the other scales ranged from .84 (memory) to .96 (arithmetic). Mean test–retest reliability was .88. Mean change in average score was 1 point; this was validated by Plaisted and Golden (1982).

4.1. Item–Scale Consistency

The question of item–scale consistency is an important one for the Luria-Nebraska. Basically, the question is whether each item correlates highest with the scale it is on or with another scale. Items within each scale intentionally vary across a number of dimensions (rather than being homogeneous, like the items on the Wechsler Adult Intelligence Scale subtests) both within and between subareas. Items were assigned to a scale on a theoretical basis; these scale–item intercorrelations offer an opportunity to verify those assignments. The scale–item correlations were determined using the same subjects employed in the split-half reliability study (and were reported in the same study). Of the total of 269 items, 250 showed their highest correlation with the scale they were on. Of the remaining 19 items, 10 showed correlations within .01 of the highest correlation on the scale they were on.

4.2. Diagnostic Validity

Most of the early studies on the Luria-Nebraska dealt with the diagnostic validity of the test in order to provide evidence to corroborate Luria's qualitative reports. In the earliest study, Golden et al. (1978) evaluated the individual effectiveness of 285 items that were considered for the test. The question under study was the diagnostic effectiveness of each item. The performance of 50 control subjects was compared with that of 50 neuropsychological patients. The groups were equal in age (control age M = 42.0; SD = 14.8; neurological age M = 44.3; SD = 18.8) but not in education (control education M = 12.21; SD = 2.86; neurological education M = 10.3; SD = 2.84; t (98) = 3.51, $p < .01$). As a consequence, comparisons were made using a one-way analysis of variance with education as a covariate.

Of the 285 items, 253 differentiated the groups at the .05 level. Of the remaining 32 items, 16 were significant at the .20 level and 16 were not. Of these latter 16 items, the neurological group performed worse on 14, while identical performance was found on 2. This study was used to shorten the battery by 16 items, to its present length of 269 items, by eliminating those that were least effective.

A second study, done as a dissertation by Thomas Hammeke (1978), used the same patients. The published version used about 90% of the same subjects but added different subjects (matched for diagnosis and severity) in order to eliminate the education discrepancy (Hammeke, Golden, & Purisch, 1978). Using optimal cutoff points, Hammeke *et al.* (1978) found the hit rates for the scales to range from 74% (expressive) to 96% (memory) in the control group and 66% (rhythm) to 86% (expressive) in the neurological patients. A discriminant analysis reported results of 100% in the control group and 86% in the neurological group, for an overall rate of 93%.

Adams (1980) has criticized this study for running separate *t*-tests on each scale without an overall multivariate *F*. To meet this criticism, another sample was drawn (Golden, 1981b) consisting of 67 neurological patients and 57 controls. The average age over all subjects was 43.87 years ($SD = 13.27$) and the average education was 11.23 years (SD EQ 2.57) with no significant group differences [t (122) = 0.89 and 1.23 respectively). A multivariate ANOVA separating the groups was run using the basic 11 scales, resulting in an $F(10, 114)$ of 8.2, $p < .001$.

The Hammeke *et al.* (1978) study had been replicated twice at the time of writing. Moses and Golden (1979) replicated the study with 50 additional control and 50 additional neurological patients. The results of the study were reported in *T*-scores, using the mean performance of the control subjects in Hammeke *et al.* (1978) as representing 50. The new control group and neurological groups were comparable to the earlier subjects in age and education. The means for the new control group varied between 48 and 52—values indistinguishable from the original control group; mean scores for the neurological patients ranged from a mean of 64 (reading) to a mean of 77 (rhythm). Using the cutoffs determined in the Hammeke *et al.* study, the hit rates for each function scale varied from those found by Hammeke *et al.* but not significantly.

A second cross-validation was performed as an as yet unpublished dissertation by Duffala (1978). This study compared normal, non-hospitalized controls to trauma victims. The author reported a hit rate of over 90%. It should be noted that this study can be criticized because of the younger age and higher education of the control group. However, corrections for age and education (discussed later) do not reduce the hit rate below 90%.

The first Luria-Nebraska study on localization was conducted by Osmon, Golden, Purisch, Hammeke, and Blume (1979). In this study Osmon compared 60 patients overall; 20 of them had left hemisphere injuries, 20 had right hemisphere injuries, and 20 had diffuse (bilateral) injuries. In general the study did not examine relatively easy-to-diagnose patients with acute lateralized disorders but examined patients who were at least 6 months postonset and in most cases more than 1 year postonset. Since these patients have recovered to some degree, their symptoms are significantly less lateralized, a characteristic of recovering brain injuries (see Golden, 1981b). In addition, hemiplegic or severely aphasic patients unable to do the test procedures or follow instructions were not included.

In looking at this study, it is necessary to examine the characteristics of the Luria-Nebraska scales. The motor scale, for example, alternates between left-hand, right-hand, bilateral, intellectual, and construction dyspraxia items; thus, one would not expect the scale score itself to lateralize. Such interpretations, as noted before, depend upon pattern configurations. Similar arguments may be made for all of the 11 basic scales. Each scale contains, according to Luria's theory, items sensitive to the functions of both hemispheres. The single closest scale to one that would lateralize would be the reading scale. However, items on this scale that assess reading paragraphs, sound synthesis, and similar processes may be affected by right as well as left hemisphere injuries.

The three special scales can also be looked at in this manner. The pathognomonic scale contains items sensitive to both right and left hemisphere damage. The last two scales, left hemisphere and right hemisphere, were theoretically chosen to represent lateralized disorders to the motor–sensory areas around the central sulcus of each hemisphere. Luria's theory would predict that the left hemisphere scale would be the most effective in that it would not be seriously impaired by unilateral right hemisphere injuries. The right hemisphere scale, however, would be affected by injuries in both hemispheres. This is because Luria assigned a major coordination role to the dominant left hemisphere, which he believed controls all motor as well as sensory behavior. Thus, left parietal injuries can lead to *bilateral* finger agnosia (loss of ability to localize touch), and left frontal injuries can interfere with left- as well as right-hand movement.

The results of the initial analysis supported Luria's theory. Of the special scales, only the left hemisphere significantly discriminated among the three groups. The reading scale was marginally insignificant [$F(2, 57) = 1.99$, p $< .10$], while the remaining primary scales were all clearly insignificant.

With these results the question still remains whether the Luria-Nebraska can lateralize brain lesions. To determine this, a discriminant analysis was employed. This analysis was able correctly to lateralize 59 of the 60 cases (98%), a rate comparable to or higher than that of any other test battery. The simple difference between the right and left scale scores (T-scores) were able to lateralize 75% of the cases by itself. (The average right–left difference for the right hemisphere group was $+11.62$; for the left hemisphere group, -14.25; for the diffuse group, $-.19$).

The remaining discriminations were based on several comparisons: visual minus intelligence (a positive score indicating right hemisphere); rhythm minus receptive (a positive score indicating right); and reading minus arithmetic (positive scores, while rare, almost always indicate left hemisphere damage). Two discriminant equations generated in this study yielded a 98% hit rate. Note that these latter comparisons are most significant in the context of the entire profile.

A follow-up study by Lewis, Golden, Moses, Osmon, Purisch, and Hammeke (1979) examined localization of function using the Luria-Nebraska Battery. The study comprised 60 patients (24 right, 36 left) with brain damage localized in one of eight brain areas. These were the frontal lobes, the sensorimotor area, the temporal lobe, and the parietal–occipital area in each hemisphere. There were 6 patients with damage to each area in the right hemisphere and 9 patients with damage to each area in the left hemisphere. The patients in the eight groups had an average age of 43.1 ($SD = 13.5$) years and education of 10.8 ($SD = 2.3$) years. The average chronicity of the patients was 210.3 ($SD = 52$) days, so all were beyond the acute stage of their disorder. No patient was tested who was unable to do simple motor movements or who was unable to follow simple directions.

These eight groups of patients were compared against a normative group of 100 controls [who also served as the control group in the Hammeke *et al.* (1978) and Moses and Golden (1979) studies]. Analysis of variance for each scale showed significant differences across the groups on all Luria-Nebraska measures. *Post hoc* *t*-tests then examined all pairs of groups on each scale to identify differences among the groups. The results from these studies were complex; the reader is referred to the original scales, which were chosen theoretically (based on lateralized sensorimotor performance) rather than being more broadly and empirically determined.

The new scales showed significant ability to discriminate lateralized injuries. Using only the differences between T-scores for the two scales, the scales correctly lateralized 87.3% of the cases in an independent cross-validation group.

A set of localization scales were proposed by McKay and Golden (1979b). In this study, the authors attempted to devise localization scales for injuries in each of the eight areas of the brain described earlier; frontal, sensorimotor, temporal, and parietal–occipital areas of the two hemispheres. Using groups of subjects ranging in size from 3 to 10—all of whom had localized injuries—for a total of 53 brain-injured subjects, comparisons were made with 77 normal subjects on each test item. The normal subjects had an average age of 41.3 (SD = 16.3) years and differed significantly only from the right temporal group mean (age 55.7) and the left sensorimotor group (age 60.7). The normal subjects had 11.9 (SD = 2.8) years of education and were not significantly different from any of the brain-damaged subjects in this regard.

Items that differentiated each of the eight localized groups of patients from the normals were then examined for overlap. Items failing on more than two of the localization scales were deleted (details of this procedure can be found in the paper). In this manner, eight localization scales with between 16 and 33 items were generated.

T-scores for each of the scales were determined by using the performance of the normal control group. Scores were then determined for each of the 53 patients used in the study. By utilizing the highest score for each patient, an attempt was made at localization. In 47 of the 53 subjects (88.7%), the localization was correct. Five out of the six errors were made in 10 subjects who showed elevations above 70 on all scales, suggesting that the focal injury was in the context of more widespread destruction (e.g., head trauma or glioma). In the remaining 43 cases, accurate diagnosis was achieved in 42 cases (97.7%).

The small sample size on which the localization scales were based necessitated the completion of a cross-validation study to demonstrate their potential clinical utility. Such a study, (Golden, Moses, Fishburne, Engum, Lewis, Wisniewski, Conley, Berg, & Graber, 1981) examined the localization scales in 87 localized cases. These cases included subgroups ranging in size from 6 to 17 subjects. Overall, the localization scales were able to classify 65 of the 87 cases correctly, for a hit rate of 74%. In addition, the localization scales classified 82 of 87 patients into the correct hemisphere (e.g., a patient whose highest score was on the right frontal scale would be classified as a right hemisphere patient), indicating that only 5 of the original 22 errors were the result of classifying the patient into the wrong hemisphere. This suggests that the localization scales may also serve as an excellent method of lateralizing brain lesions.

5. Process Studies

Beyond the obvious comparisons lies the question of diagnostic efficiency. An initial attempt at answering this question was made by the relationship between Luria-Nebraska patterns and specific neurological disorders. The first paper in this area was published by Chmielewski and Golden (1980). In this study the authors compared 40 male alcoholics to 40 male control subjects. In general, the severity of the alcoholism was not high, as none of the subjects had neurological symptoms such as ataxia. Still, differences were found between the groups on the visual, receptive language, arithmetic, memory, intelligence, and pathognomonic scales. More recent (as yet unpublished) data have suggested that these scales may only be the earliest to be affected. In chronic cases, more general and severe elevations are seen.

A study by Zelazowski, Golden, Graber, Blose, Bloch, Moses, Stahl, Osmon, and Pfefferbaum (1981) has suggested more specific relationships between scores on the Luria-Nebraska and alcoholism. Zelazowski measured the size of ventricles on CT scans of 25 alcoholics. These values were then correlated with each of the Luria-Nebraska scales. Significant correlations (adjusted for age and education) were found on the motor, visual, expressive speech, memory, intelligence, and pathognomonic scales. All the significant correlations were between .46 and .58. The multiple correlations between all of these scales and ventricular size was .70 ($p < .05$). This study suggests that Luria-Nebraska elevations are associated with neurological changes in the brain. It should be noted that, again, this group represented mild to moderate alcoholics as a whole. The maximum measure of ventricular size for an alcoholic patient in this study was 21%, well over the 3% (3 patients) average level for normals but also well under scores of 30% to 40% or more seen in severe alcoholics with prominent neurological deficits.

Berg and Golden (1981) compared the performance of normals, neurological patients without epilepsy, brain-damaged patients with epilepsy, and patients with epilepsy for whom no specific brain injury could be documented by either history, neurological examination, or radiological evaluation (idiopathic epilepsy). Significant differences were found between both epilepsy groups and the controls on all measures except motor, tactile, and the right and left hemisphere scales derived from motor and tactile. There were no differences between the two epilepsy groups on the test measures.

The study by Golden (1979) on multiple sclerosis (MS) is probably more important for its methodology than for what it reveals about "diagnoses." It was proposed that to diagnose a homogeneous neurological disorder, one needed to establish two things: (1) the presence of the expected symptoms and (2) the absence of symptoms unassociated with the disorder. Thus, Golden compared 24 MS patients to a mixed neurological group of 101 patients. From these comparisons he established two scales: items on which MS patients did better (scale B) and items on which MS patients did worse (scale W) Thus, to be diagnosed as having MS, a patient would have to do well on scale B and badly on scale W. Cutoffs were established on the basis of the performance of the MS group, so that all MS patients were diagnosed correctly. The diagnoses of the 101 neurological patients were then determined. While some were misdiagnosed by each scale alone, none were misdiagnosed using both together, for a hit rates based on the two together of 100%. Similar results were found for 74 normals and 106 psychiatric patients (73 schizophrenics, 33 others) compared in the same study. In each case, although there were individual misidentifications using only one scale, no patient was misidentified using both scales. Thus, a 100% hit rate was again achieved.

The small sample size of MS patients (24) clearly indicates the need for at least one, if not more, cross validations to determine the effectiveness of specific items on scales B and W. However, this does not diminish the possible role of what Golden (1979) termed "double discrimination scales" in diagnosing any of a large number of disorders that are more or less homogeneous in their symptoms (e.g., Parkinson's disease). Extensive research is needed in this area, but the structure of the Luria-Nebraska is ideally suited for the development of such scales.

5.1. Factor Analysis

The last area of research current at this time involves the factor analysis of the Luria-Nebraska scales. One series of studies (Golden, Hammeke, Osmon, Sweet, Purisch, & Graber, 1981; Golden, Osmon, Sweet, Graber, Purisch, & Hammeke, 1980; Golden, Purisch, Sweet, Graber, Osmon, & Hammeke, 1980; Golden, Sweet, Hammeke, Purisch, Graber, & Osmon, 1980) has attempted to evaluate empirically the subfactors that theoretically make up of each of the Luria-Nebraska scales. These studies used a population of 272 patients consisting of normal, psychiatric, and neurological patients in order to maximize range of scores so as to fully define the factors. The results in general support Luria's theoretical analysis of the scales (see, e.g., Luria, 1966, 1973; Golden et al., 1982). The factor subscales identified have potential importance both in aiding the detailed evaluation of a patient's behavior and in localization and lateralization. Current research is examining the establishment of scale norms for these subscales as well as possible profile evaluations (McKay & Golden, 1981).

6. Rehabilitation Planning and Theory

6.1. Interpretation

The standardized Luria-Nebraska offers the user several different methods of interpretation, including item analysis, scale analysis, and qualitative analysis. This has the obvious advantage of allowing for the cross-validation of conclusions within the single test, as each of the methods is largely independent of the others. The final conclusions are generally the result of the consistent trends seen between the methods (although they may be presented as the result of the method that describes the result more clearly). These steps may be done in any order, depending upon the preferences of the individual user.

6.2. Item Analysis

As presented above, the LNNB battery is suited for the specific analysis of primary skills which, according to Luria's theory, provide the basic foundation of human behavior. The purpose of this type of analysis is to identify those specific areas of the brain that have been injured and those specific brain behavior skills that have been lost. This analysis is done simply by the process of elimination. For example, if the patient shows impairment in motor speed in the initial items of the test but no impairment in tactile feedback, ability to follow instructions, ability to imitate visual presentations, and so on, one can conclude from this series of results that the patient is showing basic motor impairment. Similarly, if a patient is able to do simple phonemic discrimination and to follow simple commands but unable to follow complex grammatical instructions though intellectual status is intact, then there is likely a deficit in those skills that allow one to do grammatical and syntactical analysis. Further evaluation of the patient's specific errors and patterns of errors across the test will allow for an even more precise description of the patient's problems. In essence, one is identifying which functional system is disrupted and why. Thus, rather than talking about the loss of higher complex skills or the loss of flexibility, we may look at specific components of these skills and the intactness of the relevant functional systems. This enables rehabilitation planning to start.

The use of this method is highly dependent upon awareness of the significance of each item on the LNNB and the basic skills required to complete the item. For example, on the visual scale, a patient may be unable to name simple objects or do complex nonverbal problem solving. It could be suspected that the basic visual problem was due to an expressive language deficit rather than a basic visual disturbance. If one is familiar with the test, this can be evaluated by looking at performance in the motor section, which requires visual imitation using both sides of the body. This usually gives significant information, since both sides are rarely disrupted by motor impairment to such a degree as totally to disrupt performance of these simple items. If dominant motor skills are intact, several drawing items give additional information on basic visual skills. Similarly, several memory and intelligence items yield additional information on basic visual skills. Item analysis across scales is a very powerful technique. Reading of Luria (1980) and Christensen (1975) as well as Golden, Hammeke, Purisch, Berg, Moses, Newlin, Wilkening, & Puente (1982) will familiarize the reader with the skills involved in each item.

6.3. Qualitative Analysis

In addition to the skills measured by each item, the examiner can also gain a great deal of information by observing the patient. Luria has emphasized that it is often more important to observe the way the patient goes about doing a task than it is to know whether the patient got the right answer. The possibility for such observations is inherent in the items chosen for the test. Since the same basic skills, such as motor functions, are examined in a large number of different ways, the examiner gets the opportunity to watch the patient attempt to perform motorically under a large variety of conditions. Thus, unusual style used by the patient, bizarre approaches to problems, or attempts by the patient to find a new way of doing things will be revealed on some if not all of the items as the environmental conditions manipulating the patient's behavior are constantly changed. This constant change also allows the examiner to evaluate such important deficits as perseverations, difficulty with attention and concentration, memory disturbances, ability to follow instructions of varying degrees of complexity, inability to interact with the examiner appropriately, and the ways in which the patient reacts to frustration if unable to complete tasks. The examiner may also evaluate the patient's orientation toward goals, ability to reach goals, ability to keep tasks in mind, ability to plan sequentially in the analysis of a task, and so on. All of these are important factors in evaluating the individual but are difficult to quantify. Sensitive qualitative use of the test relies upon the examiner for these more subtle discriminations.

6.4. Scale Interpretation

In addition to the more traditional analysis presented above, the Luria-Nebraska also allows for a quantitative analysis of the patient's performance by the profile of the patient's scores on each of the 14 scales of the battery. Each scale is scored on a T-score system, with a score of 50 representing the performance of a group averaging about 42 years of age and 11 years of education. Each patient's performance, however, is compared against a critical level that is determined in a formula which takes into account his own age and education 68.8 + (.214 × age) − (1.47 × education [years]) (Golden, Hammeke, & Purisch, 1980). Scores above this level are considered abnormal. In general, more than one score above the critical point is considered evidence of brain dysfunction (see test manual for details of this objective interpretative system).

By examining the pattern of abnormal scores, basic conclusions can be reached on the nature of the patient's deficits. In turn, the pattern can be compared to patterns generated by past patients with known lesions (see Lewis *et al.*, 1979). In this way, the interpreter—depending on his experience skill, and knowledge—may generate fairly detailed descriptions of the patient's deficits.

In addition to the interpretation of the basic scales, recent research (McKay & Golden, 1979a,b) has suggested a series of localization scales based on a series of patients with specific injuries. Although highly successful in identifying the location of an injury in the original study (90%) and in cross-validation (74%), we are still in the process of studying these scales. However, they are being used experimentally to see what they can add to the objective interpretation. In general, they have been useful in identifying the locus of an injury, which in turn is helpful in defining precisely the nature of the injury (by reference to Luria's basic theoretical conceptions). It is likely that this combination of behavioral and theoretical scales will prove to be a powerful interpretive device, once adequate research has shown the specific value of each scale.

In integrating the data from these various techniques, the clinician must analyze the information so as to identify the precise behavioral deficits shown by the patient. It is not sufficient simply to note that a patient misses an item; the clinician should determine why the patient misses the item. This need arises from the basic postulates of Luria's theory that were discussed earlier; all behavior (and hence all test items) reflects the actions of all three cortical units, with each behavior reflecting different combinations of these units and different emphases upon the subareas within each unit. An error arising from dysfunction of the first unit needs to be understood and treated in a considerably different manner from an error on the same item arising from a dysfunction of the secondary auditory area of the second unit or the tertiary area of the third unit.

The process of doing this is not a simple one. One must be aware of how patients with different lesions respond to the same item; how would a first-unit lesion possibly differ from a tertiary frontal lesion, for example? Only through intensive study of neuropsychological research and theory can one become acquainted with all the possibilities in this area. A second approach is to be familiar with the results of the Luria-Nebraska and to identify patterns on the scale scores (including both the basic and localization scales) that are consistent with specific lesions. This is done through study of the test research data as well as through experience and application of results from other test procedures. This procedure, of course, is based much more on research than on application of theory. By identifying patterns of scales and items consistent with specific lesions, we can increase our understanding of the patient as well as confirm those findings suggested by theory.

It should be noted here that this process of "lesion localization" is not done for the sake of simply finding out where the lesion is physically but rather to determine where the lesion "lies" within the behavioral framework outlined earlier in this paper. Indeed, the actual localization of the lesion may be irrelevant in rehabilitation; what is important is the constellation of deficits shown by the patient. Thus, when the pattern of the Luria-Nebraska suggests a "left frontal" lesion, for example, what is important is that the patient has a series of deficits suggesting underlying problems characteristic of the left frontal area. Whether the lesion is actually there is much more important for validity research than for clinical purposes. For example, certain lesions in the temporal lobe may, because of interference with certain brain tracts, give a frontal lobe pattern of results. In other cases, the patient's brain may indeed be organized differently than the ideal model we have presented; as a consequence, lesions may not be where we expect them to be. In each case, the actual localization of the lesion is not the important factor; careful definition of the patient's deficits determines the rehabilitation program.

It should also be clear that it is impossible to divide the Luria-Nebraska items by functional units, since every item involves every unit. Only a thorough understanding of the factors outlined above allows one to make the functional breakdown necessary. It is important in this process to avoid assumptions about items measuring single skills;

such simplistic ideas can lead one to make frequent and unfortunate errors. One must continually recognize that each patient is an individual with his or her individual set of problems, deficits, and reactions to those problems. Two patients, though sustaining the same injury, will often show different test results and express the same deficits in considerably variant manners.

After one has used the Luria-Nebraska (or a similar approach) to determine the nature of the deficits shown by the patients, the actual rehabilitation process may be initiated. Luria (1973, 1980) indicates that the rehabilitation process entails the substitution of a new, intact functional system to replace the system that has been injured. The ways in which alternate functional systems can be taught and envisaged are discussed in the next section of this chapter. However, several comments are in order before leaving this section.

First, there is no way—from using the Luria-Nebraska or any other set of tests—to specify a one-to-one relationship between test results and the rehabilitation program. There are several reasons for this. First and most prominent is the observation made above that any error may arise from a wide variety of deficits. Thus, the treatment would have to be different in each case. Second, treatment must depend on the patient's intact skills. A program requiring skills that the patient does not have is not useful. "Average" programs simply are not ideal for the *individual* patient, which is where our focus ought be. Thus, while research can be done on the "left hemisphere patient," a program written for such an abstract being would not be the ideal program for all patients with injuries in the left hemisphere. With the Luria-Nebraska, the emphasis is on regarding each patient's problems as unique and giving due consideration to the patient as a whole.

In addition, there are many factors involved in rehabilitation which the Luria-Nebraska cannot predict. Such qualities as motivation, desire to improve, the question of compensation, the degree of family support, the secondary gains, and numerous other factors influence both eventual prognosis and rehabilitation planning. If the patient is more motivated or interested in one area of treatment, for example, that area might be best emphasized no matter what its overall importance. An area in which the patient refuses to work is obviously a useless one.

Finally, the test cannot decide in what ways we are to do rehabilitation. As will be shown, there are often several alternatives in any given case. One must choose between them on the basis of clinical judgment, attempting to assess which method would give the patient the greatest benefit at the least overall cost to everyone involved. Limitations on resources of both institutions and individuals must be considered, along with the emotional and practical factors discussed in the last paragraph. Such considerations require a clear conceptualization of the strengths and limitations of the patient, the institution, and the family involved as well as a clear understanding of the joint goals shared by the therapist and the patient.

With these points in mind, we will turn now to the planning of the rehabilitation program.

6.5. Establishing a Program

Once the nature of a patient's deficits has been determined, translation to a rehabilitation program turns out to be reasonably straightforward. Almost all rehabilitation tasks currently being used can be found to be effective with patients who have certain precise deficits. However, no technique is appropriate for all patients; the user of the test must be very careful to be aware of this and to remain flexible in the type of rehabilitation technique that is employed. It will also be found that, through creative understanding of brain function, many different tasks can be used to achieve the same goal. The importance lies not in the nature of the individual task itself but in its appropriateness for the individual. It is this assumption which is the basis of Luria's system of rehabilitation.

In planning a rehabilitation program for specific skills, several alternative approaches may be used by the examiner. Each of these depends upon the exact pattern of skills and deficits shown by the patient, which, in turn, is dependent upon the exact nature of the brain damage the patient has sustained. The first method, and that most often employed, simply involves the retraining of the injured skill through establishing alternative pathways in the brain. This approach is most often used in the retraining of motor skills. For example, a given patient may have destroyed significant parts of the motor and sensory areas of a given hemisphere. However, these patients can be retaught motor skills through repeated practice of the basic components. This is possible because the brain has both ipsilateral and contralateral connections for sensory and motor skills. Thus, the alternate hemisphere may be taught to take over the sensory or motor skills of the ipsilateral side of the body.

In utilizing such an approach, the first important principle is the availability to the patient of sufficient feedback. Feedback is extremely important, because the brain may have no way of evaluating whether an injured leg has moved ¼ inch or not at all after a stroke. If this information can be fed back immediately, it can reinforce the pathways that provide innervation for movement of the leg. Feedback to the patient can come in a wide variety of ways. The patient may see that the leg has moved, although this is not a very effective technique when very small distances are involved. The examiner or rehabilitation therapist working with the patient may indicate to the patient how far the leg has moved by measuring this in some way, or the patient may get feedback from biofeedback machinery set to be sensitive to small movements.

The sensitivity of the feedback necessary for assisting the patient is highly dependent upon the level at which the patient is able to start. If the patient is unable to move the muscle at first, he must first progress through stages of being able to tense the muscle slightly. Since progress at this stage is small and very difficult to determine, very sensitive measuring instruments must be employed. Later in the patient's progress, when he is able to walk a few steps, the measuring instruments can be rather gross—for example, the number of steps taken without having to use external support.

While we use motor skills as an easy example, the same type of process may be used with higher cognitive skills. For example, if the patient is unable to memorize verbal material, we might start with having the patient memorize single words, picking words that are very common to the patient and those which the patient can pronounce without difficulty, as these would be easier for the patient to remember. Then we might proceed to memorizing more difficult single words, such as words the patient is not familiar with, finally proceeding to sets of two words, then three words, and so on.

This example illustrates the second basic principle of rehabilitation: the shaping of the desired response from the specific level of skills possessed by the patient. The rehabilitation task that begins with skills the patient does not have is inappropriate; however, a rehabilitation task that demands nothing new from the patient will also have no effect. Thus, the rehabilitation task must always move slightly ahead of the patient's current level of skills, but not by such a large margin as to make it impossible for him to make that leap. This must be combined with sensitive enough feedback on progress so that the patient is constantly aware of progress.

In using the method of directly retraining a skill that has been lost, the retraining should focus directly upon those links in the functional system that have been injured. All training tasks should be put together so as to demand only one new behavior at a time. For example, in the memory task given above, reading cues would not be used to help a patient if the patient was unable to read. This would demand two new skills from the patient and would make the task too difficult to be an appropriate rehabilitation task.

In a number of situations, it will be found that direct retraining of the skill is not possible. In these situations, rehabilitation training can take two routes: the first involves training the patient to do the task using simpler, more basic level skills, while the second involves changing the skill into a higher-level ability. The selection of the appropriate approaches depends upon the task that one wishes to train as well as the intactness of other brain areas.

The substitution of more basic skills generally occurs as the result of injuries to the tertiary areas of either the second or third unit of the brain. In some cases, those areas controlling such skills as abstract spatial reasoning are injured to such a degree that the patient is unable to recover the skill or to be retrained directly in the ability. Thus, the trainer may choose to break the skill down into more simple units, using secondary- and primary-level skills that the patient retains. For example, in doing a jigsaw puzzle or block design type of task, which often requires tertiary-level abilities, the patient might be taught to break the puzzle up into certain color groups then to match certain shapes to one another, do specific types of evaluation of what has been done, and so on, in a large number of specific steps until the patient is able to follow the steps and complete the task. With time the instructions may be faded out and memorized by the patient.

In training a long series of steps, the training will ideally go step by step; the patient is taught the first step until it is overlearned, moves on to the second step until it is overlearned, and so on. Clearly, this method is highly dependent upon the ability of the rehabilitation therapist to analyze the behavior involved and to break it down into primary- and secondary-level skills, taking advantages as well of whatever tertiary skills are left. For example, one could take the same spatial task described above and turn it into a verbal task for the patient whose verbal mediation has been left primarily intact. Many of the techniques that can be used with this method are similar to those techniques used to teach children complex thinking and logical approaches to the analysis of problems (Golden, 1981b).

The substitution of higher-level skills for lower-level skills is generally used when there are injuries of the primary and secondary levels of the brain. One example of this, of course, is the use of visual analysis of lip movements to help an individual who has trouble making auditory phonemic discriminations. Here the secondary- and tertiary-level skills required in the analysis of lip movements are used to augment the information coming in through the auditory channel. Another example of this is provided by Luria (1980) for a patient who is unable to beat out a rhythmic pattern but who can count without difficulty. This patient is taught to count and to make a beat with his or her hand at each count. By controlling the rate of counting, the patient may be taught to do rhythmic patterns. Here there is a substitution of the higher-level skill of integrating expressive speech and motor output to substitute for what is basically a rhythm task.

Obviously, when one uses either of the above approaches, the elaboration of a new way of doing the task depends heavily upon the patient's skills and the ability of the therapist to envision alternate functional systems, tapping intact skills while avoiding the injured areas of the brain. This can be difficult to do unless a thorough analysis of the patient's abilities has been made and the therapist has a full understanding of the patient's disabilities and residual abilities. In some cases, a trial-and-error period is necessary in order to find the ideal task from which the patient is best able to profit. Again, however, we must caution that any task that is used must rely upon intact areas of the brain; to the extent that injured areas of the brain must play a role in the new functional system, the training will be slower and success will be less likely.

7. Case Example

The prior material has discussed the use of the Luria-Nebraska battery and the theoretical approach to rehabilitation. While it is not possible to give a general program for all patients, a case example can demonstrate the kind of conclusions that may be reached from the Luria-Nebraska battery and the results from rehabilitation programs written from the test results.

Patient: H. C.

The patient is a 19-year-old white female who, prior to an automobile accident in which she sustained multiple trauma to her head, was a sophomore-level college student. She was majoring in engineering and was maintaining a high B average. On arrival at the emergency room soon after her injury, she was noted to be comatose and to have a laceration of the right temporal area. An emergency CT scan revealed bilateral depressed ventricles with cerebral edema. Her pupils were equal and reactive, but a deviation of the eyes to the left was noted. A subarachnoid screw was maintained in place during the first 10 days posttrauma; during this period, the patient had multiple bouts of elevated intracranial pressure which were treated with hyperventilation, steroids, and mannitol.

The patient remained semicomatose for approximately three months, during which she went through a several-week period of continuous restlessness, making purposeless movements of both the upper and lower extremities on the right. Approximately three weeks after she regained consciousness, neurological evaluation was begun.

Figure 1 shows a Luria profile from the initial evaluation. The significant elevation of all subscale values is typical of what one sees on tests administered soon after the restitution of consciousness after prolonged periods of unconsciousness. However, this patient was unable to perform any of the items from the visual subscale. This subscale was, therefore, discontinued on the third item and no numerical value was assigned. Significant findings on the other subscales were as follows;

Motor. The patient was very slow in performing manual tasks such as touching each fingertip sequentially to the tip of the thumb and repeatedly opening and closing the fists. However, she was able to use kinesthetic cues to organize movement bilaterally and to use kinesthetic cues from one hand to

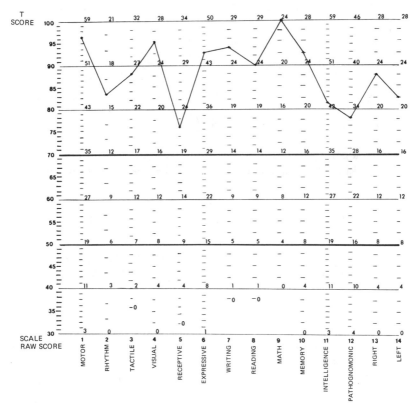

Figure 1. Profile for initial testing.

position the opposite hand. She had difficulty copying hand positions assumed by the examiner, tending to use either the wrong hand or the wrong position of the correct hand or both. She was able to pantomime complex activities such as threading a needle, although she was very slow. Her drawings of a circle, a square, and a triangle in response to a verbal command were not identifiable. Interestingly, when asked to copy these same figures from a pattern, her circle was a triangle with an extra horizontal line, her square was a star with a square beside it, and her triangle approximated a U. Oral praxis was also significantly impaired for both simple and complex oral movements.

Nonverbal Auditory. The patient could discriminate pitch patterns, but her attempts to produce pitch patterns resulted in a monotone. She could not count the number of tones in even simple patterns and, although she could reproduce rhythmic patterns verbally, she was totally unable to tap out the patterns manually.

Tactile. The patient could sense and localize touch without difficulty on both upper extremities. However, she was variable in her performance on all other tactile tasks.

Receptive Speech. The patient could discriminate phonemes and comprehend even complex grammatical structures. However, she had difficulty with essentially every item involving visual stimuli.

Expressive Speech. The patient could repeat phonemes, words, and sentences with minimal difficulty. However, she spoke in a monotone both spontaneously and on repetition. She was able to identify a single letter or word presented visually and could name objects from oral definitions, though she was unable to identify most of the pictorial visual stimuli. Automatic speech was intact, but she could not reverse the order on numbers from 20 to 1 or the days of the week. Narrative speech was also intact if visual stimuli were not involved.

Writing. The patient could not copy a single letter or word but she could write some letters and simple words to dictation. Her writing was essentially illegible.

Reading. The patient could not read letters or words.

Arithmetic. She could write numbers of up to three digits to dictation but she was less able to read numbers. All other mathematical skills were severely impaired.

Memory. Memory was impaired for both verbal and nonverbal material presented both visually and auditorily.

Intelligence. The patient again had difficulty with all items involving visual stimuli. However, she was able to interpret orally presented proverbs with fair accuracy and to identify categories and opposites. She had difficulty defining words, performing verbal analogies, and indicating similarities and differences.

Summary. This patient showed severe visual/perceptual problems including a variable ability to recognize or name visually presented objects, an inability to read or copy verbal material, and difficulty producing forms from either verbal instructions or (more profoundly) from a model. Comprehension of spoken language was essentially intact, as were her expressive language skills with the exception of those tasks involving visual stimuli (e.g., naming or describing objects or pictures). The patient was essentially acalculic and her memory for both verbal and nonverbal information was significantly impaired. Motor output was associated with significant slowing bilaterally, and discriminative tactile sensation was impaired. Although this patient was showing a generalized effect of her severe head trauma at this time, a posterior focus was also evident which (based on previous cases described in the literature) appeared to be either bilateral and/or to involve the corpus callosum (see Lewis *et al.*, 1979).

Rehabilitation at this stage focused strongly on activities of daily living, because the patient's visual perceptual difficulties caused problems for her in this area. For example, if she were not told that candy she was given had a wrapper on it, she would simply attempt to eat it wrapper and all. Interestingly, she was not observed to make attempts to compensate for her visual problems by using tactile cues (such as feeling the candy before eating it), possibly due to the tactile discrimination problems.

In addition to focusing on activities of daily living, the patient's occupational therapy program included retraining on nonverbal visual tasks such as matching objects to pictures, sorting objects by use, and so on. In speech therapy the focus was on describing pictures and naming visually presented objects as well as on improving intonational patterns of speech.

This patient was retested at intervals of approximately two months during her first year posttrauma. The Luria profile for the second administration is presented as Figure 2. As this figure indicates, all subscales remain significantly elevated. Several changes were noted in her results at the time of second testing.

1.   The visual problems remained of primary significance. Although she could now use visual cues to imitate hand positions, copying simple designs was slowed by visual aids as compared with production of the same designs from verbal instructions. For example, the patient produced a relatively good circle in 3.5 seconds on verbal command, but she subsequently took 15.5 seconds to copy a circle. She also exhibited significantly less difficulty writing if she closed her eyes and used only kinesthetic feedback to cue her than when she watched what she was writing.

2.   The patient's performance using auditory stimuli showed some deterioration during this testing as compared with the initial test. This was apparent both on nonverbal material such as pitch discrimination and on verbal material such as comprehension of orally presented grammatical structures.

3.   Tactile sensation improved considerably. The 2-point tactile thresholds remained elevated bilaterally, but the patient could discriminate sharp vs. dull and different intensities of touch with minimal difficulty. She was also able to identify 3 of the 4 verbal stimuli drawn on her wrists as well as 4 of the 6 forms. Stereognosis continued to be impaired.

4.   The ability to read individual letters improved somewhat, and the patient was able to recognize a few nonsense syllables and simple words. On the arithmetic subscale, she performed most of the simple addition, subtraction, and multiplication problems accurately as well as providing the missing signs (e.g.,

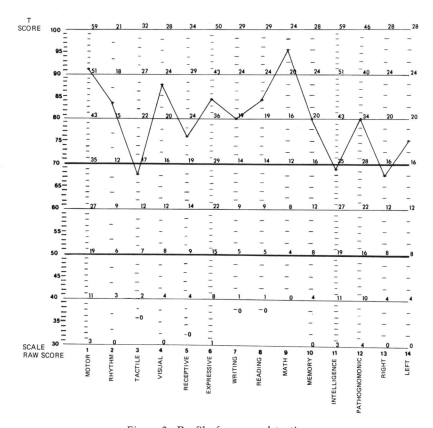

Figure 2. Profile for second testing.

=, −, ×) in some simple algebraic equations. However, arithmetic operations involving borrowing and carrying were beyond her capabilities at this time. Memory continued to be impaired, as did intellectual functioning, although quantitatively performance on both the memory and intelligence subscales showed some improvement over the two-month period.

The previously implemented rehabilitation program was changed somewhat after this evaluation because of slight improvement in visual/perceptual skills, including the emerging ability to recognize some written material. The demonstrated ability to use kinesthetic cues to write was capitalized upon in the following manner. The patient was given exercises in which she wrote letters with her eyes closed, verbalizing aloud as she worked. This was gradually modified to include the same task but with the eyes open. As the patient showed less and less deterioration in performance with eyes open, the relative time spent with eyes open as compared with eyes closed was increased. In addition, the patient was given plastic letters to feel and was asked to name them as she

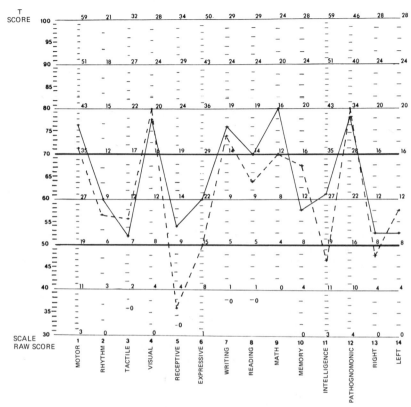

Figure 3. Profile for third and fifth testing.

felt them. This task was also performed with eyes open as well as with eyes closed. Retraining in arithmetic was also instituted at this time. The patient was given actual objects to count, add, and subtract initially, with the introduction of mathematical symbols very slowly.

A repeat CT scan at this time was read as normal and submission of this scan to a researcher who was carefully measuring ventricular size after head trauma resulted in a second normal reading. The third evaluation using the Luria showed a significant downward trend in her scores, representing improvement of overall cortical "tone." The profiles for the third and fifth test sessions are shown in Figure 3. During the period represented by these profiles, the motor subscale remained elevated, primarily due to a generalized slowing. The ability to discriminate and produce pitch patterns was slightly impaired. Tactile sensation was essentially normal, although some slight difficulty with graphognosis for letters and for stereognostic tasks requiring fine judgments (i.e., identifying the exact coin rather than simply knowing that an object was a coin) remained.

Although the profiles do not reflect a quantitative improvement, the patient's visual/perceptual skills improved significantly over the next few months. By the fourth test session she was able to perform essentially all the items on the visual subscale. However, her performance was extremely slow and thus did not allow her to get credit on the subscale. The ability to read and write also improved, but her latencies were excessive. Arithmetic skills remained impaired, as did memory.

Throughout this period the patient was maintained in physical, occupational, and speech therapies. In addition to the previous rehabilitation techniques, which were modified or deleted over time, higher-level reading, writing, and arithmetic tasks were gradually introduced. A two-month period of memory retraining techniques was also included, in which an attempt was made to teach the patient ways of organizing information to be remembered. However, at the end of the two months no significant change was noted in memory capability. Other techniques employed included reaction-time tasks in which the patient was required to decrease the time she took to perform various visual/perceptual tasks. The patient showed very little benefit from these tasks, and they were extremely frustrating to her.

8. Conclusions

As can be seen in the above case, the LNNB can be used in tracking as well as planning the course of rehabilitation. Further input can be achieved by attending to the qualitative aspects of the items as well as the pattern of item errors within the scale, combined with an understanding of basic neuropsychological processses. The LNNB should also be supplemented with further examinations into areas in which the nature of impact of the patients deficits are not clear. In all cases, the focus should be on identifying the "why" of patient errors rather than relying on empirical rules alone. In all cases, it is important to recognize the individuality of each case and to plan programs accordingly. The present chapter has presented, of course, only an overview of the possibilities in this area. Additional understanding of brain function to a much greater degree than presented here, along with supervised experience in neuropsychology, are also important aspects of planning rehabilitation.

9. References

Adams, A. "In search of Luria's Battery: A false start. *Journal of Consulting and Clinical Psychology*, 1980, *48*, 511–516.

Berg, R. A., & Golden, C. J. Identification of neuropsychological deficits in epilepsy using the Luria-Nebraska Neuropsychological Battery. *Journal of Consulting and Clinical Psychology*, 1981, *49*, 745–747.

Chmielewski, C., & Golden, C. J. Alcoholism and brain damage: An investigation using the Luria-Nebraska Neuropsychological Battery. *International Journal of Neuroscience*, 1980, *10*, 99–105.

Christensen, A. L. *Luria's neuropsychological investigation*. New York: Spectrum, 1975.

Duffala, D. *Validity of the Luria-South Dakota Neuropsychological Battery for brain-injured persons*. Unpublished doctoral dissertation, California School of Professional Psychology, 1978.

Golden, C. J. Identification of specific neurological disorders using double discrimination scales derived from the standard Luria neuropsychological battery. *International Journal of Neuroscience*, 1979, *10*, 51–56.

Golden, C. J. *Diagnosis and rehabilitation in clinical neuropsychology* (2nd ed.). Springfield, Ill.: Charles C Thomas, 1981. (a)

Golden, C. J. The Luria-Nebraska Neuropsychological Battery: Theory and research. In P. McReynolds (Ed.), *Advances in psychological assessment*. Palo Alto, Calif.: Science & Behavior Books, 1981. (b)

Golden, C. J., Hammeke, T. A., & Purisch, A. Diagnostic validity of a standardized neuropsychological battery derived from Luria's neuropsychological tests. *Journal of Consulting and Clinical Psychology*, 1978, *46*, 1258–1265.

Golden, C. J., Hammeke, T. A., & Purisch, A. *The Luria-Nebraska Neuropsychological Battery*. Los Angeles: Western Psychological Services, 1980.

Golden, C. J., Osmon, D., Sweet, J., Graber, B., Purisch, A., & Hammeke, T. Factor analysis of the Luria-Nebraska Neuropsychological Battery III: Writing, arithmetic, memory, left and right. *International Journal of Neuroscience*, 1980, *11*, 309–315.

Golden, C. J., Purisch, A., Sweet, J., Graber, B., Osmon, D., & Hammeke, T. Factor analysis of the Luria-Nebraska Neuropsychological Battery II: Visual, receptive, expressive, and reading scales. *International Journal of Neuroscience*, 1980, *11*, 227–236.

Golden, C. J., Sweet, J., Hammeke, T., Purisch, A., Graber, B., & Osmon, D. Factor analysis of the Luria-Nebraska Neuropsychological Battery I: Motor, rhythm and tactile scales. *International Journal of Neuroscience*, 1980, *11*, 91–99. (a)

Golden, C. J., Sweet, J., Hammeke, T., Purisch, A., Graber, B., & Osmon, D. Factor analysis of the Luria-Nebraska Neuropsychological Battery III: Writing, arithmetic, memory, left and right. *International Journal of Neuroscience*, 1980, *11*, 309–315. (b)

Golden, C. J., Fross, K., & Graber, B. Split half reliability and item consistency of the Luria-Nebraska Neuropsychological Battery. *Journal of Consulting and Clinical Psychology*, 1981, *49*, 304–305.

Golden, C. J., Hammeke, T., Osmon, D., Sweet, J., Purisch, A., & Graber, B. Factor analysis of the Luria-Nebraska Neuropsychological Battery IV: Intelligence and pathognomonic scales. *International Journal of Neuroscience*, 1981, *13*, 87–92.

Golden, C. J., Moses, J. A., Jr., Fishburne, F. J., Engum, E., Lewis, G. P., Wisniewski, A., Conley, F. K., Berg, R. A., & Graber, B. Cross validation of Luria-Nebraska Neuropsychological Battery for the presence, lateralization, and localization of brain damage. *Journal of Consulting and Clinical Psychology*, 1981, *49*, 410–417.

Golden, C. J., Moses, J. A., Jr., Graber, B., & Berg, R. A. Objective clinical rules for interpreting the Luria-Nebraska Neuropsychological Battery: Derivation, effectiveness, and cross-validation. *Journal of Consulting and Clinical Psychology*, 1981, *49*, 616–618.

Golden, C. J., Berg, R. A., & Graber, B. Test–retest reliability of the Luria-Nebraska

120   CHARLES J. GOLDEN

Neuropsychological Battery in stable, chronically impaired patients. *Journal of Consulting and Clinical Psychology*, 1982, *50*, 452–454.

Golden, C. J., Hammeke, T. A., Purisch, A. D., Berg, R. A., Moses, J. A., Jr., Newlin, D. B., Wilkening, G. N., & Puente, A. E. *Item interpretation of the Luria-Nebraska Neuropsychological Battery*. Lincoln: University of Nebraska Press, 1982.

Hammeke, T. A. *Validity of Luria's neuropsychological investigation in the diagnosis of cerebral dysfunction*. Unpublished doctoral dissertation, University of South Dakota, 1978.

Hammeke, T. A., Golden, C. J., & Purisch, A. D. A standardized, short, and comprehensive neuropsychological test battery based on the Luria neuropsychological evaluation. *International Journal of Neuroscience*, 1978, *8*, 135–141.

Lewis, G. P., Golden, C. J., Moses, J. A., Osmon, D. C., Purisch, A. D., & Hammeke, T. A. Localization of cerebral dysfunction by a standardized version of Luria's neuropsychological battery. *Journal of Consulting and Clinical Psychology*, 1979, *47*, 1003–1019.

Luria, A. R. *Restoration of function after brain injury*. New York: Macmillan, 1963.

Luria, A. R. *Traumatic aphasia*. Paris: Mouton, 1970.

Luria, A. R. *The working brain*. New York: Basic Books, 1973.

Luria, A. R. *Higher cortical functions in man*. New York: Basic Books, 1980.

McKay, S., & Golden, C. J. Empirical derivation of experimental scales for localizing brain lesions using the Luria-Nebraska Neuropsychological Battery. *Clinical Neuropsychology*, 1979, *1*, 19–23. (a)

McKay, S., & Golden, C. J. Empirical derivation of neuropsychological scales for the lateralization of brain damage using the Luria-Nebraska Neuropsychological Battery. *Clinical Neuropsychology*, 1979, *1*, 1–5. (b)

McKay, S., & Golden, C. J. The assessment of specific neuropsychological skills using scales derived from factor analysis of the Luria-Nebraska Neuropsychological Battery. *International Journal of Neuroscience*, 1981, *14*, 189–204.

Milner, B. Disorders of learning and memory after temporal lobe lesions in man. *Clinical Neurosurgery*, 1972, *19*, 421–446.

Moses, J. A., Jr., & Golden, C. J. Cross-validation of the discriminative effectiveness of the standardized Luria-Nebraska Neuropsychological Test Battery. *International Journal of Neuroscience*, 1979, *9*, 149–155.

Osmon, D. C., Golden, C. J., Purisch, A. D., Hammeke, T. A., & Blume, H. G. The use of a standardized battery of Luria's test in the diagnosis of cerebral dysfunction. *International Journal of Neuroscience*, 1979, *9*, 1–9.

Plaisted, J. R., & Golden, C. J. Test–Retest reliability of the clinical, factor, and localization scales of the Luria-Nebraska Neuropsychological Battery. *International Journal of Neuroscience*, 1982, *17*, 163–167.

Zelazowski, R., Golden, C. J., Graber, B., Blose, I. L., Bloch, S., Moses, J. A., Jr., Stahl, S. M., Osmon, D. C., & Pfefferbaum, A. The relationship of cerebral ventricular size to impairment on the Luria-Nebraska Neuropsychological Battery. *Journal of Studies on Alcohol*, 1981, *42*, 749–756.

4

Training the Brain-Injured Client in Behavioral Self-Management Skills

James Malec

Treatments based on clinical experience are often developed initially from theoretical assumptions exemplifying the state of the art in related scientific fields. In an area where clinical treatment of behavioral disorders following brain injury may occur without reference to the incompletely understood complex of relationships among behavioral/affective, neurological, and neuropsychological processes involved, a clear statement of assumptions on which behavioral treatments of the brain-injured are based is important. A behavior therapist, for instance, may recommend treatment for a brain-injured client based on the assumption that deviant behavior is learned and can be unlearned, but may fail to assess the effects of brain injury on the client's learning abilities. A psychiatrist may recommend psychopharmacotherapy indicated by the presence of psychoticlike symptoms while failing to appreciate the way in which brain injury may have altered the neurochemical substrate on which therapeutic chemicals are layered. A rehabilitation counselor may fail to recognize a brain-injured client's inability to perceive body schema and to function accurately and may thus incorrectly assume that, as for a spinal cord-injured person or an amputee, the brain-injured patient's emotional lability is in reaction to perceived loss of physical abilities.

James Malec • Psychiatric and Behavioral Medicine, Mount Sinai Medical Center, Milwaukee, Wisconsin 53233.

Procedures outlined in this chapter are based on the assumptions that (1) behavioral disturbances following brain injury represent inadequate personal and interpersonal self-regulatory skills that were present to varying degrees prior to injury; (2) if behavioral disturbance following brain injury represents a change from premorbid behavior, it is due in most cases to a change in cognitive functioning and learning abilities; (3) the normal stress response to severe or disabling injury depends on normal cognitive functioning and is affected by cognitive impairment; (4) disrupted self-management skills may be learned or relearned following brain injury if educational programming is designed to assist the brain-injured person to compensate for neuropsychological deficits. A corollary to this last assumption is that, if inappropriately reinforced, abnormal behavior associated with neuropsychological disabilities may become established through learning mechanisms and persist after neuropsychological abilities have recovered.

1. Behavioral Disturbance and Cognitive Dysfunction

Behavior therapists and theorists have focused considerable attention in recent years on the role played by cognitive events in behavioral disturbance in persons with presumably normal brains (Bandura, 1969, 1977; Ellis, 1973; Meichenbaum, 1977). Brain-injured persons provide an unfortunate demonstration of the manner in which a disruption of basic cognitive abilities can interfere with the complex personal and interpersonal behaviors necessary for social adjustment.

Behavioral disturbance originally presenting after brain injury appears is most often associated with impairment in one or more cognitive abilities. Lishman (1968) found only a small percentage (14%) of persons with emotional or behavioral disturbance following penetrating brain injury who did not also show identifiable cognitive impairment. Dikman and Reitan (1977) have demonstrated the close relationship between disturbed personality functioning and cognitive impairment following closed head injury. Particular types of cognitive disabilities may lead to particular behavioral problems.

Memory and concentration are abilities needed for effective self-management. In his recent review, Benton (1979) has characterized the "post-traumatic syndrome" following closed head injury as "a constellation of relatively vague complaints of impairment in concentration, disturbance in memory and emotional instability" (p. 220) often not accompanied by a specific dysphasia or other highly specific cognitive deficit. Compromised concentration and memory may have a significant impact on behavioral self-regulation.

"Impairment in concentration" acquires better definition through reference to problems in learning various stimulus discriminations. For instance, following brain trauma, a person may have difficulty attending to relevant stimuli while simultaneously ignoring the vast array of irrelevant stimuli in a given situation. Such lack of resistance to stimulus interference often results in inappropriate responses. These inappropriate responses can appear to family or staff as inexplicable or "crazy" when in fact they are correct responses to irrelevant internal or external stimulus events.

Conversely, a brain-injured person may have apparent difficulty releasing a particular stimulus from attention. The person may have difficulty shifting cognitive sets or shifting from one stimulus to another in temporal sequence. The person's behavior appears perserverative. An appropriate set of responses may be followed by a set of inappropriate responses as the person's behavior continues to be predicated on prior cues that are no longer relevant.

A particularly important type of discrimination is between correct and incorrect performances of sequential components of a behavior: the process of self-monitoring. In Luria's (1973) schema, self-generated feedback regarding the performance of motor responses is critical for ongoing motor performance and future motor planning. Poor self-monitoring probably plays a role in perseveration and interferes with self-correction of errors.

Luria (1973) has emphasized the importance of language as a primary cognitive mechanism for self-regulation. It follows from Luria's theory that compromised linguistic abilities would result in loss of some aspects of self-control in addition to the possible emergence of dysphasic symptoms. In support of this hypothesis, Levin and Grossman (1978) have noted the larger proportion of severely agitated patients among dysphasic patients by comparison with patients without dysphasia following head injury; Lishman (1968) has also reported a consistent relationship between degree of "psychiatric disability" and the presence of dysphasia. Language disturbances not typically classified as a dysphasia (i.e., certain content categories of confabulated speech) also appear predictive of later social maladjustment (Weinstein & Lyerly, 1968). In Luria's theories, language plays a central role in higher-order functions, such as prediction.

Bandura (1977) has called attention to the importance of prediction in normal behavior. Cognitive prediction of the outcome of behaviors performed under certain stimulus conditions (stimulus–response–outcome predictions) determines behavioral performance. Prediction of a positive outcome facilitates performance of a behavior. Bandura (1977) also describes the importance of self-efficacy predictions in behavioral performance. Self-efficacy predictions are assessments of one's own probable ability to perform the response necessary for a desirable response–outcome event to occur.

Other self-management abilities—such as self-reinforcement, rule development, and reasoning—appear closely tied to predictive abilities. Internalized self-reinforcement may result from covert predictions of delayed positive outcomes of immediate behaviors. When external reinforcers do not reliably follow a behavior, the behavior may be reinforced by the covert prediction of an eventual reward. Among the general population, many behaviors appear to be maintained by anticipation of relatively infrequent external reinforcers (e.g., the monthly paycheck). Self-reinforcement may also take the form of covert self-praise.

Language plays a role in the covert development of stimulus–response–outcome predictions, self-efficacy predictions, and self-reinforcement. However, these processes can conceivably occur nonverbally through covert imagery. Language may also be used to code critical and recurring stimulus–response–outcome events as verbal rules and to facilitate the storage of these rules in long-term memory. However, internalized prescriptions and prohibitions for behavior are not always coded verbally, nor are they always verbally accessible. Psychotherapists are familiar with clients whose verbal reports of personal rules and principles are either more circumspect or more permissive than the nonverbalized rules that their behavior reliably follows.

Although the degree to which verbal processes, nonverbal processes, or both are necessary and/or sufficient for prediction is uncertain, prediction does appear dependent on the more basic capacities to recall stimulus–response, response–outcome, and stimulus–outcome relationships and to recall one's own performance abilities as learned through self-monitoring. Memories of such basic discrimination learning are presumably integrated to develop predictions for the future.

When insufficient memories are available to make a prediction based on past experience, memories tied to similar stimulus conditions may be integrated through reasoning to form a prediction. Reasoning is an apparently complex process involving discrimination learning, memory, verbal mediation, and rule development as well as the creative process of modifying established internalized rules or combining internalized rules to develop symbolic models that accurately predict external events. At its best, the reasoning process appears to utilize both verbal and nonverbal processing.

Complex self-management skills involve prediction. Bandura proposes that adaptive behavior is premised on accurate, positive self-efficacy predictions, that is, self-efficacy predictions resulting in the expectation that one has the ability to perform a response that will produce a desired outcome. To continue along this line of reasoning, maladaptive or distressed behavior is premised on accurate negative self-efficacy predictions (accurate assessment of an inability to produce a reinforcement-producing response) or on inaccurate self-efficacy predictions, whether negative or positive.

Accurate negative self-efficacy predictions may lead to distress for brain-injured clients who recognize disabilities due to their injuries. However, it is probably unwise to assume that most disabled persons experience more than transient distress in reaction to sudden disabilities. Although there is little sound research available relevant to the brain injured population, a recent comprehensive review (Trieschmann, 1980) of research in spinal cord-injured persons' psychological reactions to sudden disability suggests that few spinal cord-injured persons experience clinical depression, display denial, or follow stages of adjustment following injury. In one of the few studies of brain-injured persons related to reaction to physical disability, Lishman (1968) reported no relationship between "physical disability" and "psychiatric disability."

Without elaboration, it is apparent that inaccurate negative or positive self-efficacy predictions are maladaptive. Both overestimation and underestimation of personal competencies obviously interfere with social adjustment and achievement. Furthermore, poor predictive ability interferes, in turn, with self-reinforcement, reasoning, and the development of behavioral rules.

Poor recall or learning of behavioral rules most often leads to agitated or inappropriate behavior among brain-injured clients but can eventually result in the client's withdrawal and isolation if inappropriate behaviors lead to severe or consistent punishment. If language dysfunction is present, nonverbally represented rules and predictions may be inaccessible to examination and modification through verbal channels. Following head injury, diminished self-reinforcement most often results in decreased animation, increased apathy, and a depressive complex of behaviors. Persons with a very limited capacity for self-reinforcement can become unusually dependent on external sources of reinforcement and experience significant frustration and hostility if external reinforcement is unreliable. Reasoning may be compromised by poor predictive ability or by impairment in any of the component cognitive processes on which reasoning is based. Reasoning may also be compromised by mild or minimal dysfunction in several component cognitive abilities.

Impaired reasoning has been implicated by cognitive–behavioral therapists (Ellis, 1973; Beck, Rush, Shaw, & Emery, 1979) in the development of affective disorders. In the case of clinical depression, Beck and his colleagues have defined a limited set of cognitive distortions (e.g., arbitrary inference, overgeneralization) believed to mediate the occurrence of affective features of depression. Similar cognitive distortions may occur as a result of impaired reasoning following head trauma.

Not all would agree that behavioral disturbance following brain injury is usually or typically attributable to cognitive disturbance. Some authors (e.g., Bond, 1976) argue that premorbid psychosocial disorders are more critical in the development of behavioral dysfunction following brain disorder than is the brain disorder itself, but they fail to assess neuropsychological functioning thoroughly. The Bond (1976) study, for instance, employed only measures of psychometric intelligence, which have been shown to be relatively insensitive to cognitive impairment associated with brain damage (Reitan & Davison, 1974). While commenting on the relative absence of intellectual impairment associated with the "frontal lobe syndrome" in his sample, Lishman (1968) reported a relationship between the presence of the frontal lobe syndrome and amount of brain tissue destroyed, depth of penetrating injury, and length of posttraumatic amnesia. Comprehensive neuropsychological testing would be expected to reveal more subtle, but potentially behaviorally significant, cognitive disabilities accompanying extensive frontal lobe damage (see Lezak, 1976, pp. 65–67).

Our position is that following brain trauma, behavioral disturbance is most often related to cognitive dysfunction. Principally, cognitive dysfunction disrupts behavior through disturbance of abilities to make accurate stimulus–response–outcome predictions and to develop and/or recall behavioral rules, to self-monitor and develop accurate self-efficacy predictions, to engage in appropriate self-reinforcement, and to reason and solve problems. Although cognitive dysfunction is a frequently overlooked source of behavioral disturbance following head injury, cognitive disabilities are, of course, not always the cause of behavioral dysfunction following head trauma. As mentioned previously, clients may experience transient but intense distress following accurate recognition of lasting disabilities. Another possible cause of behavioral disturbance is direct damage to midbrain structures, resulting in hyperemotionality or hypoemotionality independent of cognitive dysfunction. The improvement of cognitive skills and other coping skills, however, may assist the client with midbrain damage to learn to adapt to altered emotionality, just as the improvement of coping skills may assist disabled clients to learn to live rewarding lives despite disabilities.

Maladaptive behavior may also be the result of faulty learning without the presence of verified brain damage. Persons with presumably normal brains may fail to recognize important stimulus–response–outcome relationships and may inaccurately assess their ability to perform the required response. The phenomenon of learned helplessness (Abramson, Seligman, & Teasdale, 1978) and subsequent depression in non-brain-damaged persons is theoretically based on a failure to recognize personal behavior as a determining factor in producing positive events or avoiding negative ones.

Faulty learning leading to behavioral problems may precede or, unless learning ability is abolished, follow brain trauma. When learned maladaptive behavior precedes brain injury, the relationship between premorbid behavior and the effects of brain trauma on cognitive abilities appears to be necessarily an interactive one. Two brief case descriptions will serve as examples of the interplay between cognitive disabilities resulting from head trauma and premorbid behavior.

B. H., who will be discussed in more detail at the end of this chapter, had a premorbid history of ruminative, unproductive grief related to the death of her daughter. From report, she was premorbidly depressed and probably abused alcohol. Her depression appeared to be mediated by her conviction that her daughter's death made her own life meaningless and worthless. Following her head injury, B. H. continued to make this type of overgeneralization, but typically only when her attention was focused on her daughter's death by some external cue or prompt. In the absence of external prompting, her poor concentration and memory interfered with her ability to focus on her daughter's death. In the case of B. H., cognitive disabilities appeared to interrupt her tendency to engage in ruminative, unproductive grief, resulting in an overall improvement in her mood.

In contrast, M. H. (who will also be discussed in more detail at the conclusion of this chapter) was a woman who typically set relatively high expectations for herself prior to brain trauma. She apparently experienced no significant depression as a result of intermittent failure to meet the high standards she had set for herself. Following head trauma, she was left with severe physical disabilities, including ataxia in all extremities, but only very mild cognitive disabilities. Nonetheless, M. H. seemed unable to self-correct overgeneralizations in thinking. She tended to assume that a performance failure in some physical task indicated that she could "not do anything" and was quite "worthless." There was no evidence that M. H. was receiving consistent reinforcement at home for her self-denigration. In the case of M. H., the ability to use reason to put failure experiences in perspective appeared compromised following brain injury. Her increased tendency toward overgeneralized thinking was associated with the appearance of symptoms of clinical depression.

2. Functional Systems for Self-Management

Luria (1973) has suggested three principal functional units involved in self-regulation: a unit for arousal, a unit for memory, and a unit for prediction, programming, and monitoring. He links the third unit for programming and monitoring to linguistic mechanisms. Reference to these functional units can be useful in planning self-management training, since each makes a contribution to the performance of self-regulatory skills.

The interdependence of these three functional units must be emphasized. It is hard to imagine, for instance, how a training program for improved modulation of arousal could be developed that did not involve covert self-instruction mediated by the linguistic system, memory for these instructions, and mnemonic comparisons of present state of arousal with recall of desired state of arousal. Although a particular skill may depend primarily on a particular functional unit, all functional units contribute to the performance of most skills.

As Luria points out, a certain level of arousal is necessary for all cerebral functions, with an optimum level of arousal enhancing the performance of specific skills. Luria hypothesizes that the functional unit for arousal depends to a large extent on the integrity of midbrain structures, particularly the reticular activating system. He also suggests that level of arousal is modulated by an attentional process in which incoming sensations are matched to predictions from memory. When mismatches (unexpected stimuli) occur, arousal increases. Level of arousal and its relationship to attention appear particularly important in stimulus discrimination training, since a certain level of arousal is required to support the process of attention to relevant stimuli. Conversely, modification of a relevant stimulus may modulate arousal, as in the case where intensification or minor alteration of a stimulus is unexpected and, therefore, activating to a lethargic client.

Lethargy is not the only activation-related problem occurring among brain-injured persons. Chronic heightened arousal following brain injury can also produce undesirable consequences for the client. The hyperaroused person often seems to perceive all stimulus events as unexpected. Focusing on relevant stimuli may be difficult for such a person because irrelevant stimuli are not easily dismissed from attention and continue to be unexpected and distracting. In addition, memory dysfunction may play a role by interfering with recall of predictable stimulus events. An extremely stable, predictable training environment that does not change from day to day and week to week may facilitate attention to training stimuli in such cases.

Many of the behavioral training programs developed for our brain-injured clients are based on the premise that persons with severe cognitive disabilities can learn or relearn self-management skills if these skills are broken down into simple components. In addition to response components, behavioral self-management skills typically require a number of sequential stimulus discriminations. The sequence of stimulus discriminations begins with the discrimination of the initial cue for performance. This initial stimulus should signal two cognitions: (1) that a specific behavior will result in some positive outcome (response–outcome prediction) and (2) whether the behavior is to be executed under present conditions (stimulus–response contingency). With brain-injured clients, attention to the stimulus–response–outcome relationships must often be prompted verbally, consistently and repetitively. Prompting attention to current contingencies is particularly important following a shift from one task to another.

A stimulus–response–outcome prediction is appropriately followed by self-assessment of one's own probable ability to execute the response (self-efficacy prediction). With brain-injured clients, self-efficacy predictions may be facilitated by cuing only those responses that the client is expected to perform successfully some percentage of the time. Verbal prompting may again be necessary to help the client discriminate accurately whether he or she is potentially capable of the response.

Following the execution of a response, self-monitoring is prompted to help the client learn to discriminate correct from incorrect performances. Self-reinforcement is prompted following correct performances and is, in turn, reinforced externally. The brain-injured client must often be prompted to attend to an external reinforcer and to discriminate intended rewards from irrelevant stimuli.

Memory, the second major functional unit, also plays a critical role in discrimination learning and appears critical for most types of learning. Since memory retraining and facilitation are elaborated elsewhere in this book (see Chapter 5), memory processes will not be extensively discussed here.

The third major functional unit involves prediction, programming, and monitoring. In Luria's view, these functions are primarily linguistic. A moment of reflection on the preceding discussion of stimulus discrimination in training reveals that linguistic prediction, programming, and monitoring may occur throughout. Attention and arousal are facilitated through prompted verbal predictions of positive outcomes for response performance. Verbal coding of stimulus–response and re-sponse–outcome relationships may facilitate memory for these relation-ships. Self-monitoring, a critical function of the third functional unit, can be prompted by verbal modeling of correct and incorrect performances. Stimulus–response–outcome relationships may be linguistically coded as behavioral rules. Self-reinforcement may take the form of covertly verbalized praise or the verbally coded prediction of some future, posi-tive external event.

In response learning, verbal analysis of components of a complex behavior can be extremely helpful to both trainer and trainee by allow-ing complicated behaviors to be broken down into simple, learnable (and teachable) units. In integrating response components into a com-plex behavior, verbal analysis can facilitate forward sequencing or back-ward chaining. The verbal analysis can also be used, with slight modifi-cation, by clients to instruct themselves for correct performance, in the way Meichenbaum (1977) has shown to improve learning in hyperactive children. With prompted, then covert self-instruction, the response may be learned to a degree that its performance appears to occur automatical-ly without verbal mediation.

Language is also critical to the reasoning process. Dialogue, ques-tioning, and linguistic analysis may help correct errors in reasoning and lead to creative reanalysis of problems. Verbally mediated synthesis of existing rules or verbal models can result in new, more useful rules and models.

Although linguistic processing is unquestionably important in self-regulation, the importance of covert speech in self-regulation should not prevent the consideration of a nonverbal counterpart to verbal predic-tion, programming, and monitoring. Nearly all aspects of self-manage-ment can be observed to occur without apparent verbal mediation both in lower animals and in man. For instance, behavioral adherence to complex rules occurs in animals and in dysphasic humans, neither of whom is apparently able to state or comprehend the rule in linguistic form. Furthermore, verbal mediation does not seem to play a role in the performance of some complex tasks, such as playing a musical instru-ment or improvisational musical performance. To the contrary, some musicians can be observed to repeat a nonsensical verbal phrase during improvisational playing to help them keep rhythm and possibly to in-hibit interference from the slower, sequential verbal processing system. As mentioned previously, most clinical psychologists are familiar with clients whose behavior follows rules that are diametrically opposed to their verbal self-expectations. Although Freud's concept of the unconscious has the comfortable quality of theoretical elasticity, it has been stretched very thin to explain such clinical phenomena. Why not a nonverbal functional unit for predicting, programming, and monitoring on a par and at times competing with Luria's linguistic programming system?

The research in imitation learning (behavioral modeling) demonstrates the occurrence of response programming that is not necessarily dependent on verbal mediation. Behavioral modeling has been found effective in teaching complex responses, stimulus discriminations, behavioral rules, and appropriate self-efficacy predictions (Bandura, 1969, 1977). However, none of this research excludes the possibility that spontaneous, covert speech plays a significant role in learning through behavioral modeling. Testing the hypothesis of a nonverbal system for programming behavior may depend on investigation of behavioral modeling with aphasic patients who retain nonverbal abilities. Varney (1980) has presented preliminary evidence that dysphasic adults can imitate nonverbal behaviors and that some verbal abilities seem predicated on the ability to perform such imitations. Musical intonation therapy (Sparks & Holland, 1976) for improving oral–verbal communication provides another example of response facilitation through a nonverbal modality.

In discussing the three primary functional units, it becomes apparent that all three contribute to learning and that training cannot take place if one or another functional unit is completely nonfunctional. In the more typical case where one or more of these functional macrosystems are partially compromised, training may be directed toward facilitation of one system by another. Memory, for instance, may be facilitated by linguistic coding and verbally mediated response programming.

Within each macrosystem, various modalities can be used to support impaired modalities. Verbal memory may be facilitated through nonverbal imagery. The learning of verbal behavioral rules may be enhanced through nonverbal demonstration of stimulus–response–outcome contingencies. Internal perception of response cues may be prompted by additional external cues. Clients with difficulty predicting outcomes for their behavior may require frequent external reinforcement to learn. Previously overlearned, "automatic" behaviors may be reinstated through verbal or nonverbal cuing and modeling until extensive practice once again allows for the fading of systematic guidance. In short, verbal processes may substitute for or prompt nonverbal processes and vice versa. External cues and reinforcers may substitute for or prompt internal cues and reinforcers. Systematic guidance (external or covert) can substitute for or prompt "automatic" performance of behaviors.

Research in methods for facilitating functioning in one functional unit or modality through the workings of another functional unit or modality is limited. Possibilities for creative development of such methods are extensive. Research into new methods, however, should go hand in hand with research in the application to a brain-injured population of behavioral training methods demonstrated to be effective with normals. The following clinical case illustrations of training in behavioral self-management skills may stimulate more systematic research.

3. Training in Components of Self-Management

A simple model of the relationship between attention and arousal based on Luria's theories has been helpful in developing behavioral programs for brain-injured clients. This model specifies that, in the waking state, attention is diffuse as sensory functions scan the environment at a relatively low level of arousal. If an unexpected stimulus is scanned, arousal increases. The search of memory store for identification of the unexpected stimulus also increases. If, in this heightened state of arousal, the unexpected stimulus can be matched to a memory of the stimulus and of a previously adaptive response to the stimulus, arousal shifts to a level suitable to effect the adaptive response. Level of arousal is now determined by the planned response rather than by the stimulus. If no match for the unexpected stimulus can be found in memory, a general response (fight or flight) to unexpected stimuli is activated.

While this model is not the final word in a scientific understanding of attention and arousal, it has been of practical value in developing clinical treatments for brain-injured clients with poorly controlled arousal. For example, in the early stages of recovery from brain trauma, a person may display heightened arousal—even agitation and aggressiveness. Observation of the person gives the impression that nearly every sensation is unexpected. The proposed model suggests that the person's behavior is in response to a failure of sensations to find a match in memory. Withdrawal and intermittent agitated aggression may occur as generalized responses to a barrage of unexpected stimuli. The model further suggests that the introduction of stimuli that are more likely to find a match in memory than are unfamiliar hospital features should result in a reduction of arousal to more adaptive levels.

J. K. is a case in point. This 16-year-old youth was a fluent aphasic when first seen for rehabilitation approximately 1 month after sustaining a head trauma in a motor vehicle accident. He withdrew so quickly from stimulating therapy environments that rehabilitation training could not be conducted. His attention to a given task was estimated to be less than a minute. He was able to recognize members of his immediate family and appeared less agitated in their familiar company.

In order to provide J. K. with practice in sustained concentration, a search was begun for a task familiar enough to him to find a match in memory and produce an adaptive level of arousal. His parents suggested a hand-held, rather complicated electronic game ("Digital Derby"). J. K. had the motor proficiency to operate this game, but we doubted that his cognitive abilities would be adequate. His parents insisted that he had played the game countless times prior to his injury. Based on the premise that an extremely familiar stimulus array would match to memory and result in an adaptive level of arousal and attention, J. K. was given a try at the game.

On the first trial, he was able to play the game (on a par with staff members who were inexperienced with the game) for 10 minutes. This was in contrast to the time span of less than 1 minute in which we had observed him to participate in other tasks cued by unfamiliar stimuli in the hospital. While playing the game, he appeared at ease and engrossed. A program was initiated using the game to increase concentrated time on task to progressively longer periods of time.

In J. K.'s case, the process of comparison between stimulus events and memory was believed to occur, but his poor memory for unfamiliar stimuli caused a failure to find a match for unfamiliar stimuli in memory. For other brain-injured clients, an intermittent disruption of the matching process itself seems to occur. These persons are often inattentive. At times they fail to respond even to very unusual or threatening stimuli.

B. H., a 43-year-old woman was presented at the end of the first section of this chapter. She was admitted for rehabilitation 6 weeks after sustaining a head injury when hit by a motor vehicle. Her language abilities were intact and she had only mild motor impairment in all extremities.

Although B. H. was initially agitated following her rehabilitation admission, her agitation became increasingly intermittent and general inattention became the primary interfering factor in rehabilitation therapies. She failed to attend to many important stimuli. In particular, B. H. had difficulty monitoring her own verbal behavior, failing to recognize differences between her own sequential statements. For instance, in reporting a simple fact like her age, she would sometimes give the correct figure; at other times, she would give an alternate, incorrect figure. Even though these two contradictory statements might occur less than a minute apart, B. H. appeared unaware of the obvious mismatch between her sequential statements.

To give her practice in the process of matching events to memory, a verbal repetition task with audiotape feedback was devised. In this task, the trainer asks the client to read a short sentence into the tape recorder. Then, after a short (approximately 10-second) delay, the client is asked to repeat the sentence into the tape recorder from memory. Next both stimulus and response are replayed. The client is asked to compare the two, correcting any mismatches between the first stimulus statement and the subsequent response made from memory. As training proceeds, another step may be introduced. The client may be asked to make the comparison between the reading of the verbal stimulus and the response from memory prior to taped feedback.

By challenging B. H. in this way to recognize mismatches between expectations based on memory and more immediate events, her trainer expected to increase her level of adaptive arousal. Although the change in her observable arousal was not dramatic, B. H. did appear more able to attend to other training tasks following this exercise, which became a regular "warm-up" for social skill training.

This type of exercise can be made more challenging by increasing statement length, statement complexity, length of delays, and introducing interfering material between stimulus and response. Because both stimulus and response are tape-recorded, this task lends itself well to reinforcement of stimulus discriminations at each step in the learning process. This exercise can be interrupted at various points to reinforce the client's identification of the stimuli cuing the response, identification of the outcomes of the response, and prediction of his or her ability to perform the response. Verbal self-reinforcement can be prompted at each step. If the client appears to forget the original task demands while such general learning processes are being reinforced, the taped feedback provides a link back to the original task.

B. H.'s level of arousal was not consistently low. Although her level of adaptive arousal often appeared too low in many training situations, she continued to be highly activated, even agitated at times. In contrast, some brain-injured clients are consistently lethargic, fatigued, or chronically underaroused. This kind of client cannot be engaged in extended training sessions but may learn through a series of short, spaced trials reinforced by short rest periods.

M. J. was a 30-year-old head trauma victim with severe cognitive deficits who had been injured 6 months prior to this rehabilitation admission. Initially he was scheduled for a half hour of practice in basic

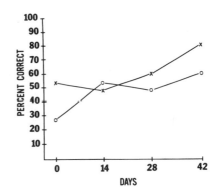

Figure 1. Performance of two clients (S. H. = ×; D. K. = ○) on 15 orientation board questions over a six-week training period.

orientation each day. During the first weeks of training, his performance continued to be inconsistent, with only mild improvement in recall of a small set of items (1, 2, 6, 7, 8, 9, 10) from the Galveston Orientation and Amnesia Test (Levin, O'Donnell, & Grossman, 1979). He frequently complained of fatigue during training, at times becoming mildly aggressive.

At this point, the trainer, who had been attempting to engage M. J.'s participation for the full half hour, changed tactics. The trainer began to follow each orientation question by prompting the correct response. As soon as M. J. imitated the correct response, this event was reinforced with praise and a 1- to 2-minute rest. Soon the prompt could be dropped for many orientation questions. Although this training process reduced the number of trials per session, it increased the number of trials resulting in correct responding and thereby facilitated learning.

Another method for spacing trials of orientation practice and for generalizing practice beyond the training environment involves use of an orientation board. The orientation board consists of a column of five orientation questions, a second column to mark correct responses, a third column to mark incorrect responses, and a fourth column with the correct answer to each question covered by a flap. The orientation board accompanies the client through the course of rehabilitation therapies each day. Therapists are asked to take 5 minutes to rehearse the questions with the client and are instructed whether to prompt the correct response. In this way, the client receives a number of spaced trials in basic orientation information in a variety of stimulus environments each day.

Figure 1 displays improvement in response to orientation questions for two male head trauma clients over a 6-week training period with the orientation board. Improvement was gradual for both clients. S. H. did

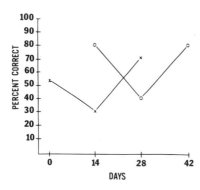

Figure 2. Comparison of S. H.'s performance on never-practiced (×) and practiced (○) orientation board questions.

not reach 100% correct performance until 13 weeks (91 days) after the orientation board program was begun. D. K., who was discharged 9 weeks (63 days) after beginning the orientation board program, had not reached 100% correct responding at that time.

To assess the degree to which improvement in orientation could be attributed to training rather than to spontaneous recovery, the orientation board programs for D. K. and S. H. were conducted in the following way. A set of 15 questions was randomly divided into three subsets of 5 questions each. Each client practiced each subset of 5 questions for two weeks using the orientation board. At the end of 6 weeks, each client had practiced all 15 questions. This method allowed for comparison of the percentage of correct responses to practiced questions with percentage of correct responses to questions not yet practiced. If spontaneous recovery were the only factor in improvement, an identical level of performance on practiced and unpracticed questions would be expected. Figures 2 and 3 show relative performances on practiced questions and on questions never practiced. The overall trend of superior performance on practiced questions supports the contention that training was a factor in improved orientation.

In addition to training procedures for use with clients with poorly modulated arousal, memory retraining may be helpful, particularly if the matching-to-memory process is compromised by poor memory. Memory retraining procedures are described in Chapter 5 of this book.

Luria's third functional unit plays a role in the matching-to-memory process through the generation of expectations based on memory. A client's capacity to predict, plan, and effect motor acts and to integrate information processed in multiple modalities can be capitalized on in training.

Of course, stimulus discrimination can also be facilitated by physical changes in the environment. Relevant stimuli may be intensified and

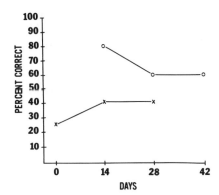

Figure 3. Comparison of D. K.'s performance on never practiced (×) and practiced (○) orientation board questions.

irrelevant stimuli deemphasized in any of a number of dimensions (size, hue, contrast, clarity, etc.). The most effective means of emphasizing or deemphasizing stimuli will vary with the client. A brighter stimulus, for instance, may be more salient to some clients but can be aversive to others.

Another method for emphasizing relevant stimulus dimensions is to involve the client in processing the stimulus through multiple or more complex modalities. If the task is to remember a short list of words, each stimulus might be emphasized by asking the client to listen to each word, look at a printed copy of the word, speak the word, and write the word or trace the letters of the printed copy. Going one step further, the client might be asked to visualize the object the word represents or use some other mnemonic technique to elaborate the stimulus. Multiple-modality processing may be particularly useful in assisting the client to make the initial discrimination that cues the beginning of the task (orientation to task).

The effectiveness of multiple-modality processing varies from client to client. For some clients, processing a stimulus in one way interferes with processing the stimulus in other ways. For example, F. W., a 38-year-old foreign language professor, was suffering from severe cognitive impairment following encephalitic brain damage. His native language was English, and he was asked to recall a list of 10 English words as part of his initial cognitive assessment. Testing with the method of selective reminding (Buschke, 1973) showed impaired verbal recall. F. W. remembered no more than 7 words (70%) in any one of five trials.

In an attempt to enhance his recall of the list, F. W. was asked to process the stimuli in a more elaborate way by repeating each word in English then giving its foreign language translation. Although he was able to translate 8 of the 10 words, translation from English did not facilitate recall. To the contrary, an interference effect was apparent. F. W.'s recall did not exceed 4 of 8 (50%) on trials with translation, despite his previous experience with the word list.

Training in divergent thinking is another approach for assisting clients to identify important stimuli. J. R. was a 57-year-old man recovering from anoxic encephalopathy following cardiac arrest. The behavior of concern to J. R. and his family was his frequently circumlocutive and tangential responses to simple questions. No other significant behavioral problems were present.

Two training tasks were defined: (1) practice in recall of basic personal and orientation information and (2) practice in alternative responses to circumlocution when he did not know the correct answer to a question. During initial training, J. R. was unable to develop alternative responses when his circumlocutions were interrupted. He seemed at a loss to find ways of arriving at an answer when direct recall failed. He did not utilize environmental stimuli to assist him in answering questions.

A modified form of brainstorming and the technique of guided search/rehearsal (each to be described later) were used to assist him in developing response alternatives to circumlocution and to use available information to develop answers to questions. In the course of training, J. R.'s circumlocutions decreased significantly. We believe the methods of guided search/rehearsal and brainstorming have assisted J. R. and other brain damaged clients with behavioral problems related to limited or stereotyped responding, but we have not undertaken a systematic investigation of this hypothesis.

Brainstorming is basically a three-step process. First, a person or group is asked to develop as many solutions or answers to the problem at hand as possible without regard to the quality of the suggestions. The idea of a quantity of ideas without regard to quality is stressed at this step. Participants are encouraged to speak up with even apparently "crazy" ideas on the premise that such ideas can often be transformed into innovative ideas and a few offbeat notions can serve to lubricate the creative wheels. Second, the list of possible solutions is reviewed and the ideas of highest quality are selected. Third, a decision is made to pursue one or two of the best solutions. A numerical ranking of the ideas selected for quality can facilitate this decision.

Brainstorming can be used with many brain-damaged clients to help them discover important stimuli and responses to which they would otherwise fail to attend. The method must be slightly modified in many cases. A brain-injured client may need frequent encouragement and reinforcement for contributing any idea to the brainstorming process. At times, potential solutions must be prompted. The trainer may offer personal suggestions as models. The client may need to be reoriented constantly to task demands of brainstorming.

An example of the initial part of brainstorming session with a brain-injured client follows. The problem is discovering the time of day.

TRAINER: There must be many ways to find out the time. How can you find out about what time it is?

CLIENT: (*No response*)

TRAINER: How can you find out what time it is? There must be loads of ways. Let's have a few wild ideas. How can you find out what time it is?

CLIENT: (*Smiles, no response*)

TRAINER: What are some ways to find out the time? Do you have a sundial?

CLIENT: A watch.

TRAINER: A watch! Good. You can look at a watch. What are some other ways to find out the time?

CLIENT: Your watch.

TRAINER: Very good. You could ask me to look at my watch. What else?

CLIENT: (*No response*)

TRAINER: I like my sundial idea. Is the sun out?

CLIENT: Outside.

TRAINER: Then is it day or night?

CLIENT: Day.

TRAINER: That narrows it down. Seeing if the sun is out helps zero in on the time.

CLIENT: (*Nodding*)

TRAINER: What part of the day?

CLIENT: I don't know.

TRAINER: How do you feel?

CLIENT: Tired.

TRAINER: Why?

CLIENT: I worked hard.

TRAINER: Where?

CLIENT: What's that called? . . . Walking therapy.

TRAINER: Walking therapy is PT. Are you done with PT for today?

CLIENT: Yes.

TRAINER: If you're done with PT, what time would it be?

CLIENT: Late afternoon, I suppose.

TRAINER: Looking at what you're doing can help you know the time, can't it?

CLIENT: Yes, on the schedule.

Throughout this process, the trainer notes down all possible solutions to be reviewed with the client for selection of three or four of the best. After such a list has been formulated, the list can be used with the client in guided search/rehearsal.

Guided search/rehearsal is simply a prompted search for relevant stimuli and rehearsal of appropriate responses. To continue with the example of orientation to time, the client is asked the time. Then he is immediately asked if he thinks he knows the answer. (He is consistently reinforced for accurately predicting whether he is able to give the correct answer or not.) If he says yes, he attempts the correct answer. If he replies no or gives a mistaken answer, he is guided through the procedures developed through brainstorming for discovering the approximate time.

TRAINER: Look at your watch.
CLIENT: It's not running.
TRAINER: Ask yourself: is it day or night?
CLIENT: (Looking outside) The sun's out. It's daytime.
TRAINER: Have you done much today?
CLIENT: A lot.
TRAINER: What does that tell you about the time?
CLIENT: It's the end of the day . . . end of the working day . . . end of the afternoon.
TRAINER: You tell me, about what time is the end of the afternoon?
CLIENT: Five o'clock.
TRAINER: "Five o'clock" is good. It's exactly four twenty-five. Knowing the time within an hour without looking at a clock is good.

Once a person has identified the appropriate response to an identified stimulus, he or she must continue to discriminate between correct and incorrect sequential components of the response. If this self-monitoring process is performed well, the person is able to self-correct for small errors made in the sequence of behavior. Accurate self-monitoring appears to be most critical during the learning of a response. With continued practice and improvement through self-correction, the response becomes stored in memory as an integrated whole that can be effected in a seemingly automatic fashion.

In the prior example of training in self-monitoring with B. H., three types of feedback were used: (1) verbal, descriptive feedback from the trainer; (2) prompted self-assessment of performance; and (3) audiotape replay. Videotape feedback is also useful with brain-injured clients, particularly in teaching social skills that have a significant nonverbal component.

As with other methods used with brain-injured clients, the type of response feedback must be selected on the basis of the client's cognitive abilities. Prompted self-assessment requires more verbal and mnemonic abilities than external feedback. Verbal feedback from the trainer can be delivered more immediately following a response than can audiotape or videotape feedback, which requires rewinding prior to replay. Taped feedback, however, provides the most accurate illustration of how the response was performed, and it can be accompanied by verbal feedback. The use of taped feedback is recommended if the client seems able for the most part to process all relevant aspects of the feedback presentation simultaneously and is not distracted by a single aspect to the exclusion of the rest.

If a client is not assisted by complex feedback, he or she may still be able to learn simple self-management skills through a highly structured system of reinforcement contingencies. Traditional operant behavior modification programs are most applicable to clients whose severe verbal, memory, and/or conceptual disabilities interfere with internal reinforcement processes (e.g., response-positive outcome predictions, covert self-praise). That behavior modification can be effective in teaching self-management skills to clients with very severe, generalized cognitive impairment has been demonstrated by Azrin's work (Azrin & Foxx, 1971; Azrin & Wesolowski, 1974) with severely mentally retarded persons.

Clients with severe cognitive impairment, however, typically require an extremely high degree of structure and consistency in the system of external contingencies. Reinforcers must often be tangible. A token or symbolic reward system is often incomprehensible to the severely brain-injured client, as are even the simplest charts and graphs used to monitor behavior. In many cases, reinforcement must occur without delay, and no acceptable response may go unrewarded without negatively affecting learning. The major drawback of behavior modification in an acute rehabilitation setting is the time demands placed on the psychologist in coordinating such a highly structured program among a large staff, who are often unfamiliar with behavior modification if not actually biased against its use.

The brain-injured client presents particular problems in the identification of reinforcers. The lethargic client may demonstrate no real preference for any type of stimulation or activity. Following brain injury, appetite may be so disturbed that not only are edibles nonreinforcing but getting the client to eat something becomes itself a problem for behavior modification. We have had best results in identifying effective social reinforcement contingencies for brain-injured clients. Even severe cognitive disturbance does not necessarily interfere with the reinforcement value of interpersonal attention.

Conversely, a cessation of social interaction (permitted withdrawal) may be a reinforcer for some brain-injured clients. Prior to the memory assessment of F. W. described previously, this client had to be helped to increase the time he spent working on any task. When F. W. arrived in the rehabilitation center, he would become agitated and aggressive if asked questions for more than approximately 3 minutes.

A program was designed to reinforce time on task. F. W. was asked no more than five simple orientation questions initially for a training period of 3 minutes. Immediately at the end of this time, he was thanked for his cooperation and left alone. He was allowed to close his eyes and withdraw, which appeared to be his preferred activity. The time of the question period was gradually increased and completion of the specified time period was always followed (and apparently reinforced) by permitted social withdrawal. In this way, the time during which F. W. was able to perform was extended to the 20 to 30 minutes necessary for his participation in the memory assessment and rehabilitation therapies.

For other clients, cessation of social interaction may be an effective punisher. We have described elsewhere (Timming, Cayner, Grady, Grafman, Haskin, Malec, & Thorsen, 1980) how an escalating system of staff withdrawal contingent on a client's tangential verbalizations was combined with a videotape-assisted social skill training program to help a head trauma patient reduce tangential remarks and improve his social interactions.

As clients recover from cognitive impairment associated with brain trauma and/or learn alternative skills for self-management, external reinforcers and punishers can become less frequent, more delayed, and more symbolic. In teaching self-control, the ultimate goal is to develop internalized self-reinforcement abilities to a degree where external reinforcers can occur at the relatively infrequent rate typical for the normal population. For this reason, internalized cognitive self-management processes are emphasized in our work with brain-injured clients to the degree that their cognitive abilities permit such internalized self-regulation. Complex self-management skills evolve from systematic training in cognitive and behavioral components of these skills. Two cases will serve to illustrate more extensive training procedures.

4. Training in Complex Self-Management Skills: Two Case Studies

B. H. was first mentioned at the end of the first section of this chapter. She was a head trauma victim with no specific language problem and only mild motor impairment in her extremities. When measured 5 months after her head injury, her full-scale Wechsler IQ was 76 (verbal, 85; performance, 67). Her case was also presented previously to illustrate training in self-monitoring.

B. H.'s difficulty in self-monitoring interfered, in turn, with her ability to converse. She often lost the thread of a conversation, becoming tangential in her replies. For her, one verbal cue seemed to lead to another in a purely sequential fashion. Her verbalizations were lengthy, with the final phrases seldom related to the initial theme.

A program was devised to teach B. H. better conversational skills. First, the behavior had to be broken down into component responses. Component responses for appropriate conversation were identified as (a) making a statement; (b) self-monitoring the statement as evidenced by the ability to repeat or paraphrase it; (c) pausing to wait for a response; and (d) if no response occurs, inviting a response by asking a question. Second, responses that interfered with conversation were identified. These were (a) repeating, (b) searching (circumlocution), (c) pausing before the end of a statement, and (d) changing the subject. Third, the client was taught to discriminate between these appropriate and inappropriate responses. Fourth, the client practiced the appropriate responses. Fifth, she learned to sequence the response components in performance of the complete behavior, "making conversation." Throughout, B. H. was reinforced for self-reinforcing after appropriate responding. Finally, she was encouraged to try out her conversational skills with self-reinforcement outside the therapy situation.

After appropriate and inappropriate responses had been identified, training in discrimination was begun, utilizing both behavioral modeling and verbal mediation. Appropriate responses (such as making a short statement) were modeled for the client, followed by her practice of the response. Because verbal self-monitoring was a particular problem for her, B. H. was involved in extensive practice in self-monitoring as described previously in this chapter. Verbal feedback from the trainer and demonstrational feedback (audiotape) were used throughout discrimination training and response rehearsal.

The naming of both appropriate and inappropriate responses aided B. H. in learning to discriminate between the two. This simple form of verbal mediation (naming) was particularly useful in helping B. H. to identify inappropriate responses in the course of conversation. The names of the inappropriate responses (i.e., repeating, searching, pausing, changing the subject) were written on index cards. When one of these responses occurred in the course of the client's conversation, the trainer would hold up the card with the name of the inappropriate response to cue her to self-correct.

B. H. practiced appropriate response components separately. After she was able to perform response components reasonably well, training in performing these responses in the correct sequence was initiated. The sequence was demonstrated by the trainer prior to its practice. Verbal feedback from the trainer and audiotape feedback followed the client's performance. In practicing response sequences, B. H. was always asked to return to the beginning of the sequence when she erred in the performance of a component in the sequence. The rationale for this procedure was to reinforce her concept of the behavior as an integrated whole to be performed as such.

Verbal rules, serving as symbolic models of the correct sequence of responses, were developed, for example: "A short statement is followed by a short pause." "If the other person makes no response, then ask a general question inviting a response, such as 'What do you think?'" As training progressed, verbal rules were further elaborated: "If the other person makes no response following a short statement, make a covert restatement of your spoken statement and ask a specific question based on the content of this statement."

With B. H., conversational skill training proceeded from discrimination learning and repetitive practice of component responses to the elaboration of increasingly complex behavioral rules. It was hoped that the development of internalized verbal rules for behavior would assist in generalization of the behavior beyond the training environment. Another method initiated to support generalization was reinforcing covert self-praise. After B. H. had performed a sequence of behavior satisfactorily, she was prompted to praise herself—first out loud, then covertly. After covert self-praise seemed to have occurred (judging from the client's facial expression), the trainer, hoping for the best and wondering what was *really* going on in the black box of B. H.'s head, praised her for having the good sense to praise herself for good behavior.

B. H.'s conversational skills improved over the course of training. As might be expected, this improvement was most obvious in the training environment and less obvious in the client's interactions with staff. Conversational skills did not improve to the degree that tangential utterances and apparent failures in self-monitoring were completely eliminated. Memory problems continued to interfere with other skills. At discharge, B. H. was not consistently able to recall the principle of self-reinforcement or the more complex behavioral rule for conversation (i.e., "If no one responds to your spoken statement, recall the statement covertly and ask a question based on the content of the statement"). At the present time, we are making arrangements to involve B. H. in an outpatient program for retraining memory, to be followed by additional social skill training.

The more complex self-regulatory functions of self-monitoring, adherence to covert behavioral rules, self-reinforcement, and predictions of self-efficacy on which socially adaptive behavior is based can be taught to brain-injured clients who do not have extremely severe cognitive deficits. The case of M. H. (who has been mentioned previously at the end of the first section to illustrate exacerbation of depressive thinking following brain trauma) can serve as an example of a training program to learn complex self-management skills.

M. H., a 35-year-old woman, was seen for additional comprehensive rehabilitation 26 months after sustaining brain damage in a motor vehicle accident. She was dysarthric but showed no specific language disturbance. She was ataxic in all four extremities. Cognitive disabilities were mild, with most in the average range. Her upper extremity movement disorder prevented administration of the performance section of the WAIS. Her verbal IQ, measured 26 months after injury, was 105.

The Pleasant-Event Schedule (PES; see Figure 4) is a clinical tool that was found to be extremely useful throughout M. H.'s training program. It is based on work at the University of Oregon (Lewinsohn, Biglan, & Zeiss, 1976) in increasing pleasant activities to counteract depression. This self-monitoring sheet has two sections, one or both of which is completed by the client on a daily basis. On the top half of the PES, the client records pleasant events occurring during the day and assigns a point value to each. On the bottom half, the client records unpleasant events that may have a long-term positive outcome. A point value is assigned to the event only if the predicted positive consequence outweighs the more immediate unpleasantness.

As described previously, the primary behavior of concern for M. H. was her tendency toward overgeneralized assessment of negative events. Her response to a small failure in some task rapidly became an indication to her that she was "worthless and unable to do anything." In addition, depressive behavior associated with such cognitions was having a deleterious effect on her marriage.

Therapy began by teaching the client to discriminate overgeneralizations and to recognize their fundamental illogic. She was taught the verbal rule that "Most—not all—generalizations are false." She was shown that reasoning from the specific to the general is a tricky business in which the truth of the general principle requires the support of each specific case. Fortunately, M. H. found such "philosophical" discussions interesting and rewarding, and her cognitive abilities allowed her active participation in and memory for these discussions.

Although most of M. H.'s cognitive abilities were unimpaired, a specific deficit in self-monitoring her own behavior was hypothesized as contributing to her tendency toward overgeneralized thinking. She

PLEASANT-EVENT SCHEDULE

Name _____ Today's date _____

List below each pleasant or rewarding event in which you are involved today. Score one point in the far right column for each event.

_____ _____
_____ _____
_____ _____
_____ _____
_____ _____
_____ _____
_____ _____

List below any unpleasant or neutral events in which you are involved today if these unpleasant or neutral events will probably result in some reward for you in the future. For example, a stressful job interview may be unpleasant at the moment but pay off with a better-paying job in the future. Score one point for each unpleasant or neutral event in which the unpleasantness in the present is outweighed by the potential reward in the future.

Unpleasant or neutral event	Potential reward	Points
_____	_____	_____
_____	_____	_____
_____	_____	_____
_____	_____	_____
_____	_____	_____
_____	_____	_____
	Total points	_____

Figure 4. The Pleasant-Event Schedule.

failed to recognize both her overgeneralized, negative self-assessments and many positive aspects of her own behavior. Following discrimination training to teach her to identify inaccurate, overgeneralized statements, a program was initiated to assist her in monitoring and limiting such statements. She carried an index card with a brief explanation of the kinds of statements she was monitoring for herself. She shared this card with each of her rehabilitation therapists and enlisted their help in calling overgeneralized statements to her attention. (Getting clients to enlist staff's help in their own behavioral programs may often be more effective in assuring staff compliance than the psychologist's recommendations and exhortations to staff.) This self-monitoring procedure, prompted and supported by staff throughout the day, resulted in a significant decrease in M. H.'s negative, overgeneralized statements.

The next step was to help her increase self-monitoring of positive events and behaviors with the PES. Although some events recorded on the PES are events over which people have no control ("It was a sunny day today"), others are intimately tied to their behavior ("I had a nice talk with another patient"). Each positive behavior that M. H. recorded served as an argument and exception to her general principle that she couldn't do anything worthwhile. By completing the PES daily, she began to recognize response–outcome contingencies resulting in positive outcomes. She also began to identify response–positive outcome contingencies in which she was capable of performing the required response. These examples of behaviors in her repertoire which reliably produced positive outcomes served as arguments for her self-efficacy in these particular tasks.

Our effort to increase M. H.'s task-specific self-efficacy predictions should not be confused with an effort to build her self-esteem. We felt that a direct attempt to increase the client's verbalizations of a general sense of self-esteem would invite failure. Suggesting to the client that she was indeed worthwhile in general because she could perform some tasks in a way that reliably produced valued outcomes was contradictory to our initial logic that the proof of general principles required a great deal of evidence with no unexplained exceptions. Accurate task-specific self-efficacy predictions did serve as arguments against her general principle that she was totally incompetent and worthless.

Her daily completion of the PES also provided an opportunity to introduce M. H. to the notion of self-reinforcement. Behaviors recorded on the top of the PES are by definition rewarding. M. H. was encouraged to recognize and verbalize positive feelings associated with these rewarding behaviors. Such affective value statements are believed to be self-reinforcing. Examination of her responses at the bottom half of the PES provided practice in another type of self-reinforcement: verbally mediated prediction of a future positive event.

Work along these lines with M. H. appeared to result in a reduction of overgeneralized negative self-statements. We also believe that, through increased self-monitoring of effective behavior, she was making more self-efficacy predictions, particularly in academic tasks, although the occurrence of such covert events cannot be easily demonstrated. The fact that M. H. attended an academic class without anxiety for the first time since her injury while in the hospital and enrolled in a class postdischarge suggests to us that her predictions of probable competency in academic situations had indeed increased.

Before M. H.'s discharge, behavioral methods were thoroughly explained to her husband. Limiting overgeneralized statements and monitoring behavioral competencies were emphasized. Because we suspect that behaviors that have been compromised by brain damage extinguish more easily following relearning, we feel it is important to provide for continued external reinforcement of relearned behavior postdischarge. Following her discharge, reports from M. H. and her husband have been positive. At last contact, her husband had enrolled in the same class as M. H. to allow them to spend some constructive and mutually rewarding time together.

This chapter began with a list of theoretical assumptions upon which described clinical treatments are based. A brief summary of clinical principles for treatment may provide an appropriate concluding statement.

Behavioral techniques can be used successfully with brain-injured clients if modified to accommodate the client's specific cognitive deficits. In order to individualize behavioral programs, a comprehensive, ongoing assessment of the client's cognitive abilities must accompany behavioral treatment. Neuropsychological tests, well validated for sensitivity to location and extent of brain tissue damage, are not well validated in predicting specific deficits in social behavior or self-management in a given social context. Neuropsychological testing should be supplemented with behavioral observation of the client, ideally within the social context to which the client is hoping to return.

Training with brain-injured clients should proceed systematically from discrimination training and teaching simple response components, through teaching response sequences and integrated behaviors, to reinforcing the cognitive representation of integrated behaviors and reinforcing accurate predictions of task-specific self-efficacy and of behavioral outcomes. The level at which the client enters this process is determined by his or her cognitive abilities. Some clients may be able to learn behaviors at the level of an integrated, sequential response. Too often, however, psychological or psychiatric treatment of the brain-injured client places expectations on the client that overestimate his or her cognitive abilities.

The importance of being systematic in our rehabilitation efforts so that we can teach each other how to provide better service to our brain-injured clients cannot be overemphasized. All the patience, compassion, and "body English" that goes into our work deserves translation into documented procedures through systematic clinical study and experimental replication.

ACKNOWLEDGMENTS

I am grateful to Charles Matthews, Ph.D., for his critical reading of the draft of this manuscript and to Kyle Stubbs, M.S., both for his review of the manuscript and his continuing assistance in developing behavioral programs for our brain-injured clients.

5. *References*

Abramson, L. Y., Seligman, M. E. P., & Teasdale, J. D. Learned helplessness in humans: Critique and reformulation. *Journal of Abnormal Psychology*, 1978, *87*, 49–74.

Azrin, N. H., & Foxx, R. M. A rapid method of toilet training the institutionalized retarded. *Journal of Applied Behavior Analysis*, 1971, *4*, 89–99.

Azrin, N. H., & Wesolowski, M. D. Theft reversal: An overcorrection procedure for eliminating stealing by retarded persons. *Journal of Applied Behavior Analysis*, 1974, *7*, 577–581.

Bandura, A. *Principles of behavior modification*. New York: Holt, 1969.

Bandura, A. Self-efficacy: Toward a unifying theory of behavioral change. *Psychological Review*, 1977, *84*, 191–215.

Beck, A. T., Rush, A. J., Shaw, B. G., & Emery, G. *Cognitive therapy of depression*. New York: Guilford Press, 1979.

Benton, A. L. Behavioral consequences of closed head injury. In Guy L. Odom (Ed.), *Central Nervous System Trauma Research Status Report 1979*. Washington, D.C.: National Institute of Neurological and Communicative Disorders and Stroke, 1979.

Bond, M. R. Assessment of the psychosocial outcome of severe head injury. *Acta Neurochirurgica*, 1976, *34*, 57–70.

Buschke, H. Selective reminding for analysis of memory and learning. *Journal of Verbal Learning and Verbal Behavior*, 1973, *12*, 543–550.

Dikman, S., & Reitan, R. M. Emotional sequelae of head injury. *Annals of Neurology*, 1977, *2*, 492–494.

Ellis, A. *Humanistic psychotherapy: The rational–emotive approach*. New York: Julian Press, 1973.

Lewinsohn, P. M., Biglan, A., & Zeiss, A. M. Behavioral treatment of depression. In P. O. Davidson (Ed.), *The behavioral management of anxiety, depression and pain*. New York: Brunner/Mazel, 1976.

Levin, H. S., & Grossman, R. E. Behavioral sequelae of closed head injury. *Archives of Neurology*, 1978, *35*, 720–727.

Levin, H. S., O'Donnell, V. M., & Grossman, R. G. The Galveston Orientation and Amnesia Test: A practical scale to assess cognition after head injury. *The Journal of Nervous and Mental Disease*, 1979, 675–684.

Lezak, M. D. *Neuropsychological assessment*. New York: Oxford University Press, 1976.

Lishman, W. A. Brain damage in relation to psychiatric disability after head injury. *British Journal of Psychiatry*, 1968, *114*, 373–410.

Luria, A. R. *The working brain*. New York: Basic Books, 1973.

Meichenbaum, D. *Cognitive–behavior modification*. New York: Plenum Press, 1977.

Reitan, R. M., & Davison, L. A. *Clinical neuropsychology: Current status and applications*. Washington, D.C.: Winston, 1974.

Sparks, R. W., & Holland, A. L. Melodic intonation therapy for aphasia. *Journal of Speech and Hearing Disorders*, 1976, *41*, 287–297.

Timming, R. C., Cayner, J. J., Grady, S., Grafman, J., Haskin, R., Malec, J., & Thornsen, C. Multidisciplinary rehabilitation in severe head trauma. *Wisconsin Medical Journal*, 1980, *79*, 49–52.

Trieschmann, R. B. *Spinal cord injuries: Psychological, social, and vocational adjustment.* New York: Pergamon Press, 1980.

Varney, N. *Assessment and classification of language comprehension deficits in aphasia.* Presented at Midwest Neuropsychology Group, May 1980.

Weinstein, E. A., & Lyerly, O. G. Language behavior during recovery from brain injury as predictive of later adjustment. *Transactions of the American Neurological Association,* 1968, *93,* 292–294.

5

Memory Assessment and Remediation in Brain-Injured Patients

FROM THEORY TO PRACTICE

JORDAN GRAFMAN

1. Introduction

This chapter will describe an approach to the assessment of memory deficits and the subsequent application of cognitive strategies/mnemonic techniques to the remediation of those deficits. We will be concerned primarily with the amnesic deficits encountered in brain-damaged patients. Amnesia can be defined loosely as the inability to retrieve information that was once comprehended and/or learned. As will be demonstrated below, there are numerous types of "amnesic deficits" depending upon injury locale and, in turn, the sensory modalities and cognitive processes represented by the involved neural system(s).

Memory impairment can be shown to be a significant factor in the functional outcome of brain-injured patients. Lewinsohn and Graf (1973) report that among disabled brain-injured patients seen at follow up by vocational rehabilitation services, approximately 40% listed memory problems as being one of several significant factors responsible for their disabled status. Bond (1975) has shown duration of posttraumatic

JORDAN GRAFMAN • Vietnam Head Injury Study, Department of Clinical Investigation, Walter Reed Army Medical Center, Washington, D.C. 20307.

amnesia to be significantly related to functional outcome (i.e., degree of independence). Levin, O'Donnell, and Grossman (1979) report that, using the Galveston Orientation Amnesia Test 2 weeks posttrauma, they were able to predict with significant accuracy the long-term outcome of severe closed head injury victims. Although no epidemiological surveys are available, it is clear that long-term memory deficits as a result of head injury, stroke, and other central nervous system disorders are a significant medical and social problem and can only increase in importance as medical advances continue to reduce the frequency of death from stroke, motor vehicle accidents, and various brain disorders (i.e., encephalitis, meningitis, etc.).

Given the significant incidence (Lewinsohn & Graf, 1973) of memory deficits among the brain-injured population, the need for careful assessment tools and remediation programs is obvious. Nevertheless, there are many obstacles to instituting such a program. For example, the time needed to administer a comprehensive retraining program is prohibitive to most practicing clinicians. In fact, as will be discussed below, to our knowledge there exists no active experimental memory retraining program for brain-injured patients besides our own. With such a documented need, this lack of attention may seem puzzling. However, until the past 15 years, psychologists have not been thoroughly integrated into hospital neurology/rehabilitation medicine departments, nor have hospitals referred patients with cognitive deficits to the psychologist's clinical practice. Part of this burden must be shared by the psychological community, which has not offered the physician a reasonable remediative alternative to traditional therapeutic methods. Another issue that must be considered is the lack of third-party reimbursement to psychologists for cognitive retraining. In the clinical setting, occupational therapists (who are usually not trained in the areas of memory theory and amnesia) have been the primary (and in some states the only) legal recipients of third-party payment for "memory/cognitive retraining."

This lack of extensive and authoritative investigation of memory retraining in brain-injured patients puts the interested investigator in a very unique position. That is, since memory retraining has not yet been demonstrated to be clinically efficacious and is not a required part of rehabilitation programs, it may be withheld (as in a control group) with reduced ethical repercussions. This is a valuable advantage for the interested researcher, since to date there have been only a few adequately controlled, published studies on the *long-term* effects of memory retraining (see the single case studies to be discussed below) and its efficacy has not been shown conclusively. Therefore, properly designed large-scale and case studies continue to be needed in order to determine whether memory retraining should advance from a topic of theoretical interest to a flowering discipline similar in scope to aphasia therapy. This is a particularly illustrative comparison since, despite more than 30 years of active practice, aphasia therapy has not produced a single convincing study proving its efficacy. That is not to say that studies such as the Veteran's Administration cooperative study (Wertz, Collins, Weiss, Brookshire, Friden, Kurtzke, & Pierce, 1979) and those by Sarno and Levita (1971), and Basso, Capitani, and Vignolo (1978) do not strongly suggest that aphasia therapy is useful, but 30 years of clinical practice now renders withholding of treatment as unethical. This forces researchers (as in the studies cited above) to use control groups that receive some form of therapy or are serendipitously excluded from the therapy process.

Thus, there is an opportunity for the application of appropriate designs in studying the effects of memory retraining. Not only would multibaseline single-case studies—as advocated by Hersen and Barlow (1976) be appropriate but also larger group studies utilizing as control conditions sham cognitive strategies or alternative therapies that could include the administration of pharmacological compounds (such as cholinergics, neuropeptides, vasodilators, etc.) thought to enhance the functioning of specific "memory systems" in the brain (Drachman, 1977; Peters & Levin, 1977; DeWied & Versteeg, 1979).

The primary purpose of this chapter will be to review pertinent literature, present a memory retraining program that has existed for several years, comment on the results of that program and point out its weaknesses, present a working theory to guide memory assessment, and suggest future guidelines for conducting research in this area. We will begin our review by presenting a brief sketch of contemporary human information processing and memory assessment of humans with brain damage, including anatomical–behavioral correlates, the varieties of amnesias, and a review of the most influential memory retraining studies to date. We shall then present the framework of the integrated neuropsychological/human information processing model of memory functioning that guides our research program. Given this theoretical model, I will then introduce our laboratory's neuromemory program, emphasizing assessment procedures, retraining and follow-up programs, and qualitative/quantitative results. The chapter concludes with a discussion of methodological requirements/constraints and suggestions for future research and clinical applications.

2. Human Information Processing and Memory

Much of the recent rationale for memory assessment of brain-injured patients is derived from the results of neuropsychological experiments that use specially devised tests such as those by Milner (1974) with temporal lobectomy patients, Butters and Cermak (1980) with Korsakoff-alcoholic patients, and Warrington (1975) with "amnesic-type" patients. Nevertheless, clinical assessment tools such as the Wechsler Memory Scale (Wechsler & Stone, 1945) remain in wide use, despite recent criticisms (summarized by Prigitano, 1978) as to its psychometric validity as a memory instrument and its applicability for brain-injured patients. In order for the clinician to decide whether a particular test is an appropriate instrument for assessment he or she should have at least a basic familiarity with human information processing models and theory. In fact, a perusal of the recent neuropsychological literature (in such journals as *Cortex, Neuropsychologia*, and *Brain and Language*) shows that many of the experimental paradigms used in memory studies are derived from the human information processing literature. We shall survey that literature briefly below. Those readers who are unfamiliar with the studies cited are encouraged to review them in greater detail.

Human information processing is a discipline that appears to be devoted to fractionating memory into distinctive processes. Perhaps the most familiar division is into sensory, short-, and long-term memory. As described by Atkinson and Shiffrin (1968), short-term memory is a limited processor characterized by phonemic storage (i.e., for linguistic processing) that is subject to rapid decay, lasting no longer than 120 to 180 seconds. Long-term memory is a far less limited processor characterized by semantic storage, with semantic information hypothetically available infinitely for recall/recognition. Sensory memory—partitioned by Neisser (1967) into echoic (auditory) and iconic (visual) stores—lasts approximately 250 milliseconds and is subject to interference by masking (i.e., by presenting a new stimulus within the 250-millisecond consolidation period). The relevance of sensory memory in memory-deficit analysis is not known, since there has been little research on this component in brain-injured patients (but see Oscar-Berman, 1980).

Support for the long-term–short-term distinction has come from experiments utilizing a free-recall word-list task (Glanzer & Cunitz, 1966). Group statistics typically yield a U-shaped recall curve. The far left side of the curve, generally represented by the first two or three list items, is called the *primary* sector and is considered to be representative of long-term memory, while the far right side of the curve, called the *recency* sector, is generally represented by the last four to five items and is considered to be representative of short-term memory. Perhaps the strongest support for the short-term–long-term distinction came from the work of Milner (1974) with H. M., a patient who had undergone a surgical procedure called bilateral temporal lobectomy (including removal of both hippocampi), which left him with "normal" short-term memory but severely impaired long-term memory. This patient will be discussed in further detail in the section on neuropsychological investigations.

A paradigm devised by Peterson and Peterson (1959) and coincidentally by Brown (1958) supported the notion of short-term memory and described its sensitivity to interference. This procedure consisted of presenting three words, consonants, or numbers to subjects and then immediately requiring them to perform a distracting task such as counting down from a three-digit number. After a variable amount of time (i.e., 6, 12, 18 seconds), recall of the stimuli was requested. As interference time increased, recall decreased up to about 3 minutes, when a floor effect was reached. It appeared that almost any verbal distracting task was sufficient to interfere with recall and that the significant variable was phonemic interference. As more time elapsed between original stimulus presentation and the onset of interference, later recall improved. Thus, a critical period appeared to be necessary for phonemic analysis and storage before long-term storage was possible. These findings, summarized by Atkinson and Shiffrin (1968), suggested that memory was a serial process requiring information to be held and analyzed in short-term memory before being encoded in long-term memory.

Recently, Baddeley and Hitch (1974) felt that a solution to some of the problems in conceptualizing short-term memory could best be offered within the context of a "working memory." Working memory was defined as containing both an active articulatory loop and an executive processor that allows for encoding and transfer of information between short-term and long-term store. The articulatory rehearsal mechanism is sensitive to phonemic interference, while the executive processor is probably most sensitive to semantic interference. This hypothesis is currently popular and has challenged the older models of short-term memory described above and in Deutsch and Deutsch's monograph (1975).

Another important distinction in memory processing was suggested by Tulving (1972), who proposed that long-term memory is composed of semantic storage or knowledge that is not "personal" but shared (such as language ability) and episodic storage or memory for autobiographical events. This distinction was only apparent in long-term memory, as both kinds of information are thought to pass undifferentiated through short-term (or working) store. This elaboration of the structural and processing properties of long-term memory stimulated Craik and Lockhart (1972) and Cermak (1972) to propose a model of memory that suggested it was the "kind of encoding operation" that the subject performed upon the stimulus that determined its later availability for retrieval. For example, a subject may choose to encode a word phonemically (via rehearsal or rhyming) or semantically (via imagery routines or by thinking about how an object functions). In general, words that are encoded semantically are more easily recalled. Tulving and Thomson (1973) have further refined this model by demonstrating that retrieval cues are most effective when they resemble the subject's method of encoding. This was called the theory of encoding specificity. Other researchers (Kintsch, 1977; Schank & Abelson, 1977) have explored the area of text processing and memory for text with results suggesting that recall of text information is dependent upon comprehension and memory for propositions (i.e., a basic linguistic meaning unit; for example, ". . . is handsome" or ". . . was touched carefully" predication about an entity) and the ability to form a schema (i.e., an archetypal plot; for example, the ability to describe how you typically dress in the morning) and to use those basic schemas to guide the process of reconstructing text as accurately as possible. The recent proliferation of "depth of processing" type theories in memory research has focused considerable interest upon the effect of encoding strategies on later retrieval of information (Tulving, 1979). Below we present an overview of the various encoding strategies that have been studied experimentally.

Perhaps the most influential and broad-based cognitive processing theory to emerge in recent years was presented by Shiffrin and Schneider (1977). They proposed that there are two basic kinds of cognitive processing. The first, entitled controlled processing, requires the subject to focus full attention to stimuli, performing various encoding operations, and later testing the subject for information accuracy and content via retrieval from long-term memory. Given a recurrent type of stimulus, this analytical process will continue until it is well learned, at which point it becomes automatized or performed with a minimum of attention. An example of this process occurs when a person moves to a new city and begins work in an environment some distance from his or her home. The first day out, attention is focused upon where the roads turn, street signs and names, facade appearances, and travel time. Over the months, as one becomes familiar with a route and schedule, the drive becomes more automatic and one may even process radio news or conversation in the car while the drive becomes a mere formality. This second kind of cognitive process, called automatic processing, allows for the expansion of processing capabilities. Shiffrin and Schneider's experiments are elegant and place the episodic-semantic distinction (Tulving, 1972) within an active processing framework; that is, episodic encoding depends upon controlled or attended processing.

What helps information to become better learned or better retrieved? One familiar style of processing is known as rote rehearsal (i.e., the various ways a person may repeat information to be remembered, with very little transformation of the basic code except for rate and/or frequency of rehearsal). Bjork (1978) has found an optimal logorhythmically spaced rote rehearsal process that he claims helped subjects recall names more successfully than other encoding strategies. Rote rehearsal or "phonemic looping" is the most obvious strategy used by amnesics and is viewed as being primitive and unsuccessful at increasing chances of recall (Cermak, 1979).

Pavio (1971) and Bower (1972) have examined the effects of imagery or so-called mental–visual representations upon recall in normal subjects. Both found that imaginal representations significantly improved recall on a variety of tasks and in comparison to a variety of other encoding strategies (i.e., rote rehearsal, etc.). A more detailed description of imaginal strategies will be discussed below.

Depth of encoding research has generally supported the claim that semantic and preferably associative encoding of stimuli creates the more opportune conditions for retrieval (Cermak & Craik, 1979). This type of mediation can take the form of synonyms, definitions, or associated words/phrases. Semantic mediation strategies have been shown to be generally superior to rote rehearsal under most retrieval conditions (Jacoby & Craik, 1979). The idea of associating words (Anderson & Bower, 1973) to provide a stronger "engram" or "trace" has received conceptual support from other models of information storage such as node–network theory (Anderson, 1976), frame theory (Minsky, 1975), schema theory (Schank & Abelson, 1977), and lexical/categorical organization theory (Rosch, 1975). Thus, both conceptually and empirically there is evidence that clearly shows the advantage of using semantic mediation strategies to improve storage and recall of information.

It appears that although defining stages, components, and dichotomous process models may help to conceptualize memory status, we must, to analyze a patient's impaired recall/recognition ability effectively, also observe and document the use of so-called cognitive strategies. As noted above, in some theoretical models such as depth of processing (Craik & Lockhart, 1972), the notion of type of encoding (i.e., phonemic or "shallow" vs. semantic or "deep") has played a crucial role in helping to formulate and test the theory. It will become apparent that differing interpretations of the amnesia deficit (e.g., due to impaired encoding), discussed in the next section, are due to the idiosyncratic theoretical model adopted.

It is also important to point out that there are several independent variables that stress the subject's response system and can be crucial in

teasing out more subtle deficits. These include rate of stimulus presentation, duration of stimulus presentation, duration of interstimulus/trial
interval, type of interference, stimulus ratings (i.e., for imagery, frequency of occurrence in the language, number of meanings, number of
syllables, etc.), divided attention, whether a cued recall or recognition
response is required, and number of stimuli administered per trial. For
example, the faster the rate of stimulus presentation and the shorter the
interstimulus duration, the more stimulus information will be lost. As
the cognitive processing system becomes stressed by time variables such
as rate and duration, it is more likely that subtle cognitive deficits will
appear. It is important to think carefully about such variables when
designing a test or experiment for discriminating power. Next we turn to
neuropsychological approaches to memory, including a brief discussion
of the neuroanatomy of memory.

3. Neuropsychological Aspects of Memory

There are several neural systems in the brain that are interdepen-
dent and contribute to the process of storing and retrieving environmental, somatic, and "subject generated" information. Since this chapter is
primarily concerned with cognitive structures and abilities, only a brief
description of these systems is offered. For a deeper and more detailed
description of neural systems involved in memory, the reader is referred
to *Amnesia* by Whitty and Zangwill, 1977.

The limbic system represents in evolutionary terms a primitive and
early developed system of structures that generally lie deep and central
in the brain adjacent to the third and lateral ventricles. Structures considered part of the limbic system proper include the hippocampus,
amygdala, fornix, cingulate gyrus, mammillary bodies, and septum
(Isaacson, 1974). The thalamus as the major sensory relay and control
system in the brain is interconnected with most of the structures previously mentioned. In addition, the hypothalamus receives from the
limbic system input that contributes to hormonal and peptide release.
The reticular formation is a highly organized midline collection of nuclei
that originates in the brain stem traversing upward to influence most
areas of the cortex and limbic system. The cortex itself has extensive
connections between different lobes and between different lobes and
subcortical structures. These systems and structures are all involved in
the encoding, storing, and retrieving of information (Luria, 1976). How

they differ in function will be illustrated in the following section describing various clinical subtypes of amnesia.

The earliest descriptions of an amnesic deficit resulted from observations of alcoholic and head-injured people. In this century, the most dramatic studies of amnesia occurred toward the end of and following World War II, when hundreds of British soldiers with head wounds were examined by Russell (1971). The resultant monograph describing their memory deficits is a classic example of how a clinical investigation can help direct future experimental investigations. Russell was able to document both anterograde (events experienced posttrauma) and retrograde (events experienced prior to trauma) amnesia. During recovery, anterograde amnesia was observed to decrease in severity, while retrograde amnesia often decreased in duration. Unfortunately, the varied types of cerebral pathology (i.e., coup, countercoup, white matter shearing, edema, hemorrhaging, frontal pole and temporal pole bruising, metabolic dysfunction, and oxygen deprivation) that can result from severe head injury usually precludes definitive clinical-pathological correlative studies.

The neuropathological study of the amnesias took a giant step forward with the neuropsychological examination of H. M., a product of a surgical procedure called bilateral temporal lobectomy (Scoville & Milner, 1957). This patient's retrograde amnesia was minimal, but his anterograde amnesia was dense and severe except in the case of "savings" on learning trials on specific motor tasks such as pursuit rotor, maze learning, and so on (Corkin, 1968). The critical brain structures thought to be responsible for this amnesia were the hippocampi, paired structures located in the medial aspect of each temporal lobe. This relationship has been confirmed in further studies (Jones-Gotman & Milner, 1977) with patients who have undergone unilateral temporal lobectomy, with differing-size excisions of the hippocampus correlated with differing levels of clinical memory loss (but see Horel, 1978, for a contrary view). Butters and Cermak (1980), following up on Talland's (1965) ground-breaking experiments, have investigated Korsakoff-alcoholic patients who have an amnesic disorder associated with medial–dorsal thalamus and mammillary body degeneration. These patients demonstrate a pronounced antegrograde amnesia and a moderate retrograde amnesia. Dementia patients of the Alzheimer's type (who have cortical and hippocampal degeneration) often display a mild anterograde amnesia as their first clinical sign (Miller, 1977). Thus, it appears that there has been a concentrated effort to describe and study the relationship between subcortical structural damage and behavioral deficits.

Recently, Shallice and Warrington (1977) summarized detailed evidence supporting the existence of an anterograde short-term memory span deficit in the absence of a long-term memory deficit. Several years earlier, Strub and Gardner (1974) had posited that this deficit was due to a phonemic processing impairment and not memory trace decay or abnormal sensitivity to interference. (See Strub and Gardner, 1974, for a discussion of these issues.) Interestingly, most of the memory deficits described above have involved neuropathology to the hippocampus, whereas the neuropathology associated with short-term memory deficit is generally cortical and particularly left temporal-parietal (Shallice & Warrington, 1977). Long-term memory loss with cortical deficits has been reported by Samuels, Butters, and Goodglass (1971), although the severity of the deficit is diminished when contrasted with those experienced by subcortical lesion patients; such loss is also more modality- and stimulus-dependent (Samuels, Butters, Goodglass, & Brody, 1971).

This brief review of memory syndromes resulting from neuropathology points out two main types of deficit: (1) retrograde amnesia impairment of memory for events that occurred prior to the onset of the central nervous system dysfunction and (2) anterograde amnesia. Within the latter category there is (a) impairment of long-term memory for events that occur subsequent to the onset of the central nervous system dysfunction and/or (b) impairment of short-term memory for events that occur subsequent to the onset of the central nervous system dysfunction. These two types of memory deficits can appear in a patient independently or interact with each other in a given central nervous system disorder. Semantic memory (i.e., skills such as vocabulary knowledge, schemas for situations, verbal reasoning, etc.) appears relatively intact in memory disorders but may be primarily impaired in aphasic disorders. This phenomenon will be discussed in some detail below.

There are at least three current theories to account for the amnesic deficit. They include encoding (Butters & Cermak, 1980), retrieval (Warrington, 1975), and consolidation (Milner, 1974) deficits. An encoding deficit implies that processing is "shallow" or predominantly phonemic and thus susceptible to interference from subsequent information and that in general these patients have difficulty in processing more than one attribute of a stimulus at a time. Butters and Cermak (1980) have suggested that, unlike normals, amnesics do not spontaneously use a semantic encoding strategy, since forced semantic encoding generally improves amnesics verbal recall. A retrieval deficit suggests, for example, that verbal information is encoded and stored but susceptible to interference due to the inability to *uniquely* code the information, so that a search of memory will not help in readily discriminating the event or stimulus to be remembered from other events or stimuli (which may result in errors of meaning or in the random selection of a response). Warrington and Weiskrantz (1973) have shown, in support of this theory, that giving patients cues has improved recall, sometimes to normal levels. The final theory, consolidation, suggests that information is irretrievable due to disorganized or degraded storage (but has not received much experimental support).

As mentioned above, purely phonemic processing of information generally does not lead to good long-term retrieval. This implies that modes of processing may exert a strong influence on the recallability of information. Imagery, verbal mediation, and general organization techniques have all been shown to affect memory processes in normals (Bower, 1972; Cermak, 1975). Pertinent to the introduction of our memory retraining program is the following review of studies that have attempted to apply mnenomic/processing strategies in order to improve retrieval of information in brain-impaired patients.

Patten (1972) worked with four patients with left hemisphere lesions and verbal memory deficits. Visual imagery techniques were used with these patients and, in each case, the patient demonstrated significantly improved scores on free-recall word-learning tasks. Three patients with midline lesions demonstrated an inability to learn the imagery strategy. Despite the lack of any experimental control, this study does represent the first attempt to remediate memory deficits in brain-injured patients. Jones (1974) taught left and right temporal lobectomy patients, two bilateral mesial temporal lobe patients, and controls to use various visual imagery instructions as an aid in the recall of verbal paired-associate stimuli. Results showed that patients with left temporal lobe lesions could partially compensate for their verbal memory deficits by using imagery, whereas amnesic patients (including H. M.; see Milner, 1968) derived no benefit from such a mnemonic. Patients with right temporal lobectomy surgery performed similarly to normal subjects. These findings provided a more appropriate methodological test of Patten's results and supported them.

Cermak (1975) attempted to extend the use of imagery mnemonics to improve retrieval in Korsakoff patients. Three learning methods were used: (1) rote learning, (2) imagery linking, (3) and cued learning (i.e., verbal mediation) to try to recall paired-associate items. Korsakoff patients performed significantly better using imagery and cued learning as opposed to rote rehearsal. Only on a recognition measure (as opposed to recall conditions) was imagery superior to cued learning. Cermak concluded that imagery could aid both storage and retrieval of verbal information for Korsakoff patients, while cued learning aids only the retrieval process (imagery being a more effective storage-process aid). Baddeley and Warrington (1973) found that their population of six amnesics were unable to benefit from imagery instructions but were able to retrieve words with taxonomic and phonemic cueing.

Lewinsohn, Danaher, and Kikel (1977), using a heterogenous brain-injury group, taught patients over three sessions an extensive six-stage program in the use of visual imagery. Training at each of the stages continued until a criterion was reached. A paired-associate learning task and a face–name task were administered. The brain-injured patients showed significant improvement on the paired-associate task but not the face–name task. Unfortunately, testing after 1 week showed no effect of imagery training. Glasgow, Zeiss, Barrera, and Lewinsohn (1977) and Lewinsohn *et al.* (1977) report on several case studies with heterogenous brain injury using a variety of mnemonic strategies (i.e., imagery, PQRST, verbal mediation, etc.) to enhance memory. Materials were standardized when possible. A step training procedure was instituted with pre- and posttraining testing. Both statistical and functional gains were made in every case. These studies represent the first attempt to remediate specific memory deficits systemically in a clinical laboratory. Lewinsohn (personal communication, 1979) reports that this program is unfortunately no longer in existence.

Shore (1979) examined the memory performances of 24 left-hemisphere-damaged patients, 24 right-hemisphere-damaged patients, and 24 neurologically normal hospitalized controls on multitrial free-recall lists in a transfer-of-training procedure after instruction on verbal and imagery mnemonics or a no-training condition. Mnemonic training dramatically improved recall performance in all groups. However, no transfer of training was evident on follow-up testing, the mnemonic strategy effect being limited to the period of training. Of note is that no particular strategy was advantageous for either group, suggesting the effectiveness of direct (i.e., trying to retrain a specific cognitive deficit) as well as compensating (i.e., training a subject to rely on nonimpaired cognitive processes) strategy training.

Gasparrini and Satz (1979) report significantly improved scores for immediate recall on a paired-associate task when imagery was used by patients who suffered left hemisphere cerebrovascular accident in comparison to verbal mediation or rote rehearsal. Nonsignificant trends suggested that learning the imagery technique enhanced recall for word lists, sentences, and paired-associates. Gianutsos and Gianutsos (1979) used a word-list retention paradigm with three left hemisphere CVA patients and one congenitally brain-damaged patient in order to assess the effects of a verbal mediation strategy upon recall. A multiple-baseline design was utilized to control for practice and recovery effects. In general, the mnemonic training program was effective in improving some aspect of task performance for all patients. Crovitz and Harvey (1979) presented a case study of a 39-year-old woman 4 years post-CVA with verbal memory deficits. In addition to her memory deficits, the patient appeared anxious and depressed. She specifically reported great difficulty in remembering things from one day to the next and in remembering intended actions. This caused her to become anxious and depressed. Visual imagery techniques, a verbal mediation technique, and relaxation training were instituted. Memory improvement occurred independent of anxiety and depression levels. Crovitz, Harvey, and Horn (1979) described the use of imagery techniques to help improve the memory of two closed head injury patients and one herpes simplex encephalitis patient. They found that slow presentation of stimuli coupled with patient-derived images were critical for success. Zarit (1979) and Poon, Walsh-Sweeney, and Fozard (1980) have discussed the use of mnemonic strategies with the aging. Their findings suggest that the use of strategies may prove effective in remediating memory deficits in such populations. A recent issue of *Experimental Aging Research* (1979) was devoted to describing a successful series of mnemonic intervention studies in the aged. As Poon (1980) carefully points out, the use of mnemonic strategies in the elderly requires an integration of human information processing theory and clinical behavioral techniques. This approach is certainly applicable to the brain-injured patient and will be discussed further below.

At this point, several general criticisms can be made of the retraining studies reported thus far. Most of the studies involved too few patients to permit generalizations, although findings even with small sample sizes may suggest several research approaches. In addition, independent test–retest data were not always available, strategies were not sufficiently described, a subject's memory complaints were often mild, functional goals were undefined, training periods were often quite brief, thorough assessment procedures to rule out other cognitive deficits often were absent, sham treatments were often missing, variables in success or failure were not determined (since few failures in retraining programs are reported), theoretical discussion was limited, independent variables were limited, and choice of stimuli was uncontrolled (i.e., for frequency, number of meanings, etc.). These criticisms are not meant to deny the significance of the studies reported. They represent a first attempt to address the issue of remediation of memory deficits in brain dysfunction patients and thus make up a significant literature. In fact, many of these same criticisms are valid for our own program, reported below. However, only by pointing out these shortcomings now can one hope that future research projects will correct for them.

The importance of memory retraining studies lies not only in the possibility that mnemonics may be of therapeutic benefit but also in their effect upon theoretical concepts of memory stages and processes. For example, if strategies such as visual imagery can help left hemisphere stroke patients overcome a documented deficit in episodic memory, we will better understand the processes necessary for the episode to be encoded, stored, and retrieved. Nevertheless, several important questions remain unanswered. For example, when statistical improvement is noted, what attributes (i.e., verbal vs. nonverbal, inferential vs. concrete, etc.) of episodic memory are stored? What is more effective, the use of retrieval cues vs. a criterion based mnemonic strategy program? Is primacy or recency improved more by strategy use? How do imagery or other mnemonic strategies affect social cognition? The search to answer these and other questions may benefit from the application of encoding and retrieval strategies in brain-injured patients.

4. Neuropsychological/Human Information Processing Integrative Model of Memory

Given the above notions of how people remember information and what brain dysfunction may do to this process, we have attempted to construct a simple model of memory along modality (vision and audition), stages, dimensions (depth of encoding), and processing (i.e., rehearsal) style differences. We are basically interested in assessing three stages of memory: immediate memory span, short-term memory, and long-term memory. We have divided long-term memory into autobiographical/episodic store and semantic/knowledge store. We find it convenient to think of people as encoding information under some individually variable optimal processing rate with directed attention to particular attributes of the stimulus. Encoding may proceed along dimensions from rote rehearsal to phonemic association (rhyming) to various forms of semantic/imagery coding. We suggest that information is independently stored in visual codes and/or linguistic–semantic codes, although production of a response can integrate all types of stored information (Baddeley & Hitch, 1974). Neuropsychological studies indicate that information is stored differentially in the brain, with higher-order complex information primarily stored cortically (Luria, 1976). To code information adequately for storage and long-term retrieval, limbic structures, particularly the hippocampal nuclei, are necessary. The left hemisphere is more involved with linguistic (i.e., particularly syntactic, parsing, and metaphorical operations) and the right hemisphere with spatial memory process and storage (Milner, 1974). The more posterior in the brain, the more the storage is visual/spatial in nature; anterior processes are more motor/inferential in nature (Luria, 1976). Relatively restricted cortical damage interferes primarily with organization and encoding of information (Schuell, 1974). Deep structure (i.e., limbic–hippocampal) damage interferes with storage and retrieval of information (Luria, 1976). Specific kinds of modality and information processing systems are dependent upon local cerebral regions (Samuels, Butters, Goodglass, & Brody, 1971). For example, damage to the right temporal lobe selectively impairs visual–spatial recognition and reproduction and nonlinguistic verbal (i.e., rhythm, pitch, etc.) recognition and reproduction (Luria, 1976). Our working model also suggests that localized, relatively restricted cortical lesions will primarily involve short-term memory mechanisms (i.e., rapid decay, temporal ordering, etc.), as opposed to localized, relatively restricted subcortical/limbic lesions, which generally compromise long-term episodic memory (i.e., recall of a particular event; Shallice & Warrington, 1977). Shallice and Warrington (1977) have argued that conduction aphasia (i.e., impaired repetition skills relative to comprehension and expressive abilities, resulting from a left temporal–parietal lesion) is actually an auditory–verbal short-term memory deficit that can be elicited by specific short-term memory probe and decay tasks. A counterargument by Strub and Gardner (1974) posits that the deficit stems from defective decoding of phonemes. This debate as to whether a short-term retrieval loop or a phonemic processor/decoder is represented in a local cortical region and selectively impaired with left temporal–parietal lesions is essentially an attempt to ascribe a specific unified description to a functional process. One way to resolve this issue might be to test linguistic vs. mnemonic strategies in patients who present with this deficit. Relative success with one approach would help support a unitary explanation.

This model of memory also implies that particular localized lesions may produce patients who present with memory deficits that coexist and/or interact with neurolinguistic deficits. Samuels and her associates (1979, 1971, 1972) have described such modality and material-specific deficits in cortically lesioned patients (both with and without aphasia). For example, it is not unusual to find aphasic patients who have semantic memory (and word-finding) deficits and long-term retrieval problems that cannot be explained by their neurolinguistic deficits (Warrington, 1975).

We stressed in the beginning of this chapter that there is a need for memory retraining programs. Historically, programs to treat memory problems are inadequately based theoretically and/or have not pro-

Table 1. Wisconsin Neuropsychology Test Battery[a]

 1. Wechsler Adult Intelligence Scale
 2. Peabody Picture Vocabulary Test
 3. Raven Progressive Matrices Test
 4. Wide Range Achievement Test
 5. Category Test
 6. Verbal Concept Attainment Test
 7. Trail Making Test
 8. Boston Speech Sound Discrimination Test
 9. Seashore Rhythm Discrimination Test
10. Knox Cube Test
11. Wechsler Memory Scale
12. Auditory–Verbal Learning Test
13. Aphasia Screening Test
14. Tactual Performance Test
15. Motor Proficiency Examination
    A. Finger Tapping Speed
    B. Dynamometer Grip Strength
    C. Pegs Fine-Motor Coordination
    D. Static Steadiness
    E. Kinetic Steadiness
16. Sensory Examination
    A. Modality Suppression and Extinction Testing
    B. Finger Recognition
    C. Fingertip Number Writing
    D. Tactile Form Discrimination
    E. Roughness Discrimination

[a]Test descriptions can be obtained by writing our laboratory.

duced published results. Based on a perceived rehabilitation need, we have used the theoretical model described above to initiate a pilot neuromemory clinical retraining program. This program and our qualitative/quantitative findings are presented below.

5. Wisconsin Neuromemory Program

The Wisconsin Neuromemory Retraining Program was established in early 1976 to meet a need that was documented by Lewinsohn and Graf (1973) and others (Barbizet, 1970) and was apparent in clinical practice. That is, memory deficits were a significant long-term factor in cognitive, vocational, educational, and interpersonal outcome. Our program was designed as a pilot study to assess the feasibility of treatment in a hospital setting, to assess the use of mnemonics in such a program, to evaluate the success of a program amelioriating memory deficits, and to determine the direction of future experimental and clinical endeavors in this area. Below we describe in detail the assessment procedures used, the retraining program itself, and the results from qualitative and quantitative analyses.

Our interest in conducting a memory retraining program was initially conveyed to physicians staffing rehabilitation medicine, neurology, and neurosurgery wards at the University of Wisconsin Hospital with the hope that patients who presented clinically with outstanding memory deficits (in light of adequate intellectual functioning) would be referred to us. Patients referred for our program were first administered a comprehensive neuropsychological test battery including measures of memory, attention, intelligence, problem solving, language, visual/spatial functioning, and motor and sensory skills (see Table 1). This would allow for assessing the relative contribution of other deficits to the memory impairment, some of which are presented in Table 2. For example, dysphasia may impair a patient's ability to express ideas verbally. This processing limitation would interfere with verbal rehearsal and cause impaired retention of material. This particular "memory deficit" would be treated differently (Schuell, 1974) than a "purer" memory problem. In addition to discriminating a "true" memory deficit from other contributing factors, the general neuropsychological examination will illustrate the patient's general problem-solving strategies, error types, presumed overall cerebral functioning, hemispheric lateralized skill functioning, and psychological status (i.e., depressed, etc.). A key determiner of patient inclusion in our program is a significant discrep-

Table 2. Types of Cognitive and Personality Disorders That May Contribute to Memory Loss

1. Depression
2. Psychotic thought disorder
3. Aphasia
   A. Broca's aphasia
   B. Wernicke's aphasia
   C. Conduction aphasia
   D. Nonspecific language impairment
4. Attention/arousal/vigilance deficits
5. Visual–spatial perceptual deficits
6. Hemispatial inattention
7. Sensory deficits (i.e., visual, auditory, tactile)

Table 3.   Wisconsin Neuromemory Test Battery[a]

 1. Selective Reminding Test
 2. Word Recognition
 3. Facial Recognition Test
 4. Recurring Figures Test
 5. 7–24 Test
 6. Visual–Sequential Coding Test
 7. Word Learning Test
 8. Sentence Recall Test
 9. Peterson and Peterson Tri-Word Recall Test
10. Paired-Associate Test (including related and unrelated pairs)
11. Story Recall Test
12. Word Fluency Test (including both letters and categories)
13. Token Test
14. Famous Events Test

[a]Test descriptions can be obtained by writing to our laboratory.

ancy between the patient's IQ (should be within normal limits) and
memory performance (at least mildly impaired on the Wechsler Memory
Scale). If the patient presented with an outstanding memory deficit and
agreed to participate in the experimental clinical memory retaining program, he or she then received an additional 3-hour test battery composed of various memory measures (see Table 3). Performance on these
tests served as a pretraining baseline, allowed for a "neuromemory
profile" detailing relative strengths and weaknesses in memory performance (i.e., relatively inferior performance on visual/linguistic long-
term memory measures), and illustrated rehearsal strategies and other
methods used by the patient to retain information. Once this analysis
was completed, the patient would enter the retraining phase of our
program.

5.1. Retraining Program

We decided that since most subjects entering in our program would
be head-injury patients with little likelihood of lateralized or restricted
lesions, there would be little advantage in using either a verbal or nonverbal strategy exclusively. In addition, our preprogram bias was that
the critical components in enhancing memory using mnemonic strategies was the organization, association, and elaboration of information
to be learned (Craik & Lockhart, 1972). The more strategies taught, the
more resources (flexibility of encoding) patients would have available to

incorporate into their day-to-day interaction. Therefore, we adopted the following strategies for our retraining program:

1. PQRSTP: an organizational strategy used with reading material.
2. Visual imagery: the utilization of mental imagery to facilitate recall of lists, actions, and chronological order of items.
3. Verbal mediation: the use of a story frame to link isolated bits of information (i.e., words) via associative (i.e., verbs, prepositions) but noncontent words.
4. Note taking: patients were required (i.e., reminded by all involved disciplines during the day and evening to take notes) to keep a "diary" to record schedules, assignments, and day-to-day events.

Another critical component in all strategies was the requirement that subjects transform/translate information into their own concepts, images, and words. They then were required to remember their self-generated "translation" of information (i.e., verbatim encoding of text or spoken words was not required). We suggest that this process of organization and transformation of material (with subsequent rehearsal of such information) is part of all mnemonic strategies and is the key to enhancing retrieval under most conditions. We next describe the four major mnemonic "strategies" used in our program in detail, including the step-by-step instruction of strategy phases.

5.2. Strategies

5.2.1. PQRSTP

This is a six-step strategy designed to organize text material. The letter "P" refers to *previewing* the text. Patients are told to skim the text, noting key headings, darkened print, orthographic emphasis (i.e., italicized phrases), and so on. They are not to return to material read earlier in the text. During this skimming phase (P), patients are taught to take the key headings, lead sentences in a paragraph, and so forth and transform them into leading *questions* (phase Q). For example, given the lead sentence "Tom was speeding into the night," several appropriate questions may be generated, such as "Where was Tom going?" "Why was Tom speeding?" or "What was Tom doing up so late?" Each question demands an answer that should be related to the essential content of the text. These questions should be written down when possible. Phase R involves *rereading* the material with the intent of writing down complete answers to the questions previously generated. During phase S, a *study* period, the text is removed and the patient is required to study *his or her* answers and questions. Phase T is the *test*. Here the patient's own questions (written earlier) are used to probe for text information presumably contained in their answers. The patient's answers should essentially form a summary of the text. The final phase (P) has the examiner *probing* for less pertinent factual or accessory information not contained in the patient's summary but inferable from its content. In capsule form, this is the PQRSTP strategy. It is necessary for the patient to have the linguistic/conceptual competence to form questions, to decide at what point in the text a question would be appropriate, to form complete and appropriate answers to his or her own questions, to devote the sustained attention necessary for study and rehearsal, and to recognize the relationship and story flow between their answers. As mentioned above, the key factor in this strategy is the step-by-step *visible* organization of information to be remembered. The materials that we use initially are standardized (for grade levels 1 through 8) stories from the Gates-McKillop reading test. Once the patient achieves a criterion recall at a specific level, he or she advances to more difficult material. When the highest level is attained (based on premorbid functioning), we introduced simple stories selected from the *Reader's Digest*. Patients may then progress to magazine articles (i.e., *Time* magazine, *Sports Illustrated*, etc.), and finally material pertinent to job or school. Patients in our program usually progressed rapidly through the standardized material (Gates-McKillop and *Reader's Digest*) and first encounter retention problems with the introduction of more difficult current events material and job- or school-related texts (see Lewinsohn, Glasgow, Barrera, Danaher, Alperson, McCarty, Sullivan, Zeiss, Nyland, & Rodrigues, 1977, for another description of the utility of this strategy).

5.2.2. Visual Imagery

We introduce patients to the concept of visual imagery by asking them to close their eyes and imagine a living object such as a cow (many of our patients live in rural Wisconsin). We probe the subject's image by asking him or her to describe its color, how big it is, its texture, the surrounding environment, the weather, and—if an animate object—how it moves. After some initial hesitation, patients are usually able to accomplish this task. It is important to stress that the patient make a mental image of the object and to note that responses to questioning are not offered too quickly (or with eyes open). That might suggest that the patient is merely offering a verbal definition instead of describing a "mental image." An important component of this initial exposure to the concept of visual imagery is the requirement that the patient report many details of the image, necessitating constant refocusing with relative continuity of the image framework and components. After several experiences with imaging animate objects, we introduce word lists. During this phase of the strategy, the subject is required to report the image of each word heard, but with no time-limit restrictions. The next phase requires the patient to form images of each word initially within 15 seconds, with the time allowed being gradually restricted to 3 seconds. During this stage of the training, patients receive the word list without imagery instructions in a selective reminding task for two initial trials. They are then instructed for the next two trials to use the individual images of each word to try and remember the word. In the next phase of the training, patients are taught to generate interactive images (see Figure 1) containing no more than two to three words (from the list). Examples are first provided by the therapist, then patients are encouraged to generate their own (obviously) unusual but not bizzare interactive images (Wood, 1967). Following criterion-based improvement, patients are taught the final strategy phase—the method of loci. The method of loci requires the patient first to reliably describe (several times over several days) a familiar route he or she has taken (i.e., from home to work) with at least four to five landmarks or a detailed description of his or her bedroom. The patient is then told to place the first interactive image (from a word list) in some relationship (e.g., resting on/hanging from) to the first landmark on the route or in the bedroom (i.e., the first piece of furniture to the left of the door and continuing around the room in a clockwise fashion). The stimuli used in all word lists come from the Pavio, Yuille, and Madigan (1968) imagery ratings and are segregated into word lists of different imagery values. After a patient achieves criterion recall during a particular phase of the imagery program on the highest imagery value list, a list more difficult to image is introduced. Since imagery appears to be most effective with lists (Pavio, 1971), all manner of material to be learned (from instructions to current events) is reduced to steps in a list, minimizing step length to as few words as possible. As the material used changes from standard rated lists to information needed to function adequately at home, school, or work, criterion levels change from approximately 75% recall to 90% recall.

5.2.3. Verbal Mediation

This strategy requires the patient to form a story from isolated words or noun phrases. The patient is told that it is preferable to use only verbs, prepositions, and similar function words to connect the

Figure 1. An illustration used as an example in teaching patients how to utilize imagery. They are taught to first image individual objects and later to combine several objects (no more than three) into one image. (Illustration by Tessa Lindsay.)

nouns. The examiner first has the patient form the story and repeat it back aloud, noting which words belong to the list. Gradually the patient is encouraged to subvocalize the story, repeating aloud only the word he or she believes to be on the list. As with the imagery strategy training, word lists are composed of nouns rated for imagery and of materials relevant to the patient's job, education, and domestic responsibilities.

5.2.4. Environmental Strategy

The last organizational strategy we use is environmental, requiring the patient to use a diary, to have a large appointment calendar on a

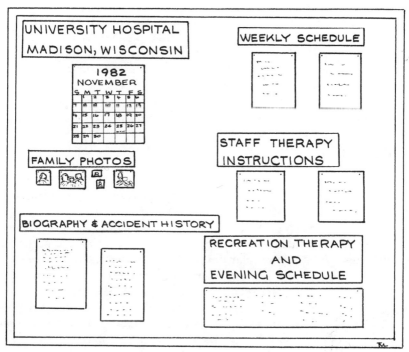

Figure 2. A drawing of the orientation board (1 × 1 meter; cork board with wood frame) that is placed in a brain-injured patient's room to facilitate cognitive/memory functioning. (Illustration by Tessa Lindsay.)

room wall, and to construct a poster board for room wall mounting containing pertinent biographical, instructional, and injury information (see Figure 2). This strategy, which uses external aid, supplements the endogenous strategies described above.

5.3. Schedules

Patients enrolled in our program are seen for at least three (but usually five) hour-long sessions per week. In addition, overnight and weekend homework assignments are given, with the patient using stimuli provided by the examiner and administered by hospital staff and/or family members schooled in the strategy techniques and applications. The program is designed to last 12 weeks. The environmental aids are constructed/assigned at the beginning of the program. The strategies are introduced serially in the order presented above. Each subsequent strategy is introduced when the patient demonstrates proficiency in the one currently used. Our program stresses the need to learn and use the strategies 24 hours a day, seven days a week. That is, the patient is quizzed constantly by staff, family, and therapists to recount the practiced strategies. The point of this intensive program is to force the strategies to become context-independent, unlike the episodes and facts the patient is exposed to during the hospital/institutional stay. Patients are told that they must immerse themselves in the learning of a second "language." Language usage, as opposed to learning a particular therapist's name, is of course generally context-free.

The importance of context-free (or independent) learning is that once the information is learned, it does not require a specific instance or stimulus to be instantiated. The only requirement is that the learned information be utilized automatically when necessary. For example, if an amnesic patient is taught a specific task (e.g., a route from his hospital room to the speech pathology department), that knowledge becomes tied to a specific context (e.g., a speech therapy session at a particular hospital, usually at a particular time). Since we have described the amnesic deficit as constituting a primary impairment of episodic storage, several problems associated with teaching a specific contextual task may become evident. For example, it is unlikely that such a context-dependent skill will be generalized. It is also likely that the skill may become disassociated from the context. Therefore, a patient may be unlikely to instantiate the skill, since there would be no association to time and place without some kind of external cuing (e.g., a reminder from a staff person that it is time to go to speech therapy). The importance of teaching a context-free strategy becomes obvious. If you teach a patient so that the key stimulus becomes information or a situation to be remembered as opposed to a specific route or event, the patient should utilize the strategy more often, in a generalized fashion. In a sense, we use language to communicate in a general fashion (e.g., only specific slang or lexicons such as computer terminology become context-dependent); thus, amnesics generally have normal language. It is hypothesized that memory-impaired patients can use mnemonic strategies to remember information in the same way they use language to communicate. By being urged to use encoding and retrieval mnemonics constantly, as in our program, selected memory-impaired patients should demonstrate improved encoding and retrieval skills.

Adequate staff/family training and education is considered essential for operationalizing and maintaining the use of mnemonic strategies. For example, the family is taught to be cautious regarding the patient's apparent improvement during a weekend pass. Since the strategies are detailed and laborious to carry out, family members may point to a patient's improvement at home to justify their hope that he can improve "on his own" without needing to learn the strategies. The family is told that the patient's sudden improvement is due to familiarity with the overlearned home environment and routines and to the basically intact ability to use learned scripts (Schank & Abelson, 1977) in unfamiliar surroundings. That is, a patient may respond to a question about lunch by reporting that she ate in the cafeteria, had a nice waitress, the food was good, the bill was reasonable, and so on. This reply amounts to a brief restaurant script (i.e., a series of statements that are typical of all lunches). Yet the patient would probably be unable to tell you when, where, or what she ate, since this is context-dependent information.

Professional hospital staff may also be "taken in" by the patient's appropriate interpersonal conversation and situational interactions. It is only when *new* and context-dependent information is introduced that the patient's impaired organizational and retrieval strategies become apparent. It is the failure of these patients to retrieve episodic (context-dependent) events that we hope to ameliorate by immersing them in a mnemonic strategy program. They should then be able to instantiate these strategies when encoding and retrieving information, and this will, one hopes, allow them to improve their functional status.

5.4. Subjects

A total of 48 patients have entered our memory retraining program (as described above) and completed it. All patients entered were judged to have an outstanding memory deficit. We have seen approximately 25 other patients in our role as consultants, making a total of 73 patients treated by the author in the 4 years since the initiation of our program. Data will be reported for those 48 patients who entered our program and completed it. Of the 48 patients entered, 29 had sustained a severe head injury, 10 suffered a cerebrovascular accident, 3 were referred with suspected dementia, 3 experienced an anoxic episode, 2 were referred following encephalitic episodes, and one suffered from partial complex epileptic episodes. There were 30 males and 18 females. The average age was 33.8 years. The average amount of education was 1 year of college (13.0), with most subjects (19) reporting graduation from high school only. The average entry point into our program was 31.6 months post-trauma. Twelve subjects were seen at least 4 years from the time of trauma. The average full-scale IQ (based on the Wechsler Adult Intelligence Scale) of subjects in our program was 89.2, with a verbal IQ score of 94.4 and a performance IQ score of 83.1. These scores can be contrasted with an entry Wechsler Memory Scale $\bar{X}$ Memory Quotient of 75.6. This Wechsler Memory Scale score is significantly inferior (t,

$P \leq .05$) to the estimated IQ levels. Eighteen patients in our program had a Wechsler Memory Scale memory quotient between 50 and 65, a severely impaired performance.

Success in our program was indicated by one of two criteria. The first was defined as functional. That is, patients had to demonstrate functional improvement at work, home, or school. This was assessed at the program's termination during a follow-up evaluation. Patients had either to document that they now earned a bigger paycheck, worked significantly more hours, had been given more responsibility at work, improved their grade point average at least one full grade in school, and/or increased their class load from part time to full time while maintaining the same grade point average, or taken on more of a work load at home (i.e., assuming more responsibility for house care such as cooking, cleaning, etc.). The second criterion required significant improvement (at least one standard deviation) on at least half the tests used in our memory battery.

These measures of success in our program are obviously not rigorous in light of available methodological designs. Nevertheless, due to the pilot nature of the program, we were unable to control such variables as patient personality characteristics, length of hospital stay, matching location and size of lesion, or time since central nervous system lesion onset. The author has spent over 2,500 hours with these patients, and it was felt that given the pilot nature of the study, the established criteria for success along with the experience of treating these patients allowed for sufficient data to explore the *possibility* that the use of mnemonic strategies could help amnesic patients better retain information and improve their functional status.

5.5. Qualitative Assessment

Clinical observations revealed that most patients in our program demonstrated improved test scores and/or reported improved memory for daily activities *only* after 1 to 2 weeks of the program. Initially, homework assignments were often forgotten or ignored. Patients often did not realize the severity of their deficits and refused to participate fully; occasionally they became temporarily depressed upon realizing the magnitude of their memory impairment or showed that they were unable to understand how they would benefit from the program. Therefore, *prolonged* intensive training appeared to be a necessity. Once a patient learned the various strategies, he or she often began to apply them spontaneously in daily activities even prior to the therapist's instructions. Unfortunately, patients who remained disoriented to time, place, personal experience, or current events were generally unable to learn the strategies despite good attendance and hospital staff/family participation. This will be commented on further below.

5.6. Quantitative Assessment

Of 48 patients in our program, 19 (or approximately 40%) demonstrated significant functional *and* quantitative (improvement on 50% of memory tests administered on follow-up evaluation) improvement following completion of the memory retraining program. This is the first reported evidence that a significant percentage of patients enrolled in a memory retraining program can show meaningful improvement in memory ability. There was no obvious trend toward success when specific "control" variables were considered (i.e., sex, posttrauma duration, education, or Weschler Memory Scale) with the possible exception of age and full-scale IQ. That is, 63% of the subjects with improved performance were younger than 40 and had a full-scale IQ score above 95 (X^2 = 12.5, $P<.006$). Thus at least in our uncontrolled sample, the younger and more "intelligent" (independent of premorbid education) subject was, the better the chance of improvement in memory functioning following a retraining program.

To our knowledge, no other pilot study has looked at such a large group of patients with such promising results. The importance of increasing a patient's functional skills need not be discussed; the advantage to the family and society is obvious. Nevertheless, we suggest cautiousness in generalizing from our largely uncontrolled study. More studies are needed (including studies utilizing large numbers of patients) to assess the cost-effectiveness of a memory retraining program. Below we present three case studies (two successes, one failure) to highlight our clinical approach. The two successful patients' programs were serendipitous ABAB designs, making their improvement particularly noteworthy.

5.7. Case Studies

5.7.1. Patient 1

M. S., a 25-year-old college-educated male, was evaluated in our laboratory in March 1978. He had suffered a severe head injury in an auto accident 3 months earlier. During his neuropsychological examination, the examining technician described the patient as very slow to respond and as needing continual repetition of instructions. Despite the patient's reasonably adequate performance on a short aphasia screening battery, his speech was described as slow and slightly slurred. He often seemed to use long words inappropriately and occasionally punctuated his responses to test questions with inappropriate sentences or expressions. Both his cooperation and effort throughout the testing were described as quite variable. Nevertheless, the patient was able to perform many of the neuropsychological tests typically given adult patients. On the Wechsler Adult Intelligence Scale, he obtained a verbal IQ of 90, a performance IQ of 67, and a full-scale IQ of 79. Despite his college education, he was found to be able to recognize words only at the eighth-grade level. He gave a clearly impaired performance on a variety of cognitive measures, including verbal concept formation, perception of speech sounds, and alphabetic-numeric sequencing. His performances on a visual sequencing task and a rhythm discrimination task were within normal limits, suggesting that his attention span was reasonably adequate on tests where no competitive or intervening responses were required. M. S. demonstrated a severely impaired performance on the Wechsler Memory Scale, a task sampling both verbal and nonverbal recall. The few items he was able to recall initially from two narrative stories were totally lost to recall after 1 hour. In summary, the patient's testing suggested recovery of some cognitive and adaptive functioning since the time of injury. His overall performance was described as severely impaired, with specific difficulties in short- and long-term recall, concept formation, and bilateral motor/sensory functions. Despite the patient's general confusion on some test items, he was able to complete the MMPI; the resultant profile was felt to be valid and a reasonable estimate of his personality status. Aside from some indication of rejection of commonly held social and family norms, the MMPI was felt to be within normal limits.

Rehabilitation medicine staff then requested that M. S. receive a more extensive memory evaluation. His cooperation on this evaluation also ranged from fair to good. He interrupted the testing numerous times to ask questions (i.e., "What time is it?" "where am I?" "Am I going back to the fraternity?" "How do I make up my classes?" etc.).

A test of language comprehension (the token test) was performed within normal limits. M. S.'s score of 24 on a word fluency test is moderately impaired when compared with an average score of 46 for a normal control group. The patient's immediate verbal memory span as reflected by a digit span scale score of 9 was only minimally below average. M. S. was also given a series of tests designed to assess memory for words, sentences, stories, and word associations. These tests were presented orally and visually and required recall or recognition of items. The patient's performance on these tests was moderately impaired, particularly when the required response followed a poststimulus distractor interval. Sentence recall was superior for visual vs. auditory presentation, but no distinct trends occurred when complexity of the stimuli was taken into account (i.e., words, sentences, stories). The patient was unable to recall any story material a half hour after presentation, despite being cued with the principle characters. Both related and unrelated paired-associate tests were performed at a moderately impaired level.

Tests of a visual–spatial nature were also administered. On the recurring figures test (a test that required the patient to recognize repeated nonsense and geometric designs), M. S. performed at a level that is consistent with moderate impairment. His score on the facial recognition test also reflected a moderately impaired performance. On a visual figure retention test, the patient's scores were borderline for immediate reconstruction and impaired for delayed reconstruction. On the 7-24 test (which required the patient to arrange plastic chips in an array identical to one previously shown), his performance was slightly impaired, but he did exhibit good learning skills and was able to create a match following only a few presentations. M. S. was able to copy a series of four symbols on the visual sequential coding test accurately (copying a series of crosses and squares arranged in a particular order with increasing complexity).

Two tests requiring recall for famous events were administered. M. S. was able to answer correctly only 30 out of 114 questions. This is far below the expected score for a person with his education, although no pattern of results could be discerned. During clinical questioning, the patient referred to himself as a student presently living in a fraternity on campus (i.e., a retrograde amnesia of 2 years). He did not recall his accident, his preaccident employment, or his reason for being in a hospital. These findings represent a substantial posttraumatic amnesia for episodic events and a general loss for extrapersonal events (i.e., orientation to time and place).

In summary, M. S.'s performance is indicative of impaired memory for new events, particularly when recall is preceded by an interfering task. He showed good learning skills where explicitly required on several tests. There was little evidence of perseveration, although his verbal production was limited at times. This dysfluency could have been a contributing factor in his poor recall scores. There was a substantial posttraumatic amnesia for personal events and a more general loss of information for famous events. It was felt that M. S. would be an appropriate candidate (i.e., in light of his average verbal IQ) for memory retraining.

M. S. was enrolled in the full program as described above. A key deficit that was influential in the outcome of M. S.'s training program was his ongoing disorientation to time and place. Following his 3-month program, M. S. was reevaluated on the neuromemory test battery with some trend toward improved visual–spatial recognition but generally an unimproved or worsened performance on tests of linguistic memory. Despite all efforts to teach him the various memory strategies and all attempts at cuing, M. S. was unable to use any of the suggested strategies spontaneously and was continually disoriented while in the hospital, unable to learn any staff members' names or any *new* skills in recreation therapy. A CT scan of this patient's brain showed bilaterally enlarged ventricles and sulci. He also presented with a left temporal–parietal slow-wave focus on EEG recording. It is suggested that M. S.'s chronic and multiple CNS problems, implicating both cortical and limbic sites, were responsible for his severe disorientation, lack of metamemory (i.e., see Flavell & Wellman, 1977), and inability to learn and retain new information (i.e., including the mnemonic strategies).

5.7.2. Patient 2

B. S., a 24-year-old woman, had suffered brain damage secondary to anoxia following an assault and strangulation. She was admitted to the University of Wisconsin Rehabilitation Medicine Service approximately 1 year posttrauma. The patient presented with quadriparesis, dysarthria, perceptual deficits, and mild dysphasia.

On formal neuropsychological testing, B. S. attained a Wechsler Adult Intelligence Scale verbal IQ estimate of 68 and a Wechsler Memory Scale memory quotient of 56. She was oriented to personal and current events but not time or place. The rehabilitation medicine staff requested that B. S. receive a more extensive memory evaluation. The patient exhibited good cooperation and effort during the examination, but testing was limited due to time contraints and the patient's inability to manipulate objects effectively.

The patient was given the first four parts of the token test, a test of receptive language ability. She made 15 errors on this test, which is in the moderately impaired range. Recall for words was mildly impaired both for visual and auditory presentation. Recall for sentences was in the borderline normal range for auditory presentation and moderately impaired for visual presentation in both immediate and delayed conditions. A paired-associate task was performed in the mildly impaired range. On a word-recognition task, the patient's performance was in the moderately impaired range. B. S. correctly identified 6 out of 8 originally presented stimuli but also endorsed 23 false-positives.

Several visual–spatial tests were also administered. On the 7-24 test (which calls for the correct reproduction of a spatial array of chips), over several trials, B. S. proved unable to remember a simple design after only a brief interval. A test of facial recognition was performed in the severely impaired range of scores, as was a recurring figures test. On the recurring figures test, B. S. adopted a "yes" response bias, which accounted for 64 false-positive answers.

During a clinical interview, the patient was oriented to time and place. She was animated in discussing her past with the examiner, who was familiar with the urban area that the patient had resided in. When asked if she had any memory problems, B. S. responded that she did not think so. She rated her memory as falling in the average range.

In summary, B. S. presented with several cognitive deficits. Of these, the most significant was of a visual–perceptual nature. This was evident on the facial recognition, 7-24, and recurring figures tests. A second cognitive deficit was a mild to moderate memory deficit. The more complex the stimuli, the more apparent this deficit became. This held true for both visually and verbally presented stimuli. However, when stimuli were presented visually, her perceptual deficits would aggravate the memory deficit. Her third cognitive deficit was a mild dysphasia, B. S. exhibited word-finding difficulties and occasional paraphasic utterances. Her poor token test performance was due to 13 errors on part IV of the token test. Commands for this section are more complex than for others, and can be said to present a challenge to memory as well as syntactic parsing mechanisms. We interpreted her performance on this test as reflecting both memory and language deficits.

Despite several interactive cognitive deficits, we were pleased to try a trial memory retraining program upon the request of the referring physician. Training focused on imagery and verbal mediation, although the PQRSTP method was also taught. It became necessary to focus on B. S.'s auditory–verbal memory due to her dyslexia, perceptual deficits, and spasticity. The patient initially was recalling only 40% to 50% of word lists, sentences, and paragraph material. B. S. showed an excellent grasp of verbal-mediation instructions and volunteered examples during training sessions. The patient was extremely cooperative and practiced frequently overnight with the assistance of hospital nursing staff. The patient was reevaluated 4 months following the initiation of our retraining program.

To best summarize the patient's improved performance on our tests, performances on two measures (hit rate vs. false-positive rate), two modes of presentation (visual and auditory), and two types of stimuli (linguistic and visual–spatial) will be described. B. S. correctly recalled or recognized more items (hits) than on baseline testing on 60% of our verbal memory tests. She also significantly reduced her false-positive response rate on these same tasks. We interpret the patient's improved performance on these tasks to increased storage capacity (facilitated by verbal coding strategies and logical organization of stimulus material) and a more reasonable decision criterion for items to be positively identified as belonging to a set of stimuli shown earlier. The patient dramatically improved her recall and recognition of *linguistic* stimuli presented *orally*. However, information presented visually continued to cause the patient difficulty in both basic decoding (dyslexia) and memory (particularly for nonverbal stimuli).

Following this evaluation, B. S. stopped utilizing the strategies because of "time constraints." When retested, no improvement over postprogram testing was seen. It was recommended that B. S. reinitiate strategy practice, and she was retested again after she had studied the various mnemonic strategies for several weeks. On this last testing, 6 months after her initial Wechsler Memory Scale evaluation, the patient demonstrated a 33-point increase over her first evaluation, giving her a memory quotient of 89 (plus additional significant gains on 30% of our memory battery when compared with her prior evaluation after she had "dropped the program"). The patient is now employed in a sheltered workshop, has passed her GED examination (a lifelong goal), and is about to attempt an independent living situation. She attributes these functional gains to her improved recall and retention of verbal information.

5.7.3. Patient 3

J. L., 20-year-old right-handed female, was referred from rehabilitation medicine 6 months after an anoxic encephalopathic episode due to propane gas intoxication. On a neuropsychological evaluation, the patient achieved a

Wechsler Adult Intelligence Scale IQ score of 80, a prorated performance IQ score of 39, and a prorated full-scale IQ score of 60. J. L. did not show evidence of being able to make any purposeful movements. She achieved a Wechsler Memory Scale memory quotient of 57. On that task, she was oriented to place but not to time. Her performance was mildly impaired on the digit span task, moderately impaired for recall of paragraph information and paired associates, and severely impaired for figure reproduction. In addition, J. L.'s performance was moderately impaired on the Rey auditory–verbal learning task.

The patient also received a detailed memory evaluation. She demonstrated good cooperation and effort during this testing. The patient was able to produce only 14 words on a word fluency test. This score falls into the severely impaired range of scores. As on the majority of the tasks administered, the patient's mistakes consisted primarily of semantic errors, perseverations, and paraphasic responses. On the facial recognition test, the patient's automatic (1, 2, 3, 4, 5, 6 consistently repeated) and perseverative responses would not allow the test to be completed. When I questioned the patient regarding these error responses, she answered, "They are so familiar to me, they just come out, can't be helped." The patient performed in the moderately impaired range with auditory presentation and in the severely impaired range on visual presentation. Her memory for sentences also fell into the moderately impaired range for auditory presentation and in the severely impaired range for visual presentation. A word-learning task was performed in the moderately impaired range. On a word-recognition task, the patient correctly identified 3 out of 8 words but also had 18 false-positives, indicating an extremely low criterion for identifying previously shown stimuli. The patient was moderately impaired on short-term paragraph recall but severely impaired on long-term paragraph recall. On a selective reminding recall test, the patient's total recall depended on short-term memory.

In summary, J. L. was moderately impaired on short-term recall tasks and severely impaired on long-term recall tasks. Visual presentation of stimuli to be retrieved was much more difficult for this patient than auditory presentation. Because of J. L.'s rapidly improving cognitive and physical status and at the request of her physician, she was enrolled in our memory retraining program. J. L. responded to the retraining program with enthusiasm and, by the time the program was completed, her performance on over 50% of the tests in the memory battery had significantly improved, with most of the test performances now falling in the normal range of scores. Her Wechsler Memory Scale score had increased to 93, a significant jump in performance. On this test, her ability to recall paired associates was now within normal limits, while paragraph recall and figural reproduction were only mildly impaired. A word-learning task was now performed in the borderline impaired range.

Following her participating in our program and in conjunction with her return home, J. L. reportedly abandoned the use of mnemonic strategies and returned to finish her second year of college. After several weeks of attending classes, J. L. contacted our laboratory complaining that she was not able to retain the information she was being taught in classes. We asked her to return for more memory testing. On that evaluation, J. L.'s scores on many of our tests had dropped significantly, although not to her pretraining program levels. We strongly suggested that she begin the retaining program again at home with the addition of her family's participation. She agreed and returned 8 weeks later to our laboratory for another memory evaluation. At this time, J. L.'s performance was back to postprogram levels; in addition, she now reported that her grade average on tests for several classes had improved from a C average to an A–B average. She attributed these gains to her memory remediation program and environmental suggestions (i.e., homework time, organization, and location) made by neuropsychological staff. This serendipitous ABAB design emphasizes the practical necessity for some patients to continue to use these strategies after they leave the program and provides an example of how effective they can be for someone who is enrolled in an academic program.

6. Conclusions

This chapter has presented an overview of the "infant" research discipline of memory retraining from one laboratory's point of view. Research in our laboratory and others is encouraging in that at least some brain-injured patients demonstrate statistical and/or functional gains following a variable period of memory retraining. These gains have been seen with single-case-study designs, in patients of different posttraumatic durations, in patients of different etiologies, and with patients of differing cognitive status. In addition, both individually and in combination, mnemonic strategies seem to have some positive effects that are not apparent when a patient uses only simple rote rehearsal strategies.

Despite this cautious optimism, several caveats are in order. Most research reports have presented only their successes, not their failures. In order to understand why strategies succeed, we need to analyze why they fail in certain patients. A hasty dismissal of a patient based on failure in three or four study sessions is premature. As Meudell and Mayes (1980) have recently shown, even Korsakoff patients, given enough time to learn, can increase their learning and retention scores to near normal levels.

While the case-study approach is extremely useful in providing acceptable controls by which to judge changes in memory status following a retraining program, it cannot offer a rationale for the appearance of a discipline. This can only be accomplished by additional epidemiological and large-scale studies. Epidemiological studies are needed to document the incidence of memory deficit in central nervous system disorders and its long-term effects regarding vocational/educational placement barriers and interpersonal behavioral restrictions. Large-scale studies are necessary to compile the kind of data that can help tease apart the critical patient, disease, and mnemonic characteristics allowing some patients to improve and others not. Both the epidemiological and large-scale study approach will require agency/foundation funding to support the staff necessary to carry out such programs.

The large-scale study approach should include the following methodological controls:

1. Clearly defined lesion groups.
2. Age, sex, and education covaried, matched, or contrasted.
3. Only patients who have a documented, defined memory deficit should be included.
4. Documented neuropsychological status (exclusive of memory deficit) should be necessary prior to admittance to a memory retraining program.
5. Mnemonic strategies must be carefully defined.
6. Baseline data must be gathered.
7. The retraining program features and duration must be defined.
8. The patient's posttrauma duration period must be defined.
9. Appropriate statistical analyses such as multiple regression should be used to discover the most important predictor variables in recovery of memory mechanisms.
10. Functional and experimental criteria for success (besides statistical significance) must be established.

These controls form the bare minimal constraints to be met in large-scale studies such as recommended above. Case studies should continue to use the kind of case designs advocated by Hersen and Barlow (1976) and Gianutsos and Gianutsos (1979).

Language therapy with adult aphasics is currently undergoing a self-critical period, with problems inherent in a discipline that grew up too quickly, skipping the methodological steps necessary to ascertain its own usefulness scientifically. That is not to deny its potential and actual contribution to language remediation, only to note the problems that accompany the growth of a discipline without scientific (controlled experimentation) constraint and to contrast it with the opportunity we now have to ensure the controlled growth of a "possible discipline" (i.e., memory retraining).

We have not discussed orientation procedures in disoriented patients, although we have collaborated with James Malec (see his chapter in this book) in developing such a program. Much work remains to be done in this area. We have also not discussed the necessity of including a behavioral reinforcement program (again, see J. Malec's chapter) with some patients, although a published case study is available (Timming, Cayner, Grady, Grafman, Haskin, Malec, & Thornsen, 1980) that utilized this approach successfully. Finally, another area not discussed fully is the patient's ability to "realize" that he or she cannot remember, so-called "metamemory" (Flavell & Wellman, 1977). It may be essential for patients to have an adequately functioning metamemory in order to succeed in a memory retraining program such as ours. Clinical observations have revealed that patients who are not aware of their documented memory deficits have a tendency to participate less in the program than patients who are aware of their memory problems. Less participation in our program frequently results in less success. In summary:

1. There is an apparent need for some kind of memory retraining program for patients with specific kinds of brain pathology or dysfunction.
2. In order to conceptualize memory problems adequately as well as to construct assessment tools and plan remediation programs, a familiarity with memory and information processing theory is necessary.
3. Neuropsychological analysis of memory deficits points out the "fractional" nature of processing and storage of information.
4. An *integrated* neuropsychological/human information processing model was proposed.
5. Memory retraining programs should include both case studies and large-scale evaluation efforts.
6. Data should be analyzed for both quantitative and functional gains.
7. Success in treating memory impairment was noted in a significant number of patients over several studies.

This chapter should have stimulated more questions than answers. Memory remediation is an emerging area of clinical research and application; it will be necessary to attract more professionals and research funding to it if it is to expand and prosper. In conjunction with pharmacological attempts to improve memory and education of family and health professionals, cognitive–memory retraining attempts to alleviate one of the most serious consequences of central nervous system lesions—loss of memory.

Acknowledgment

I would like to thank Mrs. Teri Dolecki for her persistence in typing the manuscript.

7. References

Anderson, J. R. *Language, memory and thought*. Hillsdale, N.J.: Erlbaum, 1976.

Anderson, J. R., & Bower, G. H. *Human associative memory*. Washington, D.C.: Winston, 1973.

Atkinson, R., & Shiffrin, R. Human memory: A proposed system and its control processes. In K. Spence & J. Spence (Eds.), *Advances in the psychology of learning and motivation research and theory* (Vol. 2). New York: Academic Press, 1968.

Baddeley, A. D., & Hitch, G. Working memory. In G. H. Bower (Ed.), *The psychology of learning and motivation* (Vol. 8). New York: Academic Press, 1974.

Baddeley, A. D., & Warrington, E. K. Memory coding and amnesia. *Neuropsychologia*, 1973, *11*, 159–165.

Barbizet, J. *Human memory and its pathology*. San Francisco: Freeman, 1970.

Basso, A., Capitani, E., & Vignolo, L. A. Influence of rehabilitation language skills in aphasic patients. *Archives of Neurology*, 1979, *36*, 190–196.

Bjork, R. A. The updating of human memory. In Bower, G. H. (Ed.), *The psychology of learning and motivation* (Vol. 12). New York: Academic Press, 1978.

Bond, M. R. Assessment of psychosocial outcome after severe head injury. In CIBA Foundation Symposium 34 (new series), *Outcome of severe damage to the central nervous system*. New York: American Elsevier, 1975.

Bower, G. H. A selective review of organizational factors in memory. In E. Tulving & W. Donaldson (Eds.), *Organization of memory*. New York: Academic Press, 1972.

Brown, J. A. Some tests of the decay theory of immediate memory. *Quarterly Journal of Experimental Psychology*, 1958, *10*, 12–21.

Butters, N., & Cermak, L. S. *Alcoholic Korsakoff's syndrome: An information-processing approach to amnesia*. New York: Academic Press, 1980.

Butters, N., Samuels, I., Goodglass, H., & Brody, B. Short-term visual and auditory memory disorders after parietal and frontal lobe damage. *Cortex*, 1970, *6*, 440–459.

Cermak, L. S. *Human memory: Research and theory*. New York: Ronald Press, 1972.

Cermak, L. S. Imagery as an aid to retrieval for Korsakoff patients. *Cortex*, 1975, *11*, 163–169.

Cermak, L. S. Amnesia patient's level of processing. In L. S. Cermak & F. I. M. Craik (Eds.), *Levels of processing in human memory*. Hillsdale, N.J.: Erlbaum, 1979.

Cermak, L. S., & Craik, F. I. M. (Eds.). *Levels of processing in human memory*. Hillsdale, N.J.: Erlbaum, 1979.

Corkin, S. Acquisition of motor skill after bilateral medial temporal-lobe excision. *Neuropsychologia*, 1968, *6*, 255–265.

Craik, F. I. M., & Lockhart, R. S. Levels of processing: A framework for memory research. *Journal of Verbal Learning and Verbal Behavior*, 1972, *11*, 671–684.

Crovitz, H. F., & Harvey, M. T. *Case report: Memory retraining in a woman with anterograde amnesia after cerebrovascular accident using relaxation and home-practice in visual imagery mnemonics*. Unpublished manuscript, 1979.

Crovitz, H. F., & Harvey, M. T., & Horn, R. W. Problems in the acquisition of imagery mnemonics: Three brain damaged cases. *Cortex*, 1979, *15*, 225–234.

Deutsch, D., & Deutsch, J. A. *Short term memory*, New York: Academic Press, 1975.

DeWied, D., & Versteeg, D. H. G. Neurohypophysical principles and memory. *Federation Proceedings*, 1979, *38*, 2348–2354.

Drachman, D. A. Memory and cognitive function in man: Does the cholinergic system have a specific role? *Neurology*, 1977, *27*, 783–790.

Experimental Aging Research, 1978, 4(4), 233–319.

Flavell, J. H., & Wellman, H. M. Metamemory. In R. V. Kail, Jr., & J. W. Hogen (Eds.), *Perspectives on the development of memory and cognition.* Hillsdale, N.J.: Erlbaum, 1977.

Gasparrini, B., & Satz, P. A treatment for memory problems in left hemipshere CVA patients. *Journal of Clinical Neuropsychology,* 1979, *1,* 137–150.

Gianutsos, R., & Gianutsos, J. Rehabilitating the verbal recall of brain injured patients by mnemonic training: An experimental demonstration using single-case methodology. *Journal of Clinical Neuropsychology,* 1979, *1,* 117–135.

Glanzer, M., & Cunitz, A. R. Two storage mechanisms in free recall. *Journal of Verbal Learning and Verbal Behavior,* 1966, *5,* 351–360.

Glasgow, R. E., Zeiss, R. A., Barrera, M., Jr., & Lewinsohn, P. M. Case studies on remediating memory deficits in brain injured individuals. *Journal of Clinical Psychology,* 1977, *33,* 1049–1054.

Hersen, M., & Barlow, D. H. *Single case experimental designs: Strategies for studying behavioral change,* New York: Pergamon Press, 1976.

Horel, J. A. The neuroanatomy of amnesia: A critique of the hippocampal memory hypothesis. *Brain,* 1978, *101,* 403–445.

Isaacson, R. L. *The limbic system.* New York: Plenum Press, 1974.

Jacoby, L. L., & Craik, F. I. M. Effect of elaboration of processing at encoding and retrieval: Trace distinctiveness and recovery of initial context. In L. S. Cermak & F. I. M. Craik (Eds.), *Levels of processing in human memory.* Hillsdale, N.J.: Erlbaum, 1979.

Jones, M. K. Imagery as a mnemonic aid after left temporal lobectomy: Contrast between material-specific and generalized memory disorders. *Neuropsychologia,* 1974, *12,* 21–30.

Jones-Gotman, M., & Milner, B. Design fluency: The invention of nonsense drawings after focal cortical lesions. *Neuropsychologia,* 1977, *15,* 653–573.

Kintsch, W. *Memory and cognition.* New York: Wiley, 1977.

Levin, H. S., O'Donnell, V. M., & Grossman, R. G. The Galveston Orientation and Amnesia Test. *Journal of Nervous and Mental Disease,* 1979, *167,* 675–684.

Lewinsohn, P. M., & Graf, M. A follow-up study of persons referred for vocational rehabilitation who have suffered brain damage. *Journal of Community Psychology,* 1973, *1,* 57–62.

Lewinsohn, P. M., Danaher, B. G., & Kikel, S. Visual imagery as a mnemonic aid for brain injured persons. *Journal of Consulting and Clinical Psychology,* 1977, *45,* 717–723.

Lewinsohn, P. M., Glasgow, R. E., Barrera, M., Danaher, B. G., Alperson, J., McCarty, D. L., Sullivan, J. M., Zeiss, R. A., Nyland, J., & Rodrigues, M. R. P. Assessment and treatment of patients with memory deficits. JSAS Catalog of Selected Documents in Psychology, 1977, *7,* 79. (Manuscript No. 1538.)

Luria, A. R. *The neuropsychology of memory.* Washington, D.C.: Winston, 1976.

Meudell, P. R., & Mayes, A. R. Do alcoholic amnesic patients passively rehearse verbal information? *Brain and Language,* 1980, *10,* 189–204.

Miller, E. *Abnormal aging: The psychology of senile and presenile dementia.* London: Wiley, 1977.

Milner, B. Memory. (From Milner, B., & Teuber, H. L., Alteration of perception and memory in man: Reflections on methods.) In L. Weiskrantz (Ed.), *Analysis of behavioral change.* New York: Harper & Row, 1968.

Milner, B. Hemispheric specialization. In F. O. Schmitt & F. G. Worden (Eds.), *Scope and limits, in the neurosciences Third Study Program.* Cambridge, Mass.: MIT Press, 1974.

Minsky, M. L. A framework for representing knowledge. In P. Winston (Ed.), *The psychology of computer vision.* New York: McGraw-Hill, 1975.

Neisser, U. *Cognitive psychology.* New York: Appleton Century Crofts, 1967.

Oscar-Berman, M. The neuropsychological consequences of long-term chronic alcoholism. *American Scientist*, 1980, *68*, 410–419.

Pavio, A. *Imagery and verbal processes*. New York: Holt, 1971.

Pavio, A., Yuille, J. C., & Madigan, S. A. Concreteness, imagery, and meaningfulness values for 925 nouns. *Journal of Experimental Psychology Monograph*, 1968, *76* (1, Pt. 2).

Patten, B. M. The ancient art of memory: Usefulness in treatment. *Archives of Neurology*, 1972, *26*, 25–31.

Peters, B. H. & Levin, H. S. Memory enhancement after physostigmine treatment in the amnestic syndrome. *Archives of Neurology*, 1977, *34*, 215–219.

Peterson, L. R., & Peterson, M. J. Short-term retention of individual verbal items. *Journal of Experimental Psychology*, 1959, *58*, 193–198.

Prigatano, G. P. Wechsler Memory Scale: A selective review of the literature. *Journal of Clinical Psychology*, 1978, *34*, 816–832.

Poon, L. W. A systems approach for the assessment and treatment of memory problems. In J. Ferguson & C. B. Taylor (Eds.), *Advances in behavioral medicine*. New York: Spectrum, 1980.

Poon, L. W., Walsh-Sweeney, L., & Fozard, J. L. Memory skill training for the elderly: Salient issues on the use of imagery mnemonics. In L. W. Poon, J. L. Fozard, L. S. Cermak, D. Arenberg, & L. W. Thompson (Eds.), *New directions in memory and aging: Proceedings of the George A. Talland Memorial Conference*. Hillsdale, N.J.: Erlbaum, 1980.

Rosch, E. Cognitive references points. *Cognitive Psychology*, 1975, *7*, 532–547.

Russell, W. R. *The traumatic amnesias*. London: Oxford University Press, 1971.

Samuels, I., Butters, N., & Goodglass, H. Visual memory deficits following cortical and limbic lesions: Effect of field presentation. *Physiology and Behavior*, 1971, *6*, 447–452.

Samuels, I., Butters, N., Goodglass, H., & Brody, B. A comparison of subcortical and cortical damage on short term visual and auditory memory. *Neuropsychologia*, 1971, *9*, 293–306.

Samuels, I., Butters, N., & Fedio, P. Short term memory disorders following temporal lobe removals in humans. *Cortex*, 1972, *8*, 283–298.

Sarno, M. T., & Levita, E. Natural course of recovery in severe aphasia. *Archives of Physical Medicine*, 1971, *52*, 175–178.

Schank, R., & Abelson, R. *Scripts, plans, goals, and understanding*. Hillsdale, N.J.: Erlbaum, 1977.

Schuell, H. Aphasia theory and therapy. In *Selected lectures and papers of Hildred Schuell*. Baltimore: University Park Press, 1974.

Scoville, W. B., & Milner, B. Loss of recent memory after bilateral hippocampal lesions. *Neuropsychologia*, 1957, *20*, 11–21.

Shallice, T., & Warrington, E. K. Auditory–verbal short term memory impairment and conduction aphasia. *Brain and Language*, 1977, *4*, 479–491.

Shiffrin, R. M., & Schneider, W. Controlled and automatic human information processing: II. Perceptual learning, automatic attending, and a general theory. *Psychological Review*, 1977, *84*, 127–190.

Shore, D. L. Memory deficit remediation in patients with unilateral brain damage. *Archives of Physical Medicine and Rehabilitation*, 1979, *60*, 542. (Abstract)

Strub, R. L., & Gardner, H. The repetition defect in conduction aphasia: Mnestic or linguistic? *Brain and Language*, 1974, *1*, 241–255.

Talland, G. A. *Deranged memory: A psychonomic study of the amnesic syndrome*. New York: Academic Press, 1965.

Timming, R. C., Cayner, J. J., Grady, S., Grafman, J., Haskin, R., Malec, J., & Thornsen, C. Multidisciplinary rehabilitation in severe head trauma. *Wisconsin Medical Journal*, 1980, *79*, 49–52.

Tulving, E. Episodic and semantic memory. In E. Tulving & W. Donaldson (Eds.), *Organization of memory*. New York: Academic Press, 1972.

Tulving, E. Relation between encoding specificity and levels of processing. In L. S. Cermak & F. I. M. Craik (Eds.), *Levels of processing in human memory*. Hillsdale, N.J.: Erlbaum, 1979.

Tulving, E., & Thomson, D. M. Encoding specificity and retrieval processes in episodic memory. *Psychological Review*, 1973, *80*, 352–373.

Warrington, E. K. The selective impairment of semantic memory. *Quarterly Journal of Experimental Psychology*, 1975, *27*, 635–657.

Warrington, E. K., & Weiskrantz, L. An analysis of short term and long term memory defects in man. In J. A. Deutsch (Ed.), *The physiological basis of memory*. New York: Academic Press, 1973.

Wechsler, D., & Stone, C. P. *Wechsler Memory Scale*. New York: Psychological Corporation, 1945.

Wertz, R. T., Collins, M., Weiss, D., Brookshire, R. H., Friden, T., Kurtzke, J. F., & Pierce, J. *Veterans Administration cooperative study on aphasia: A preliminary report on a comparison of individual and group treatment*. Presented at the Annual Meeting of the American Association for the Advancement of Science, Washington, D.C., February 1978.

Whitty, C. W. M., & Zangwill, O. L. *Amnesia*. Boston: Butterworth's, 1977.

Wood, G. Mnemonic systems in recall. *Journal of Educational Psychology*, 1967, *58*(6), 1–27.

Zarit, S. Helping an aging patient to cope with memory problems. *Geriatrics*, 1979, *4*, 82–90.

6

The Physical Rehabilitation of the Brain-Damaged Elderly

A BEHAVIORAL APPROACH

Erica M. Sufrin

1. Introduction

Chronic disease and physical disability will seriously affect the lives and function of almost half of those living in the United States at some point in their lifetimes. Of the 20 million disabled people living in the United States, 40 percent are aged 65 or older (Henriksen, 1978). The United States Public Health Service indicates that during a 10-year period, a person in 1 of 10 households will fall victim to stroke (Levenson, 1971). Estimates of the annual incidence of stroke among people aged 65 to 80 range between 870 and 3,430 new cases per 100,000 population (Kurtzke, 1976). In brief, many older people are faced with serious disruption of motor, sensory, and cognitive functions secondary to stroke or other disabling conditions.

In contrast to neurologically disabled children who have had no prior learning in areas such as speech, sensory experience, emotional behavior, or motor control, adults who suffer the residual effects of a stroke can face a considerable disruption of already learned functional, performance, emotional and social abilities. Since physical rehabilitation is dependent on the patient's learning or relearning adaptive behaviors and often "unlearning" maladaptive or inefficient behaviors, the de-

Erica M. Sufrin • Department of Psychiatry, Albany Medical College, Albany, New York 12208 and Department of Psychology, Russell Sage College, Troy, New York 12180.

crease in learning efficiency that often accompanies brain damage becomes an important consideration. Impairment of the reception and processing of incoming information, interference with association to previously acquired information, and ineffective retrieval or memory impairment are all factors that can greatly hamper an individual's rehabilitation program (Fordyce, 1971). This chapter will review issues relevant to the physical rehabilitation of stroke patients—in particular, elderly stroke patients. The use of behavioral techniques in physical rehabilitation as well as training and implementation issues will be discussed. The reader should keep in mind, however, that in spite of this chapter's emphasis on the rehabilitation of brain-damaged elderly, much of what is said can be readily adapted to other treatment programs for the elderly as well as to physical rehabilitation programs for people of all ages.

2. Comprehensive Behavioral Program Planning for the Neurologically Impaired Elderly

While old people are seen by many in the medical and paramedical profession as suffering from numerous, progressive, or irreversible, and often untreatable physical and emotional disorders, they often do not receive adequate rehabilitative treatment (Mock, 1977). The reasons for this often include the myths that old people are crotchety, stubborn, unmotivated, and probably unwilling to engage in active treatment programs. To put it succinctly, old people with physical and/or emotional problems are often seen by physicians and other health care personnel as suffering from the "normal," expected consequences of aging. Intervention in such circumstances is often nonaggressive in the area of diagnosis as well as in treatment or rehabilitation. It is beyond the scope of this chapter to review the work dealing with the psychological and social changes that accompany senescence. However, numerous researchers have documented the extent of a negative bias against the elderly and described the social "climate" surrounding the aging individual (See Birren & Schaie, 1977; Brantl & Brown, 1973; Busse & Pfeiffer, 1977; Eisdorfer & Lawton, 1973; Howells, 1975; and Usdin & Hofling, 1978).

Numerous physical changes are associated with normal aging. Approximately 86 percent of those over the age of 65 have one or more chronic illnesses (Busse, 1973). In a study described by Estes (1977), approximately 30 percent of those over age 65 considered themselves limited in one or more activities of daily living due to the effects of a chronic disease. Yet many aspects of a rehabilitation program for an elderly person will involve considerations related to the general consequences of normal aging while also being concerned with diagnostically determined treatments and concomitant chronic illnesses.

2.1. Sensory and Motor Considerations

Older people tend to demonstrate a decrease in their peripheral vision, are more affected by glare, have diminished dark-adaption abilities and poorer visual acuity, and have more limited visual accommodation and contrast sensitivity abilities (Fozard & Thomas, 1975). Special attention must be paid to lighting a treatment area so that illumination is adequate but not glaringly bright. To ensure that one is within an elderly patient's visual range, it is best to stand directly in front of him or her. Sudden moves from brightly to dimly lit areas should be avoided, and patients should be encouraged to illuminate their homes with even, adequate light. On stairs, the elderly person may have difficulty discerning the edge of each step. To compensate, a bright yellow or white stripe may, for example, be painted along the edge of any step frequently used by an elderly person having a visual disturbance.

Older people are also likely to demonstrate a diminution of pitch discrimination, a decrease in auditory acuity, and some difficulty in speech perception. Frequency response deficits, however, usually involve frequencies higher than those used in normal speech. Strax and Ledebur (1979) found that some degree of motivational and performance improvement could be achieved simply by correcting a patient's hearing deficit; this was implicit in their procedural description. This author's experience is that paranoid thinking and its related agitation or depression may often occur in the elderly solely because of a hearing deficit.

In any clinical situation, there are some routine procedures that should be followed when any patient is suspected of having hearing impairment. First, the patient should undergo an ear examination to determine whether impacted ear wax is present. If the ears are clear and auditory impairment persists, an audiometric examination is indicated. In the meantime, a quick, informal examination may be conducted by having the patient wear a stethoscope while the clinician speaks into the bell at a somewhat soft to normal speaking volume. It is important not to speak too loudly into the stethoscope, since the resulting amplification could be painful for the patient. If the patient can hear through the stethoscope, it is likely that a correctible, mechanically caused hearing deficit is present. Should the patient not be able to hear even with the stethoscope, it is probable that the deafness is due to nerve damage. The "stethoscope test" is described here because there is often an immediate need for a clinician either to assess a patient's auditory acuity or to talk with a patient. Such is the case when an elderly patient is seemingly agitated and uncooperative with the nursing staff. If a mechanical deafness is present, talking to a patient through a stethoscope and perhaps explaining whatever hospital procedures are being attempted can immediately calm a very agitated person who simply did not understand what was going on and could not hear what was being explained. For the most part, hearing deficits due to nerve damage will usually not be improved by hearing aids or surgical procedures. Deafness due to mechanical factors such as scarring or bony changes is likely to be treatable with surgery or hearing aids.

Although it seems obvious, it must be mentioned that, in talking with a hearing-impaired patient, it is necessary to face the person and to speak in a loud, clear voice at a moderately slow pace. Parenthetically, it is not uncommon for an older person to own a hearing aid yet avoid its use because of problems with fit or noise. Also, an elderly person who has experienced a gradual decline in auditory acuity may not to notice the change in his or her ability to hear. Again, whenever there is a question regarding auditory function, it is essential that an adequate audiometric examination be conducted.

Motor function may also be affected by aging. An increase in simple reaction time—that is, the time it takes a person to make a single response to a single stimulus event—is commonly seen in the elderly and has a potential impact on motor performance. Complex, coordinated motor responses and actions are necessary for normal, purposeful movement. A motor response usually involves many discrete components. If each individual component of a complex motor response is affected by a very slight delay in reaction time, a larger cumulative effect should be noticed. It has been speculated that such delays are due to central rather than peripheral nervous system factors and account for the motor performance decrements commonly noted in the elderly. Such decrements carry functional implications in situations such as regaining one's balance after stumbling. And as motor tasks are made more difficult, the discrepancy in response latencies between old and young people increases (Fozard & Thomas, 1975), compounding the disabilities resulting from an elderly person's stroke.

2.2. Goals in Physical Rehabilitation

Effective rehabilitation treatment is predicated on the development of residual or alternative abilities, not simply the treatment or management of disabilities and deficiencies. The elderly person with a serious physical disability may have a very supportive family that can be worked with to great advantage. Or the person requiring institutionalization may have the capacity to engage in social interactions. With the appropriate environmental manipulations (prompting, encouragement, or reinforcement), this ability may be more fully developed or realized (McDonald, 1978). In short, the rehabilitation requirements of the elderly are complex but can be dealt with creatively and productively when thoughtfully considered.

Regardless of the patient or condition being worked with by the physical rehabilitation team, the goal of any program is to maximize functional abilities, minimize pain and discomfort, and maintain existing abilities. Much work by rehabilitation personnel is conducted with young, relatively able, or active patients who have a high likelihood of good recovery. Some disorders—such as many orthopedic or dermatologic problems—often produce relatively little impairments in social or vocational functioning. With severely disabled children or younger adults, vocational training or rehabilitation often becomes an integral part of a rehabilitation program. Young-adult and middle-aged patients usually have families and, in many cases, have job skills and/or hold gainful employment. The elderly person is frequently somewhat different. The elderly person who has suffered a stroke is likely to have other chronic disorders. He or she is not likely to have a job to return to and, if the patient lacks a family or interested relatives or is impaired psychologically, can present a major challenge to the members of a rehabilitation team. The difference often seen between older and younger patients (and "old" has all sorts of connotations for both old and young) is that the elderly patient probably has a greater degree of total disability and fewer resources or supports than does a younger person.

The resolution of a patient's medical problems does not guarantee that other problems areas (i.e., vocational, social, or psychological) will improve. It has been observed, however, that success in dealing with one area of an individual's behavior often influences outcomes in other areas (Grove, 1970; Spencer, 1969). Rice, McDaniel, and Denny (1968) suggested that most patients must find ways to improve their motor functioning before their cognitive functioning can be studied. In rehabilitation, it is especially important that a careful analysis be performed on the kinds of information a patient can or cannot receive and utilize. Corresponding adjustments in instructions and feedback must be made with patients who have language, sensory, perceptual, memory, or motoric impairment (Fordyce, 1971; Goodglass & Kaplan, 1972).

To accomplish such goals, many kinds of personnel are required. A rehabilitation team may be comprised of physicians, including but not limited to physiatrists and surgeons; nurses; physical, occupational, and speech therapists; psychologists; audiologists; vocational counselors; social workers; academically trained therapy assistants; and clinically trained aides. Few personnel who engage in physical rehabilitation treatment are typically members of such a large team. Multidisciplinary treatment teams are usually found in large general or university hospitals or in rehabilitation centers. Yet it is quite common for those requiring physical rehabilitation services to be patients in smaller hospitals or nursing homes or to be at home. Some elderly may be hospitalized for an illness or disability; where acute care is no longer required, however, they may find themselves transferred to an extended-care facility or to their homes with limited home aide, visiting nurse, or visiting therapist assistance. Small hospitals, extended care facilities, and visiting or public health nursing programs may have limited access to physical rehabilitation professionals and—on a routine basis—may have regular access only to a physical therapist. Such situations require comprehensive, versatile, and innovative evaluation and treatment services by those available to provide rehabilitation services.

2.3. Stroke Treatment

Once a person has suffered a stroke, the initial task of the rehabilitation team will be to evaluate the patient, determine appropriate treatment goals, and develop a plan by which to achieve them. Ideally, the initial rehabilitation evaluation of a stroke patient will occur at bedside as soon as any emergency medical or surgical procedures have been completed. Thus, a stroke patient might undergo an initial evaluation before regaining consciousness and while still in an intensive care unit. Regardless of where a patient undergoes evaluation, there should be space enough to permit a full active and passive range-of-motion evaluation. During any evaluation or treatment of a stroke patient, distracting sights and sounds should be kept to an absolute minimum. Early interventions may be limited to active or passive range-of-motion exercises, bed positioning (including the proper use of pillows), positional rolls or footboards, the prevention or treatment of decubitus ulcers and contractures, and a thorough evaluation of premorbid levels of physical, social, emotional, and vocational functioning. The patient's and family's understanding of the process of stroke and their long-term expectations should be explored, and explanations or clarifications should be made as needed. The actual evaluation and determination of a sensorimotor prognosis may, as the patient's condition changes or improves, actually take several weeks or even months. For this reason, the evaluation and treatment process must remain fluid and must be modified whenever any of the patient's needs, abilities, or disabilities dictate. As treatment progresses, thorough evaluations of kinesthetic, proprioceptive, and vibratory senses should be made. Visual perception, pain, touch, and temperature sensations also need to be evaluated. Muscle testing and functional "activities of daily living" (ADL) evaluations should be performed at regular intervals. A general physical evaluation must be performed to ascertain whether other medical problems coexist with the effects of the stroke. Concomitant disorders often seen in hemiplegic patients are myocardial infarction, congestive heart failure, hypertension, diabetes, and bowel or bladder incontinence. Also, with elderly stroke patients it is imperative that the irreversible impairments related to aging be differentiated from the disabilities of a treatable disease or process (Gryfe, 1979). For comprehensive discussions of the methods and procedures utilized in a physical rehabiliation evaluation, see Krusen, Kottke, and Ellwood (1971) and Bonner (1974).

Possible consequences of stroke include either a flaccid or spastic paralysis. In addition to attempts to retrain muscle function and prevent a subluxation or dislocation of an involved shoulder, training to inhibit muscle spasticity might be undertaken; also, the need for bracing, especially of the leg or ankle, must be evaluated. If able, patients must be taught to transfer in and out of beds, on and off toilets, and in and out of wheelchairs or other chairs. Those having the potential should be taught to stand, balance, and walk. In time, patients may be taught to climb stairs, to step on and off curbs, to navigate ramps, and to perform the myriad movements involved in the dressing, cooking, and cleaning activities that are necessary for independent function. Treatment planning must be a flexible process, with individually set goals that may be revised at any time (Levenson, 1971). Each patient will have his or her own level of function and potential for improvement.

Numerous factors can affect the outcome of a physical rehabilitation program. A patient's physical and cognitive abilities and deficits, the thoroughness or adequacy of the diagnostic evaluation, and the quality of the rehabilitation program or treatment plan are certainly of primary importance. The patient's social, economic, and vocational resources can have an impact on a rehabilitation program. Patient and family attitudes toward illness or disability, as well as staff attitudes, can affect treatment outcome. The elderly person suffering from a stroke is obviously, as described earlier, a candidate for misunderstanding. Negative bias toward the patient or the patient's disability on the part of family members, care providers, or even the patient can seriously hamper treatment efforts or temper the success of rehabilitation treatment. Perhaps one of the biggest problems in geriatric rehabilitation is that both patients and rehabilitation personnel often equate treatment success with "cure" or a patient's return to an independent level of function. Such goals are often unrealistic. On the other hand, there are occasions where independence is incorrectly considered to be an unrealistic treatment goal for an elderly person simply because the person is old and may, for instance, already reside in an extended-care facility rather than at home. Or the patient may have few social and economic resources with which to offset some degree of the disability. In some cases, treatment goals are set too low: a good rehabilitation program might concentrate on the development of limited standing, ambulation, or ADL function even though total independence will never be a realistic treatment goal. Sometimes treatment staff will perform a task for a patient rather than assisting in or guiding the patient in the performance of ADL activities. This is often mistakenly perceived as a means of expediting care and treatment. What is saved in time in such situations, however, certainly does not offset what a patient loses in both sense of autonomy and in opportunity to practice ADL skills. Strax and Ledebur (1979), seeing that elderly patients were frequently perceived as lacking in motivation, attributed this perception to the failure of others to expect anything from the elderly. They saw this failure, combined with a decreased sense of responsibility among the patients, as leading to the development of inappropriate social behavior and an intensification of psychosomatic complaints among elderly patients.

Yet treatment goals can be set too high. When patients or care providers set unattainable goals, a chronic sense of failure among both staff and patients may permeate all rehabilitation activities. Each needs to be aware of realistic, achievable treatment goals. Initially, limited goals may have the effect of saddening or depressing a patient. If such a reaction is not excessive, it is to be expected and forms the basis for a patient's adjusting to disability. Treatment gains should be pointed out routinely or made evident to the patient. Hope need not be withheld from a patient but should be maintained within the realm of possibility. In the long run, excessive false hope can only be destructive.

2.4. Learned Helplessness

It is interesting that after weeks of nonimprovement on a general treatment ward, elderly patients often improve rapidly in a geriatric treatment ward or setting. Reasons for improvement may include factors such as attention and encouragement from the staff and other patients. Patients who do well on a geriatric unit often find themselves the focus of much attention. This is in sharp contrast to the attention which, on more acute wards, is often directed at complainers and dependent patients. The traditional focus of attention on an acute ward may be a consequence of what might be termed "medical-model thinking," whereby it is primarily pain and illness or complaining behavior that attracts attention from health care providers. The adoption of this model often leads to a situation where independence of function or lack of complaint can result in a benign neglect by staff, who associate quiet with "better," "nondisruptive," or "good." Such thinking may unconsciously foster maladaptive or "sick behaviors," since it may teach patients that behaving in a sick or dependent manner assures them of staff attention. Learned helplessness (Seligman, Klein, & Miller, 1976) and institutionalization are two concepts that may clarify the basis for some of the behavior seen in the elderly. People confined to institutions such as nursing homes or hospitals are likely to find their independence, initiative, or even active participation in their own care are no longer encouraged. A patient may find that he or she is bathed, rather than being allowed to bathe alone, because an aide can perform the task more quickly. Or a patient may find that complaining about tasteless institutional food effects no changes in the dinner menu but does serve to condemn him or her to being considered an uncooperative complainer by the ward staff. The behaviors that institutional settings often foster are apathy and complaint—dependent behaviors that make a patient "more manageable" but certainly less of an individual. In summary, being housed in an unfamiliar setting such as hospital or a nursing home may have serious detrimental effects on an elderly patient (Lawton, 1977; McDonald & Butler, 1974).

Successful rehabilitation with the elderly should involve regular treatment team meetings to reassess the patient's status and program. Whenever possible, patients should be involved in the planning of their treatment program and given some choice of or control over the activities in which they engage. Group treatment or treatment classes attended by several patients at a time can serve as an adjunct to or substitute for some individual treatment sessions. Treatment groups offer patients an opportunity for social interaction while also providing a setting in which to meet other patients with similar disabilities. Once in a group, it is usually not long before patients will start to talk with each other about their illnesses, fears, expectations, failures and accomplishments. Peer pressure can serve as a motivating force and lead to the development of new desirable behaviors as well as the suppression of socially undesirable behaviors such as complaining or refusal to participate in a program. Peer approval coupled with staff approval can be an exceptionally potent motivating force (Strax & Ledebur, 1979, and Wright, 1979).

2.5. *Behavioral Disturbance in the Elderly*

A discussion of geriatric rehabilitation would not be complete without some mention of the psychological and neurological conditions that, when present, can have a potentially significant impact on the treatment and/or management of an elderly person.

Although exact prevalence figures are not available, it has been estimated that between 4 and 6 percent of people over the age of 65 suffer from a definite organic brain syndrome and that an additional number suffer from milder degrees of impairment (Busse, 1973). The symptoms of organic impairment may include confusion or disorientation to time, place, and person; defects in memory (especially recent memory); intellectual and cognitive impairment in such areas as comprehension, learning, calculation, judgment, and problem solving; and emotional lability. Occasionally, a seemingly minor stress—such as relocation from a familiar room or home to an unfamiliar room, hospital, or other location—may lead to the development or exacerbation of the symptoms of dementia in what seemed to be a well-functioning individual. Such an occurrence can indicate that a well-compensated underlying decrement was previously present. Depriving an elderly person of sensory stimulation and social interaction is likely to lead to the development of confusion or an apparent organic psychosis. Reality orientation training is a valuable intervention and helps to avoid or alleviate confused and disoriented behavior (Holden & Sinebruchow, 1978).

While the elderly may exhibit any of the psychiatric disturbance seen among younger adults, most of the psychiatric disturbances seen in the elderly fall into the category of affective or mood disorders. At least one study concluded that depression, rather than being simply a response to a motor disability, may be a more specific complication of stroke (Folstein, Maiberger, & McHugh, 1977). Paranoid disorders, hypochondriasis, adjustment disorders, acute and chronic anxiety disorders, and alcoholism are also not uncommon among elderly people. A detailed discussion of how to deal effectively with such psychiatric disturbances can be found in Busse and Pfeiffer (1973, pp. 109–144).

Confused, delusional, or disoriented people do not respond well to angry, threatening, or forceful behaviors. Staff behavior seen as firm or authoritative by persons suffering from nonorganic behavioral disturbances may seen very frightening to the organically impaired, anxious, or psychotic person. Such patients may not immediately comprehend or follow instructions. To speed things along, therapists and aides may try to rush the patient in performing an activity and, when going somewhere with a patient, may even try to pull him or her along. Such an approach virtually guarantees noncooperation and can prompt assaultive or aggressive behaviors. Therefore the use of verbal or physical force on the part of staff are to be avoided in favor of less demanding, more supportive, clear and gentle but firm approaches. Should a patient present rehabilitation personnel with seriously disruptive behaviors that are not easily manageable, the rehabilitation personnel would do well to seek psychological or psychiatric consultation or assistance.

2.6. Summary

In summary, the older person is particularly vulnerable to both biological and psychological problems. Social losses, retirement and its subsequent diminution of professional status and income, loss of a spouse through death, and other losses involving grown children who move away or the deaths of friends often characterize the lives of older people. One may be fairly safe in assuming that an older person will probably lack many of the economic, social, familial, and vocational resources that are integral to the development of the comprehensive rehabilitation programs designed for most younger people. The net effect of these factors, coupled with the biological and pathological physical states of an older person who suffers a stroke, is that the development of a physical rehabilitation program for such an individual requires special attention.

3. Behavior Modification and Rehabilitation with the Elderly

Agras (in Pomerleau, 1979) has noted that, as has long been known, behavior affects both the maintenance of health and the development of disease, but until recently the behavioral sciences have contributed little to clinical medical care. The development of behavior therapy, however, has permitted the introduction of innovative and effective treatment procedures through the application of the research methods and the findings of experimental psychology.

Traditionally, anyone who has been injured and/or needs to acquire new skills to increase his or her effectiveness is usually assumed to "want to" or to "be motivated" to acquire these new skills and is expected to be "reinforced" by signs of achievement. Using this paradigm, failure to achieve is usually thought of as resulting from a personality difficulty and is often referred to as a "motivational problem." The intervention of a psychologist or psychiatrist is often requested at this point to help guide the patient's family and to motivate the patient (Fordyce, 1968). Working with the emotional problems that accompany physical disability and may interfere with recovery or rehabilitation is necessary for successful rehabilitation. Researchers have demonstrated the importance of considering the influence of such factors as mood, cooperation, and mental status as well as a variety of other factors—ranging from the nature of the disability to age of onset and psychological assets and liabilities prior to onset—to success in rehabilitation (Cain, 1969; Grossman, 1968; Masterman, 1958; Meyerson, Michael, Mowrer, Osgood, & Staats, 1960). However, seeking the internal impetus to motivation has not proven fruitful. Researchers and clinicians have turned to methods that promote more direct behavior (Fordyce, 1968, 1971).

A current trend in physical rehabilitation is to seek explanations for behavior seen with the assimilation of or adjustment to disability, using a learning model rather than or in addition to the traditional medical model. Actually, the new field of behavioral medicine is developing in response to the recognition that a multidisciplinary, biopsychosocial approach in medical and health care is an efficient, effective course to follow (See Matarazzo, 1980, and Pomerleau, 1979). A major distinction between the medical and learning models is that the medical or disease model approach emphasizes the modification of the etiological causes of symptoms or underlying feelings and attitudes, permitting the reduction or removal of symptoms or the appearance of new behaviors. In contrast, the learning model seeks to change undesirable symptoms or behaviors and has no direct concern with effecting changes in the ostensible underlying causes of a disorder.

Traditional approaches to physical rehabilitation have emphasized treatments that, when performed by motivated patients, were expected to have positive effects. Patient motivation was viewed as an internal state that, when it was present, guaranteed active participation by the patient in that treatment program. Patients who failed to actively participate in their treatment programs were termed "unmotivated"; in many cases they were seen as not warranting aggressive treatment until such time as they became motivated. This conceptualization of motivation has its obvious shortcomings. Many patients suffering from physical disabilities are depressed, hopeless, tired, and in pain. Many are uncertain as to what is expected of them or what they can expect of themselves with regard to physical performance.

A number of researchers who have utilized learning theory and behavior modification principles in their work in physical rehabilitation have affected the way concepts such as treatment and motivation have come to be viewed by many rehabilitation practitioners. Behaviorists have stressed the importance of utilizing measurable or observable behaviors as the criteria by which treatment outcomes be measured (Fordyce, 1971; Fordyce, Fowler, Lehman, & DeLateur, 1968; Meyerson, et al., 1960; Trotter & Inman, 1968). It is true that human beings demonstrate covert behaviors that are observable only by the individual (e.g., they think). However, most covert responses can be translated into measurable or somewhat objectified terms by addressing their overt concomitants (Ince, 1976).

Let us take the example of an elderly person who has suffered a stroke with the consequence that she has developed a painful shoulder. She is afraid to exercise for fear of experiencing an increase in pain, even though she knows exercise is a requirement for both the ultimate relief of pain and any improvement in muscular function in her arm and shoulder. In the past, such a patient, if she complained loudly and frequently enough, would probably have been seen as uncooperative and unmotivated (i.e., she complained and refused to participate in her exercise program). Looking at this patient in behavioral terms, we see a woman suffering from fear, pain, and anxiety (all internal states) who complains and refuses (overt behavior) and has impaired strength and range of motion (overt, measurable behavior). From a behavioral perspective, one could define the behaviors of interest (target behaviors) and then set about developing ways of measuring them. For example, self-report of fear or pain or exercise performance as indirect measures of pain (assuming that less pain means more exercise) or physiological measures such as heart rate or galvanic skin resistance as indirect measures of anxiety could serve as measurable or quantifiable target behaviors. Put succinctly, behavioral approaches view the organism as being controlled by its external environment, private events (cognitions), and history of interaction with the environment. By controlling the environmental antecedents (public and private) of an individual's behavior as well as the consequences (public and private), one can occasion desired behaviors or at least increase their probability of occurrence. But this is getting ahead of ourselves. Let us return to our discussion of other fundamental behavioral considerations in physical rehabilitation.

3.1. Maladaptive Disability-Related Behaviors

Disabled individuals often have some degree of prior learning. During rehabilitation, relearning—as opposed to learning from a state of total naivete—may be indicated (Meyerson *et al.*, 1960). Some patients may have a great deal of prior learning but because of their disability may be unable to utilize this knowledge. Other patients may have prior learning that is adaptive to their current disabled state, while others may have prior learning that is maladaptive to their present state. For example, in contrast to the recently disabled patient who has not had a chance to develop ineffectual behaviors relative to his disability, the patient who has had his disability for a long period has probably developed maladaptive behaviors that are reinforced and maintained with considerable strength.

The development and maintenance of ineffective disability-related behaviors in disabled individuals can be attributed to a variety of "causes." First, the patient's environment (i.e., the hospital or wheelchair) may serve to remove any reinforcement opportunities—otherwise normally encountered in daily life. Removal of primary and secondary reinforcers, can lead to the development of apathy, depression, and lethargy (Seligman, Klein, & Miller, 1976). In such situations it would be important to modify the patient's environment (McDonald & Butler, 1974) and to supply some minor reinforcers that existed in the patient's prior situation (Meyerson *et al.*, 1960). McDonald and Butler (1974) successfully used social reinforcement to modify staff (environmental) expectations and thus to increase independent walking behavior in institutionalized elderly people who generally utilized wheelchairs as their preferred method of transport. If a patient is confined to a wheelchair, environmental manipulations might be made, permitting easier access to areas that he or she finds reinforcing, such as areas of social activity or of privacy. Each patient will have his or her own particular areas or activities that are reinforcing. These must be individually determined for every patient.

Michael (1970b) discussed a form of social "ping-pong" sometimes played by a disabled individual with friends. In this case the patient receives constant reassurance and attention from friends following expressions of discouragement. Such attention to the patient's complaining behavior is reinforcing to the patient in producing certain desired consequences (e.g., increased social interaction). The complaining behavior may interfere drastically with the patient's rehabilitation program but may be very difficult to remove from the patient's behavioral repertoire, since it does lead to a great deal of attention for the otherwise essentially alienated patient. The disabled elderly person—who may lack adequate diversions, activities, or social interactions—is a likely candidate for the development of such behaviors.

Therapists and physicians often fall into this same trap. Traditionally, physical and occupational therapists have surrounded patients indiscriminately with attention and encouragement. The less patients may try to do for themselves, the more encouragement and attention they may receive from the therapist, who is trying to convince them to be independent. Patients in such situations soon learn that as they do become more independent and as their self-care abilities do improve, there is a corresponding decrease in the attention forthcoming from their therapists, since the therapists in this situation often withdraw and leave the patients on their own (Trombly, 1966).

Ayllon and Michael (1959) pointed out that disruptive behavior by patients can often prevent staff from dealing with the patient's basic problems. One large-scale study illustrated that the attentional component of the doctor–patient relationship inadvertently reinforced illness behaviors and concluded that the attention accompanying the doctor–patient relationship can reinforce an emphasis on either health or ill health (Hallauer, 1972). That is, reinforcers that can be effective when applied properly can also serve to maintain sick or disabled behavior when improperly used (Ayllon & Michael, 1959; Fordyce et al., 1968; Fowler, Fordyce, & Berni, 1969; Rice, McDaniel, & Denney, 1968).

3.2. Operant Conditioning in Rehabilitation

Rehabilitation lends itself to the use of operant conditioning principles (i.e., reinforcement, extinction, discrimination, generalization) and the counterconditioning of incompatible behaviors (Goodkin, 1970; Grove, 1970; Hall & Broden, 1970; Meyerson et al., 1960; Michael, 1970b; and Reese, 1966). Piggott (1969) has discussed the conceptual basis for using a behavioral analysis system in rehabiliation, and Cushing (1969) provided examples of its successful use in a vocational setting. Rice et al. (1968) stated that one advantage to an operant rehabilitation program is that once a response is shaped to the therapist's satisfaction, it can be practiced or maintained by an essentially untrained person such as a parent. An individual's having skill, or the ability to emit certain behaviors, does not guarantee that he or she will use it.

Before behaviors can be changed one must clearly define a patient's rehabilitation goals in operational terms (Fordyce, Fowler, Sand, & Trieschmann, 1971; and Michael, 1970a). Operant conditioning involves the enginnering of relationships between behavior, its antecedents, and its consequences. Behavioral interventions have been demonstrated to be effective in numerous health-related areas such as obesity, tachycardia, seizure disorders, neuromuscular disorders, sexual function problems, headache, and adherence to a treatment program (Pomerleau,

1979). Except for work in the areas of electromyography and biofeedback training as used in muscle reeducation of the treatment of pain (Basmajian, Regenos, & Baker, 1977; Blanchard & Young, 1974; Bowman, Baker, & Waters, 1979; Cushing, 1969; Fordyce, 1968; Fordyce *et al.*, 1968; Fordyce, 1976; Fordyce, Fowler, Lehman, Delateur, Sand, & Trieschmann, 1973; Inglis, Campbell, & Donald, 1976; Keefe & Surwit, 1978; Mroczek, 1976; Mroczek, Halpern, & McHugh, 1978; Peck, 1976; Wolf, Baker, & Kelly, 1979), recent literature related to the use of behavior modification or operant techniques in the area of physical rehabilitation is surprisingly scant. Apparently only Ince (1976) has treated the role of behavior modification in rehabilitation medicine in a relatively complete fashion. This paucity of literature reflects an apparent inattention of psychological researchers to physical rehabilitation issues, in spite of the fact that behavior modification has settled in as an accepted tool in psychology's treatment armamentarium. General motivation and performance issues in physical rehabilitation are certainly problematic to patients and treatment personnel and most certainly lend themselves to behavioral interventions and research.

3.3. Treatment Programs

Medical rehabilitation is involved neither in curing disease nor in intervening in functional pathology for symptom removal. Instead, it is concerned with increasing functional capacities for the emission of behaviors necessary to daily social and vocational activities, living, and survival (Fordyce, 1968). Physical therapists, occupational therapists, speech therapists, and related rehabilitation personnel are involved with helping the disabled develop new skills. Their educative and management functions can be broken down into two main activities. First, there is the analysis of a selected skill into its component parts and the arrangement of the components into an effective sequence (Goodkin, 1966; Michael, 1970b; Taylor & Persons, 1970). This is followed by the selection of a mechanism for quantifying it. Management must include differential consequences—reinforcement and/or punishment—for correct vs. incorrect or good vs. poor performance (Michael, 1970b; Taylor & Persons, 1970). All the problems encountered in a rehabilitation program do not have to be addressed at the outset. It is unrealistic to expect that all clinical problems can be so clearly defined at any point in time that a comprehensive behavioral treatment plan can always be implemented. Instead, treatment programs may be partial and must remain fluid and subject to constant evaluation and revision. However, utilizing an oversimplified model can preclude the observation of some aspects or classes of behavioral phenomena (Meyerson et al., 1960).

3.4. Generalization

In implementing a behavioral treatment program, it is important to remember that a major treatment goal is likely to be the performance of newly acquired behaviors in a variety of settings. This carryover is termed "generalization," which, as relevant to rehabilitation, involves the performance of disability-appropriate behavior across nontraining settings. The approximation of the natural environment during rehabilitation training or a modification of the environment to provide appropriate reinforcement contingencies upon the performance of disability-appropriate behaviors are means of achieving generalization (Fordyce, 1971). "A behavioral change is said to have generality if it proves desirable over time, if it appears in a wide variety of possible environments, or if it spreads to a wide variety or related behaviors" (Baer, Wolf, & Risley, 1968). Generalization is crucial if what patients learn in a clinical setting is to benefit them in their natural environment and is to allow them flexibility and adaptability.

Varying degrees of a systematic approach to ensuring generalization have been utilized. It is not safe to assume that newly learned skills will generalize simply because they are useful (Stokes & Baer, 1977). Since behavioral treatments lend themselves well to institutional settings and institutionalized people are likely to be older persons in a hospital or nursing home, this concern with generalization of treatment effect should be of particular concern to those working with the elderly. To some degree their task is made easier by the fact that their patient's natural environment is limited to the institution, a self-contained potentially controllable environment. On the other hand, the very structural, social, and other limitations of an institution (i.e., high staff turnover, staff shortages, untrained staff, or poor programming), can make the task of fostering generalization of learned skills a difficult one.

A final note regarding the carryover of behaviors newly learned in a rehabilitation setting to the natural environment is that home visits while a patient is confined to an institution and home treatment programs following inpatient discharge are useful methods to ensure that newly learned behaviors are appropriate to and will be performed in the patient's natural environment. Ideally, at least one home visit in the company of a staff member is made by any patient being prepared for inpatient discharge from any hospital, rehabilitation, or long-term care setting.

3.5. Staff Concerns

In spite of the fact that operant conditioning principles are well suited to rehabilitation training and treatment, their use is not always met with enthusiasm by rehabilitation personnel. Few rehabilitation workers have had much or any training in the clinical application of operant principles and many are put off by the unfamiliarity of the concepts utilized and what is incorrectly perceived as the impersonal, mechanistic nature of behavior modification programs. Roberts, Dinsdale, Matthews, & Cole (1969) described ways of minimizing some of the objections to behavioral modification programs in rehabilitation through (1) a discussion of the program with the rehabilitation staff, (2) the staff's demonstration of similar programs working successfully with other patients and the fact that the patients did not object to such programs, and (3) demonstrating the simplicity of an operant program as a major advantage in facilitating their acceptance of such programs by therapists. Behavioral analysis offers goal-oriented approaches to treatment with measurable and often observable objectives. Moreover, the means to achieving objectives and attaining goals are easily specified. These factors are appealing to clinicians and should be clearly specified when discussing operant conditioning programs with rehabilitation staff.

3.6. Motivation, Performance, and Reinforcement in Rehabilitation

3.6.1. Motivation

Empirical evidence supports the notion that the ways and means of implementing marginal motivation is the single most important problem in rehabilitation (Diamond, Weiss, & Grynbaum, 1968; Fishman, 1962). In a discussion of the management of rehabilitation patients, Meyerson *et al.* (1960) defined the problem of motivation in behavioral terms as "the task of specifying adequate reinforcers." Fordyce (1968) operationalized one's being motivated as engaging in the behavior of interest at an acceptable rate. The operant model conceives of marginal motivation as being exclusively a case of poorly arranged, inefficient, or insufficient reinforcement. Motivation of the patient can be achieved by arranging the environment so that its desirable features are available only upon engagement and/or achievement in rehabilitation training.

What are the specific factors involved in the motivation, performance, and reinforcement aspects of physical rehabilitation? Patients must often learn to do or perform in different ways than they have been used to doing. Sometimes new behaviors must be learned; sometimes existing behaviors must be changed. A major problem arising in rehabilitation is determining how to motivate and pace individuals so that they perform as expected. Disabled people are often afraid that they cannot learn new skills and sometimes fear that they will be unable to relearn behaviors to the level of their premorbid skills. A patient's avoidance of the fact or denial that he or she has residual disabilities may lead to a reluctance to try a rehabilitation program. Conversely, some individuals may overlook the fact that they have been left with some residual abilities in addition to their disabilities. Age-related decrements in performance have been observed in animal studies. Whether this is due to loss of motivation or to changes in various kinds of capacities is unclear (Jakubczak, 1973). There is an extensive human research literature that also demonstrates the slowing of response speeds in later life. These findings bear no apparent relationship to intelligence test results (Botwinick, 1977). In the elderly, therefore, physical disability may be compounded by age-related performance decrements. When these factors are considered in conjunction with the realities of the environments of the disabled elderly, which often preclude the use of powerful reinforcers, one can see how motivational problems can arise and how patient management can be complicated (Belmont, Benjamin, Ambrose, & Restuccia, 1969; Masterman, 1958; McDaniel, 1969; Meyerson et al., 1960; Wilmore, 1968). Fordyce (1971) explored the possibility that motivational problems may arise when the disabled individual finds his or her disability to be punishing because of the loss of prior sources of positive reinforcement. In such a situation, a patient may avoid punishment by engaging in behaviors that keep him or her out of rehabilitation programs. Similarly, when participating in rehabilitation activities, escape behaviors by the patient can serve to terminate the aversive aspects of the disability (e.g., pain) and rehabilitation programs (e.g., exercise).

Other problems encountered in attempts to modify patients' behaviors are exemplified by situations in which patients appear to understand what it is they are supposed to do but often do not seem to perform in consonance with this understanding. Many rehabilitation problems arise when attempts to modify people's behavior are made by explaining or telling the individual something instead of altering the environment (Brunner, 1969) in conjunction with providing verbal instructions. Another means of influencing the patient's behavior might be the utilization of performance feedback (Madison & Herring, 1960).

Elderly poststroke or other CNS-damaged patients often have sensory and motor disturbances and possible mood or affective disturbances as well as other disabilities unrelated to their stroke. They constitute a group who may represent particularly difficult motivational problems to rehabilitation personnel. Whether such a patient's apparent withdrawal or disinterest in a rehabilitation program is due to actual boredom, fear, depression, or neurological factors is not always certain. That such symptoms may well lend themselves to behavioral interventions is clear.

3.6.2. Performance

An objective means of looking at a patient's involvement and success in a rehabilitation program is to observe and quantify the patient's activity performance. An assessment of performance should not be confused with an evaluation of ability, as having the ability to do something does not guarantee that it will be done. Performance is the observable, quantifiable means by which we can assess the patient's success at his or her rehabilitation program. It is operationalized in terms of what specifically the patient is doing, how frequently, at what rate, at what speed, and so on. Someone may have the physical and mental capacities to learn a technique, but until he or she has learned to do so, that ability does not exist. Unless a patient demonstrates an ability, its performance cannot be evaluated. It should be obvious that a great many variables (e.g., strength, cognitive processes, attitudes, pain, and so forth) can influence both a patient's abilities and performance (Berger & Layne, 1969; Cain, 1969; Fordyce, 1971).

Welford (1977), in a detailed discussion of motor performance and the elderly, noted that there is some reason to believe that simple reaction times in the elderly seem to demonstrate a greater degree of change than do reflex times, indicating that the changes are due to central processes. There is also evidence that changes in sensory and perceptual mechanism in the elderly are fairly constant across sensory modalities, implying either some commonality of change affecting all sensory and perceptual mechanisms or some central change. Slowness in old age, Welford (1977) states, is unrelated to a lack of motivation. With regard to the increases in reaction time seen in the elderly, it is unclear whether changes in performance strategy, such as increased cautiousness, or a general sensorimotor deterioration account for these changes. And finally, there is ample evidence that exercise can increase physical capacities in the elderly (Welford, 1977). Thus, it is obvious that factors such as the sensorimotor changes or slowing of response times seen in normal elderly people might become especially important to consider in the elderly who have experienced a stroke or other neurological insult. How to evaluate, instruct, interact with, and treat such a patient, and what to expect in terms of clinical outcome, are all factors that hinge on age-related sensorimotor changes as well as the pathological events the patient has experienced.

3.6.3. Reinforcement

A variety of factors that may influence a patient's performance have been delineated. The etiology of such performance-impedance is not the crucial issue in rehabilitation. What is most important is how to maximize the patient's performance and to learn specifically what to do in the event that a patient is not fully cooperative in carrying out programs involving existing skills or in programs geared towards the development of new skills.

Generally defined, a reinforcement is an event that increases the likelihood of the response which it follows. As rehabilitation is concerned precisely with the issue of how to change the frequency or likelihood of response, it is the nature of these reinforcers to which we shall now shift our attention. Rehabilitation may require the performance of tasks that in and of themselves may be aversive or unrewarding. One cannot rely upon any intrinsically rewarding aspects of training to increase performance gains. In addition, the natural environment is not as likely to reinforce rehabilitation behaviors as other behaviors.

To learn, change, or maintain a behavior, different reinforcers may be required following the development of a disability. The chronically ill or those suffering physical injury or disability may have marked changes in their systems of reinforcement following hospital admission and resulting from the withdrawal or many learned and primary reinforcers. The main task in working with such individuals becomes finding ways of reinstituting a system of reinforcers to permit the shaping of desired behaviors (Meyerson et al., 1960; Staats, 1966). Ideally the rehabiliation process should utilize reinforcers that supersede the specific training situation and incorporate secondary motivating properties for continuing the behavior. The application of reinforcers of this type will increase the likelihood that a patient will maintain a behavior after treatment and in a variety of situations. In other words, developing secondary motivating properties will increase the likelihood that target behavior performance will generalize to nontreatment settings.

Another consideration when choosing reinforcers for rehabilitation programs involves an examination of the individual undergoing treatment. The reinforcers traditionally used with psychiatric populations or children may not be maximally effective with physically handicapped adults. Primary and secondary reinforcers may exert differential effects on similarly handicapped individuals in the same age groups (Meyerson *et al.*, 1960). A major problem encountered by rehabilitation personnel is one of determining specifically what contingencies can be utilized to lead to greater accomplishments in rehabilitation. Treatment and contingency programs must be individualized, clearly specified, and systematic in their monitoring of behavior and application.

A variety of researchers have examined the problem of determining optimally effective reinforcers in a rehabilitation setting. Perseverance at a task has been found to differ with the patient's objective evaluation of the task as difficult or easy. This differential effect is attenuated when approval is given for successful performance or failure rate is manipulated (Wyer, 1968). Social reinforcement has been described as an effective (Baltes & Barton, 1977; McDonald & Butler, 1974; and McDonald, 1978) but often mismanaged reinforcer (Ayllon & Houghton, 1962; Kerr, Meyerson, & Michael, 1965, pp. 366–370). Improvement may not always be an effective reinforcer, since maximal recovery may in some cases be far below premorbid levels of function (Michael, 1970a), seeming to the patient, and perhaps to the therapist, a relatively unimpressive accomplishment.

Various primary reinforcers have been evaluated for effect on exercise performance (Rushall & Pettinger, 1969). Rest pauses serve as effective reinforcers for both normal and handicapped persons (Azrin, 1960; Kerr & Meyerson, 1964). Token reinforcements have been favorably discussed, as they can be used in a variety of situations, are available immediately upon behavior performance, can be used in the absence of reinforcers in the natural environment, and can be used where other forms of reinforcement may be inadequate (Fordyce *et al.*, 1971; Goodkin, 1970; Greenberg, Scott, Pisa, & Friesen, 1975; Michael, 1970a; and Rice *et al.*, 1968). Libb and Clements (1969) demonstrated that token reinforcement can successfully be used with geriatric exercise patients.

In some situations it is of interest to reduce the frequency or rate of undesirable behaviors in addition to facilitating the development of desired behaviors. Time out from positive reinforcement has been explored as one successful means of achieving such response suppression, although its benefit can be diminished in situations where the behavior to be decreased is an operant response simultaneously maintained by another positive reinforcer (Baer, 1962; Ferster & Appel, 1961; Holz, Azrin, & Ayllon, 1963).

Ideally, once an individual has undergone a rehabilitation program, the learned behaviors will generalize to other situations and be maintained over time. In short, the goal of rehabilitation is the achievement of maximal independence. A step that facilitates the realization of these goals is the specification of treatment objectives, clarifying them for the benefit of both therapist and patient. Goal specification simplifies performance and the process of progress evaluation (Fordyce, 1971). Although it has been demonstrated that many complex behaviors can be learned in the absence of an understanding of what is to be done (Meyerson et al., 1960), there is merit to the argument that inadequate knowledge of the task as well as unclear self-knowledge interfere with an individual's ability to plan and execute a behavior most efficiently (Franks, 1969; Kanfer & Marston, 1961; Kanfer & Phillips, 1970; Taylor & Parsons, 1970). Meyerson et al. (1960) discussed the merits of self-esteem achieved through feedback as being a type of intrinsic, self-monitoring, self-dispensing reinforcer that is much more desirable in terms of portability, generalization, and maintenance of behavior than any extrinsic reinforcer (Franks, 1969; Goldiamond, 1965; Meyerson et al., 1960). The concept of self-reinforcement is especially pertinent to the treatment of the handicapped, as such individuals have already suffered loss of function with concomitant losses or self-esteem. To develop or redevelop such self-esteem in the handicapped furthers their psychological as well as their physical well-being—that is, if the two can truly be separated.

3.7. Supportive Experimental Evidence for the Use of Behavior Modification in Physical Rehabilitation

Behavior modification has been defined as the systematic application of reinforcement theory and behavioral principles to bring about desired changes in behavior. Token reinforcement has been successfully used with a cerebral-palsied patient (Kolderie, 1971). External reinforcement has been successfully used with patients suffering sensory deficit. Feedback has been effectively used in orthotics (bracing) training (Trombly, 1966), to teach minimal weight bearing in gait training and also to teach head control to a wheelchair-bound mentally and physically handicapped child (Grove, 1970).

Behavioral management has been successfully used in the treatment of tilt-table patients complaining of dizziness and to increase the fluid intake of spinal-cord-injured patients (Fordyce, 1968). Pain, often a serious interference to physical treatment, has been controlled with reinforcement techniques (Fordyce, 1968; Fordyce et al., 1968). Pain and disruptive behaviors have been diminished by the manipulation of social reinforcement in a physical therapy setting (Hollon, 1973). Further work has been done with hygienic activities, activities of daily living, and exercise activities (Cain, 1969; Cushing, 1969; Fordyce, 1971; Trotter & Inman, 1968). Behavior modification programs have been used for speech instruction and with mute individuals (Kerr, Meyerson, &

Michael, 1965), with aphasic individuals, and also to train patients' spouses as supplemental speech therapists (Goodkin, 1966, 1970). Grove (1970), in his work with cerebral-palsied children, found that ambulation (walking) and wheelchair propulsion behaviors could be initiated, increased, and maintained through behavior modification techniques. And Garber (1971) made successful use of operant procedures in his attempt to modify drooling behaviors in a cerebral-palsied adolescent. Goodkin (1966) taught stroke and Parkinson's disease patients to write, keypunch, propel their wheelchairs, speak more clearly, and minimize perseverative speech using behavior modification techniques. Feldman and DiScipio (1972) successfully used desensitization and relaxation techniques to control the anxiety and fear of falling which had interfered with a parkinsonian patient's physical therapy program. Rotondi (1978) demonstrated that systematic desensitization used in conjunction with either muscle tension or muscle relaxation were effective in reducing the social fears of handicapped persons.

As mentioned earlier, several studies involving the use of electromyography (EMG) and biofeedback have been conducted. Although the auditory and visual displays provided by the EMG were found to be effective aids in improving electromyographic muscle activity in hemiplegics, a more limited effect was noted on functional retraining (Mroczek et al., 1978). Skrotzky, Gallenstein, and Osternig (1978) found EMG feedback useful in muscle training with cerebral-palsied patients but expressed concern about what may have been a failure by their patients to transfer newly acquired motor skills to their ADL. In other studies, Basmajian et al. (1977) and Kiester (1976) showed that biofeedback could be utilized successfully to reduce the spasticity associated with hemiplegia. All of these studies were conducted with relatively small patient samples. In a larger study utilizing 52 stroke patients, Wolf et al. (1979) found that numerous variables such as age, duration since stroke, or duration of previous rehabilitation had no significant effect on treatment outcome, whereas biofeedback training did. Their treatment effects were more apparent in lower than in upper extremities. As Fernando and Basmajian (1978) commented, EMG feedback can serve as an attention getter, general motivator, and evaluation tool for both patients and therapists. As to the state of the art, Inglis et al. (1976) commented that EMG biofeedback may be regarded with cautious optimism as a treatment for neuromuscular disorders, as EMG studies, on the whole, lack methodological rigor. Many studies have not utilized control groups and often little information has been provided regarding the condition of the patients, feedback procedures, or possible placebo effects of treatment. Yet almost all EMG biofeedback studies demonstrate that virtually all patients who had failed to respond to other forms of physical therapy did respond to biofeedback training. Biofeedback would seem to be most effectively utilized in conjunction with, not in lieu of, traditional physical rehabilitation treatments. Further experimental study of these procedures is certainly warranted (Keefe & Surwit, 1978).

Baltes and Barton (1977) reviewed various operant and nonoperant research and concluded that operant research has demonstrated its potential efficacy with regard to the modification or reversal of behaviors in old age. Hoyer, Mishara, and Reibel (1975) observed that "despite the general acceptance of the efficacy of behavior modification techniques and approaches by clinical psychologists, little if any mention is made of behavior therapy in recent reviews of clinical psychology of aging." Yet they went on to demonstrate that behavior modification techniques are becoming increasingly accepted as a treatment alternative for use with elderly people. Behavior modification has been used successfully in the reestablishment of verbal interactions among elderly nursing home residents; in the increasing of exercise, eating, walking, and verbal behavior; and in the decreasing of self-injurious behaviors and urinary incontinence. The resocialization of elderly nursing home residents has also been effected using operant techniques (Mueller & Atlas, 1972). Although the establishment of token economies for elderly persons has been rare, they have been found to be more effective than no-treatment controls. Mishara (1978) found that both a token economy as well as a milieu program could bring about desired behavioral changes in demented nursing home residents. An important outcome of his study was the demonstration that many chronically debilitated elderly patients who were previously thought to have no rehabilitation potential did in fact improve. Urinary incontinence and requirements for staff assistance were shown to improve with treatment. And the highly structured token economy system had the apparent effect of making the treatment staff feel as if they were successful in their effort, probably because observable goals were defined and evaluated. Thus, even when rehabilitation gains are modest, they can become evident to both staff and patients.

3.8. Behavior Modification Treatment with Neurologically Impaired Older Adults

In a previously unreported study, this author examined the effects of behavior modification treatment program on a neurologically handicapped population (Sufrin, 1975). The subjects were 57 men and 3 women with a mean age of 61 years. All were patients from a general hospital rehabilitation program and all underwent physical therapy treatment at least three times a week for a minimum of 6 weeks. Of the 60 subjects, half had nonneurological (primarily orthopedic) diagnoses and half CNS (primarily stroke) diagnoses. Pretreatment evaluations were conducted on all patients. Following this, goal behaviors and intermediate target behaviors were designated for each subject in the areas of mobility training, active exercise, and active resistive exercise.

This experiment employed a nested design whereby the subjects were divided into four treatment groups. Groups I and III consisted of neurologically involved patients while Groups II and IV were composed of those with nonneurological diagnoses. Experimental Groups I and II were treated with a behavior modification paradigm and control Groups III and IV were exposed to a traditional treatment program that included randomly assigned, response-independent reinforcement for predesignated tasks. The reinforcers to which all patients were exposed included performance feedback (poster-sized progress charts), rest (time out from the physical therapy program), and social attention (by staff). These reinforcers were chosen because they were readily available in a natural physical therapy setting. Randomized sequencing of behavior-reinforcement pairs determined the temporal order in which the various behaviors were treated at a rate of one every 2 weeks for a duration of 6 weeks. Patient assignments were made in the manner usually employed in the treatment facility. Other than the use of a contingent reinforcement paradigm in the experimental groups, there were no differences in the physical therapy activities performed by the experimental and control groups.

The physical therapy staff who were to provide the evaluation and treatment of all subjects were instructed in the underlying principles and mechanisms for conducting a behavioral treatment program. Throughout the experimental program, the primary researcher was frequently available in the physical therapy clinic to advise and supervise the staff physical therapists about dispensing reinforcers and maintaining initial and weekly evaluation records on all subjects. Nontherapist behavioral observers were utilized to monitor and record patient behaviors.

Following the completion of the experimental period, each subject was rated as to whether his or her performance at that time was greater than, equal to, or less than the levels expected at the time target behaviors were defined. When the behaviorally treated, neurologically involved experimental Group I was compared to its control Group III, the subjects in Group I were found to have accomplished or exceeded their behavioral objectives significantly more frequently than did control sub-

jects. Similarly, behaviorally treated, non-neurologically involved patients in Group II were found to have accomplished or exceeded their
behavioral objectives significantly more frequently than did control subjects in Group IV.

Further analyses revealed that rest was a more effective reinforcer for
brain-damaged patients, while social attention and feedback were found
to have equal reinforcement value for both diagnostic groups. Brain-
damaged people frequently display a greater degree of fatigability than
do orthopedic patients. Fatigue can lead not only to a loss of physical
stamina but also to an inability to concentrate on activity performance.
This effect is usually seen to a lesser extent with the non-brain-damaged
and may have accounted for the greater reinforcing value of rest for brain-
damaged patients. Clinically, rest is an ideal reinforcer, as it is freely
available. If rest is to be used as a reinforcer, it should be specified as such
and treatment activity performance should be required to meet criterion
before a patient is permitted to rest. If treatment programs overtax a
patient, they become aversive, thereby becoming negatively reinforcing
when the program is stopped for rest periods. In clinical situations, it
might be worth experimenting with modifying treatment sessions or
making them shorter to lessen their degree of aversiveness when rest
periods might be disruptive to a treatment program.

Active exercises are range-of-motion activities performed by the patient with or without the elimination of gravity. Active–resistive exercises are range-of-motion activities performed against manual or mechanical resistance. Both active and active–resistive exercise task
performance levels were found to be significantly affected by the use of
contingent reinforcement with brain-damaged and non-brain-damaged
patients. Mobility training was not found to be affected by the use of
contingent reinforcement in either diagnostic group. A consistent program of reinforcement used with stroke patients can help them supplement their own impaired sensory input with alternative feedback to aid
them in assessing and modifying their own performance.

In summary, the findings of this study demonstrated that behaviorally treated subjects were more likely than traditionally treated subjects to reach the treatment goals set for them by their therapists. The
question might be raised here as to whether the goal-setting behaviors
used by physical therapists or other allied health or medical personnel
might not be affected by the characteristics of the institutions for which
or within which they work. Such variation could lead to somewhat
limited goals being set for a patient in an acute-care facility, while a
rehabilitation center patient might have a treatment plan that incorporated comprehensive, long-term goals. A patient in an extended-care

facility might have a program consisting of only maintenance and non-aggressive treatment goals. One could speculate that even if a nursing home patient were to accomplish rehabilitation goals, his or her ADL performance might not make a corresponding shift. That is, for some patients in some facilities, improvement might not lead to discharge, independent living, or—on a more modest scale—a different existence within the long-term-care setting itself. It is for these reasons that the adoption of behavior modification programs—with their clearly specified treatment goals, objective monitoring of progress, and accompanying contingencies—might make a welcome addition to many less clearly defined rehabilitation programs. The principles of contingency arrangement, record keeping, treatment success, treatment failure, and program revision are present in all clinical settings. The introduction of systematically applied behavior modification programs as a component of or adjunct to existing treatment programs might be a welcome and necessary addition.

3.9. The Utilization and Training of Rehabilitation Staff as Behavioral Engineers

Physical rehabilitation is a teaching–learning process. All the ingredients needed for the implementation of a behavior modification program are present in every rehabilitation program, but they are often not arranged in a maximally effective manner. Most rehabilitation personnel have not received training in the form of behavior modification programming. Most rehabilitation staff people are rightfully proud of the warm and caring atmosphere that characterizes most rehabilitation settings and staff–patient interactions. Of all the treatment services a physically disabled patient is likely to receive, that of physical rehabilitation is apt to be the most frequent, ongoing, and supportive interaction and is one that has great potential for affecting a patient.

However, years of observation by this author, as both a physical therapist and as a clinical psychologist, indicate that staff attention is often mismanaged in clinical situations. Boisterous or disruptive patients are often the recipients of considerable attention from staff, while quiet, withdrawn, or aphasic patients infrequently have conversations or interactions initiated by staff beyond those minimally required by the therapeutic interaction. Sometimes a therapist working with a nonverbal patient will chat with another patient while for the most part ignoring the patient being treated.

The psychologist who is interested in introducing behavioral techniques into physical rehabilitation or long-term-care settings might be well advised to utilize such behavioral observations when making initial contacts with those whom he or she intends to persuade that benefit can be derived by the modification of traditional treatment procedures. Many rehabilitation personnel are resistant (as are most of us) to suggestions that tried and true ways be changed or, even more distressingly, that the traditional ways of working with patients might be less than optimally effective. Keeping these factors in mind, it should be recognized that the success of any treatment program will only be as good as are the efforts of those providing direct treatment services. Department head support does not guarantee line worker commitment.

Couch and Allen (1973) discussed some of these considerations with regard to the implementation of a behavior modification program in a rehabilitation facility. They emphasized the importance of staff training and continuing in-service or consultant availability when conducting such a program. Other authors have commented on different but relevant aspects of such program implementation. Reppucci and Saunders (1974), in their excellent discussion of the difficulties encountered with the establishment of a behavior modification program in a natural setting, stressed that a program lacking the support of its staff members cannot possibly survive. An example of attitudinal difficulties encountered by Sufrin (1975) was exemplified by the comment of one staff physical therapist who stated, "I don't think it would do the physical therapist any good to have to stand with him [the patient] on his bad days giving him chips. . . . it would be a waste of time to put the patient on an experimental program." Sufrin (1975) found that her frequent availability for both supervision and procedural clarification during the entire duration of the study served to answer questions or alleviate the uncertainties that the physical therapy staff had regarding the implementation of a behavior modification program. Such availability also served to improve and maintain the accuracy and skill with which the program was conducted.

For potentially beneficial techniques such as behavior modification to be taken from the laboratory to a clinical setting, attention to staff training, patience, and flexibility is necessary. Without a fully informed and maximally cooperative staff, the psychologist or behavioral engineer has no control over any aspect of behavior or contingency management. Behavioral program development in a physical therapy department must take into account that the staff involved in the program are professionals with previously learned clinical and technical knowledge. Staff members may approach the development of a new program with enthusiasm or may feel threatened or inadequate if the suggestion is made that their approach to patient care may require revision or modification.

Such diverse attitudes can exert a variety of influences on the manner in which a program may be conducted as well as on its subsequent outcomes.

Conflicting demands on the physical therapist, or any other involved rehabilitation personnel, may exist at any time. Demands by other patients, a schedule that is too full, or simply a lack of cooperation may seriously disrupt that prescribed pattern of dispensing reinforcers. It is necessary for the psychologist or behavioral engineer to be aware of these potential difficulties and to provide adequate instruction, supervision, and consultation, so that as many potential problems as possible may be avoided. For a behavior modification program to be successfully implemented in a natural setting, the psychologist who will be involved would be well advised to meet the staff informally and get to know the nature and peculiarities of the treatment setting before formulating plans with any great degree of specificity. Initially focusing on areas with which the rehabilitation staff would welcome some assitance will facilitate entry into the setting. Disruptive, aggressive, or uninterested patients, preferably those who show likelihood of responding to a behavior modification program, could be the first patients worked with. Once the psychologist has become familiar with the treatment setting and the staff and once the rehabilitation staff has made clear its preferences for interventions, then and only then is it time to embark on the prerequisite staff training and treatment program development. And, as in any instructional setting, ongoing supervision and guidance of the treatment staff by the psychologist is essential to the success of any program. If these conditions are met, both staff and patients might find themselves pleasantly surprised with the results of behavior modification rehabilitation programs.

4. Summary and Conclusions

The prevalence of physical disability and brain damage secondary to stroke among elderly people has been reviewed. Numerous issues surrounding physical rehabilitation programs and those providing them have been discussed. The successful rehabilitation of elderly people has been shown to require comprehensive and cooperative treatment programs. The principles of learning, contingent reinforcement, and techniques of behavior modification have been shown to be potentially valuable assets in the development of physical rehabilitation programs for the brain-damaged elderly. Considering the number of issues associated with the treatment of brain-damaged or other chronically ill elderly, relatively little clinical psychological research has been conducted with these groups. Further research in the area of treatment for such people is needed, as is further work in the area of comprehensive rehabilitation program development suitable for implementation in the great variety of treatment settings that serve elderly individuals.

ACKNOWLEDGMENT

The author wishes to thank Laura Carstensen for her valuable comments and editorial assistance during the preparation of this chapter.

5. References

Ayllon, T., & Houghton, E. Control of behavior in schizophrenic patients by food. *Journal of the Experimental Analysis of Behavior*, 1962, 5, 343–352.

Ayllon, T., & Michael, J. The psychiatric nurse as a behavioral engineer. *Journal of the Experimental Analysis of Behavior*, 1959, 2, 323–334.

Azrin, N. H. Use of rest periods as reinforcers. *Psychological Reports*, 1960, 7, 240.

Baer, D. M. Laboratory control of thumb sucking by withdrawal and representation of reinforcement. *Journal of the Experimental Analysis of Behavior*, 1962, 5, 525–528.

Baer, D. M., Wolf, M. M., & Risley, T. R. Some current dimensions of applied behavioral analysis. *Journal of Applied Behavioral Analysis*, 1968, 1(1), 91–97.

Baltes, M. M., & Barton, E. M. New approaches toward aging: A case for the operant model. *Educational Gerontology*, 1977, 2, 383–405.

Basmajian, J. V., Regenos, E. M., & Baker, M. P. Rehabilitating stroke patients with biofeedback. *Geriatrics*, 1977, 32(7), 85–88.

Belmont, I., Benjamin, H., Ambrose, J., & Restuccia, R. Effect of cerebral damage on motivation in rehabilitation. *Archives of Physical Medicine and Rehabilitation*, 1969, 50, 507–511.

Berger, R., & Layne, R. Strength and motor ability as factors toward physical education. *Research Quarterly*, 1969, 40, 635–637.

Birren, J. E., & Schaie, K. W. (Eds.). *Handbook of the psychology of aging*. New York: Van Nostrand-Reinhold, 1977.

Blanchard, E. B., & Young, L. D. Clinical applications of biofeedback training. *Archives of General Psychiatry*, 1974, 30, 573–589.

Bonner, C. D. *Medical care and rehabilitation of the aged and chronically ill* (3rd ed.). Boston: Little, Brown, 1974.

Botwinick, J. Intellectual abilities. In J. Birren & K. W. Schaie (Eds.), *Handbook of the psychology of aging*. New York: Van Nostrand-Reinhold, 1977.

Bowman, B. R., Baker, L. L., & Waters, R. L. Positional feedback and electrical stimulation: An automated treatment for the hemiplegic wrist. *Archives of Physical Medicine and Rehabilitation*, 1979, 60, 497–502.

Brantl, V. M., & Brown, M. R. (Eds.). *Readings in gerontology*. St. Louis: C. V. Mosby, 1973.

Brunner, B. Personality and motivating factors influencing adult participation in vigorous physical activity. *Research Quarterly*, 1969, 40, 464–469.

Busse, E. Organic brain syndromes. In E. Busse & E. Pfeiffer (Eds.), *Mental illness in later life*. Washington, D.C.: American Psychiatric Association, 1973.

Busse, E. W., & Pfeiffer, E. (Eds.). *Mental illness in later life*. Washington, D.C.: American Psychiatric Association, 1973.

Busse, E. W., & Pfeiffer, E. (Eds.). *Behavior and adaptation in late life* (2nd ed.). Boston: Little, Brown, 1977.

Cain, L. Determining the factors that affect rehabilitation. *Journal of the American Geriatrics Society*, 1969, *17*(6), 595–604.

Couch, R. H., & Allen, C. M. Behavior modification in rehabilitation facilities: A review. *Journal of Applied Rehabilitation Counseling*, 1973, *4*, 88–95.

Cushing, M. When counseling fails—then what? *Journal of Rehabilitation*, 1969, *35*, 18–20.

Diamond, M. D., Weiss, A. J., & Grynbaum, B. The unmotivated patient. *Archives of Physical Medicine and Rehabilitation*, 1968, *49*, 281–284.

Eisdorfer, C., & Lawton, M. P. (Eds.). *The psychology of adult development and aging*. Washington, D.C.: American Psychological Association, 1973.

Estes, E. H. Health experience in the elderly. In E. Busse & E. Pfeiffer (Eds.), *Behavior and adaptation in late life*. Boston: Little, Brown, 1977.

Feldman, M. C., & DiScipio, W. J. Integrating physical therapy with behavior therapy: A case study. *Physical Therapy*, 1972, *52*(12), 1283–1285.

Fernando, C. K., & Basmajian, J. V. Biofeedback in physical medicine and rehabilitation. *Biofeedback and Self-Regulation*, 1978, *3*(4), 435–455.

Ferster, C. B., & Appel, J. B. Punishment of S$^\triangle$ responding in matching to sample by time-out from positive reinforcement. *Journal of the Experimental Analysis of Behavior*, 1961, *4*, 45–56.

Fishman, S. Amputation. In J. F. Garrett & E. S. Levine (Eds.), *Psychological Practices with the Physically Disabled*. New York: Columbia University Press, 1962.

Folstein, M. F., Maiberger, R., & McHugh, P. R. Mood disorders as specific complications of stroke. *Journal of Neurology, Neurosurgery and Psychiatry*, 1977, *40*, 1018–1020.

Fordyce, W. E. *The learning model and psychology's role in medical rehabilitation*. Paper presented at a meeting of the American Psychological Association, San Francisco, 1968.

Fordyce, W. E. In *Report No. 5*, Region IX Rehabilitation Research Institute, January, 1970.

Fordyce, W. E. Psychological assessment and measurement. In F. H. Krusen (Ed.), *Handbook of physical medicine and rehabilitation* (2nd ed.). Philadelphia: Saunders, 1971.

Fordyce, W. E. *Behavioral methods for chronic pain and illness*. St. Louis: Mosby, 1976.

Fordyce, W. E., Fowler, R. S., Lehman, J. F., & DeLateur, B. J. Some implications of learning problems in chronic pain. *Journal of Chronic Diseases*, 1968, *21*, 179–190.

Fordyce, W. E., Fowler, R. S., Sand, P. L., & Trieschmann, R. B. Behavior analysis systems in medical rehabilitation facilities. *Journal of Rehabilitation*, 1971, *37*, 29–33.

Fordyce, W. E., Fowler, R. S., Lehman, J. F., DeLateur, B. F., Sand, P. L., & Trieschmann, R. B. Operant Conditioning in the treatment of chronic pain. *Archives of Physical Medicine and Rehabilitation*, 1973, *54*, 399–408.

Fowler, R. S., Fordyce, W. E., & Berni, R. Operant conditioning in chronic illness. *American Journal of Nursing*, 1969, *69*, 1226–1228.

Fozard, J. L., & Thomas, J. C., Jr. Psychology of aging. In J. G. Howells (Ed.), *Modern perspectives in the psychiatry of old age*. New York: Bruner/Mazel, 1975.

Franks, C. M. (Ed.). *Behavior therapy: Appraisal and status*. New York: McGraw-Hill, 1969.

Garber, N. B. Operant procedures to eliminate drooling behavior in a cerebral palsied adolescent. *Developmental Medicine and Child Neurology*, 1971, *13*, 641–644.

Goldiamond, I. Self-control in personal behavior problems. *Psychological Reports*, 1965, *17*, 851–868.

Goodkin, R. Case studies in behavioral research in rehabilitation. *Perceptual and Motor Skills*, 1966, *23*, 171–182.

Goodkin, R. *The modification of verbal behavior in aphasic subjects.* Paper presented at a meeting of the American Psychological Association, Miami, 1970.

Goodglass, H., & Kaplan, E. *Assessment of aphasia and related disorders.* Philadelphia: Lea & Febiger, 1972.

Greenberg, D. J., Scott, S. B., Pisa, A , & Friesen, D. D. Beyond the token economy: A comparison of two contingency programs. *Journal of Consulting and Clinical Psychology*, 1975, *43*, 498–503.

Grossman, M. Rehabilitation and psychiatry: A symposium. *American Journal of Psychiatry*, 1968, *124*, 1369–1374.

Grove, D. N. *Applications of behavioral technology to physical therapy.* Paper presented to the American Psychological Association Physical Therapy Symposium, Miami, 1970.

Gryfe, C. I. Reasonable expectations in geriatric rehabilitation. *Journal of the American Geriatrics Society*, 1979, *27*(5), 237–238.

Hall, V., & Broden, M. Behavior changes in brain-injured children through social reinforcement. In R. Ulrich, T. Stachnik, & J. Mabry (Eds.), *Control of human behavior* (Vol. 2). Glenview, Ill.: Scott, Foresman, 1970.

Hallauer, D. S. Illness behavior—An experimental investigation. *Journal of Chronic Diseases*, 1972, *5*, 599–610.

Henriksen, J. D. Problems in rehabilitation after age sixty-five. *Journal of the American Geriatrics Society*, 1978, *26*(11), 510–512.

Holden, U. P., & Sinebruchow, A. Reality orientation therapy: A study investigating the value of this therapy in the rehabilitation of elderly people. *Age and Aging*, 1978, *7*, 83–90.

Hollon, T. H. Behavior modification in a community hospital rehabilitation unit. *Archives of Physical Medicine and Rehabilitation*, 1973, *54*, 65–68.

Holz, W. C., Azrin, N. H., & Ayllon, T. Elimination of behavior of mental patients by response-produced extinction. *Journal of the Experimental Analysis of Behavior*, 1963, *6*, 407–412.

Howells, J. C. (Ed.). *Modern perspectives in the psychiatry of old age.* New York: Brunner/Mazel, 1975.

Hoyer, W. J., Mishara, B. L., & Reibel, R. G. Problem behaviors as operants: Applications with elderly individuals. *The Gerontologist*, 1975, *15*, 452–456.

Ince, L. *Behavior modification in rehabilitation medicine.* Springfield, Ill.: Thomas, 1976.

Inglis, J., Campbell, D., & Donald, M. W. Electromyographic biofeedback and neuromuscular rehabilitation. *Canadian Journal of Behavioral Science*, 1976, *8*(4), 299–323.

Jakubczak, L. F. Age and animal behavior. In C. Eisdorfer & M. P. Lawton (Eds.). *The psychology of adult development and aging.* Washington, D.C.: American Psychological Association, 1973.

Kanfer, F. H., & Marston, A. R. Verbal conditioning ambiguity and psychotherapy. *Psychological Reports*, 1961, *9*, 461–465.

Kanfer, F. H., & Phillips, J. S. *Learning foundations of behavior therapy.* New York: Wiley, 1970.

Keefe, F. J., & Surwit, R. S. Electromygraphic biofeedback: Behavioral treatment of neuromuscular disorders. *Journal of Behavioral Medicine*, 1978, *1*(1), 13–24.

Kerr, N., & Meyerson, L. *Learning theory and rehabilitation.* New York: Random House, 1964.

Kerr, N., Meyerson, L., & Michael, J. A procedure for shaping vocalizations in a mute child. In L. P. Ullman & L. Krasner (Eds.), *Case studies in behavior modification.* New York: Holt, 1965.

Kiester, M. E. Facilitation of neuromuscular retraining of patients with stroke-related spasticity through electromyographic augmentation of feedback. *Dissertation Abstracts International,* 1976, *37*(1), 1957.

Kolderie, M. L. Behavior modification in the treatment of children with cerebral palsy. *Physical Therapy,* 1971, *51*(10), 1083–1091.

Krusen, F. H., Kottke, F. J., & Ellwood, P. M. (Eds.). *Handbook of physical medicine and rehabilitation* (2nd ed.). Philadelphia: Saunders, 1971.

Kurtzke, J. R. An introduction to the epidemiology of cerebrovascular disease. In F. Scheinberg (Ed.), *Cerebrovascular diseases.* New York: Raven Press, 1976.

Lawton, M. P. The impact of the environment of aging and behavior. In J. Birren & K. W. Schaie (Eds.), *Handbook of the psychology of aging:* New York: Van Nostrand-Reinhold, 1977.

Levenson, C. Rehabilitation of the stroke hemiplegia patient. In F. H. Kruzen, F. J. Kottke, & P. M. Ellwood, Jr. (Eds.), *Handbook of physical medicine and rehabilitation* (2nd ed.). Philadelphia: Saunders, 1971.

Libb, J., & Clements, C. Token reinforcement in an exercise program for hospitalized geriatric patients. *Perceptual and Motor Skills,* 1969, *28*, 957–958.

Madison, H. L., & Herring, M. B. An experimental study of motivation. *American Journal of Occupational Therapy,* 1960, *14*(5), 253–255.

Matarazzo, J. D. Behavioral health and behavioral medicine: Frontiers for a new health psychology. *American Psychologist,* 1980, *35*(9), 807–817.

Masterman, L. E. Some psychological aspects of rehabilitation. *Journal of Rehabilitation,* 1958, *24*, 4–6, 26.

McDaniel, J. *Physical disability and human behavior.* New York: Pergamon Press, 1969.

McDonald, M. Environmental programming for the elderly. *The Gerontologist,* 1978, *18*(4), 350–354.

McDonald, M. L., & Butler, A. K. Reversal of helplessness: Producing walking behavior in nursing home wheelchair residents using behavior modification procedures. *Journal of Gerontology,* 1974, *29*(1), 97–101.

Meyerson, L., Michael, J. L., Mowrer, O. H., Osgood, C. E., & Staats, A. W. Learning, behavior and rehabilitation. In L. H. Foquist (Ed.), *Psychological research and rehabilitation.* Washington, D.C.: American Psychological Association, 1960.

Michael, J. Principles of effective usage. In R. Ulrich, T. Stachnick, & J. Mabry (Eds.), *Control of human behavior.* (Vol. 2). Glenview, Ill.: Scott, Foresman, 1970. (a)

Michael, J. L. Rehabilitation. In C. Neuringer & J. Michael (Eds.), *Behavior modification and clinical psychology.* New York: Appleton Century Crofts, 1970. (b)

Mishara, B. L. Geriatric patients who improve in token economy and general milieu programs: A multivariate analysis. *Journal of Consulting and Clinical Psychology,* 1978, *46*(6), 1340–1348.

Mock, M. B. Rehabilitation of the elderly cardiac patient hampered by bias. *Geriatrics,* 1977, *32*(12), 22–23.

Mroczek, N. S. A treatise on psychology and voluntary motor behavior with an investigation of biofeedback effects on hemiplegias resultant from cerebrovascular accident. *Dissertation Abstracts International,* 1976, *37*(6), 3116–3117. (Abstract)

Mroczek, N., Halpern, D., & McHugh, R. Electromyographic feedback and physical therapy for neuromuscular retraining in hemiplegia. *Archives of Physical Medicine and Rehabilitation,* 1978, *59*, 258–267.

Mueller, D. J., & Atlas, L. Resocialization of regressed elderly residents: A behavioral management approach. *Journal of Gerontology*, 1972, 27(3), 390–392.

Peck, D. F. Operant conditioning and physical rehabilitation. *European Journal of Behavioral Analysis and Modification*, 1976, 3(1), 158–164.

Piggott, R. A. Behavior modification and control in rehabilitation. *Journal of Rehabilitation*, 1969, July–August, 12–14.

Pomerleau, O. E. Behavioral medicine—The contribution of the experimental analysis of behavior to medical care. *American Psychologist*, 1979, 34(8), 654–663.

Reese, E. P. *The analysis of human operant behavior*. Dubuque, Iowa: Brown, 1966.

Reppucci, N. D., & Saunders, J. T. Social psychology of behavior modification—Problems of implementation in natural settings. *American Psychologist*, 1974, 29, 649–660.

Rice, H., McDaniel, M., & Denney, S. Operant conditioning techniques for use in the physical rehabilitation of the multiply handicapped retarded patient. *Journal of the American Physical Therapy Association*, 1968, 4, 342–346.

Roberts, A., Dinsdale, S., Matthews, R., & Cole, T. Modifying persistent undesirable behavior in a medical setting. *Archives of Physical Medicine and Rehabilitation*, 1969, 50, 147–153.

Rotondi, J. M. The differential effectiveness of three methods of behavior therapy in reducing social fear in physically handicapped adults. *Dissertation Abstracts International*, 1978, 38(12), 7238–7239. (Abstract)

Rushall, B., & Pettinger, J. An evaluation of the effect of various reinforcers used as motivation in swimming. *Research Quarterly*, 1969, 40, 540–545.

Seligman, M. E. P., Klein, D. C., & Miller, W. R. Depression. In H. Leitenberg (Ed.), *Handbook of behavior modification and behavior therapy*. Englewood Cliffs, N.J.: Prentice-Hall, 1976.

Skrotzky, K., Gallenstein, J. S., & Osternig, L. R. Effects of electromyographic feedback training on motor control in spastic cerebral palsy. *Physical Therapy*, 1978, 58(5), 547–551.

Spencer, W. Changes in methods and relationships necessary within rehabilitation. *Archives of Physical Medicine and Rehabilitation*, 1969, 50, 566–580.

Staats, A. A case in and a strategy for the extension of learning principles to problems of human behavior. In L. Krasner & L. Ullman (Eds.), *Research in behavior modification*. New York: Holt, 1966.

Stokes, T. F., & Baer, D. An implicit technology of generalization. *Journal of Applied Behavior Analysis*, 1977, 10, 349–367.

Strax, T. E., & Ledebur, J. Rehabilitating the geriatric patient: Potential limitations, *Geriatrics*, 1979, 34(9), 99–101.

Sufrin, E. M. The effects of a behavior modification treatment program on a neurologically handicapped population (Doctoral dissertation, University of Southern California, 1975). *Dissertation Abstracts International*, 1975, 36(6-B), 3077.

Taylor, G. P., & Persons, R. W. Behavior modification techniques in a physical medicine and rehabilitation center. *Journal of Psychology*, 1970, 71, 117–124.

Trombly, C. Principles of operant conditioning: Related to orthotic training of quadriplegic patients. *American Journal of Occupational Therapy*, 1966, 20, 217–220.

Trotter, A., & Inman, D. The use of positive reinforcement in physical therapy. *Journal of the American Physical Therapy Association*, 1968, 4, 347–352.

Ullmann, L. P., & Krasner, L. (Eds.). *Case studies in behavior modification*. New York: Holt, 1965.

Usdin, G., & Hofling, C. K. (Eds.). *Aging: The process and the people*. New York: Bruner/Mazel, 1978.

Welford, A. T. Motor performance. In J. Birren & K. W. Schaie (Eds.), *Handbook of the psychology of aging*. New York: Van Nostrand-Reinhold, 1977.

Wilmore, J. Influence of motivation on physical work capacity and performance. *Journal of Applied Physiology*, 1968, *24*, 459–463.

Wolf, S. L., Baker, M. P., & Kelly, J. L. EMG biofeedback in stroke: Effect of patient characteristics. *Archives of Physical Medicine and Rehabilitation*, 1979, *60*, 96–102.

Wright, W. B. The psychology of rehabilitation. *Lancet*, 1979, *2*, 1179.

Wyer, R. Effects of task reinforcement, social reinforcement and task difficulty on perseverance in achievement-related activity. *Journal of Personality and Social Psychology*, 1968, *8*, 269–276.

7

Strategies for Intervention with Families of Brain-Injured Patients

MITCHELL ROSENTHAL

The advent of rapid advances in the acute neurosurgical management of head-injured adults during the past decade has given rise to an ever-increasing number of survivors of severe brain injury. Epidemiological studies have indicated that the vast proportion of this population are young adults, usually between the ages of 15 to 30 (Rimel, 1979). Despite a prolonged period of unconsciousness (usually a week or more) and resultant evidence of focal or diffuse brain damage, a majority of the survivors regain the ability to ambulate and perform most self-care activities independently (e.g., bathing, grooming, dressing, etc.). However, unlike other severely disabled adults (e.g., spinal cord injury), the brain-injured adult usually displays a variety of cognitive and behavioral deficits that adversely affect the patient's ability to function effectively within the community and family system. Such deficits are often of indefinite duration and can result in prolonged dependence on family members. This state of dependence is often linked to the inability of the head-injured adult to achieve an adequate measure of social and vocational rehabilitation.

MITCHELL ROSENTHAL • Department of Rehabilitation Medicine, Tufts University School of Medicine, Boston, Massachusetts 02111.

Research on the nature and effects of traumatic brain injury has often been directed toward describing the specific medical, functional, and vocational outcomes following brain injury (Jennett & Teasdale, 1976; Najenson, Mendelson, Schechter, David, Mintz, & Grosswasser, 1974; Evans, Bull, Devenport, Hall, Jones, Middleton, Russell, Stichbury, & Whitehead, 1976; Levin & Grossman, 1978). However, little attention has been directed to the impact of the disability upon the family system and toward identifying potential strategies for minimizing family stress and maximizing family adaptation. Yet the most heroic of early neurosurgical efforts and subsequent physical rehabilitation may be of little consequence if the patient cannot be successfully integrated into the family unit and regain a useful function within society.

Past research conducted by Bond (1976); Romano (1974); Panting and Merry (1972); Oddy, Humphrey, and Uttley (1978); and Rosenbaum and Najenson (1976) has attempted to describe the impact of brain injury upon the family. Romano (1974) reported the prevalence of denial as a defensive strategy for families of 13 head-injured adults. Relatives tended to deny both the presence of disability and the potential permanence of deficits. Initially, this may be viewed as an effective coping strategy, inasmuch as full recognition of the presence of brain damage and likelihood of lifelong disability might be overwhelming during the initial stages of recovery. However, the continued utilization of denial for 1, 2, or 3 years postinjury may result in the family's failure to effectively assist their relative in regaining a productive role in society.

Bond (1976) studied 52 patients with severe brain injury and found that mental, rather than physical, deficits were most closely associated with a lack of family cohesion. Panting and Merry (1972) reported that 61% of families interviewed after brain injury reported that they were under considerable stress as a result of the head trauma and its consequences. Oddy *et al.* (1978), in a study of 54 head-injured patients and their families, noted that the stress did not appear to diminish over time (e.g., 1 year postinjury). Level of stress was unrelated to length of hospitalization, degree of physical disability, or severity of stress. Finally, Rosenbaum and Najeson (1976) studied the reactions of wives of brain-injured soldiers in Israel and found that they had a more restricted social life than either the wives of males with spinal cord injuries or of control subjects.

This brief review suggests that head injury can result in significant problems for the families of the head-injured adults and that methods for managing these problems need to be developed to optimize the rehabilitation of these patients.

1. Significant Cognitive and Behavioral Deficits Affecting Family Functioning

To intervene successfully with the families of brain-injured adults, it is critical initially to identify the nature and variety of cognitive and behavioral deficits that can create stress and disrupt the family system. The following listing is not all-inclusive; rather, it is a brief summary of selected deficits that can create maladaptive interactions within the family system.

1.1. Disorders of Communication

An important factor in the successful reintegration of the brain-injured patient into the family is open, effective communication. In the case of the brain-injured adult, communication disorders are usually less severe than are the results of other acquired neurological disorders (e.g., stroke, tumor). Nonetheless, disorders such as aphasia, dysarthria, and apraxia can impair the patient's ability to cope and communicate. Impaired communication skills can adversely affect a person's ability to function independently in activities of daily living or in vocational pursuits and thus create a greater burden for significant others.

1.2. Emotional Regression

As Symonds (1937) noted in his discussion of brain-injured adults, the patient is often observed to be "less of a man and more of a child." It is frequently the case that the newly brain-injured adult demonstrates behavior patterns reminiscent of childhood and adolescence. The patient may display childlike dependency, crave constant attention, display inappropriate affect, or engage in violent temper tantrums. The parent or spouse of the patient may be dismayed and confused by this behavior and express confusion as to the appropriate methods of managing it. Often, significant others may unwittingly contribute to the maintenance of these behaviors by providing attention and positive reinforcement when they occur.

1.3. Frontal Lobe Behavior

Often a patient with brain injury displays a constellation of behaviors identified as a "frontal lobe syndrome." As described by Freedman, Kaplan, and Saddock (1975, pp. 218–219), damage to the frontal lobes may result in a variety of behaviors including aspontaneity, lethargy, flat or dulled affect, irritability, loss of initiative, and lack of goal-directedness. In addition, there may be a loosening of inhibitions, lack of regard for social graces and moral standards, impaired ability to abstract, and inappropriate sexual behavior. The following case example illustrates several components of the frontal lobe syndrome:

Patient: Mr. S.

Mr. S. was a 48-year-old man who received a closed head injury in an automobile accident and sustained bifrontal injuries. Though the patient recovered most of his physical and self-care skills within a short time, his behavior within the rehabilitation hospital was reflective of frontal lobe behavior, such as lack of initiative, aspontaneity, dull affect, and so on. Upon discharge to the home environment, he tended to spend the entire day sitting in front of the TV not speaking unless spoken to, displaying indifference toward his wife and children. He was unable to persist at a household task for more than 15 minutes, after which he lost interest in it. Frequently, he walked outside his home and wandered aimlessly, which caused his family great concern about his safety and welfare.

The patient with frontal lobe behavior tends to need constant supervision and is a considerable burden to family members. Such a patient has the worst prognosis of all traumatically brain-injured patients for return to independent living and vocational productivity.

1.4. Withdrawal from Social Contacts

The patient with severe brain injury suffers a severe blow to his or her self-esteem on account of apparent physical or mental deficits, as well as a perceived loss of self-worth and identity as a productive, well-functioning, competent individual. Usually, feelings of decreased self-esteem are reinforced by the loss of peer contact and social relationships (which often occurs within 3 to 6 months after return to the community). Brain-injured adults perceive themselves as different, handicapped, brain-damaged, and unattractive and tend to isolate themselves or be isolated from their peer groups in the community. The following case example illustrates this problem:

Patient: Miss H.

Miss H., an attractive, intelligent 16-year-old, was injured in an automobile accident and sustained a severe closed head injury. Premorbidly, she was described by family as an outstanding student, musician, and cheerleader and had a very active social life. The only apparent physical residual of the brain injury was a small facial scar and lack of hair (caused by the neurosurgical intervention). Prior to the accident she took great pride in her appearance, especially her long blond hair. Other deficits included a slightly impaired gait and a mild dysfluency in speech. On account of the loss of hair, she viewed herself as extremely unattractive and refused to venture outside the home for approximately 12 months postinjury.

Because of the patient's self-imposed social isolation, the burden was upon the family to provide a meaningful, rewarding, active program within the home setting. The stress experienced by family members who accept this responsibility is truly enormous and usually increases throughout the first 2 years of recovery.

1.5. Presence of Cognitive Deficits

Perhaps the most persistent deficits following traumatic brain injury are cognitive. Though significant recovery of formal intellectual function is observed during the first year postinjury, residual problems in maintaining attention, processing complex information, storage and retrieval of information, problem solving, and inability to use conceptual and abstract thinking are often present and present significant obstacles to the patient and family. In some cases, there is a generalized deficit in intellectual functioning. Since brain injury is most frequently observed between ages 15 and 30, it is likely that such patients are in the prime of their educational and vocational careers. Thus, the brain injury may impose a variety of cognitive deficits that create a seemingly insurmountable hurdle on the road to maximal recovery. The lack of adequate community programs to serve these needs and facilitate educational and vocational restoration creates a situation where the brain-injured person is homebound much of the time. Often families experience anguish and despair in their extensive search for innovative programs that can remediate cognitive deficits and restore premorbid function.

1.6. Inappropriate Social Behavior

As mentioned earlier, the behavior of the brain-injured adult often resembles that of a young child or adolescent. In observing the behavioral patterns of brain-injured adults, one notes that such patients are unaware of the consequences and implications of their behavior. Often the patient engages in verbal or motor perseveration, pathological laughter, or inappropriate sexual behavior. The presence of this con-

stellation of behaviors is a source of embarassment and frustration for
the family. Inappropriate sexual behavior is especially troublesome for
families who are confused as to its etiology (functional or organic) and
uncertain as to the best method of managing it.

1.7. Depression

Often the recovery of the brain-injured adult is accompanied by a
gradually progressive awareness of the multifaceted loss in physical and
mental functioning imposed by the injury. Despite the restoration of
mobility skills, the young adult may be less able to participate in strenuous physical exercise (e.g., athletic activities). Though the person can
perform most self-care activities independently, residual perceptual–motor problems can preclude the resumption of driving an automobile. On account of prophylactic seizure medication (e.g., Dilantin,
Phenobarbitol), the young adult is often asked to restrict or eliminate
alcohol intake. Often, the injury results in changes in cosmesis, such as
scars and cranial defects, that can greatly alter body image and self-
concept. Due to the persistence of cognitive deficits such as memory
impairment and slower rate of information processing, the patient may
have an acquired learning disability that will interfere with the successful resumption of academic pursuits.

The result of this recognition of loss in psychosocial function and
rewarding activities is frequently an onset of depression. Depression
may be observed in the form of decreased activity level, self-derogation,
negative affect, feelings of worthlessness, and occasionally suicidal idea-
tion. The brain-injured person may say "I wish I were still in a coma" or
"Why did they save my life if there's nothing for me." The presence of
depression may have a major impact upon the family, who feel impotent
and frustrated. The brain-injured person who experiences depression is
likely to be more passive, dependent, and less productive, thus imposing a greater burden on family members, who feel a sense of responsibility for maintaining the emotional well-being of their loved one.

1.8. Inability to Resume Premorbid Role within the Family

Because of such deficits, the brain-injured adult is usually prevented from resuming premorbid roles within the family. In the marital
relationship, it is often observed that the brain-injured husband who
was formerly the assertive partner is now the passive one. Whereas the
brain-injured patient may have been a "breadwinner," the family may
now be dependent on federal and state agencies for financial support.

Frequently, siblings experience guilt feelings about their brain-injured relative and will report dismay at the changes in role relationships that occur. The likelihood of alterations in role relationships is greatly enhanced when the patient sustains significant cognitive or behavioral deficits. The observed changes in the patient can be a stimulus for marital discord. Whereas, in the initial 6 to 12 months postinjury, the spouse may be quite willing and able to accept these changes, the realization that the partner "may never be the same" is an overwhelming stress on the spouse's coping mechanisms. The recognition that certain mental changes may be permanent is extremely difficult for parents to recognize and accept.

The cognitive and behavioral deficits described represent a sampling rather than an exhaustive listing of the potential problems of the brain-injured adult that can impair the functioning of the family unit. It is noteworthy that the impact of these deficits is rarely experienced by the patient or family unit until discharge from the rehabilitation hospital into the community. At that point, however, contact with the health care team is probably diminished, and the family feels alone in dealing with these overwhelming problems. Families may be reluctant to seek out appropriate professional help. It is therefore imperative that health care professionals anticipate family distress and establish the appropriate mechanisms for providing family support prior to discharge from the hospital.

2. Assessing the Need for Family Intervention

Just as early neurological diagnosis and surgical intervention is often necessary to save the life of the brain-injured patient, so is early assessment of the need for the family intervention and selection of the appropriate intervention technique. The diagnostic process may be viewed as consisting of at least three major components: (1) analysis of premorbid history of patient and family; (2) identifying the severity and potential duration of mental and physical deficits; and (3) understanding "signals" from the family that would appear to reflect a need for intervention.

2.1. Analysis of Premorbid History

The complexity of the process of rehabilitation of the brain-injured adult is partly attributable to the uniqueness of each patient and family.

In the case of brain injury, it has often been observed that the head-injured population seems to consist of a significant percentage of young people with a history of antisocial behavior or impulse-control problems. It is not surprising that excessive alcohol intake is correlated with the occurrence of brain injury (Rimel, 1979). In other cases, drug intake may be a contributing factor to the events surrounding a traumatic brain injury. By interviewing family members or significant others, it is often possible to obtain a detailed (though not completely objective) picture of both patient and family prior to the injury. Important components of this history might include a description of intellectual and academic function; peer, marital, and family relationships; vocational history; avocational activities; and antisocial or unusual behavioral problems. Though less sophisticated and accurate than an x-ray or CT scan, the resulting profile provides a necessary baseline for the assessment of the patient and family. It is often the case that a strong correlation exists between a newly disabled person's premorbid history and level of postmorbid adjustment. Therefore, the 19-year-old head-injured victim who had a poor work history, impaired peer relationships, and/or had shown frequent antisocial or rebellious behavior may be prone to significant postinjury adjustment problems. Conversely, the 19-year-old who was successfully employed, had an active and rewarding social life, and had good peer and family relationships may achieve a satisfactory adjustment to the injury. Though this is an oversimplification, it is often observed in clinical practice that there is an important relationship between premorbid history and postmorbid adjustment.

In this regard, it would also be useful to understand the patient and family's ability to handle stress. Did the presence of stress stimulate an expression of aggression, avoidance, or denial? Could the patient tolerate certain stresses better than others (e.g., work vs. family)? The presence of chronic disability secondary to brain injury poses a continuous series of stresses that would greatly tax the resources of an intact individual (i.e., non-brain-injured).

2.2. Identifying the Severity and Duration of Deficits

The ability to predict recovery of mental and physical function is still a very problematic area in brain-injury research. Though Jennett and Bond (1975) and others have developed tools, such as the Glasgow Coma and Outcome Scales, that help predict outcome, it is still difficult to specify the extent, nature, and duration of specific mental and physical deficits for any single patient. This issue is of central importance for the patient and family who are struggling to accept the permanence of the injury and effectively plan for the future.

Though physical deficits are often greatly reduced at 6 months postinjury, residual deficits in vision, hearing, mobility, self-care, strength, coordination, and balance may exist. The patient whose vision may be compromised as a result of the injury and prove to be insensitive to remedial measures may be greatly limited in ADL or vocational productivity, thus requiring a greater dependence on family for supervision of daily activities. Helping the patient and family acknowledge and accept these limitations can be a formidable yet critical task for the helping professional.

The prediction of residual mental sequelae is even more difficult due to a variety of factors, including a generally slower and less consistent pattern of recovery, environmental factors that may aid or adversely affect the recovery process, and problems in objectively measuring the course of recovery in such areas as memory, social skills, and personality. The family is often informed that *some* mental sequelae of head injury are likely to exist indefinitely. Such information is frequently provided by physicians and is difficult for family members to accept. Within the context of a psychotherapeutic relationship, it is incumbent upon the identified professional (e.g., psychologist, social worker, or counselor) to be prepared to help the family understand the recovery process and provide as honest and accurate information as can be determined and tolerated. An assessment of the family's willingness to accept and utilize this information is crucial to the determination of the appropriate intervention strategy.

2.3. Understanding "Signals" from the Family

Within a rehabilitation setting, it is a rare event when the family of a patient approaches the staff to request assistance in coping with the catastrophic effects of the brain injury. Yet, if the family is to play a central role in the rehabilitation process, it is necessary that rehabilitation specialists recognize certain expressed concerns that may signal a need for family intervention. These concerns may be verbalized to any member of the rehabilitation team (i.e., physician, physical therapist, nurse), as opposed to the identified psychosocial team member (i.e., psychologist, social worker).

A frequent signal may be the expression of *anxiety or fear about prognosis*. Statements such as "I don't know if I can manage if he can't recover" or "Will my son ever be the same?" are indications that the family is having difficulty. Another need for family intervention may be observed when the family expresses *confusion and helplessness concerning observed behavioral problems*. As mentioned earlier, behavioral deficits are often upsetting and alarming to families who do not understand why the behavior is occurring. Assistance may be required to explain the nature of these deficits—their etiology and relationship to premorbid behavior—and in helping the family to manage their problems. Another concern expressed by families involves the *change in role relationships*. This is especially the case in marital relationships, where one partner may have been the dominant, assertive individual and now becomes the passive-dependent one. This is also the case where the brain-injured victim was an important figure in the life of a sibling and can now no longer be relied on for emotional support and assistance. These alterations in role relationships are likely to create disruptions in family functioning. Often, as discharge from the inpatient rehabilitation setting approaches, there is a sudden realization of family members as to the level of *emotional/physical dependency* demanded by the injured relative. Though families are often quite willing and able to assume a great burden of responsibility and care, the recognition of the scope of the problem is often overwhelming. A family member frequently has to relinquish a job, hire home health aides, or adopt a much more restricted lifestyle than in the past. A parent may become consumed with the burden of care and thus lose perspective on his or her own needs. Such a situation can create tension and stress within the family system.

3. High-Risk Families

Certain patients and families may be considered in greatest need for family intervention due to "high-risk" factors. The term "high-risk" reflects the greater probability that such families would probably become disrupted by the advent of the brain injury and therefore be less equipped to facilitate the recovery process.

The first category of high-risk families would be those with a *premorbid history of dysfunction* or with *evidence of maladaptive interaction patterns*. Families with a history of alcoholism, marital discord, or antisocial behavior would be apt to be overwhelmed by the burden of adjusting to the presence of a brain-injured relative. Also included within this category would be patients whose premorbid behavior tended to be impulsive, reckless, and reflective of poor social judgment. The presence of brain injury has often been observed to intensify these maladaptive behaviors due to the disinhibition caused by many brain injuries.

Another group of high-risk families are those in which the patient demonstrates *severe, chronic cognitive and/or behavioral deficits.* For example, a patient with a frontal lobe injury is likely to be perceived as an entirely different individual, lacking in drive, affect, and initiative. The presence of such behaviors is likely to greatly disrupt the day-to-day functioning of the family unit. A patient with severe cognitive deficits, such as memory loss, is likely to require intensive assistance and supervision in everyday activities. A point may be reached where the constant care and emotional support required cannot be provided consistently or effectively. Such a family is clearly in need of intervention.

Finally, those *families in which denial is utilized for a prolonged period* have great difficulty in realistically planning for the future. In such cases, the inability to accept the permanence of the deficit may cause family members to develop unrealistic expectations for their relative, unwittingly creating additional frustration and unrewarding experiences. This problem is illustrated by families who insist that their brain-injured relative is capable of returning to work or school when in fact the reverse is often the case. Feelings of failure and pessimism are felt by the patient when such return to work or school is premature and inappropriate.

4. Types of Family Intervention Techniques

Four categories of family intervention strategies may be proposed. These include (1) patient–family education, (2) family counseling, (3) family therapy, and (4) family support groups.

4.1. Patient–Family Education

Though this technique may be considered a routine part of modern rehabilitation, it is certainly not systematically utilized by many rehabilitation facilities. It is significant to note that Oddy *et al.* (1978) reported that families often expressed dissatisfaction with the communication between themselves and medical staff. The most frequent complaint was the need for greater information regarding the nature and extent of brain injury and the rate of recovery of premorbid function. Several approaches may be considered. In the case of spinal cord injury, families are often given written brochures and reading material detailing the nature of spinal cord injury. However, this is not the case with brain injury because of the lack of widely available written materials or films on the topic. Individualized family teaching is widely employed by rehabilitation nurses, physical therapists, occupational therapists, and speech pathologists.

In the past several years, many rehabilitation centers have developed patient–family education group programs. These sessions are designed to provide basic information about the nature of brain injury and its consequences and to help families gain a greater understanding and acceptance of the disability and the rehabilitation process. Usually sessions are held at the rehabilitation facility during the evening hours (to allow for maximal attendancy by family members). The sessions usually comprise a series of 1- to 2-hour meetings covering a wide range of topics. A model for patient–family education was developed by Diehl (1978) and her colleagues at the Medical College of Virginia. In this program, patients with brain injury (e.g., stroke and head injury) and their families attend 10 sessions over a period of 5 weeks. The format is a combined lecture–discussion approach, with actual demonstrations of techniques and procedures as well as audiovisual aids and handout materials. During these sessions, a wide variety of topics are presented and discussed, including the nature of brain injury, the rehabilitation process, the recovery process, psychosocial deficits, mobility skills, perceptual–motor deficits, and community resources. Because the material is presented in a structured educational format, patients and families react positively to the program and feel comfortable in sharing their own frustrations and experiences. Though the group is primarily educational in design and focus, peer support is a natural by-product. This method of intervention has been well-received and is likely to benefit most families within the early stages of recovery from brain injury.

4.2. Family Counseling

Another level of intervention often practiced by rehabilitation professionals is family counseling. This type of intervention is often directed toward the family of the brain-injured patient. The purpose of family counseling is to assist the family in dealing with their overwhelming feelings of loss and helplessness. The purpose of family counseling is to assist the family in understanding and accepting the disability and its potential consequences (e.g., increased dependence, impaired cognitive and behavioral functioning, decreased physical abilities). Often, this intervention is initiated by the psychosocial member of the rehabilitation team. It is useful to commence family counseling sessions within the inpatient rehabilitation program, though precise timing will vary according to the needs and desires of the individual family.

In these sessions, family members (often the parents or spouse of victim) are given the opportunity to express their feelings of guilt, anguish, anger, sadness, and loss. The family is given the opportunity to ask questions about the nature of the disability, prognosis, and level of care that may be required. An additional goal of family counseling is to provide much-needed emotional support. Families that experience head injury and subsequent prolonged periods of hospitalization are often taxed to the limit of their adaptive resources. Seemingly endless visits to the hospital may necessitate changes in family work schedules, impose strain on marital and parent–child relationships, and create physical stresses that may lead to psychosomatic illnesses. Often, perceived progress is painstakingly slow and the ultimate goal of restoration of premorbid function appears to be an "impossible dream." As discharge approaches, families become apprehensive, since they have been given an implicit or explicit message that a "plateau" has been reached. During the transition from hospital to community, the counselor can play a key role in assisting the family to anticipate future problems and be more psychologically and physically prepared to assume the burden of care. Frequently, the patient and family may maintain unrealistic expectations that restoration of function will magically occur once the patient can return home. To prevent an experience of overwhelming disappointment and frustration, the counselor can gently prepare the family for the realities of life with a brain-injured relative and maintain close communication to provide support during this most difficult transition period. It is important to schedule periodic follow-up sessions with the family to provide the additional support so often needed but rarely requested.

Patient: J. G.

J. G., a 23-year-old unmarried male, was a passenger in a car driven by his roommate on the way home from a party; both men were injured in a collision. J. G. sustained a severe brain injury resulting in 4 weeks of coma and diffuse brain damage, and his roommate also sustained a severe brain injury. After 3 months of hospitalization, the patient was independent in ADL and mobility skills but continued to experience mild residual deficits in cognitive functioning, dysarthria, impaired coordination, decreased motor speed, periodic violent outbursts, and inappropriate sexual behavior. During the hospitalization, the family met weekly with a psychologist in family counseling sessions. The family vented its anger about the circumstances surrounding the injury, particularly toward the roommate who was driving the car while intoxicated. Fears about the patient's ultimate mental recovery were expressed as well as concern about his future ability to return to work and live independently. Upon J. G.'s discharge, sessions were continued for several months. Many concerns were discussed, including questions about the patient's ability to drive an automobile and/or to resume drinking, effects of seizure medication on arousal, sexual functioning, ability to be left alone, and so on. Methods of managing inappropriate behavior were suggested.

This case illustrates the variety of needs for ongoing family counseling and emotional support during the hospitalization and after discharge into the community. In many cases, families are resistant to participating in a counseling relationship during the hospitalization, perhaps due to the presence of denial. After discharge, however, the family is often confronted with the reality of living with a brain-injured relative and are more likely to acknowledge the presence of problems and experience feelings of helplessness. Uncertainty regarding appropriate management techniques can often lead to inconsistency and feelings of guilt and inadequacy. Maintenance of ongoing contact in periodic family counseling sessions can help minimize the deleterious effects of these problems and their disruptive impact upon the family.

4.3. Family Therapy

Another technique that may be utilized to assist the families of brain-injured patients is family therapy. Glick and Kessler (1974, p. 4) define family therapy as "a professionally organized attempt to produce behavioral changes in a disturbed marital or family unit by essentially interactive, non-physical methods." The chief objective of family therapy is to alter maladaptive communication and interaction patterns within the family system. The focus in family therapy is directed toward developing an increased understanding of the family's current mode of interaction and providing active intervention to resolve the dysfunctional communication and produce more satisfying and rewarding family relationships. In contrast to family counseling, the focus in family therapy is on the family system as a whole rather than the identified patient (i.e. brain-injured patient).

In cases involving traumatic brain injury, family therapy may be limited to a select number of families where there is "high risk" (as described earlier) and wherein the "identified patient" is cognitively intact to the degree that he or she can meaningfully participate in the sessions. The goals of family therapy include but are not limited to the following:

1. To provide a supportive environment where all family members

can freely verbalize feelings about the trauma and its effects upon the family

2. To educate the family about the nature of the deficit in communication and interaction and develop methods for resolving conflicts within the relationship patterns of the family system

3. To examine and clarify role relationships and restructure roles and responsibilities within the family system

Ideally, family therapy is initiated prior to discharge, since the need for this type of intervention should have been clearly defined. However, in reality, it is difficult for the family to express readiness to participate in this process until the patient has returned home and specific problems become manifest. Some specific techniques that can be employed in family therapy include these:

1. Emphasizing the mutuality of responsibility for the maladaptive communication and interaction within the family—shifting the burden of guilt and blame from the identified patient to the family system

2. Analyzing and emphasizing the positive aspects of the family system—reinforcing evidence of appropriate and healthy interaction that occurs within the sessions

3. Exploring dysfunctional patterns of interaction by reenacting family conflicts and assisting family members in problem solving to alleviate conflicts

4. Prescribing "homework assignments" for the family to practice outside the sessions so as to foster generalization of behavior change. Homework assignments may be defined as specific tasks that family members are asked to perform between sessions to create desirable behavior change. These tasks may include altered methods of communication between parent and child, specific problem-solving techniques to employ when conflicts arise, or perhaps alternative and more adaptive ways of expressing feelings and frustrations

The following case example is presented to illustrate some of the above concepts.

Patient: R. B.

R. B., a 17-year-old high school senior, sustained a left frontal subdural hematoma in a diving accident. The patient had been a star athlete and had plans to attend college on an athletic scholarship. The brain injury resulted in deficits in attention, abstraction, memory, judgment, drive, motivation, affect, and problem solving. He had regained strength and endurance but could not return to school or resume his athletic endeavors. Both the patient and family had great difficulty accepting the injury and its devastating consequences. Shortly after discharge, the patient and his family agreed to participate in family therapy sessions. Initially, the sessions were focused on the expression of anger and frustration caused by the injury and how each family member was affected by it. Family members were gradually able to support each other and ultimately able to accept the notion of disability. The patient was surprised and comforted by his family's expression of support. Maladaptive behaviors within parent–child relationships and sibling relationships were explored. When the patient resisting the idea of seeking out part-time employment and expressed great anger at his parents and sisters for pressuring him, a behavioral contract was developed. This contract specified the expectations of the patient and family members and attached specific contingencies for compliance and noncompliance. Within a week, the patient found a position and started to work. Several sessions focused on the reactions of siblings who were suffering from the loss of attention they experienced and were having significant academic and social difficulties.

Family therapy helped to establish a more open communication system within the family and allowed the burden of responsibility for the care of the patient to be shifted to the entire family system. The therapy sessions provided a nonthreatening atmosphere in which the patient could communicate his feelings and achieve greater self-esteem. The behavioral contract was helpful in that it was a written understanding of the behavioral expectations of each family member and the contingencies that would be provided. In addition, members of the family were able to clarify their roles and responsibilities and became more comfortable in relating to each other.

4.4. Family Support Groups and Organizations

The preceding intervention strategies are described as helpful methods that rehabilitation professionals might consider for incorporation into their overall treatment programs. However, for a variety of reasons, health care professionals are not always the ideal resource for families. In recent years, the notion of peer counseling and support has gained prominence within the field of rehabilitation.

Within the past few years, parents and spouses of the brain-injured patient have joined together to form support groups and "grass-roots" organizations to address the unmet needs of this population. Within the United States, one of the first examples of consumer-initiated programs for the brain-injured was the High Hopes Recovery Group in southern California. This organization was founded by the parent of a traumatic brain-injured adult. A major task accomplished by High Hopes was the establishment of a prevocational workshop program designed to retrain cognitive and vocational skills as well as improve social skills. In addition, parents of the brain-injured clients are involved in an active parent support group.

Very recently, families of several head-injured victims in Massachusetts coalesced to form an organization known as the National Head Injury Foundation. This organization is developing a wide variety of services to aid the families of brain-injured patients. Some of the planned activities include:

1. Providing a centralized resource and clearinghouse for the gathering and dissemination of information related to head injury for parents and others responsible for the care of head-injured persons
2. Providing emotional support to families and others responsible for the care of their head-injured loved ones
3. Encouraging the formation of family groups throughout the United States as chapters of the organization
4. Developing parent support groups and "hot line" counseling services

At present, regional support groups conducted by parents of the head-injured have been developed throughout Massachusetts. The purpose of a family support group is to provide peer support, exchange of information, practical problem solving, and mutual assistance in coping with the unsettling realities and frustrations associated with the burden of care for the brain-injured person. Similar support groups run by consumers have been established in other parts of the country and have been found to be a much needed resource for families.

Support groups and self-help organizations run by consumers provide an important alternative source of counseling and support that may be more effective than services provided by health care professionals. The perspective provided by families is unique, since they have experienced the anger, frustration, despair, and uncertainty associated with the process of recovering from brain injury. The opportunity to attend regular support groups or meetings with those experiencing similar problems decreases feelings of social isolation and helplessness.

5. Conclusions

The field of rehabilitation has recently awakened to the serious plight of the brain-injured person. Both clinicians and researchers are devoting a great deal of effort to determining the best methods for restoring the brain-injured person to a useful place within society. Thus far, physicians have provided the means to sustain life in spite of severe brain injury. With the aid of the natural recovery process, rehabilitation therapists have been successful in restoring mobility, self-care, and communication skills to a level that is often close to the brain-injured person's premorbid level of function. Yet it is so often the case that serious mental sequelae in the form of cognitive, behavioral, and social deficits persist and significantly impair the brain-injured person's capacity to live independently and return to a meaningful, satisfying, and productive life-style.

The presence of these deficits often compels the family of the brain-injured victim to assume a central role in the care and management of their loved one's life. Thus, the needs of family members must be addressed so that the newly rehabilitated brain injured patient will not be placed in a chaotic, inconsistent, unstructured environment. The usually persistent presence of cognitive and behavioral deficits long after the injury places many demands and stresses upon the family; these are likely to lead to disruption of the family system unless the necessary psychosocial intervention is provided.

The preceding discussion has presented a model for family intervention that can be applied to the rehabilitation of the brain-injured adult. Within the early phases of recovery from brain injury within the hospital setting, patient–family education would be the treatment of choice. At this point, most families are interested in learning about the nature of brain injury and the recovery process but not yet ready to confront the rather frightening problems that lie ahead. The brief, focused, educational group format allows families to gain an understanding of the injury and ask questions about the future.

As the patient approaches the end of inpatient rehabilitation, many families can benefit from periodic family counseling sessions. These sessions are useful in identifying problems that may be encountered when the patient returns home. The counselor can aid the family in developing a realistic assessment of the patient's abilities and limitations. In addition, the counselor can help family members "work through" their grief and the feelings of loss accompanying a growing recognition of the significant and perhaps permanent changes in cognitive and behavioral functioning manifested by their loved one.

A select number of families are in need of family therapy, which involves a psychotherapeutic process whereby communication and interaction patterns within the family are explored and, one hopes, altered. This type of intervention is usually effective only when the entire family unit, including the patient, can participate in the sessions. It is recommended for "high-risk" families, in which there is a significant premorbid history of family dysfunction or a persistent tendency to deny the disability and its consequences. The goal of family therapy is to shift the focus from the identified patient to the family system and to develop specific techniques to alter maladaptive patterns of interaction within the family.

A newer form of family intervention has been developed by the consumer community (i.e., families of the head-injured). Organizations have been developed by parents and spouses of the head-injured to provide education, referral information, and peer support. Family support groups have been developed where emotional support is provided in an environment that may be less threatening and provide greater reassurance than is available in the traditional health care setting.

The inclusion of family intervention in the broad scope of treatment provided for the brain-injured is a relatively new concept. To date, studies have not been conducted demonstrating that family intervention significantly alters the ultimate prognosis, outcome, and quality of life for the brain-injured victim. However, there is an increasing body of clinical evidence suggesting that family intervention should be considered as a primary rather than secondary or optional mode of treatment in the comprehensive rehabilitation management of the brain-injured patient.

6. References

Bond, M. R. Assessment of psychosocial outcome of severe head injury. *Acta Neurochirurgica*, 1976, *34*, 57–70.

Diehl, L. *Patient–family education.* Paper presented at 2nd Annual Conference on the Rehabilitation of the Traumatic Brain Injured Adult, Williamsburg, Va., June 1978.

Evans, C. D., Bull, C. F., Devenport, M. J., Hall, P. M., Jones, J., Middleton, F. R., Russell, G., Stichbury, J. C., & Whitehead, B. Rehabilitation of the brain damaged survivor. *Injury*, 1976, *8*, 80–97.

Freedman, A. M., Kaplan, H. I., & Saddock, B. J. *Comprehensive textbook of psychiatry* (Vol. 1). Baltimore: Williams & Wilkins, 1975.

Glick, I. D., & Kessler, D. R. *Marital and family therapy.* New York: Grune & Stratton, 1974.

Jennett, B., & Bond, M. R. Assessment of outcome after severe brain damage. *Lancet*, 1975, *1*, 480–484.

Jennett, B., & Teasdale, G. Predicting outcome in individual patients after severe head injury. *Lancet,* 1976, *1,* 1081–1084.

Levin, H., & Grossman, R. G. Behavioral sequelae of closed head injury, *Archives of Neurology,* 1978, *35,* 770–727.

Najenson, T., Mendelson, L., Schechter, I., David, C., Mintz, N., & Groswasser, Z. Rehabilitation after severe head injury. *Scandinavian Journal of Rehabilitation Medicine,* 1974, *6,* 5–14.

Oddy, M., Humphrey, M., & Uttley, D. Stresses upon the relatives of head-injured patients. *British Journal of Psychiatry,* 1978, *133,* 507–513.

Panting, A., & Merry, P. II. The long-term rehabilitation of severe head injuries with particular reference to the need for social and medical support for the patient's family. *Rehabilitation,* 1972, *38,* 33–37.

Rimel, R. *An assessment of recovery following head trauma.* Paper presented at the 3rd Annual Conference on the Rehabilitation of the Traumatic Brain Injured Adult, Williamsburg, Virginia, June 1979.

Romano, M. D. Family response to traumatic head injury. *Scandinavian Journal of Rehabilitation Medicine,* 1974, *6,* 1–4.

Rosenbaum, M., & Najenson, T. Changes in life patterns and symptoms of low mood as reported by wives of severely brain-injured soldiers. *Journal of Consulting and Clinical Psychiatry,* 1976, *44,* 881–888.

Symonds, C. P. Mental disorders following head injury. *Proceedings of the Royal Society of Medicine,* 1937, *30,* 1081–1092.

8

Psychological and Neuropsychological Interventions in the Mobile Mourning Process

CRAIG A. MUIR AND WILLIAM J. HAFFEY

It has become axiomatic that cognitive and psychosocial deficits severely retard recovery from traumatic brain injury. Jennett's (1975) review of the management of traumatically head-injured patients reported persistent cognitive losses as the main contribution to social disability. He also cited the apparent failure to recognize the extent of family disruption resulting from a trauma to one of its members. Lundholm, Jepsen, and Thornvak (1975) reported that in 80% of patients followed 8 to 14 years posttrauma, social rehabilitation was impeded by reductions in mental capacity. Oddy, Humphrey, and Uttley (1978) found that the two most common stresses experienced by families 6 and 12 months posttrauma concerned the trauma patient's current and future deficits. Their findings suggested that families desired "more details regarding the extent and nature of the brain damage" (p. 511). They also stated that the families complained about the lack of continued psychological counseling "other than through the usual psychiatric channels which they regarded as inappropriate" (p. 511). Our clinical experience is consistent with these findings.

CRAIG A. MUIR AND WILLIAM J. HAFFEY • Neuropsychology Service, Casa Colina Hospital for Rehabilitative Medicine, Pomona, California 91767.

Psychological responses to traumatic brain injury have enormous impact on the recovery process. These responses are highly variable and charged with emotion. The professional is often inundated by a confusing welter of questions and opinions from all sides as patient, family members, and others attempt to find some tenable way to deal with the nature and magnitude of the trauma. For the trauma is not "just" the damage to the brain but also the effects of that physical trauma and its behavioral sequelae on the lives of the patient and those closely tied to the patient.

The purpose of this chapter is to share some conceptual formulations that have helped us make sense of the intense and varied array of responses from brain-injured patients and their families. These formulations have emerged over the course of treating some 90 to 100 traumatically brain-injured patients annually for the past 4 years as members of the specialized Brain Injury Program of Casa Colina Hospital for Rehabilitative Medicine. The concepts represent our attempts to integrate into a coherent clinical approach the existing literature in various fields and the experiences of our patients and their families. Studies on reaction to death or to the loss of a loved one, behavioral approaches to changing response styles, and so on have all been drawn upon. But our patients and their families have taught us that the losses subsequent to traumatic brain injury are unique. These losses, and the persons suffering from them, cannot be fully understood solely by the application of findings or theories from other situations.

We will begin by briefly describing some of the specific needs faced by patients and families. This is followed by explanations of the concepts of personal system, partial death, and mobile mourning. The next section briefly describes a clinical neuropsychological approach. The final section outlines some of the ways these concepts are used in treatment.

1. The Personal System

Each brain-injured individual coming for treatment brings in tow a unique personal system (Muir, 1978b) of pretraumatic experiences, abilities, aspirations, family members, friends, lovers, and so on. It is a system in that the elements interact with one another. A change in one area creates changes in all the other areas. Each personal system interacts with the event of head injury in ways that are unique. Each person's history and personality are unique; the family constellation and interrelationships are in many ways different from any other; no two brain injuries are exactly the same, nor are their functional sequelae.

The purpose of treatment at Casa Colina Hospital for Rehabilitative Medicine is to minimize the damage to each patient's personal system. That includes minimizing the patient's cognitive and functional sequelae, of course; more broadly conceived, it also means minimizing the damage inflicted on all the people who are adversely affected by a single medical trauma. It involves not only helping the patient to become as capable and functional as possible but also dealing with the hopes, aspirations, and relationships that may be affected by traumatic brain injury. This treatment involves all staff members on the rehabilitation team, not just those whose primary accountability is psychosocial adjustment.

Each patient is a part of this larger entity called a personal system, so a traumatic brain injury involves not just the individual but the entire system. The relative importance of various aspects of the injury, including the functional sequelae, is determined by the specific characteristics of each patient's personal system. For example, a lesion resulting in slow, halting ambulation will have a different meaning for the patient who premorbidly supported the family as a physical laborer than for the patient who had a more sedentary occupation. Ambulation difficulties in the former may require drastic changes in roles, financial comfort, and so on, whereas in the latter it may cause less disruption. Even in this simplified example, it is clear that the brain injury affects not only the patient. In Moos's (1977) formulation, it is not the injury *per se* but rather the perceived meaning of it that affects the patient and family members.

The members of the personal system are tied together in systemic fashion. That is, a change in one element of the system causes changes in other areas. In the previous example, a patient's loss of ability to produce income caused other changes, such as a spouse having to switch roles in order to replace the lost income or to alter life-styles to accommodate lower income. If there are children in the family, they also must adjust to the diminished economic outlook; parents of the patient may have to dip into retirement savings to help out. The single injury can be seen to reverberate throughout an extended family as people shift to accommodate the changed role of the patient. Personal systems, like individuals (Caplan, 1964; Lindemann, 1979), operate at levels of equilibrium or homeostasis, and the brain injury disrupts that equilibrium.

Unfortunately, this simplified example only elucidates the fact of systemic relationships; it does not begin to describe the degrees of dislocation caused by traumatic brain injury or the complexity of those systemic interrelationships. People are not like chess pieces that can be moved about when a loss occurs; nor can the effects of a brain injury be adequately remediated by addressing only the obvious physical/cognitive sequelae and their superficial factual implications. The fabric of the personal system comprises interwoven emotional needs, expectations, hopes, aspirations, reinforcement histories—in short, the psychodynamics of its members. The complexity of these relationships is often lost in the immediate need to restore physical function (Rochlin, 1965). Though it cannot be denied that physical restoration is vital, excessive focus on it, or on the obvious factual implications of the physical loss, can exclude the other elements of the personal system to the point of obstructing traditional physical rehabilitation. A case history may serve to illustrate this point of view.

In the previous example, it was pointed out that decreased ambulation might have more effects on the personal system of a physical laborer than on that of an accountant or psychologist. For example, R. T., a 28-year-old bookkeeper, illustrates the danger of this oversimplification. His case will be discussed at length throughout the chapter because his situation is typical of the problems encountered by so many of our patients and their families.

R. T. was married and had one child. While on vacation, he had an off-road motorcycle accident resulting in severe head injury. After stabilization in a general neurosurgical service, he was referred for treatment of the sequelae of right frontoparietal and left inferotemporal lesions. Left hemiparesis resulted in a dysfunctional gait that was predicted to improve with treatment to the point that he could walk, perhaps using a cane and a short-leg brace. He could return to his previous employer as a bookkeeper regardless of his gait. He had been pursuing part-time studies in business and planned to continue doing so if his cognitive deficits could be sufficiently remediated. His gait problems should have been the least of his worries, since he had substantial cognitive deficits that might prevent his return to work, let alone his lifelong ambition to obtain a master's degree in business administration.

Referral information from another rehabilitation center variously described R. T. as depressed, unmotivated, highly motivated, manipulative, charming, and hostile. The therapists applying those labels were aware that some of the disagreements in their assessments of the patient's emotional state were due to the fact that he reacted differently to different therapies. However, there was no basis for integrating these observations.

R. T.'s parents were perceived as "unrealistic" in their expectations for his total recovery. His wife was described as still being in the "denial stage" and as being unable to cope with the burden of her husband's disability.

R. T. received a thorough psychological evaluation as part of the standard initial work-up at Casa Colina Hospital for Rehabilitative Medicine. The psychological evaluation focuses on the premorbid psychodynamics of the patient and extended family. Comments from the patient and from family members were gathered by occupational and physical therapists. Often the members of the personal system are freer in their comments to nonpsychologists in a physical rehabilitation setting. We have learned to value the psychological insight of nonpsychological therapists, just as they have learned to bring their observations—not labels—to team conference. R. T. also had a neuropsychological assessment by a speech–language pathologist and a neuropsychologist. At the initial outpatient conference and subsequent team meetings, the following picture of the personal system emerged.

R. T.'s father had always felt insecure about his own intellectual abilities, especially in relation to the patient's mother. Consequently, the patient had received positive reinforcement for academic abilities only from his mother. His father reinforced a model of manhood that required vigorous physical activity coupled with financial–professional success. Males who did not show some sort of physically aggressive behavior were seen as weak and dominated by their wives.

R. T.'s wife was unaccustomed to handling the family finances but was beginning to manage well. What bothered her most was her husband's devaluation of himself, including his frequently stated belief that surely she would abandon him for someone who was more sexually attractive.

The response within this patient's personal system to his recovery was as follows. His mother was concerned almost exclusively with return of cognitive abilities, while the father was overcome by the conviction that his son "could never be a man again." Based on these two disparate points of view, mother and father entered into fierce arguments about the patient's treatment program. The mother felt that everyone should be grateful for so much recovery and be reasonable about such minor losses as the poor gait. The father felt that the situation was virtually hopeless. Neither understood the basis for the other's viewpoint.

The patient settled into a state of deep "depression" that interfered with his cognitive retraining and other therapies. He began to drink heavily, to be quarrelsome with his wife, and to make inappropriate sexual advances to other women. His wife was deeply hurt and confused by his behavior toward her, as he had always been considerate and sexually faithful. She felt that her diligence was being rewarded with rejection. She was unable to respond to the needs of their 4-year-old son, which provoked additional loss of self-esteem.

R. T. had already quit one rehabilitation program. His father wanted him to stay in occupational and physical therapy until he recovered all premorbid physical abilities. His mother was agitating for a speedy return to college. His wife was considering a trial separation. If the patient's personal system had not been assessed and treatment structured accordingly, rehabilitation would have failed. Traumatic brain injury can thus be seen to affect the patient's entire personal system of people, hopes, aspirations, and so on. Each personal system is unique and must be treated as such if the number of victims and amount of damage from any one injury are to be minimized.

2. Partial Death

Traumatic brain injury is a "partial death" (Shneidman, 1974). As the phrase suggests, partial death is the loss of some more or less important aspect of one's life. This may include the loss of function, a major change in a personal relationship, a death in the family, a change in lifestyle, and so on.

Partial deaths run a gamut in all of our lives, from rather minor events, such as graduating from college to major changes such as getting married or losing a loved one. Likewise, the partial deaths encountered by the personal systems of brain-injured patients range from scarcely noticeable decreases in cognition or coordination to the other end of the spectrum, where the individual as he was experienced by others—and probably by himself—ceases to exist. "Such endings short of death . . . often involve mourning and grief as intense as the mourning caused by death itself, and as appropriate" (Shneidman, 1974). In R. T.'s case, for example, the loss of physical function represented the death of a crucial part of himself, even though to the outside world he was recovering very well, considering the severity of his head injury.

Traumatic brain injury produces particular forms of partial death. There are at least five major ways in which traumatic brain injury assaults the personal system:

1. The suddenness of the event
2. The severity and complexity of the trauma
3. Physical regression
4. Changes in "personality"
5. Uncertainty of recovery patterns

Some of these assaults are common to other kinds of partial deaths, but the combination appears unique. A cerebrovascular accident, for instance, may cause physical regression to infantile needs for care and may cause personality changes. But it usually occurs in people who know they are in a high-risk category, and the course of recovery is comparatively predictable. Multiple injuries and multiple brain lesions also occur less frequently in cerebrovascular accidents.

An example of the kinds of partial death brought on by traumatic brain injury is B. N., a patient in his late twenties, admitted 4 years ago to Casa Colina Hospital for Rehabilitative Medicine's inpatient Brain Injury Program. His wife had been accustomed to getting up early, making her husband's lunch, and sending him off to his job as a telephone lineman. She then did her housework, took care of their 3-year-old daughter, and spent her afternoons in a business she operated from the home. This young couple was progressing well financially, had just purchased their first home, and were planning on more children. All were in good health. One day, as the afternoon waned and the patient's wife began to get dinner ready, there was a knock on the door. A telephone pole had broken off when her husband was on top of it, and he had suffered a severe head injury.

Her life changed irrevocably in that moment. Her husband hovered close to death for weeks, then slowly progressed to a point where he only needed the complete care of an infant, not that of an intensive care unit patient. He had suffered multiple brain lesions and fractures to both legs, one of which required multiple surgeries. By the time he reached Casa Colina Hospital for Rehabilitative Medicine 7 months later, he had recovered enough to be a candidate for a rehabilitation program. However, he was far from being the person who had left for work on that typical morning 7 months before. In addition to his physical and cognitive deficits, he threw temper tantrums; demanded constant attention from his wife, mother, father, and nursing staff; and was volatile with his daughter.

His wife's response to the sudden disorder in her universe was to question her very fundamental belief in a just God and to feel increased fear for her daughter's safety. She was constantly distressed when she visited the patient because she could not bring the daughter along—given the patient's response—but at the same time she was terrified that something would happen to the child if she were out of sight.

The severity of the brain trauma had produced medical bills that wiped out their savings and forced them into debt. The patient had required the care and supervision usually needed only by an infant for many months. As so often happens, physical regression resulted in increased egocentricity. The more demanding he became, the more conflictual was the situation for his family. Mother, father, and wife alternately felt a desperate need to relieve the patient's distress, or resentment at the increasing demands. The patient appeared to be a different person charcterologically from the one who had worked and planned for the happiness of his family (Lezak, 1978).

Perhaps worst of all, there was little certainty about his recovery. Despite major research efforts to establish statistical trends of recovery after head injury (Jennett, Teasdale, Galbraith, Pickard, Grant, Braakman, Avezaat, Maas, Minderhoud, Vecht, Heiden, Small, Caton, & Kurze, 1977; Jennett, Teasdale, Braackman, Minderhoud, Heiden, & Kurze, 1979), no one would say with a very high degree of probability what the recovery course for this one individual would be (Bond, 1980).

3. Mobile Mourning

The partial deaths in the personal system caused by traumatic brain injury result in a characteristic pattern of grieving. We have chosen to call this mobile mourning (Muir, 1978a) because its central characteristic is uncertainty. Mobile mourning has many similarities to other types of grief. It is a variation on a theme, not a totally new concept. The process also varies somewhat as each personal system varies, but there seem to be some common themes.

Partial death is unlike the definitive event of a complete death, which may produce definite stages of mourning (Kübler-Ross, 1969). Clinicians and researchers now argue about how definite those stages really are. However, there is some consensus that after the short-range oscillation among the stages of mourning, in the long term most people go through a reasonably ordered process (Bowlby, 1975, pp. 292–309). There are many responses following traumatic brain injury that are common to other grief reactions (Schoenberg, Carr, Peretz, & Kutscher, 1970; Szalita, 1974, pp. 673–684), but the overall picture is much more disorganized. Indeed, one must ask what "short-term" and "long-term" mean in light of the extended course of uncertainty following traumatic brain injury. Should members of the personal system grieve for the patient's loss of ability to use a limb? Return to work? Resume care of himself or herself? What if these functional losses are recovered by the patient? Many members of the personal system reject what little certainty there may be because it seems to be a betrayal of the patient, a giving up of hope.

The single most common response of members of the personal system is the search for a certainty of a different kind: certainty of recovery. This may be seen in behaviors that are frequently characterized as "denial of disability." For example, family members tend to give meaning to objectively uninterpretable events. The flickering of an eyelid, the reflex movement of a limb, are taken to be evidence of improvement. The failure of the patient to respond consistently when staff are present may be blamed on the poor observation powers of the staff. To admit otherwise is to be once again cruelly disappointed. As Rochlin (1965) notes, attempts at restitution are "often made through fantasy of achievements that will be forthcoming with recovery" (p. 129). The patients and those close to them seem endlessly stuck between euphoric hope and resignation (Forbes, 1978). As Lezak (1978) says, they are not allowed to mourn decently.

This burden of alternating hope and despair continues for many months, even years. The very length of time involved accentuates the feelings of rage at the patient. Yet one is not allowed freely to admit anger toward someone who is sick. The anger may be projected onto staff or other members of the personal system, or it may come out obliquely at the patient. As one husband said to me of his severely injured wife, "Sometimes I've thought of just smothering her so she wouldn't have to go through all this agony." The patient, however, was virtually unresponsive. She was not going through any discernible distress. The person experiencing the agony was the spouse, caught between his love for his wife and his rage at this patient in the bed, who seemingly would neither live nor die but stay in limbo, and he trapped with her.

Just as the brain injury is a collision of an event with a more or less stable personal system, so also are there collisions within each personal system. Breakdowns of individual defense structures follow the lines of each personal system, as was evident in the case of R. T. The links among members can also break apart, often where they were premorbidly weakest, and trivia can come to seem all-important. The sister of a brain-injured patient announced one day that she had stopped speaking to her parents. Since she had been the family communicator and "counselor" up until that time, it at first seemed that something momentous must have occurred. It turned out that her fury was triggered when her parents sold out her brother's motorcycle parts business. They had not consulted her. In her opinion they had received a very low price for his merchandise, much lower than if they had allowed her to manage the sale. Actually, the patient's assets totaled no more than $3,000. He was in a persistent vegetative state, so the money was objectively unimportant to him. The importance of this seemingly trivial event was that the sister and the patient had banded together premorbidly when their parents had rejected the patient for his long hair and rebellious behavior. The sister had defended him to their parents in a protective way. When the motorcycle stock was sold, the sister took this as another condemnation of the patient. Since he was unable to defend himself, she came to his "rescue" and refused to speak to her parents.

The severity and complexity of traumatic brain injury frequently lead to learned helplessness. Far from being able to do anything to help, patient and family members usually cannot even understand the nature of the deficits. For example, "memory" is perceived as returning if the patient recalls premorbid events. Members of the personal system seldom realize that retrograde amnesia is different from the inability to learn new material. Inconsistencies in functional responses, especially of a higher cortical nature, are particularly confusing. R. T., for example, could read quite well until he made an error. He then "got stuck" and was unable to proceed, regardless of how much his family coached him. The sudden inability to function, coupled with the family's inability to assist him, increased their feelings of helplessness.

In summary, mobile mourning is the particular variation of the grieving process that follows traumatic brain injury. Each personal system experiences the grief somewhat differently, but there are some frequently observed themes: the search for certainty of recovery, virtually endless fluctuations between euphoria and despair, exacerbated feelings of rage, breakdowns in the often tenuous links in the personal system, and learned helplessness.

4. Neuropsychological Approach

The recovery of impaired physical and cognitive abilities is of paramount importance to the members of the personal system and is one of the central issues of the mobile mourning process. That recovery requires the acquisition of the behavioral skills necessary to overcome the effects of the trauma. Since the disabling behavioral deficits result from brain damage, rehabilitative interventions should be based on the brain's capacity to process information in ways that will permit the performance of behaviors essential for functional recovery.

Our neuropsychological approach seeks to help rehabilitative specialists achieve their physical and medical restorative goals in order to reduce the disabling physical sequelae of the brain trauma. The remediation of the disabling cognitive deficits rests on the neuropsychological data regarding the effects of the brain lesions on specific cognitive processes and on the brain's potential for performing the tasks in a way that could be subserved by intact or partially intact brain structures. We also utilize the neuropsychological data to help the members of the personal system understand the patient's behavioral deficits. Given this understanding, they can more readily adjust their behaviors and expectations to match the patient's current processing and production capacities. We have found that such interventions facilitate the mobile mourning process.

4.1. Definition of Terms

Neuropsychology is the study of brain–behavior relationships (Davison, 1974, pp. 1–18). Clinical neuropsychology attempts to translate research data regarding brain-behavior relationships into clinically efficient and effective assessment and treatment methods. Our principal goal in neuropsychological assessment is to generate data that will help define the *focus* and the *means* of rehabilitative training and help shape the psychological and behavioral responses of the members of the personal system. Cognitive retraining is the application of the neuropsychological assessment data to the remediation of behavioral deficits resulting from traumatic brain damage, both in the acute rehabilitative inpatient phase and in the more protracted outpatient phase.

4.2. Theoretical Foundations

Luria (1963; 1969, pp. 277–301; 1970, 1975, pp. 335–361; and Luria, Nayden, Tsvetkova, & Vinarskaya, pp. 368–433, 1969) elaborated a model of remediation based upon a theoretical conception of brain–behavior relationships. Luria (1973) conceived of the brain as being composed of three functional units: (1) a unit for regulating tone or alertness; (2) a unit for reception, coding, and storage of information; and (3) a unit for planning, regulating, and verifying behavior.

The reticular activating system and the corticoreticulocortical connections form the brain structures of the first unit. The posterior cerebral cortex (parietal, temporal, occipital regions and their interconnections) subserves the second unit. The cerebral cortex anterior to the Rolandic fissure is the foundation of the third unit. All human activity involves the concerted working of each of these units, with each zone of each unit contributing differentially in accord with its structures and function.

Traumatic brain injury results in the disturbance of the dynamic working of the brain. A lesion will result in a disruption of the brain processes dependent upon the physiological function of the damaged cells. The secondary effect of such a lesion is that all the cognitive skills reliant upon the damaged cells will be affected in accord with the particular contribution of those cells.

For example, Luria (1970, 1973, 1976) proposed that a lesion in the left temporal lobe (Brodmann's area 22 and part of area 21) results in the loss of the ability to discriminate phonemes that differ in only one feature. This primary deficiency in phonemic discrimination leads to secondary effects such as deficits in understanding speech, in naming objects, in expressing a thought, and in writing to dictation. These secondary symptoms appear because the behaviors require adequate phonemic discrimination. Conversely, behaviors that are independent of phonemic discrimination ought to be intact. Thus, the capacity to discriminate musical tones or to perform a visual–spatial discrimination task would not be inhibited by a superotemporal lesion. More recent research indicates that other variables also contribute to brain processing strategies (Hirschkowitz, Earle, & Palen, 1978; Hardyck, Tzeng, & Wang, 1978; Moore & Haynes, 1980; Willis, Wheatley, & Mitchell, 1979).

The performance of any complex human behavior requires the coordination of various brain processes. A symptom is the behavioral manifestation of an inability to perform a task. Noting that a patient cannot write, however, is insufficient for planning a rehabilitative strategy (Luria, 1965, pp. 689–754; Luria et al., 1969) or for explaining the deficit to the members of the personal system. Lesions in the temporal, occipital, parietal, postcentral, or premotor cortex can result in a disturbance in writing.

A temporal lesion producing phonemic discrimination difficulties would impair the ability to write to dictation in a different way than an occipitoparietal lesion resulting in difficulties in organizing the visual–spatial characteristics of the letters (graphemes). Damage to the premotor area would impair the coordination of the smooth motor movements necessary for writing. The nature of the deficit must be delineated before therapy can be planned.

The identification of the underlying deficit that gives rise to the behavioral symptom (dysgraphia) would assist the rehabilitative specialists in defining the focus of the treatment (for example, phonemic discrimination versus visual–spatial discrimination, etc.). By helping the members of the personal system understand why their relative cannot write, they could see why they got no results from urging the patient to practice writing words they said to him. Additionally, the members of the personal system could be helped to understand that the ability to write automatic stereotypic material such as the patient's name and address might not be the significant milestone of improvement that they believed it was. Finally, once a treatment strategy had been constructed, they could be guided in their interactions with the patient so as to complement the formal treatment interventions. Thus, their need to be actively involved could be met; their expectations could be modified to approximate the patient's response capacities more closely; and their beliefs that nonrelated behaviors were indicators of improvement or regression could be reduced.

The rehabilitation of the behavioral deficits following traumatic brain injury rests upon identifying the behavioral symptoms and, if possible, the underlying, damaged brain processes giving rise to these symptoms. The *focus* of the rehabilitative interventions should be the deficient brain functions underlying the behavioral symptoms. The *means* of achieving rehabilitative goals are determined by the brain's current processing capacities and by the matching of task demands to the information processing parameters.

4.3. Clinical Applications

The neuropsychological approach to assessment and treatment exists on two levels in our clinical practice. The initial stage involves defining the parameters of a trauma patient's information processing capacities. The subsequent stage focuses on a complete syndrome analysis (Luria, 1966; Luria & Artemyeva, 1970).

4.3.1. Information Processing Stage

The majority of tramatically brain injured patients whom we serve enter rehabilitation soon after they have become medically stable and demonstrate some level of responsiveness to environmental stimuli. The goal of the initial neuropsychological assessment is to define the parameters of their brain's capacity to process information, so that rehabilitation interventions may be shaped.

We evaluate the neuropsychological status of the three principal functional units described above by observing behavioral responses to quasiexperimental conditions. The clinical data reported by Luria and his colleagues and the research data generated by western neuropsychology (Hécaen & Albert, 1978; Heilman & Valenstein, 1979) direct our choice of test conditions and our testing of hypotheses.

The investigation of attention will serve as an example of our evaluation process. Luria (1973, pp. 256–275) divided attentional processes into involuntary attention (arousal, orienting reaction) and voluntary attention (selective attention, intention). The first unit subserves involuntary attention, whereas the third unit is seen as the foundation for voluntary attention. Western neuropsychological findings (Bowers & Heilman, 1980) that envision arousal, attentiveness, and activation as components of attention are consistent with such a formulation.

The clinical neuropsychological assessment begins with elementary stimulus–response conditions (e.g., "when I squeeze your hand, squeeze my hand"). Although it is difficult to dissociate the components of attention precisely without reliance on electrophysiological techniques such as average evoked potentials (Rappaport, Hall, Hopkins, Belleza, Berrol, & Reynolds, 1977; Rappaport, Hopkins, Hall, Belleza, & Berrol, 1978), we observe behaviors like eye opening, eye fixation, head and body position, performance over multiple trials, and so on as measures of arousal. The examination involves systematic manipulation of task and stimuli characteristics (e.g., "When I squeeze your hand once, you squeeze twice"; "When I say 'red' squeeze my hand; when I say 'green' do nothing"). The behavioral observations include such factors as latency of response time, maintenance of instructional set and response set, initiation of response, contamination of subsequent tasks by previous task demands or response parameters, learning of task, retention of task under delayed conditions without repetition of task, instructions with a variety of interposed tasks, and differential performance capacities as a function of task–stimulus interactions.

The neuropsychological investigation surveys the processing capacities of the three functional brain units across a variety of task and stimulus conditions. In addition to attentional factors, the assessment covers learning and memory, perception, motor functioning, language processing and production, extralinguistic communication, problem-solving and reasoning, and the capacity to program response strategies and to verify the outcomes of such programs. In each of these broad areas, we attempt to define the conditions under which performance reliably occurs and those under which performance is deficient.

This initial investigation results in the delineation of the individual's current processing and production capacities. The next stage in the establishment of a rehabilitation program is the analysis of the task demands of the target behaviors (e.g., walking, transfers, dressing, bowel and bladder control). The neuropsychologist works with the rehabilitative specialists to match the information processing capacities of the individual to the task demands of the target behaviors so as to arrive at the most probable means of evoking the target behavior.

To illustrate an elementary application of the neuropsychological assessment data to treatment, a review of the described differential disturbances in attention with respect to the target behavior of bladder continence may be instructive. H. R. and C. M. were both bladder incontinent, much to the distress of the rehabilitative specialists (especially nursing) and the members of the personal system. C. M. was an inpatient on Casa Colina's Brain Injury Unit; H. R. was seen as an outpatient after discharge from another inpatient rehabiliation center. Both patients were described by staff and relatives as having poor attention span.

Patient H. R.

H. R.'s incontinence had led to severe disruption in the personal system. His wife refused to sleep with him or to engage in conjugal relations because H. R. consistently urinated while they were in bed. H. R.'s in-laws, with whom he and his wife were living, were embarrassed by his incontinence, so they gradually stopped having friends and relatives visit their home. Conflicts arose between H. R.'s wife and her parents; the incontinence became the focal point of all of their responses to the disruption wrought by the trauma. H. R. was sent to a nursing home, where he was residing when he was referred for an outpatient evaluation.

Neuropsychological testing revealed severe disruptions in levels of arousal. Regardless of the nature or level of difficulty of tasks, H. R. would periodically evidence the following behaviors: his eyes would close, his head would drop, and he would appear asleep. After a pause ranging from 60 seconds to as much as 10 minutes, he would lift his head and return to the task at hand with no evidence of a loss of instructional and response sets. His performance capability was adequate for every task presented in the assessment.

If the examiner called his name loudly immediately after he closed his eyes, he could be aroused approximately 75% of the time. However, if allowed to put his head down, the external stimulus was minimally successful in arousing him. During the examination he was incontinent, but he continued working on the task at hand as if nothing untoward had occurred.

H. R. also demonstrated highly irregular latency times ranging from a few seconds to as much as 250 seconds. These latency times did not appear to be task- or stimuli-dependent. Moreover, his response adequacy did not vary as a function of his response latency. Whether this was a function of arousal or intentional problems could not be assessed reliably. However, in naturalistic settings, when not given a task, H. R. would rarely initiate purposeful behaviors that he was capable of performing. And when inactive, his periods of diminished arousal were reportedly more frequent and of longer duration. Thus, the initiation of purposeful behavior was also involved.

The treatment program was aimed at the arousal rather than the intentional mechanisms. Timed voiding programs could not rely on H. R.'s self-monitoring, given his arousal problems. Consultation with staff physicians resulted in the suggestion that a trial of Ritalin might be warranted. The program was delayed until a previously scheduled cranioplasty was performed. For as yet unexplained reasons, H. R.'s arousal level improved significantly. Treatment then shifted to his intentional problems.

The increased level of general alertness resulted in a significant decrease in his urinary incontinence. A timed voiding program could now be implemented under H. R.'s self-direction to curb the remaining periods of incontinence. The decrease in incontinence also enabled the members of H. R.'s personal system to examine the psychological conflicts among themselves for which the urinary problems had served as a symbolic focus. Premorbid psychopathological patterns, which had been exacerbated by the trauma and the psychological stresses of the mobile mourning process, could now be addressed psychotherapeutically.

Patient C. M.

C. M.'s neuropsychological data revealed a different pattern. He was an individual with multiple cerebral deficits. His arousal level was intact. Indeed, his orienting response was pathologically enhanced in that he attended to as many different environmental stimuli as possible. Behaviorally, this was manifested as extreme distractibility. However, his ability to initiate selective, purposeful activity was severely impaired. His bifrontal cerebral damage (the third functional unit) was at the root of his selective attentional deficit. Thus, he was unable to initiate purposeful activity on the basis of sensory messages indicating a full bladder. Since he could propel his wheelchair and talk, nursing aides were angered by his seeming indifference to their interventions. A sample discussion between C. M. and an aide after an incident of urinary incontinence illustrates the situation:

AIDE: Do you know when you have to go to the bathroom?
C. M.: Uh-huh.
AIDE: Do you like being wet so much?
C. M.: Nope.
AIDE: Then why don't you tell us when you have to go?
C. M.: I don't know.

When the neuropsychological information was communicated, the aide understood that she was asking him to perform in a way that was outside his capacity. She not only became less angry, she also became an effective teacher. By instituting a timed voiding program that began with all the initiation of activity being provided by staff, C. M.'s behavior was gradually shaped to the point where he was continent when discharged. The external structuring began by removing him from the treatment unit every 15 minutes to a quiet room with a minimum of environmental distractors. Attention was focused on the toilet by flushing it. He was then guided to perform a transfer and was left on the toilet for 3 minutes whether or not he urinated. Social reinforcement for urinary behavior was provided, moving eventually to an intermittent reinforcement schedule. After 3½ weeks of treatment, he began to initiate the movement of his wheelchair to his room, where he would sit in front of the bathroom door. Within 6 weeks, he was using a urinal at half-hour intervals and remained continent.

The members of C. M.'s personal system had attributed various meanings to his lack of initiation. His father felt that he was not trying hard enough, which he connected with premorbid "laziness." His mother felt his problems were based on his stubbornness and adolescent rebellion from their authority. Nonetheless, she would excuse his lack of response to her husband as she had premorbidly, which generated further conflict. His brother's approach was to take C. M. to the bathroom and hand him the urinal after unzipping his pants. He saw the patient's capacity to urinate as a measure of recovery. If he came to visit and found his brother had been incontinent, he took that as a sign that the nursing staff was being neglectful. He would then berate any aide who was in the vicinity for mistreating his brother.

When the neuropsychological information was shared with these members of this personal system, they could see that the lack of initiation was a function of the brain trauma. This helped reduce their erroneous attributions, decreased the intrafamilial conflict, and eliminated much of the deflection of their anxiety onto the nursing staff. Moreover, they were trained in the procedures and became active members of the treatment team. This helped them feel useful and laid the foundations for maintaining a timed voiding program upon C. M.'s discharge to their home.

4.3.2. Higher Cortical Functions

The second stage of the neuropsychological assessment focuses on deficiencies in target behaviors of a higher cortical nature (effective communication in extended discourse; comprehension of an expanded text or utterance, integration of cross-modal information processes for mechanical tasks, utilization of information organization to compensate for defective memory, etc.). The assessment parallels what Luria described as a syndrome analysis. This involves hypothesis formulation and testing regarding the potential underlying deficits that result in the behavioral symptoms.

The integration of the clinical data generated by Luria and his colleagues, western neuropsychological research data, and the knowledge bases of related fields such as cognitive psychology, linguistics, speech-language pathology, artificial intelligence, special education, and so on guide the assessment and the programming of remediation strategies.

Patient R. T.

The case of R. T. provides a brief illustration of this approach to the remediation of higher cortical functions (Haffey, 1980). Return to college and success in a profession were of paramount importance to R. T. and his family. His personal system was experiencing severe disruptions due to conflicts over treatment priorities. Consequently, of the cognitive deficiencies manifest in the assessment, the target behaviors chosen for cognitive remediation were the abilities to (1) extract the "sense" of the author's communication from an expanded text and (2) recall the information contained in such an expanded text well enough to return to some kind of academic program.

The neuropsychological investigation revealed that R. T. failed to incorporate many of the information bits contained in a paragraph, even though his language skills were adequate for decoding the surface syntactical structure of sentences. One aspect of his processing deficits seemed based on breakdowns in decoding at the level of the deep syntactical structure and the semantic representation of the text (Luria, 1976). R. T. also demonstrated deficiencies in the amount of linguistic information he could store in working memory when decoding multiparagraph material. Further complicating the symptom picture was his response pattern, which was characterized by a persistence of initial responses. That is, R. T. demonstrated a paucity of response alternatives in his decoding: once he realized or was cued that his first approximation of the material was incorrect, he could not generate an alternative response. R. T. also experienced periodic minor seizure activity. EEG results indicated an epileptiform focus in the right frontoparietal area. On occasions he would lose track of what he was processing and have to begin anew in his efforts to comprehend the flow of information.

Since his decoding of the morphological and surface syntactical aspects of sentences was reasonably intact, the cognitive retraining strategies assumed this skill level. The first stage of treatment required him to extract information by answering "WH" questions about the material (e.g., who, what, why, when, and so on). The second stage required him to decode the relationships among separate information bits by consciously asking himself questions such as, "Why did the author bother to tell me this information?" "How is the author building his story?" and "How is this new information related to what I already know?" The answers to these questions enabled him to construct an outline. The main headings were drawn from the answers to the first questions. The information bits under each heading were organized in response to the last question. After constructing a complete outline, he was taught to create a summary. He followed the same strategy but used the outline as his referent rather than using the extended text. Recall was then trained by focusing on the relationships between information bits as organized in the outline, relying on associative thinking to assist information retrieval.

R. T. was trained to generate alternative hypotheses by inhibiting his repetition of initial responses. He referred to what he had already written down and produced additional responses in a quasi-free-association manner. Limitations in working memory and interruptions in processing due to seizure activity were handled by reference to the information already contained in the outline rather than beginning the entire text anew.

After 6 months of treatment, R. T. could perform these tasks as long as the decoding was not dependent on inferential reasoning. That is, if the decoding was dependent on information not explicitly stated by the author, R. T.'s performance capability decreased significantly. Nonetheless, he could organize explicitly stated information sufficiently to appreciate the "sense" of the text and to retrieve the information days later.

The effects of R. T.'s participation in the cognitive retraining program on the members of his personal system were widespread. Since the focus of the treatment related to academic skills that might permit him to resume his pursuit of a professional career, both his mother and father could cope better with the results of his trauma. His mother had been exerting intense pressure to have him enrolled in an academic program, regardless of evidence pointing to probable failure. She had been doing this to deflect the grief associated with the potential loss of a goal she prized highly. Since she viewed the cognitive retraining as a means of restoring his academic potential, the symbolic value of immediate enrollment in a university was reduced. His father accepted the cognitive retraining as opening the possibility of R. T. becoming a professional businessman. Both parents could then begin to grieve the losses that most likely would persist (e.g., physical disability). The conflicts born out of their individual psychological needs were substantially reduced.

R. T.'s grieving was also assisted by the cognitive retraining. Whereas previously he had been unreceptive to psychotherapy, he openly discussed his losses during the course of cognitive retraining sessions. As he perceived that he was making progress, his self-esteem improved. He could not only begin to mourn his losses but also had less of a need to "act out" sexually. When he ceased this behavior, he and his wife could begin to cope with the disruptions wrought in their relationship. Premorbid weaknesses in their relationship that were exacerbated by the brain trauma could also be addressed therapeutically.

5. Interventions in the Mobile Mourning Process

We have given a few examples illustrating that each personal system defines and faces the partial deaths caused by traumatic brain injury in its own way. Nonetheless, there are some commonalities shared by personal systems as their members go through the mobile mourning process. What follows is a description of some of the interventions we have found to be helpful in facilitating mobile mourning. Psychological and neuropsychological assessments are necessary to provide the data on which to base the interventions.

These data also serve other functions. Both sources of information are important for designing treatment to meet physical restorative goals and cognitive remediation goals. However, this chapter focuses on interventions in the mobile mourning process.

Recovery from loss really means restitution, not acceptance (Rochlin, 1965). There is no need for a patient or family to give up hope for the future if they can change the focus of that hope. The better we understand the mourning process and each personal system, the better we can help our patients and those tied to them to place some of their hopes in more immediate, realizable achievements. We cannot remove the emotional pain of grieving; our job is to make it tenable.

Each personal system—and each person involved—needs different assistance in rebuilding a foundation upon which to construct new interrelationships, new hopes, new aspirations. The most valuable service we can render has become a cliche: to listen. However, "listening" does not mean sitting for hours hearing someone pour out grief. That may be the task of some staff members, but most do not have the time, and most members of the personal system will not do it anyway. It is more important to "listen" to brief glimpses provided by offhand remarks and behaviors.

Such "listening" includes hearing the messages behind the words. For example, the mother of a 6-year old traumatically brain-injured patient stated in a recent counseling session, "If I really thought he was not going to be like he used to be, I couldn't bear it." Knowing how fragile her premorbid adjustment had been and how much her life had been centered around her son, what she meant was clear. She needed, for the time being, to cling to the image of her son as he used to be. The therapist was being instructed by this mother that she had had enough facts for one day, that he should leave her "denial" alone for awhile.

There can be no rush to enable patients and loved ones to see the losses "realistically." There can only be a measured progress toward restitution. This mother's role need not change immediately because her son had brain damage. He could still be the center of her life. They could still communicate in affectionate ways if she could be helped to settle into a pattern of tenable grief rather than wild fluctuations between euphoria and despair.

If she were not able to carry out the grieving process, her son's injury could alter the delicate balance of their relationship in very destructive ways. Prior to the accident, there was a mild degree of excessive dependency. But she had sufficient insight to know that he had to grow away from her and gradually become more independent. She was already preparing herself to lose him to adulthood. During the first week she had reluctantly allowed him to ride his bike in the street, he was hit by a car. This event plunged her into severe guilt. She felt responsible for his injury and gave up all of her own gratifications to be with him long after it was medically necessary. She stopped seeing the man she had been dating because "he doesn't understand why my boy needs me to be with him so much," and stopped going out to dinner with friends.

When the boy was transferred to Casa Colina, all her time away from work was spent at the hospital. As she gave up more and more of her own life, her resentment deepened. Her anger produced more guilt, which she tried to assuage by concentrating even more on her son's "needs." His every movement, his every smile, was announced as a sign of impending recovery; his every silence brought fear of death.

Her dependency slipped rapidly toward symbiosis. We have seen this cycle all too often, so every effort was made to stave off the drift toward severe psychopathology. Other patients' families were very helpful in the family support group. She, in turn, was able to perceive her own behavior more clearly in the reflections of other families' problems, which mirrored her own. Psychotherapy sessions continued biweekly while her son was an inpatient. They focused on the patient's need to do as much as he could for himself as well as on the potential destructiveness of her reactions.

Psychotherapy was offered to her after discharge. She agreed but did not return for regular sessions. When she did drop in, however, she indicated that she was working full time again, that her son was in day care after school, and that "my old boyfriend asked me out again and I knew I'd catch hell from you so I said yes." Two years after her son's discharge from the hospital, she continues to mourn, but our knowledge of the personal system permitted interventions that have at least minimized the human loss resulting from the trauma.

Neuropsychological information has also proven particularly helpful in facilitating the mobile mourning process. The specificity of the clinical neuropsychological assessment enables members of the personal system to replace some of their justifiable uncertainty about the future with an understanding of the present. In R. T.'s case, for example, his parents, after reviewing the neuropsychological findings, felt less confused about the impact of the brain damage on his ability to function. The information gave them something to hold onto. Showing them pictures of the brain in a large atlas and describing R. T.'s specific injury helped reduce their fear of the effects of "brain damage." Sharing the proposed cognitive retraining program with them encouraged the feeling that something specific was being done to help their son. They could become involved in the concrete details of the present plan, which they could value since it provided some hope for the future. They were able to shift their focus from an unknown future to a present with some felt degree of certainty.

It does not help to tell these people not to think about the losses. They were plunged into a world of chaos when the brain injury occurred. We cannot give them a road map of the recovery process, nor can we predict the ultimate outcome. But we can help them understand the present. This must be done concretely enough to permit rational thought in the face of intense anxiety that numbs their ability to think abstractly. The restitution of their personal system takes place slowly, incorporating the evolving status of the brain-injured member.

Specific cognitive remediation techniques can reduce feelings of helplessness by giving members of the personal system something constructive to do. Rather than becoming euphoric about R. T.'s ability to understand what he read or despondent when he "got stuck," he and his family could participate together in his cognitive retraining program. They may have been helpless to remove all the losses, but at least they could be of use in some specific, immediate ways.

Patients often express the feeling that they are "stupid" or "retarded" when they are unable to do tasks that were in their premorbid repertoire. It seems to reduce their self-denigration to conceive of their problem more specifically, that is, to know that a part of their brain is working and a part is not. Some particular parts of a specific organic system are dysfunctional. The person, the self, can then receive high regard for the hard work required in the pursuit of cognitive remediation. Any loss of function brings grief; the neuropsychological assessment helps to focus the grief on actual losses, leaving room for restitution.

Cognitive retraining has also resulted in some rather dramatic changes in responsiveness to counseling. In several cases, we had terminated counseling due to lack of progress. When we focused our efforts on cognitive retraining, we found the patient and family wanting to talk about emotions whose very existence they previously denied. In R. T.'s case, for example, he simply refused to discuss future limitations or his reactions to what had happened to him. When we switched our contract with him to include only cognitive retraining, he began to express deep feers about his future, his marriage, and so on.

Operating on the limited data base of a few such cases, we can only guess at the underlying mechanisms. Our current hypotheses are that by focusing on restoration, the therapist comes to be viewed as an ally and that the focus on restoration allows the process of restitution to begin.

The focus on restoration is one of the strongest arguments that all treatment staff are involved in the mobile mourning process. Each member of the personal system chooses members of the treatment team to talk to, listen to, confide in. Each treatment team member will be involved with each personal system to a greater or lesser extent, depending on the idiosyncrasies of each personal system.

R. T.'s physical therapist would have been less effective if she had simply labeled him as unmotivated when he wanted to withdraw from therapy. Being a sophisticated therapist, she searched for positive reinforcers, but that search would have failed without knowledge of his particular reinforcement history or background. Therapists are often caught up in the interpersonal conflicts emanating from a personal system. They have a right to know what is going on psychologically and neuropsychologically if they are to avoid entrapment in the dynamics of the personal system, let alone maximize their effectiveness.

6. Summary

The conception of the event and sequelae of traumatic brain injury as a partial death involving the members of the personal system has provided a framework for understanding our patients' experiences and needs. The unique characteristics of traumatic head injury plunge the personal system into a grieving process which we have called mobile mourning. Psychodynamic and neuropsychological assessment data have proven useful in designing specific interventions to facilitate this mobile mourning process.

7. References

Bond, M. *Mental consequences of brain-injury.* Paper presented at the 4th Annual Post-Graduate Course on the Rehabilitation of the Traumatic Brain-Injured Adult, Medical College of Virginia, Williamsburg, Virginia, June 1980.

Bowers, D., & Heilman, K. Material-specific hemispheric activation. *Neuropsychologia*, 1980, *18*, 309–319.

Bowlby, J. Attachment theory, separation anxiety, and mourning. In S. Arieti (Ed.), *American handbook of psychiatry* (Vol. 6). New York: Basic Books, 1975.

Caplan, G. *Principles of preventive psychiatry.* New York: Basic Books, 1964.

Davison, L. Introduction. In R. M. Reitan & L. A. Davison (Eds.), *Clinical neuropsychology: Current status and applications*. New York: Wiley, 1974.

Forbes, L. M. Personal communication, 1978.

Haffey, W. J. *Qualitative neuropsychological assessment: Implications for rehabilitation strategy*. Paper presented at the 4th Annual Conference on the Rehabilitation of the Traumatic Brain-Injured Adult, Medical College of Virginia, Williamsburg, Virginia, June 1980.

Hardyck, C., Tzeng, O. J. L., & Wang, W. S-Y. Cerebral lateralization of function and bilingual decision processes: Is thinking lateralized? *Brain & Language*, 1978, *5*, 56–71.

Hécaen, H., & Albert, M. L. *Human neuropsychology*. New York: Wiley, 1978.

Heilman, K., & Valenstein, E. *Clinical neuropsychology*. New York: Oxford University Press, 1979.

Hirshkowitz, M., Earle, J., & Paley, B. EEG alpha asymmetry in musicians and non-musicians: A study of hemispheric specialization. *Neuropsychologia*, 1978, *16*, 125–128.

Jennett, B. Who Cares for Head Injuries? *British Medical Journal*, 1975, *3*, 267–270.

Jennett, B., Teasdale, G., Galbraith, S., Pickard, J., Grant, H., Braakman, R., Avezaat, C., Maas, A., Minderhoud, J., Vecht, C. J., Heiden, J., Small, R., Caton, W., & Kurze, T. Severe head injuries in three countries. *Journal of Neurology, Neurosurgery and Psychiatry*, 1977, *40*, 291–298.

Jennett, B., Teasdale, G., Braakman, R., Minderhoud, J., Heiden, J., & Kurze, T. Prognosis of patients with severe head injury. *Journal of Neurosurgery*, 1979, *4*, 283–289.

Kübler-Ross, E. *On death and dying*. New York: Macmillan, 1969.

Lezak, M. Living with the characterologically altered brain injured patient. *Journal of Clinical Psychiatry*, 1978, *39*, 592–598.

Lindemann, E. *Beyond grief: Studies in crisis intervention*. New York: Jason Aronson, 1979.

Lundholm, J., Jepsen, B. N., & Thornvak, G. The late neurological, psychological, and social aspects of severe traumatic coma. *Scandinavian Journal of Rehabilitation Medicine*, 1975, *7*, 97–100.

Luria, A. R. *Restoration of function after brain injury*. Oxford, England: Pergamon Press, 1963.

Luria, A. R. Neuropsychological analysis of focal brain lesions. In B. B. Wolman (Ed.), *Handbook of clinical psychology*. New York: McGraw-Hill, 1965.

Luria, A. R. *Higher cortical functions in man*. New York: Basic Books, 1966.

Luria, A. R. The neuropsychological study of brain lesion and restoration of damaged brain function. In M. Cole & I. Maltzman (Eds.), *A handbook of contemporary soviet psychology*. New York: Basic Books, 1969.

Luria, A. R. *Traumatic aphasia: Its syndrome, psychology and treatment*. The Hague: Mouton, 1970.

Luria, A. R. *The working brain*. New York: Basic Books, 1973.

Luria, A. R. Neuropsychology: Its sources, principles and prospects. In F. G. Worden, J. P. Swazey, & G. Adelman (Eds.), *The neurosciences: Paths of discovery*. Cambridge, Mass.: MIT Press, 1975.

Luria, A. R. *Basic problems in neurolinguistics*. The Hague: Mouton, 1976.

Luria, A. R., & Artemyeva, E. Two approaches to an evaluation of the reliability of psychological investigations: Reliability of a fact and syndrome analysis. *Soviet Psychology*, 1970, *8*, 271–283.

Luria, A. R., Nayden, V. L., Tsvetkova, L. S., & Vinarskaya, E. N. Restoration of higher cortical function following local brain damage. In P. J. Vinken & G. W. Bruyn (Eds.), *Handbook of clinical neurology* (Vol. 3). Amsterdam: North-Holland, 1969.

Moore, W. H., & Haynes, W. O. A study of alpha hemispheric asymmetries and their relationship to verbal and nonverbal abilities in males and females. *Brain and Language.* 1980, *9*, 338–349.

Muir, C. A. *Mobile mourning: Psychodynamics of family and patient in brain trauma.* Paper presented at the Western Psychological Association, San Francisco, California, April 1978. (a)

Muir, C. A. *Mobile mourning: Response of the personal system to partial death due to brain injury.* Paper presented at Second Annual Conference on the Rehabilitation of the Traumatic Brain-Injured Adult, Medical College of Virginia, Williamsburg, Virginia, June 1978. (b)

Moos, R. H. *Coping with physical illness.* New York: Plenum Press, 1977.

Oddy, M., Humphrey, M., & Uttley, D. Stresses upon the relatives of head-injured patients. *British Journal of Psychiatry,* 1978, *133*, 507–513.

Rappaport, M., Hall, K., Hopkins, K., Belleza, T., Berrol, S., & Reynolds, G. Evoked brain potentials and disability in brain-damaged patients. *Archives of Physical Medicine and Rehabilitation,* 1977, *58*, 333–338.

Rappaport, M., Hopkins, K., Hall, K., Belleza, T., & Berrol, S. Brain evoked potential use in a physical medicine and rehabilitation setting. *Scandinavian Journal of Rehablitation Medicine,* 1978, *10*, 27–32.

Rochlin, G. *Griefs and discontents, the forces of change.* Boston: Little, Brown, 1965.

Schneidman, E. S. *Deaths of man.* Baltimore: Penguin Books, 1974.

Schoenberg, B., Carr, A. C., Peretz, D., & Kutscher, A. H. *Loss and grief: Psychological management and medical practice.* New York: Columbia University Press, 1970.

Szalita, A. B. Grief and bereavement. In S. Arieti (Ed.), *American handbook of psychiatry* (Vol. 1). New York: Basic Books, 1974.

Willis, S. G., Wheatley, G. H., & Mitchell, O. R. Cerebral processing of spatial and verbal analytic tasks: An EEG study. *Neuropsychologia,* 1979, *17*, 473–484.

9

A Rehabilitation Program for Brain-Injured Adults

William J. Lynch

1. Introduction

It has been estimated that one person in 200 will require medical care for a head injury each year, and that each day about 1% of the work force is disabled because of head injury (Peterson, 1975, pp. 1093–1108). A majority of these injuries occurs in people under 40 years of age, and many brain-injured patients survive 30 to 40 years beyond the initial trauma (Jennett, 1975, pp. 3–21). These factors are responsible for the increasing numbers of those suffering late effects of traumatic brain injury.

Early investigations in the area of treatment of traumatically brain-injured were limited to individual case studies or anecdotal observations on small groups of patients. Typically, these studies had little in common insofar as observational or assessment techniques were concerned. Other potentially meaningful variables—such as type of lesion, criteria for inclusion in the treatment program, treatment techniques, outcome measures, and follow-up procedures—were highly variable from one investigation to another.

With the development of clinical neuropsychology, it became possible to evaluate patients more comprehensively and reliably. First with the test batteries of Halstead (1947) and Reitan (1955) and later with the publication in this country of Luria's Neuropsychologic Evaluation (Christensen, 1975) and the Luria-Nebraska (Golden, Purisch, & Ham-

WILLIAM J. LYNCH • Brain Injury Rehabilitation Unit, Veterans Administration Medical Center, Palo Alto, California 94304.

meke, 1979), the use of some sort of standardized assessment procedures became commonplace. More will be said about these procedures in a later section.

Certain other key variables in determining degree of brain dysfunction have been found to be easily quantified. For example, the concept of posttraumatic amnesia has been shown (Jennett & Teasdale, 1981, p. 326) to be a significant factor in prediction of outcome. Posttraumatic amnesia is defined as the time between onset of the head injury and return of day-by-day memory. Levin, O'Donnell, and Grossman (1979) have published a scale, known as the Galveston Orientation and Amnesia Test, which measures the presence and the degree of posttraumatic amnesia.

Similarly, there have been attempts to quantify such heretofore unreliable variables as coma and treatment outcome. The Glasgow Coma Scale (Teasdale & Jennett, 1974) has gained fairly wide acceptance as an objective measure of level of consciousness. The Glasgow Coma Scale is a 15-point scale which encompasses the variables of eye opening, verbal responsiveness, and best motor response. The Glasgow Outcome Scale (Jennett & Bond, 1975) provides a standardized manner of categorizing eventual outcome of treatment of patients with head injuries. The Glasgow Outcome Scale consists of five levels of outcome, each of which has certain defining characteristics (Jennett, 1976):

- *Death*
- *Persistent Vegetative State:* The patient does not respond meaningfully, although his or her eyes are open and he or she appears to be awake. The limbs may remain flexed. There is no attempt to speak.
- *Severe Disability:* The patient is dependent upon others for survival due to either physical or mental disability (or both). These patients are usually (but not necessarily) hospitalized.
- *Moderate Disability:* At this level, the patient is independent with regard to daily functions, can use public transportation, and is able to work in a protected setting. Some of the deficits evidenced by such patients would be dysphasia, hemiparesis, memory deficits, cognitive deficits, and personality disorders.
- *Good Recovery:* The patient is able to resume normal life functions at or near the premorbid level.

With the widening popularity of these measures of posttraumatic amnesia, coma, and outcome there has been a trend toward more collaborative research, both at national and at international levels. In this chapter, I will describe one type of rehabilitative program for brain-impaired persons. This is an outpatient program which deals primarily with persons who are 3 or more months postinjury and are medically stable. The assessment and treatment procedures which will be described will be representative of similar programs around the country, although numerous variations in specific tests or treatment methods will always exist.

2. A Rehabilitative Program for Brain-Injured Adults

2.1. Assessment

2.1.1. The Referral Process

The first step in the rehabilitation process is one of the most important—selecting patients who are able and likely to benefit from treatment. The suitability of a patient for treatment depends upon the overall scope of the program in question. For example, an acute-care program may not wish to accept patients who are more than 6 months or a year postonset. Similarly, more chronic-care programs may accept the long postonset patient, while being unable to accommodate recent-onset patients who demand continual skilled medical–nursing care. Jennett and his colleagues (Jennett, Teasdale, Galbraith, Pickard, Grant, Braakman, Avezaat, Maas, Minderhoud, Vecht, Heiden, Small, Caton, & Kurze, 1977) have shown that by 3 months postonset 60% of their traumatically injured patients have reached their highest level on the Glasgow Outcome Scale (GOS), while 80% to 90% reach their highest level by 6 months postonset. Although it must be granted that *within* GOS categories there is certainly room for change beyond the 6-month period, it is also true that a patient who has stayed well within one of the GOS categories for 6 to 12 months is not likely to improve sufficiently to reach a higher level.

Some variables that need to be considered in evaluating a referral (aside from administrative or legal eligibility criteria) include the following:

2.1.1.1. *Type of Injury.* Studies of the effects of angle of impact upon cerebral injury (Lewis, 1976, pp. 300–302) have revealed that a greater amount of tissue damage occurs following a rotational (or oblique) rather than a linear (front-to-back/back-to-front) plane of impact. Shearing effects in rotational impacts appear to result in more substantial damage to both cortical and brain stem structures. Similarly, closed head injuries (i.e., those in which the dura remains intact) tend to have a more favorable prognosis than penetrating lesions such as depressed skull fractures or missile wounds. This is due partly to the fact that substantial force must be exerted upon the head in order for penetration to occur. In addition, there is a greater risk of intracranial infection with penetrating injury.

2.1.1.2. Location of Injury. Traumatic lesions that are relatively circumscribed tend to have a better prognosis than those which are bilateral or diffuse (Golden, 1978, p. 187). A recent study (Miller & Miyamoto, 1979) suggested that brain lesions that are deep or central (using a horizontal frame of reference) are more apt to result in greater and more lasting deficit than lesions in superficial or peripheral areas. Additional considerations include the presence and degree of brain stem involvement as well as involvement of language centers. The former can result in persistent impairment of consciousness, alertness, and attention; the latter can make rehabilitation difficult due to the difficulty in communicating with the patient.

Other investigators (Smith, 1971) have pointed out that patients with mixed cerebral dominance are better able to adapt to focal cerebral lesions because of a greater degree of decentralization of cortical functions in the hemispheres.

2.1.1.3. Chronicity of Lesion. It is generally accepted that rehabilitation is more effective with lesions of recent—as opposed to remote—onset (Jennett and Teasdale, 1981, p. 308). As mentioned earlier, it is unlikely that a patient will improve sufficiently to move from one outcome category to another on the Glasgow Outcome Scale (GOS) after 6 months beyond the date of onset. Certainly, it can be argued that these GOS categories are rather broad and that patients may evidence improvement *within* as well as *between* categories. The 6-month figure applies more to structural than to functional recovery and does not take into account the myriad of secondary effects or maladaptive behaviors relating to—but not caused directly by—abnormal brain activity. We have never rigidly applied a time-since-onset criteria for admission. Indeed, there have been patients in our program whose onset was during World War II.

Russell (1979) discusses the concept of diaschisis as it relates to the chronicity of brain lesions. Diaschisis is defined as the situation in which abilities or functions dependent upon remote brain areas are temporarily impaired by a lesion elsewhere in the brain. Russell's point is that we must bear in mind that the *acute effects* of a brain lesion should not be assumed to be reflective of the areas of the brain that have been permanently damaged. Essentially, the initial effects of a lesion are a result of some permanent (or relatively permanent) structural changes in brain substance in addition to temporary changes that occur as a result of transient brain swelling, vascular spasms, or mass effects. The clinician must be careful not to base decisions regarding either acceptance into treatment or long-term prognosis upon neuropsychologic data gathered immediately following onset of a traumatic lesion.

In this connection, it has recently been pointed out (Bricolo, Turazzi, & Feriotti, 1980) that such variables as duration in and stages of recovery from posttraumatic coma may not be as strongly related to eventual outcome as is commonly believed. These investigators found that, aside from patients who showed immediate and profound coma following head injury, there was no clear relationship between traditional prognostic indices and actual duration of coma or ultimate outcome. They attribute this finding to the varying secondary effects of coma—such as medical complications, which vary in their incidence and impact depending upon the individual's state of health—as well as the intensity of the early medical diagnostic and treatment effort.

In summary, then, the data do not permit rigid prognostic inferences based upon chronicity of traumatic brain lesions. Although it may be true that patients will tend to reach their maximum outcome level by the sixth month postonset, there is sufficient room for variation *within* categories to justify accepting patients in treatment long beyond this traditional 6-month period.

2.1.1.4. Age of Patient. It is generally accepted that, in an absolute sense, older patients perform more poorly than younger patients on neuropsychologic tests (Hamsher & Benton, 1978). Younger patients tend to demonstrate greater and more rapid improvement after cerebral trauma than do older patients (Teuber, 1975, pp. 155–190). Golden (1978, p. 186) has suggested that aside from neurophysiologic differences between the two groups, older patients may fare more poorly due to a higher incidence of brain deterioration, inadequate financial resources, and lack of optimism on the part of the staff. In our program, we tend not to consider age to be a sufficiently meaningful variable in isolation, although we are hesitant to accept patients who are well beyond age 70. This is due partly to the fact that significant aging effects are apt to be in process at this point (Golden, 1978, p. 186).

2.1.1.5. Presence of Other Disabilities. Patients who have other disabilities will require additional and special care during the rehabilitation effort. The list of potential conditions is virtually limitless; it includes mental disorders, substance-abuse disorders (alcohol and drug abuse), heart disease, liver disease, blindness, paraplegia/quadriplegia, emphysema, and uncontrolled diabetes. These conditions often result in slowed improvement due to special accommodations required and lim-

Table 1. Summary of Some Important Variables to Consider in Evaluating Likely
Outcome of Rehabilitation of Brain-Injured Adults

Variable	Outcome tends to be	
	More favorable if:	Less favorable if:
Angle of impact	Linear	Oblique/rotational
Type of injury	Closed	Penetrating
Location of injury	Focal	Diffuse/bilateral
Brain stem involvement	None/minimal	Significant and permanent
Cerebral dominance	Mixed	Lateralized to injured side
Chronicity of lesion	New/recent	Old/remote
Age	Younger (<65)	Older (>65)
Presence of other disabilities	None	Any
Motivation	High	Low

itations of the activities in which these patients can become involved. In our program, patients who are active substance (alcohol or drug) abusers, dangerously violent, or suffering a major mental disorder (affective disorder or schizophrenia) are not accepted for treatment.

In many cases of craniocerebral trauma, brain stem and/or cerebellar dysfunction may result in deficits involving cranial nerves, muscular tone, or coordination. Such patients require special attention in transportation, feeding, toileting, and manipulation of testing or retraining materials. These conditions are usually not sufficient to exclude a person from treatment, however.

2.1.1.6. Level of Motivation. It seems obvious that one must consider the patient's level of motivation when deciding about his or her appropriateness for treatment (Benton, 1960; Luria, 1963, pp. 223–262). In much the same fashion as we consider ego strength an important factor in prognosis for psychotherapy, psychodynamic variables must be considered in rehabilitation.

In patients with inadequate motivation, it is often helpful to utilize techniques such as praise and feedback. This can be accomplished by providing frequent opportunities for encouragement and recognition for improved performance. By establishing specific treatment goals, the patient's progress toward a goal can be monitored by means of comparing his or her baseline performance with current level of performance. In addition, the development of rapport with the patient tends to stimulate him or her to put forth a greater and more sustained effort. Table 1 summarizes the variables to be considered in evaluating likely outcome of rehabilitation.

In addition to considering the above criteria for suitability of a referral, it is also necessary to review the patient's medical record and to interview any people who are familiar with the patient's past and present status. This enables us to determine exactly what happened to the patient, when it happened, what evaluations have been done, and what kind of person he or she was prior to the injury. At this point, an initial decision as to the need for further evaluation must be made.

2.1.2. The Basic Work-up

2.1.2.1. History. In actual practice, it is necessary to obtain three histories for each patient. The first is a traditional medical history, preferably one that conforms to a standard, structured format. Figure 1 illustrates a portion of such a structured history form.

Particular emphasis is placed upon premorbid functioning, date and type of the head injury in question, presence of other medical conditions, medication history, and results of any neurodiagnostic procedures. A second history is concerned more with psychologic and neuropsychologic data such as handedness, school performance, previous head injuries, results of previous standardized tests, job performance, and current behavioral deficits. The third history focuses upon psychosocial factors. Data pertaining to early childhood and adolescent development, mental health history, adult adjustment, interpersonal relationships, integrity of defenses, and ego strength attributes are among the points of interest here.

Certainly, it is preferable to combine two or all three of these histories into one comprehensive form. However, in most settings the various histories can be obtained by the appropriate discipline (i.e., nurse or physician for medical history; and a social worker, psychologist, or psychiatrist for the psychosocial history).

2.1.2.2. Neuropsychologic Assessment. The two principal neuropsychologic batteries in general use in the United States today are the Halstead Reitan Battery (and its variants) and Luria's Neuropsychological Investigation (and its variant).

The original Luria procedures were organized and published by Christensen (1975). Although it represented a valiant attempt to consolidate and partially standardize the techniques employed by Luria in his 40 years of clinical work in the U.S.S.R., Christensen's publication of Luria's Neuropsychological Investigation (LNI) met with mixed reviews among the neuropsychologic community in the United States (cf. Reitan, 1976). The procedures are frequently described ambiguously or vaguely, so that one is not certain whether the stimuli are being present-

Patient's name: _____

Age: _____ Born: _____ Sex: _____

Marital: S   M   Sep   D   W

Education: _____ Religion: _____

Occupation: _____

Referred by: _____

Reason for referral: _____

_____

Home address: _____

_____

Family order:

   Brothers: _____ Age _____

   Sisters: _____ Age _____

Handedness:

   Patient: _____ Mother: _____

   Father: _____ Sibs: _____

Military Service: no   from _____

   Branch _____ to _____

Place of examination: _____

Previous mental health contacts:

_____

_____

_____

Drugs at time of testing: _____

_____

Glasses: No   Yes   Type: _____

Test behavior:

	Low			High	
Activity level:	1	2	3	4	5
Cooperation:	1	2	3	4	5
Effort:	1	2	3	4	5

Speech defect: none   Type:

_____

Hearing defect: none   Type:

_____

Visual defect: none   Type:

_____

Additional laboratory data:

   Skull films: normal   abnormal

      Findings: _____

_____

   EEG: normal   abnormal

      Findings: _____

_____

   Brain Scan: normal   abnormal

      Findings: _____

_____

Filled out by _____

Date _____

Echo: normal   abnormal

   Findings: _____

Pneumo: normal   abnormal

   Findings: _____

Other: normal   abnormal

   Findings: _____

Birth and developmental history:

Pregnancy and delivery:

   Pregnancy complications: none

   Diseases: _____

_____

   Other: _____

   Delivery:

      Term: full   _____ months

      Labor: _____ hours

      Delivery: _____

      Incubator: no   yes _____

      Weight: _____ lbs.

      Condition: healthy   other:

_____

   APGAR rating: _____

Development:

   Neonatal feeding problems: none

      Type: _____

   Milestones (age of, in months):

Holding up head:	_____	(1–2)
Sitting up:	_____	(4–7)
Crawling:	_____	(10)
Talking: words:	_____	(12)
sentences:	_____	(18)
Standing: help:	_____	(8)
no help:	_____	(14)
Walking:	_____	(15)
Toilet trained:	_____	(5 years)

Illnesses and accidents:

   Illnesses:

Tuberculosis	no	yes
Meningitis	no	yes
Encephalitis	no	yes
Polio	no	yes
Diabetes	no	yes
High blood pressure	no	yes
Heart disease	no	yes
Rheumatic	no	yes

Chorea	no	yes	Fainting spells (4+): _____	
Scarlet fever	no	yes	Knocked unconscious: _____	
Other: _____			_____	

Operations:	Head injuries: _____
Type: _____	_____
Age: _____ Complications: _____	_____
_____	Convulsions (epilepsy): no yes
Type: _____	Age first seizure: _____
Age: _____ Complications: _____	Frequency: _____
_____	Duration: _____
High fever (104°+): _____	Aura, warning: _____

Near drowning: _____	Pattern, if any: _____
Near overcome by gas: _____	_____

Figure 1. Neuropsychological History Form.

ed in a reliable fashion. Normal performance was often hinted at but not specified. Scoring is not considered essential but appears to consist of a dichotomous pass–fail or plus–minus system. A concise but coherent discussion of the differences between the Soviet (Luria) and American approaches to clinical neuropsychology was published recently by Luria and Majovski (1977).

Recently Golden and his associates published a major revision and reorganization of the LNI under the title of the Luria-Nebraska Neuropsychological Battery (Golden, Purisch, & Hammeke, 1979). Briefly, the Luria-Nebraska consists of 269 items divided into 14 subscales:

Motor functions	Reading functions
Rhythm functions	Arithmetical functions
Tactile functions	Memory functions
Visual functions	Intellectual processes
Receptive language	Pathognomonic scales
Expressive language	Right hemisphere
Writing functions	Left hemisphere

Each item is scored according to a three-point scale: 0 = normal, 1 = intermediate, and 2 = impaired. The raw scores are then translated into T scores and are plotted on profiles. Generally, scores that fall below a T score of 60 are considered normal; 60 to 69 is considered as borderline; and 70 or above, impaired.

It is not the purpose of this chapter critically to compare the Luria Neuropsychological Investigation, Luria-Nebraska, and Halstead-Reitan procedures. The reader is referred to discussions by Adams (1980a,b); Golden (1980); Golden, Hammeke, and Purisch (1978); Luria and Majovski (1977); Reitan (1976); and others (Hayden, Kalisky, & Hess, 1980) for a more thorough treatment of this delicate issue. Suffice it to say that there seems to be an unfortunate schism developing between those who characterize themselves as being faithful to Luria's original intent (i.e., the traditionalists) and those who have "Americanized" the original version to accommodate our demand for administrative and scoring precision (the revisionists).

One solution which I have employed is to have all of the patients who are accepted for treatment undergo both Luria-Nebraska and Halstead-Reitan examinations. At a later date, a decision will be made as to the relative contribution of the two procedures to the overall diagnostic and treatment process. The remainder of this section will be devoted to the tests or procedures which I typically utilize in evaluating potential rehabilitation patients.

The Halstead-Reitan Battery (Reitan, 1966, pp. 153–218) consists of seven principal measures in addition to a number of other specialized procedures. The reader may be familiar with most or all of the tests comprising the Halstead-Reitan Battery, therefore I will not describe them at great length. Items in the Halstead-Reitan Battery:

Halstead tests:
  Category
  Tactual Performance Test (3 measures)
  Rhythm Test
  Speech Perception Test
  Finger Oscillation (Tapping) Test
Other measures:
  Trail Making Test
  Aphasia Screening Test
  Sensory–Perceptual Examination
  Strength of Grip
  Wechsler Intelligence Scale (WAIS-R or WISC-R)
  Wide Range Achievement Test (WRAT)
  Minnesota Multiphasic Personality Inventory (MMPI)

As happens in most locations, I have made some additions and adjustments to this basic battery, partly as a result of special requirements of the patient population with which I deal but also due to a desire to improve the quality and utility of the data obtained. For example, we may employ the Peabody Individual Achievement Test (Dunn &

Markwardt, 1970) rather than the Wide Range Achievement Test (Jastak & Jastak, 1978), since the former employs a multiple-choice format requiring a simple pointing response on most items. This paradigm does not unfairly penalize patients with expressive speech or motor problems. Another example would be our use of the multiple choice version of the Visual Retention Test (Benton, Hamsher, & Stone, 1977) rather than the standard version (Benton, 1974), which requires the patient to draw the design to be recalled.

Measures of Language Functions. I have found the Porch Index of Communicative Ability (PICA) (Porch, 1967) to be an extremely useful assessment tool for determining the integrity of the patient's total communicative system. The PICA consists of 18 subtests that evaluate visual and auditory input as well as gestural, verbal, and graphic output by presenting 10 standard objects in various situations requiring responses as simple as responsive naming and as complex as composing a sentence describing the function of an object. In all, there are 180 separate observations, each of which is assigned a numerical score based on Porch's Multidimensional Scoring System (Porch, 1971). The scores are then grouped and averaged, resulting in four separate summary measures: overall, gestural, verbal, and graphic. The data can then be transposed onto various profile forms, including a rating of communicative deficit, ranked response summary, modality response summary, and aphasia recovery curve. Porch and his colleagues (Porch, Collins, Wertz, & Friden, 1980) have recently published data, based upon the PICA, that permit reasonably accurate early prediction of eventual level of recovery of aphasic patients. Although not all speech pathologists are in agreement regarding the utility of the PICA (see for example, Martin, 1977), I have found it is without peer insofar as reliability and objectivity of scoring is concerned. The PICA was not designed to *diagnose* aphasic syndromes as were, for example, the Boston Diagnostic Aphasia Examination (Goodglass & Kaplan, 1972) or the Minnesota Test for the Differential Diagnosis of Aphasia (Schuell, 1965). Rather, the PICA's strength lies in its ability to accurately quantify language behavior in a way that permits reliable data comparison within and between patients.

The Token Test (De Renzi & Vignolo, 1962) is another useful measure of verbal comprehension in patients with apraxia of speech, motor impairment of the arms, or dysarthria. The procedure for administering the test varies slightly from one institution to the other but essentially involves presenting verbal commands of systematically varying complexity to touch, pick up, or move one or more variously colored and shaped plastic tokens. We have found the Token Test to be useful in detecting subtle deficits in auditory comprehension in patients who are unable to attend to the more complex examinations such as the PICA, Boston Diagnostic Aphasia Exam, or Minnesota Test for the Differential Diagnosis of Aphasia.

Measures of Memory. It has been argued that neither the Halstead-Reitan battery nor the Luria's Neuropsychological Investigation nor the Luria-Nebraska adequately assesses memory (Hayden, Kalisky, & Hess, 1980). I agree with this criticism and consequently have sought to thoroughly evaluate the ability of patients to register, store, and retrieve information. The principal measure I employ is the Wechsler Memory Scale (Wechsler, 1945), with age-weighted total score and subtest norms (Osborne & Davis, 1978) and 30-minute delay norms for the Logical Memory and Visual Memory subtests (Russell, 1975). In addition, I use the list-learning procedures of both Rey (1964, pp. 353–356) and Buschke and Fuld (1974). The Rey test is quite useful in that it contains both a postinterference and recognition trial—elements absent from most popular memory measures. The Buschke is described as a "selective reminding" procedure that assesses both long- and short-term information storage, retention, and retrieval. Another set of helpful measures of auditory memory is the Goldman, Fristoe, Woodcock Auditory Memory Tests (Goldman, Fristoe, & Woodcock, 1974). Memory for content and sequence and Recognition memory are measured. Norms are provided for a wide range of age groups, and since all three subtests are presented by audio cassette tape, there is excellent reliability in test administration.

For evaluating visual memory, I find the Benton Visual Retention Test (Benton, 1974) to be most useful. The availability of three parallel forms, age- and IQ-weighted norms, and a recently published multiple-choice format (Benton, Hamsher, & Stone, 1977) are important advantages. The importance of evaluating a patient's memory functions cannot be exaggerated. It is imperative to obtain a careful determination of the efficiency of the patient's ability to register, store, and retrieve information. The entire treatment process depends, to some extent, upon the patient's ability to retain and later apply information that has been presented to him or her by each therapist. By identifying the patients who have serious memory impairment, special efforts can be made either to reduce the complexity of the information to be retained or to simplify the process of retrieving the information once it is registered. In our program, about 80% of the patients are in need of formal memory retraining as a separate treatment module.

Measures of Motor Functions. In addition to the HR finger-tapping test and strength-of-grip examination, I have included the following motor measures: the Purdue Pegboard (Tiffin, 1968) and the Grooved

Pegboard and Foot Tapping tests (Beardsley, Matthews, Cleeland, & Harley, 1972). The former two tests provide useful information regarding fine manual dexterity, visual–motor integration, and possible lateralization of motor dysfunction (Costa, Vaughn, Levita, & Farber, 1963). The foot-tapping test is a useful complement to the finger-tapping test. It is helpful to compare finger- and foot-tapping speed performance in patients with motor dysfunction.

    2.1.2.3. Personality Assessment. It is important to determine the presence of current or potential behavioral abnormalities in head-injured patients. In addition to the standard Minnesota Multiphasic Personality Inventory (MMPI), I have found both the MMPI-168 (Overall & Gomez-Mont, 1974) and the OBD-168 (Sbordone & Caldwell, 1979) to be useful brief screening devices. Patients may also be given portions of the Personality Research Form (PRF; Jackson, 1974) as a way of determining need for assertiveness training. Lately, I have begun to use the SCL-90-R (Derogatis, Lipman, & Covi, 1973) as a way of determining a patient's subjective level of distress. The Brief Psychiatric Rating Scale (Overall & Gorham, 1962) is used as a guide for interviewing and providing a quantified evaluation of the presence and severity of maladaptive behavior patterns.

    Information from family, friends, and job associates is solicited in order to determine the patient's premorbid level of functioning. Behavioral problems severe enough to impede rehabilitative progress are treated directly by individual or group psychotherapy or by behavior modification techniques. Medication may be employed, but this is considered only after behavioral treatments have failed to take effect.

    Depression is a common psychopathologic symptom observed in brain-injured patients (Hendrie, 1978). The nature and extent of depression is determined by interview and various psychometric methods such as the SCL-90-R, Zung Self-Rating Depression Scale (Zung, 1965), Beck Depression Inventory (Beck & Beck, 1972), or the Depression (especially the Depression-Subtle) scale from the MMPI. The need to evaluate and treat depression cannot be overemphasized. Progress in treatment can be attenuated, even stalled entirely, if the patient is not given prompt and effective treatment for this problem.

    Another common behavioral deficit in brain-injured patients is inappropriate assertion—either aggressiveness or, more commonly, passivity (Wells & Duncan, 1980, pp. 195–197). As an operational definition of the presence of either trait, I have opted for a psychometric measure in addition to certain other self-report techniques. The assessment tool I am currently employing consists of the Abasement, Dominance, and Aggression scales of Jackson's Personality Research Form-R (Jackson,

1974). These scales, along with a validity scale, constitute the "Assertiveness Index." By convention, scores on the three principal dimensions which fall outside the range of T score 40 to 60 are considered to indicate a need for intervention.

Finally, all the behavioral assessment information obtained is collated so that the patient's relative strengths and liabilities can be articulated. The personality data are summarized by means of standard-score profiles (such as MMPI or SCL-90-R) or by preparing a list of assets and liabilities as they apply to level of independence and adaptibility. An attempt is made to avoid reliance upon psychodynamic language and to employ more readily understood terms that describe how the patient acts or will act in certain situations. This information is invaluable in the designing of an appropriate treatment program. Assets—such as high self-sufficiency, strong motivation, friendliness, and talkativeness—may be used to the patient's advantage by arranging treatment modalities that will exploit these traits. The wider use of independent study (in which the patient works alone on an assigned task) as opposed to one-to-one therapy with such patients would be one way of making use of his or her assets. Similarly, liabilities such as low self-sufficiency, low motivation, and social introversion would require an altogether different rehabilitative strategy.

2.1.2.4. Consultations. In any rehabilitative program, consultation with various members of the rehabilitation team is vital. In the following sections, I will describe how this is carried out in the Brain Injury Rehabilitation Unit (BIRU).

Neurologic Evaluation. A clinical neurologic examination is obtained on all patients at the time of admission. The importance of obtaining a current, thorough neurologic examination is clear (Rohmer & Buchheit, 1975). The neurologic examination provides information regarding integrity of the sensorimotor system, presence of normal or pathologic reflexes, and some information regarding mental status. The examination is carried out either by a neurologist or by a specially trained and certified neurologic nurse. The nurse/examiner follows a strict protocol which she helped to develop and, as a result, the data gathered are complete and consistently organized for each patient. A copy of this form can be obtained on request from the author. An electroencephalogram (EEG) will be ordered if there is reason to suspect that a lesion detectable by this procedure exists. The EEG can help to determine the relative abnormalities of two or more brain areas. All patients with a positive history for seizures are referred for an EEG, of course. If the lesion is already well documented and delineated by other means and if seizures are no longer an issue, the EEG is not typically obtained.

Radiology and Nuclear Medicine. Routine skull x-rays are not obtained. This is due partly to the fact that virtually all patients referred for rehabilitation will already have had a series of skull films and also to the fact that "routine" skull x-rays have not been shown to be sufficiently informative to justify either the cost or additional cranial radiation involved (Tsai & Tsuang, 1978).

The radiologic study of choice is the computed tomographic (CT) scan of the head. This study is noninvasive, painless, and virtually free of any mortality or morbidity factor (Osborn, 1979). The data obtained are very useful, both for understanding the type and location of the brain lesion(s) present and for objectively determining any changes in brain structure over time. The CT scan is able to determine relative density of brain tissue as well as the size and possible displacement of the cerebral ventricles. Clearly, such data regarding the integrity of cerebral structures are critical in making cogent decisions regarding admission and treatment approaches.

Miller and Miyamoto (1979) have presented data on the use of the CT scan in the prediction of functional recovery following stroke. Bigler (1980) described the technique of incorporating CT scan results with neuropsychologic test data in determining rehabilitation potential. Despite the obvious usefulness of CT scanning in diagnosis, the clinician should not uncritically accept normal or abnormal CT scan results as being conclusive in determining potential for change or outcome from treatment (Adams, Brown, & Jacisin, 1980; Tsushima & Popper, 1980).

In certain instances, it is desirable to obtain a traditional (isotope) brain scan. This procedure provides the clinician with data pertaining to the location of breakdowns in the blood–brain barrier as well as some indication of efficiency of cerebral blood flow (Oldendorf, 1978).

Angiography, pneumoencephalography, or ventriculography is rarely necessary in a long-term rehabilitative setting, particularly in view of the fact that the CT scan is available. There may be occasions, however, when these studies are necessary. Angiography is clearly the study of choice for suspected aneurisms, carotid stenosis, or vascular spasms, for example (Oldendorf, 1978).

The information gained by these various neurodiagnostic procedures is used to confirm our understanding of the exact type, location, and extent of the lesion(s) present. These data will often be helpful in explaining the specific pattern of abilities that are retained, impaired, or lost. In a sense, while the neuropsychologic evaluation can tell us *what* the patient can and cannot do, the neurodiagnostic evaluation can tell us *why* this is so. Changes in the patient's neurodiagnostic studies may portend changes in behavior. In the instance of CT scans showing enlarged cerebral ventricles, surgical procedures such as shunting excess cerebrospinal fluid from the ventricles may be indicated. Currently, the correlation between CT scan findings and behavior is not sufficiently strong to permit prediction of one from the other. Indeed, we can recall a patient in our program whose discharge CT scan was considered *worse* than one done on admission but who was clearly improved clinically.

Psychiatry. I feel strongly that a psychiatrist with special expertise and interest in organic brain disorders should be part of the rehabilitation team as a consultant if not as a full-time team member. All of the prospective patients for BIRU treatment are referred for a psychiatric examination. The purpose of the evaluation is twofold: first, to obtain a "second opinion" regarding the patient's current mental state (presence of a mental disorder, functioning of defenses, judgment, etc.) and, second, to evaluate past and current medication status. The psychiatrist is asked to determine what medications the patient has taken, what is currently being taken, and what he or she should continue to take. The psychiatrist's knowledge of medication effects, appropriate dosage levels, and drug interactions is called into play at this point. This psychiatric evaluation serves as a useful cross-check to validate or call into question the neuropsychologist's evaluation of the patient's personality structure and mental status.

Audiology. Although routine audiometry is obtained on most patients in most centers, I have found that additional procedures such as speech reception threshold, filtered speech perception, binaural fusion, dichotic competing sentences, and alternating speech perception are often helpful in delineating the presence and extent of auditory processing deficits (Willeford, 1977; Welsh, Welsh, & Healy, 1980). Techniques such as auditory evoked potentials are becoming more common in many centers and are potentially quite helpful in providing reliable diagnostic and prognostic information regarding the integrity of the entire auditory system (Starr, 1978).

Speech Pathology. Referral for a formal evaluation by a speech pathologist is mandatory in any patient with an obvious or suspected language disorder. In our unit, the Boston Diagnostic Aphasia Examination (Goodglass & Kaplan, 1972) is routinely administered. This complements the brief aphasia evaluation from the HR battery and provides additional information to that obtained from the PICA. The speech pathologist is asked both to arrive at a diagnosis of the problem and to make specific recommendations as to the type and frequency of speech/language therapy indicated (if any).

Physical Therapy.   Any patients with weakness, spasticity, or ataxia should be referred for a thorough physical therapy (PT) evaluation. Recommendations by PT as to need for therapy or for assistive or prosthetic devices are helpful in treatment planning. In many instances PT may make suggestions to the staff and/or family regarding exercises that can be carried out at home or by unit staff aside from regularly scheduled PT appointments.

Occupational Therapy.   The primary goal of rehabilitation in general is to maximize independence in daily living. It is the objective of the occupational therapy (OT) evaluation to assess the patient's skill in various actitivies of daily living (ADL). The traditional OT evaluation is supplemented by an objective assessment of independence known as the Rating of Patient's Independence (ROPI; Porch & Collins, 1974). The ROPI consists of 15 separate activities (such as dressing or eating), which are, in turn, subdivided into five discrete tasks. All tasks are rated upon a 15-point multidimensional scale, the results being plotted upon a profile that indicates whether an activity is carried out at all and, if so, whether the patient requires direct assistance or merely supervision while carrying out the act in question. Many of the activities are evaluated directly by structured behavioral samples. Hearsay by relatives is relied upon only as a final resort. The ROPI provides a comprehensive and objective measure of ADL and can easily be repeated for purposes of pre-, post- or serial testing.

A less detailed but quite promising measure that evaluates various categories of disability is the Disability Rating Scale (Rappaport, Hall, Hopkins, Belleza, & Cope, 1982). The Disability Rating Scale evaluates the following five categories:

1. Arousability
2. Awareness and responsibility
3. Cognitive ability for self-care activities
4. Dependence on others
5. Psychosocial adaptability

2.1.3. Organizing the Data

All the information gathered from our initial evaluation and consultations is analyzed by myself and the head nurse in order to articulate the patient's assets and liabilities. In many cases, the data are transformed into profiles for more rapid analysis. Figures 2 and 3 illustrate the profiles used for summarizing data from the Halstead-Reitan (HR) battery and other neuropsychologic tests as well as the Rating of Pa-

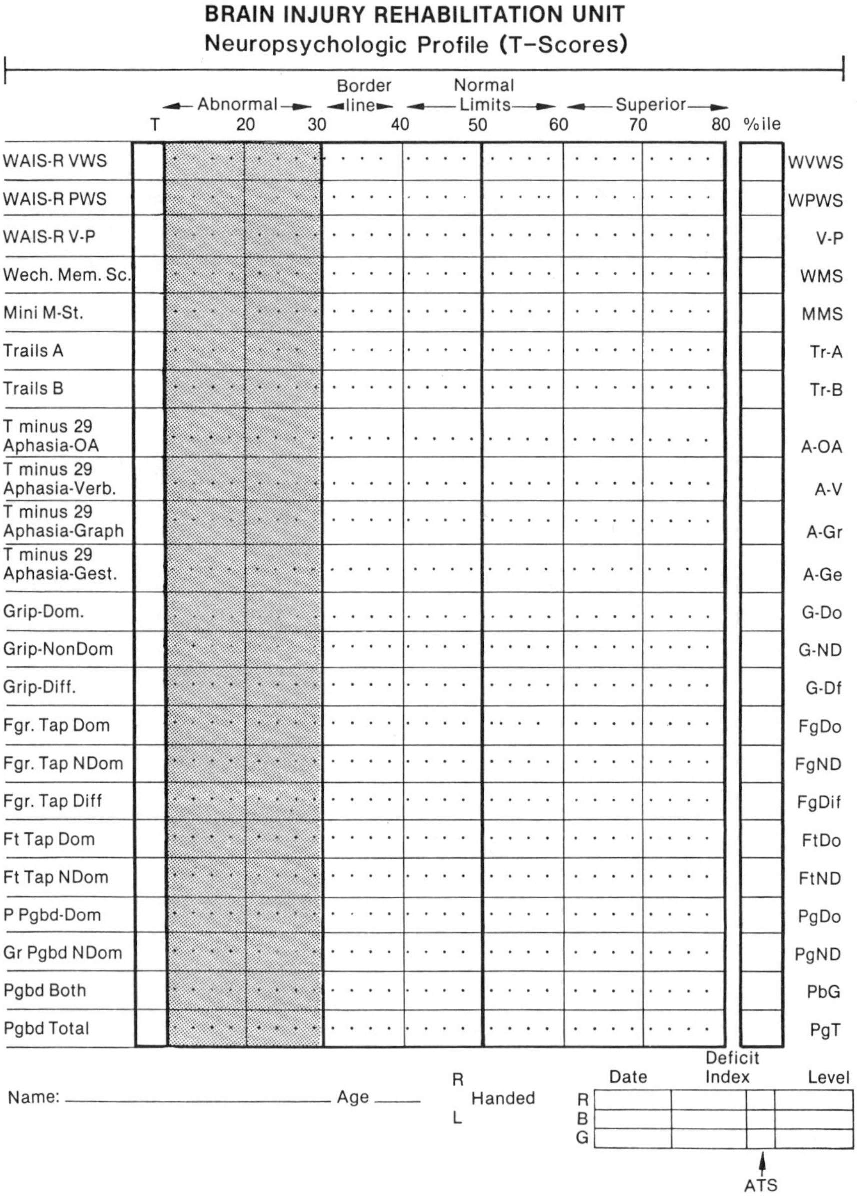

BRAIN INJURY REHABILITATION UNIT
Neuropsychologic Profile (T–Scores)

	T	20	30	40	50	60	70	80	%ile
		◄— Abnormal —►		◄line►	◄— Normal Limits —►		◄— Superior —►		
WAIS-R VWS									WVWS
WAIS-R PWS									WPWS
WAIS-R V-P									V-P
Wech. Mem. Sc.									WMS
Mini M-St.									MMS
Trails A									Tr-A
Trails B									Tr-B
T minus 29 Aphasia-OA									A-OA
T minus 29 Aphasia-Verb.									A-V
T minus 29 Aphasia-Graph									A-Gr
T minus 29 Aphasia-Gest.									A-Ge
Grip-Dom.									G-Do
Grip-NonDom									G-ND
Grip-Diff.									G-Df
Fgr. Tap Dom									FgDo
Fgr. Tap NDom									FgND
Fgr. Tap Diff									FgDif
Ft Tap Dom									FtDo
Ft Tap NDom									FtND
P Pgbd-Dom									PgDo
Gr Pgbd NDom									PgND
Pgbd Both									PbG
Pgbd Total									PgT

Name: _____ Age _____   R Handed   L

	Date	Deficit Index	Level
R			
B			
G			

ATS

Figure 2. Neuropsychologic Profile (T-scores).

	1	2	3	4	5	6	7	8	9	10	11	12	13	14	15
Overall rating		•	•	•	•	•	•	•	•	•	•	•	•	•	•
Self-care		•	•	•	•	•	•	•	•	•	•	•	•	•	•
Socialization		•	•	•	•	•	•	•	•	•	•	•	•	•	•
Communication		•	•	•	•	•	•	•	•	•	•	•	•	•	•

	Can't Do	Direct Assist	With Supervision				Independent								
SELF-CARE:															
A. Dressing		•	•	•	•	•	•	•	•	•	•	•	•	•	•
B. Grooming		•	•	•	•	•	•	•	•	•	•	•	•	•	•
C. Toilet activities		•	•	•	•	•	•	•	•	•	•	•	•	•	•
D. Ambulation		•	•	•	•	•	•	•	•	•	•	•	•	•	•
E. Eating		•	•	•	•	•	•	•	•	•	•	•	•	•	•
SOCIALIZATION:															
A. Scheduling		•	•	•	•	•	•	•	•	•	•	•	•	•	•
B. Interpersonal activities		•	•	•	•	•	•	•	•	•	•	•	•	•	•
C. Transportation		•	•	•	•	•	•	•	•	•	•	•	•	•	•
D. Occupation/ avocation		•	•	•	•	•	•	•	•	•	•	•	•	•	•
E. Personal business		•	•	•	•	•	•	•	•	•	•	•	•	•	•
COMMUNICATION:															
A. Speech		•	•	•	•	•	•	•	•	•	•	•	•	•	•
B. Understanding		•	•	•	•	•	•	•	•	•	•	•	•	•	•
C. Reading		•	•	•	•	•	•	•	•	•	•	•	•	•	•
D. Writing		•	•	•	•	•	•	•	•	•	•	•	•	•	•
E. Gestural		•	•	•	•	•	•	•	•	•	•	•	•	•	•

Patient: _____   Date(s) Evaluated _____

Figure 3. Rating of Patient's Independence—Summary Profile.

tient's Independence. Attention is paid not only to functions that are normal or relatively normal but also to those that are impaired. Although treatment will focus upon problems, it is necessary to take note of unaffected abilities as well, so that rehabilitative efforts can be most effectively focused. In the following sections, I will outline the process of translating the mass of data into a coherent treatment plan.

2.2. Treatment

2.2.1. The Treatment Plan

Soon after all the data from neuropsychologic testing and the various consultations have been collected and organized, a treatment plan is devised. A first step in this process is the enumeration of a problem list. There are various problem lists in existence (Meldman, McFarland, & Johnson, 1976; Reinstein, Staas, & Marquette, 1975), and not all rehabilitation settings make use of a problem-oriented medical record (POMR) system (Reinstein, 1977). It seemed that the POMR would be an efficient system for use with brain-injured patients, but a standard list of problems that applied to this particular population was not readily available. After considerable discussion, the head nurse and I were able to develop a standard list of problems (Lynch & Mauss, 1981). This provides standard terminology for most of the problems one encounters in brain-trauma rehabilitation; for each problem, one or more common treatment approaches are provided. Finally, a standard technique for determining outcome of treatment is listed. Table 2 provides a portion of the problem list. The complete list of problems, treatments, and outcome measures may be obtained by contacting the present author.

In practice, we use the list as a checklist (i.e., the list is gone through, problem by problem, for every newly admitted patient). This technique is not as tedious as it might appear, particularly once one becomes familiar with the process. It will occur to the reader that rather lengthy problem lists are apt to result from this procedure. This does, in fact, occur; but my feeling is that a patient's problems need to be enumerated, if not treated, as thoroughly as possible. This is not to say that all problems will be treated initially or even at all. Once the list is completed, logical and practical priorities are set and an initial treatment schedule is developed. Problems such as "Impaired use of transportation" or "Job impairment" are clearly not priorities in the first stage of a rehabilitation program. Frequently problems that are closely related— such as expressive language deficits or problems related to weakness, ambulation, or general physical conditioning—are consolidated with re-

Table 2.   The BIRU Standard Problem List[a]

I. Cognitive problems
  A. Memory difficulty
    1. Auditory
    2. Visual
    3. Spatial
    4. Temporal disorientation
  B. Impaired receptive language in:
    1. Reading comprehension
    2. Word recognition
    3. Auditory comprehension
  C. Impaired expressive language in:
    1. Writing
    2. Word finding
    3. Fluency
    4. Spelling
  D. Math difficulty
II. Sensorimotor problems
  A. Impaired sensory analysis
    1. Visual
      a. Field cuts
      b. Suppression/inattention
      c. Low acuity
    2. Impaired hearing
    3. Impaired body awareness
  B. Impaired motor function
    1. Constructional apraxia
    2. Impaired fine motor coordination
    3. Impaired gross motor coordination
    4. Extremity weakness
    5. Impaired physical conditioning
    6. Impaired flexibility
    7. Impaired ambulation
    8. Difficulty swallowing
    9. Dysarthria
III. Medical conditions, e.g.:
  A. Seizures
  B. Hypertension
  C. Diabetes
  D. Heart disease
  E. Chronic lung disease
  F. Substance abuse
IV. Emotional problems
  A. Depression/anxiety
  B. Low self-esteem
  C. Nonassertion; faulty assertion
  D. Aggressive behavior
  E. Family discord
  F. Sexual dysfunction

(continued)

Table 2.   (Continued)

V. Social problems
   A. Impaired self-care (dressing, grooming, toileting, eating)
   B. Impaired interpersonal skills
   C. Impaired independent living
      1. Clothing
      2. Finances
      3. Food
      4. Housing
   D. Impaired use of transportation
   E. Job impairment

---

[a]The Brain Injury Rehabilitation Unit treatments and outcome measures are not shown. For complete list, please contact the author.

gard to the treatment prescribed. In these examples, speech therapy and corrective therapy, respectively, may be the treatments. Although no empirical data are available as yet concerning the utility of the standard problem list, it does appear that treatment planning is expedited by use of such a list. In addition, communication among both the treatment teams and allied services seems to be enhanced by the use of standard terminology.

Goals of treatment are necessary, although in many settings they are not universally set forth prior to treatment. There are certain advantages to the practice of establishing these goals clearly and objectively. One advantage is that the clinician is required to make a commitment to a specific endpoint of treatment. This can easily be communicated to the patient, her or his family, and other members of the treatment team, providing all concerned with a view of the treatment process that is finite rather than indeterminate. Patients commonly express frustration at not knowing why they are in treatment or when they will be discharged. Specific treatment goals provide ready (although perhaps not always accepted) responses to these questions. In a sense, patients are better able to comprehend where they are in the treatment process when they know what the endpoint is.

Another advantage of specification of goals is that treatment outcomes can be readily determined for research or program evaluation applications. One useful aid to accomplish this specification of goals is the Goal Attainment Follow-up Guide (Kiresuk & Sherman, 1968). Figure 4 illustrates the format of the guide as it would appear in its completed form. The problems noted at the head of each column are obtained from the standard list mentioned previously. The decision as to what the "expected level of outcome" should be is determined by vari-

Levels of predicted attainments	Scale 1 Nonassertion	Scale 2 Impaired receptive language/ word recognition
Much less than the expected level of outcome	On assertion index: All scales out of normal range $(T \geq 60 \leq 40)$	Wide Range Achievement Test— Reading $T = 19$ or less
Somewhat less than the ex- pected level of outcome	2 of 3 scales out of normal range	Wide Range Achievement Test— Reading $T = 20-29$
Expected level of outcome	1 scale out of nor- mal range	Wide Range Achievement Test— Reading $T = 30-39$
Somewhat more than the ex- pected level of outcome	0 scales out of nor- mal range	Wide Range Achievement Test— Reading $T = 40-49$
Much more than the expected level of outcome	0 scales out of nor- mal range	Wide Range Achievement Test— Reading $T = 50$ or more

Figure 4. Goal Attainment Follow-up Guide. Outcome measures: for Scale 1— the Assertion Index (Abasement, Aggression, and Dominance scales from Jackson's Personality Research Form (1974); for Scale 2—Wide Range Achievement Test (WRAT) reading score, converted to T-score.

ous factors such as premorbid level of functioning, likely frequency and duration of treatment, and numerous prognostic variables, such as chronicity of the injury, age of the patient, and type of lesion. At the bottom of each column, a notation is made as to when and by what means the outcome will be determined. Typically, these goal-attainment sheets are completed prior to admission so that the patient and his or her family can be permitted to inspect them at the admission staffing.

Following treatment, the goal-attainment sheets are consulted to determine the problem-by-problem success of the rehabilitative effort. The goal-attainment system is an effective method for determining success or failure of each treatment. As such, it provides a useful basis for calculating outcome data for patients completing a particular treatment program. Table 3 presents outcome data on a small sample of BIRU

Table 3. Outcome Data for a Mixed Group of 10 Patients Treated at the Brain Injury Rehabilitation Unit

Patient	General diagnostic category	Problems treated	Total treatment hours[a]	Outcome[b] +	−	?	Success rate (in percentages)[c]
1	Vascular	12	102	10	1	1	85
2	Vascular	11	141	6	1	4	55
3	Degenerative	4	162	2	2	0	50
4	Vascular	12	348	8	1	3	67
5	Neoplastic	8	147	4	3	1	57
6	Vascular	8	141	3	4	1	38
7	Vascular	12	221	6	4	2	50
8	Traumatic	8	62	6	1	1	75
9	Infectious	12	270	10	2	0	83
10	Traumatic	13	476	4	8	1	44

[a]Mean: 207; median: 154.5; range: 62–476.
[b]Outcome categories: + = Treatment goal reached; − = Treatment goal not reached; ? = Outcome undetermined/insufficient data.
[c]Mean: 60.2; Median: 56; Range: 38%–85%.

patients with various etiologies. The "success rate" was calculated by dividing the successful outcomes (that is, where the treatment goal was achieved or exceeded) by all other outcomes (where treatment goal was not achieved or not determined). Means, medians, and ranges for total treatment hours as well as success rate are provided at the foot of the appropriate column. The reader is referred to the various publications concerned with the Goal Attainment Follow-up Guide for a more thorough description of its construction and application (Garwick, 1977).

2.2.2. Strategies of Treatment

Various investigators have developed ingenious treatment strategies for working with brain-injured patients (Diller, Ben-Yishay, Gerstman, Goodkin, Gordon, & Weinberg, 1974; Golden, 1978; Gudeman & Craine, 1976; Luria, 1963). Our approach is by no means unique, and, in fact, draws heavily from these sources. With few exceptions, the treatment techniques employed in most centers are based on the concepts of simplification, amplification, feedback, substitution, or redundancy.

2.2.2.1. *Simplification.* This term refers to the strategy of reducing the requirements of a task to a level at which the patient can perform adequately. Training then proceeds by gradually increasing the complexity of the task as the patient masters each increment of difficulty. As elementary as this principle may appear, it is not uncommon to encounter therapists who opt for the "keep trying until you get it right" philosophy, whereby the patient is drilled repeatedly with material that is beyond his or her current capabilities. Such an approach guarantees frustration for the therapist and negativism and feelings of failure for the patient. The concept of shaping (i.e., eliciting a target behavior by systematically reinforcing successive approximations of that behavior) is basic to the concept of simplification.

One example of simplification would be the employment of the Peabody Individual Achievement Test (PIAT; Dunn & Markwardt, 1970) as a training tool for patients with spelling or arithmetic deficits. The PIAT is presented in a multiple-choice format that requires no verbal or graphic response. In addition, both the spelling and arithmetic sections begin at a very basic level, assessing knowledge of elementary letter and number concepts. Many patients who perform poorly on more difficult achievement tests such as the Wide Range Achievement Test (WRAT) are able to demonstrate some ability, once the methods of data presentation and responding are sufficiently simplified. The reader is referred to the excellent work by Diller *et al.* (1974) for numerous other examples of this technique.

2.2.2.2. Amplification. This involves the enhancement of a stimulus in order to ensure timely and accurate reception by the patient. Much as we would increase the size of visual stimuli or loudness of auditory stimuli for people who have impaired vision or hearing, we can often improve the detectability of a stimulus by augmenting its characteristics. This may involve highlighting or emphasizing subtle cues that the patient is no longer able to utilize. For example, bright red tags may be placed on the left-hand margin of a printed page so that patients with left-sided visual neglect or inattention will take note of the margin each time they scan from right to left. Patients with arousal or attentional deficits may benefit from slightly louder auditory or more vivid visual inputs. With regard to clothing, buttons or zippers can be made larger so that they can be manipulated more easily.

2.2.2.3. Feedback. This is one therapeutic concept that should occur throughout all phases of rehabilitation. In retraining, feedback should be continuous and immediate. The purpose of feedback is to provide regulatory information to the individual at the time he or she is performing a task. Thus, while learning to transfer or walk, the patient should be provided with feedback by the therapist to be certain that training is taking place and to ensure maximum impact of the information. Words of encouragement, as well as constructive criticism, are often the only form of feedback a patient receives. We have experimented with the use of videotape in teaching patients to walk, fall, and arise properly. Videotaping is not only useful for reviewing the patient's progress but also provides a vivid record of the patient's appearance and abilities on admission, for comparison with his or her condition at the end of treatment. While we have not used videotape with a sufficient number of patients to permit us to reach a conclusion regarding its effectiveness, it does appear to be a potentially useful adjunct to the rehabilitation process.

There are devices on the market, such as the Perceptuomotor Pen (Wayne Engineering, Skokie, Ill.) designed to give both auditory (tone) and visual (digital tally of cumulative errors) feedback during writing or drawing tasks. Performance on memory tests can be plotted on graph paper so that the patient can continuously monitor his or her progress over time. Numerous other devices and techniques are available for virtually any number of applications. Electromyogram (EMG) biofeedback has been used for treating some patients with spasticity (Dunn, Davis, & Webster, 1980). And there are simple microswitch devices that can be attached atop a set of earphones in order to monitor head position while simultaneously providing reinforcement (pleasant music) for holding the head upright.

2.2.2.4. Substitution. This is the technique whereby one intact system or behavioral ability is substituted for another that has been damaged or destroyed. Luria, Naydin, Tsvetkova, and Vinarskaya (1969, pp. 368–433) describe situations in which the patient can be taught to carry out particular motor acts by utilizing a different set of muscles or a different sequence of movements. On a different level, patients who can no longer operate an automobile must be taught alternate modes of transportation, such as taking a taxi, bus, subway, or train. Likewise, patients who cannot walk must be taught ambulation with crutches, a walker, or a wheelchair. Patients who are cortically "blind" or are suffering severe visual agnosia may be able to enjoy "reading" once again by making use of tape-recorded "talking books." (These are available through the Division for the Blind and Physically Handicapped, Library of Congress, Washington, D.C. 20542.)

Patients who cannot dress or undress themselves easily may be provided with special adaptive clothing. Other adaptations may also be useful. For example, one patient in our program suffered considerable brain stem and cerebellar dysfunction following a combination of a brain tumor and cerebrovascular accident. Due to severe spasticity and ataxia, he was unable to stand or walk without continual direct assistance. Rather than persist in what appeared to be a vain effort at teaching him to ambulate, we eventually settled for a more practical alternative: an electric wheelchair. And patients with severe nonfluent aphasia without dyspraxia can be taught sign language or use of an electronic communicator as a substitute for verbal communication.

2.2.2.5. *Redundancy.* Redundancy—or repetition—is a useful technique in many phases of rehabilitation. Physical therapy and occupational therapy utilize repetition as a means of strengthening skills relating to ambulation or ADL skills. In retraining higher cognitive functions, there are numerous instances in which redundancy is employed. Perceptual–motor skills training, memory retraining, and speech or language therapy are prominent examples. The overall aim of redundancy or repetition is to enhance the development of more automatic performance of motor, cognitive, or speech skills—that is, to reduce the need for plodding, strenuous effort in carrying out these activities. It is helpful to provide as much extra feedback as possible. The mere repetition of a correct activity will provide kinesthetic, proprioceptive, and either visual or auditory feedback. The clinician should attempt to enhance the basic feedback inherent in the task by utilizing the other input channels. For example, speech therapy sessions can be conducted in front of a mirror, on videotape, or on audiotape with a volume monitor to provide immediate visual feedback to the patient who is attempting to improve articulation or loudness. In this fashion, the impact of each repetition of a task can be greatly increased.

2.2.3. The Role of the Family

The vital role played by the patient's family is all too often overlooked. Fortunately, there are a number of excellent papers in the literature that address the interactive effects between the head-injured patient and his or her family. Lezak (1978) emphasizes the need for family counseling both prior to and after the patient's discharge. She points out several of the common psychologic sequelae of head injury, many of which serve as sources of irritation, puzzlement, or fear among family members. Feelings of guilt, depression, isolation, or anger may occur at various times in most spouses and children of head-injured patients. The need for realistic expectations regarding recovery is stressed both by Lezak and others (Bond, 1975, pp. 141–153). Patients who are agitated or prone to violence require special understanding and treatment, both by the rehabilitative team and the family (Fauman, 1978).

The clinician should strive to include the patient's family in all phases of the treatment process. This includes attendance at all staff meetings or conferences during which the patient's treatment is discussed. Further, we have found that it is a welcome and informative practice to provide the family with photocopies of certain test profiles or samples of test performance.

To offer families an opportunity to ventilate frustration, seek support from other families, obtain advice regarding finances, and so forth, we instituted a "family support group" that meets twice monthly for 90 minutes each session (Mauss-Clum & Ryan, 1981). As Lezak (1978) points out, these group sessions provide the clinician with a vivid impression of the often devastating effects that brain injury has upon the family structure as a whole and upon each family member individually.

We have found that with regard to identifying family pressures and conflicts, selective psychologic assessment of immediate family members can often complement the testing routinely carried out with the patient. The Minnesota Multiphasic Personality Inventory (MMPI) is often not appropriate; therefore, in such instances, we employ the Taylor-Johnson Temperament Analysis, which permits individuals to rate themselves as well as other family members on a number of bipolar traits such as "nervous–relaxed" (Taylor, 1968).

2.2.4. Duration of Treatment

The decision as to when to terminate treatment should not be a difficult one if the treatment plan and goals are set forth correctly. In a sense, the patient—by having attained all of the goals established at the onset of treatment or, conversely, by failing to evidence improvement over a reasonable interval—provides us with the rationale for either continuing or discontinuing treatment. We tend to rely upon the Goal Attainment Follow-up Guide to determine objectively the need to continue treatment. In actual practice, however, there are some complicating factors influencing the timing of termination of treatment. For example, the patient must have a place to live, means of support, access to transportation, and access to follow-up treatment. It is advantageous to attempt to synchronize the establishment of out-placement and follow-up facilities with the anticipated termination of treatment. The patient and family should be given an initial estimate as to the proposed length of treatment. This estimate can be revised upward (or downward) if needed, but any such changes should be communicated promptly and clearly to the patient and family. In any event, the clinician should provide a minimum of a month's notice prior to discharge. In our program, the typical length of stay is about 9 months, with 3 months being our preferred minimum.

2.2.5. Outcome Measures

Rehabilitation outcomes can be measured in a number of ways. What is often difficult to determine, however, is the appropriate measuring device. It is helpful to bear in mind that rehabilitation has change as its primary goal. Thus an outcome measure must be sensitive to change in some relevant area(s). It follows that the precision required of a measuring device is a function of the need for detecting minor, vs. major, change in the patient's condition.

One approach to measuring outcome is to simply readminister most or all of the psychometric and/or behavioral assessments that constituted the initial or baseline evaluation. Improvement in standard scores on the order of one standard deviation could be declared sufficient to conclude that change had occurred between admission and discharge. Neuropsychologic assessment lends itself readily to this form of analysis because of its use of quantiative measurements and the availability of norms that, in turn, permit the derivation of standard scores. The use of standard score profiles is a routine practice in many centers, both with Halstead-Reitan (see Figure 1) and Luria-Nebraska data (Golden et al., 1979). The difficulty with limiting outcome measurement to psychometric indices is that occasionally the test data do not seem to reflect the patient's actual level of functioning. This variability is due in part to the imperfect (or improperly understood) validity of some of the traditional neuropsychologic measures with regard to predicting extra-test behavior. Another pertinent factor is the notorious variability in level of performance of brain-injured patients due to fluctuations in attention, motivation, mood, and general energy level. The combined influence of these two factors frequently produces unusual test patterns, such as a sudden decline in test scores after a period of continual improvement and without clinical evidence of newly developing pathology. It is not uncommon, for example, to observe increases in depression just prior to discharge in long-term patients who have developed a certain degree of dependency upon the hospital.

In order to avoid the possible pitfall of overreliance upon purely psychometric measures, it is advisable to adopt additional measures of adaptive functioning. There are a number of these measures available, such as the Burke Stroke Time-Oriented Profile (BUSTOP; Feigenson, Polkow, Meikle, & Ferguson, 1979), the Barthel Index (Mahoney & Barthel, 1965), or the PULSES (an acronym representing key functional areas such as physical condition, upper limb and lower limb functions, sensory components, excretory functions, and support from family) profile (Moskowitz & McCann, 1957). More recently, Rappaport and others

(Rappaport *et al.*, 1982) have developed the Disability Rating Scale, which is an excellent tool for defining level of disability during various stages of rehabilitation. An excellent source for vocational rehabilitation outcome measures is a monograph by the Institute for Research Utilization (Backer, 1977).

As mentioned previously, we prefer to use the Rating of Patient's Independence (ROPI) as both a baseline and an outcome measure. The ROPI provides a comprehensive portrait of the patient's abilities, with an emphasis upon practical functional skills relating directly to capacity for independent living. The numerical scoring system also lends itself readily to statistical analysis.

Jennett (1976) points out that certain commonly employed outcome criteria are not universally appropriate. For example, "return to work" is not necessarily a reliable index of success or failure, since some able-bodied patients may be unable to find work; likewise, an impaired patient may be placed in a highly structured, sheltered work setting at a level far removed from his premorbid occupation. Jennett and Bond's (1975) Glasgow Outcome Scale (described previously) attempts to avoid such unreliable criteria, and, instead, consists of broad, behaviorally derived categories.

In conclusion, with the number of measuring instruments and systems available, it would appear that most rehabilitation programs should be able to find one that fits their needs fairly closely.

2.2.6. Follow-up

Since the ultimate goal of rehabilitation is to effect change that is relatively permanent, there is a need to determine long-term outcome in patients who are discharged. In a sense, we are more concerned with what the discharged patient *does* than what he or she is deemed *capable* of doing. A patient who does not choose to establish an independent residence, go to work, or drive a car is really no better off than the patient who *cannot* perform these tasks due to physical limitations.

In our program, we attempt to follow patients monthly for a year after discharge. This is effected by either personal visit, telephone contact, or mail. A standard form, compatible with all three types of contact, is completed for each follow-up. Figure 5 shows the front of the BIRU follow-up form. We do not employ a separate follow-up team but, instead, strive for continuity by maintaining the same staff coordinator who dealt with the patient throughout the active treatment phase. Informal or irregular follow-up should be carried out indefinitely as long as the patient is willing and able to maintain contact with his or her coordinator.

3. Current and Future Trends in Rehabilitation of Brain-Injured Patients

3.1. Assessment and Diagnosis

Probably the most important recent trend in neuropsychologic assessment has been the increase in popularity of the Luria assessment procedures (Christensen, 1975; Golden et al., 1979). Yet there are a number of other developing trends that show signs of becoming more prominent in the next few years.

3.1.1. Automated Neuropsychologic Assessment

Investigators in both Canada (Knights & Watson, 1968) and the United States (Russell, Neuringer, & Goldstein, 1970) have developed computer programs for tabulation and analysis of neuropsychologic test data. Knights later (1973) described an ingenious method of storing and retrieving previous cases for comparison with current cases. Termed "profile matching," the technique requires a computer to match the pattern of data from a current case to all other cases in its memory. A coefficient of profile similarity is calculated and a list of the five most highly correlated cases—along with a capsule description of the findings in each—is then printed. This technique represents a sophisticated attempt to arrive at a profile typology for neuropsychologic data, much like the system of frequent code types for the MMPI.

It seems clear that computer-assisted analysis of neuropsychologic data will become the rule in the coming years. Complex statistical procedures and data storage and retrieval requirements are such that computer assistance is mandatory (Swiercinsky, 1978, pp. 13–29).

Another related area is that of outcome prediction. Various studies have attempted to arrive at statistical formulas to aid in predicting outcome from severe head injury (Jennett, Teasdale, & Knill-Jones, 1975, pp. 309–324); Stablein, Miller, Choi, & Becker, 1980). Thus far, the results seem promising, although some conceptual and statistical problems are yet to be resolved. With regard to actuarial prediction of change in speech therapy, Porch and his colleagues (Porch et al., 1980) have used a stepwise multiple regression procedure to predict change after 3, 6, and 12 months postonset.

MEDICAL RECORD	PROBLEM ORIENTED PROGRESS NOTES OVERPRINT- BIRU #43
PROBLEM DATE NO.	Format - Problem title (Do not abbreviate) S - Subjective O - Objective A - Assessment P - Plans. (All notes must have signature and title of person making entry.) Continue on reverse.

STANDARD FOLLOW-UP FORM - BIRU

Today's Date: _____   Completed by: _____
          Mo.   Day   Year
Please answer the following questions the best you can:

1. WHAT ARE YOUR MAIN PROBLEMS NOW? _____
   a. _____
   b. _____
   c. _____
   d. _____

2. WHERE ARE YOU LIVING NOW? _____
   Same as before? Yes_____ No_____
   Present address: _____
   _____Phone: _____

3. ARE YOU WORKING NOW?   Yes_____   No_____
   Part time?   Yes_____   No_____
   Full time?   Yes_____   No_____
   Where do you work: _____

4. ARE YOU ATTENDING CLASSES ANYWHERE?   Yes_____   No_____
   If yes, at College_____ Junior College____ Other_____
   Name of institution: _____
   How many hours per week? _____hours.

5. HOW ARE YOUR FINANCES (ANY MONEY TROUBLES)?
   (Circle): OK   Getting by, but some problems   Need help*
   Describe problems, if any: _____

*Optional: How much do you receive each month now from:
   VA_____ $_____
   Social Security ___ $_____
   Health Insurance___ $_____
   Other Sources_____ $_____
   Total each month ___ $_____

PROBLEM ORIENTED

PROGRESS NOTES

VA FORM 10-7978 i
FEB 1976

EXISTING STOCK OF VA FORM 10-7978i,
OCT 1974, WILL BE USED.

DATE	NO.	CONTINUE FORMAT SAME AS ON FACE OF FORM

DO YOU WANT HELP WITH GETTING MONEY FROM THE VA OR STATE?   Yes␣No␣

6. ARE YOU TAKING ANY MEDICINE(S) NOW?   Yes*_____   No_____

*Optional: If yes, what kinds_____   How many per day?_____
_____ How many per day?_____
_____ How many per day?_____

*ARE THE MEDICATIONS/PILLS HELPING YOU?   Yes_____   No_____

*ARE YOU HAVING ANY PROBELMS, SUCH AS DIZZINESS, HEADACHE, OR
FEELING SICK TO YOUR STOMACH - DUE TO YOUR MEDICATIONS?   Yes_____ No_____

7. ANY OTHER PROBLEMS NOT MENTIONED SO FAR?_____

8. PLEASE CALL BACK OR WRITE TO ME IN A MONTH,_____

   BY_____, 19_____.

9. MAIL THIS FORM IN THE ATTACHED VA ENVELOPE TO:_____

     Brain Injury Rehabilitation Unit (205B1)
     Veterans Administration Medical Center (MPD
     3801 Miranda Avenue
     Palo Alto, CA 94304

                  Patient Signature

WL:ht(1)8-13-79(100) (4-28-80-X100)

Figure 5. Sample of standard BIRU follow-up form.

3.1.2. Neurophysiologic Techniques

John (1977) has advocated a more rigorous approach to assessment, utilizing a combination of electroencephalograms and cortical-evoked potentials (CEP). This approach, while intriguing, remains unavailable to many rehabilitative centers because of the costly equipment and expert technical staff required to run and maintain a CEP laboratory. The wealth of information available for CEP evaluations, however, more than compensates for the expense involved. Information regarding level, lateralization, and localization of lesions is obtained. In addition, more process-oriented data regarding efficiency of information processing by either hemisphere alone or in combination can be generated. A major advantage of CEP evaluations is that no verbal or gestural response is necessary and no language comprehension is required. Thus, many patients considered untestable by traditional neuropsychologic assessment can be evaluated by CEP studies. CEPs have been applied to the assessment of patients with severe head trauma with considerable success (Greenberg, Mayer, Becker, & Miller, 1977; Greenberg, Becker, Miller, & Mayer, 1977).

3.2. Treatment: Some Newer Strategies

3.2.1. Methods

As mentioned above, numerous devices that utilize the principles of reinforcement and feedback as a means of altering the patient's behavior are available. Mechanical devices are becoming more sophisticated and less expensive with the development of microcircuitry. There are already in existence devices permitting the quadriplegic patient to operate a wheelchair, the blind patient to "see" by using a device that transforms visual images to tactile patterns, and the aphasic patient to "speak" by using an electronic communicator. We are experimenting with the use of commercial video games as a therapeutic aid and can foresee the increased reliance upon computer-controlled test *administration*, as well as scoring and interpreting, in rehabilitation.

3.2.2. Pharmacologic Therapy

Various chemical agents have been proposed as being beneficial in the treatment of organic brain disorders. Physostigmine has been mentioned by Luria *et al.* (1969) as well as Peters and Levin (1977, 1979) as being potentially effective in enhancing impaired memory. Vasodilators and other drugs with both vasodilator and metabolic effects have met with mixed success in the treatment of patients with dementia (Gaitz, Varner, & Overall, 1977; Yesavage, Tinklenberg, Hollister, & Berger, 1979). More recently, Chute (1980) has explored the role of cyclic AMP (adenosine-monophosphate) as a memory facilitator. He mentions both the administration of cyclic AMP and the inhibition of its enzyme (phosphodiesterase) by other drugs as methods which should result in enhancement of new learning. Definitive studies with humans have not yet been carried out, however.

3.3. Closing Comments

It is hoped that increased public awareness and understanding of brain-injured people will lead to more immediate, skilled treatment of acute head injuries. There is clear evidence, for example, that immediate, intensive surgical/medical intervention results in a greater number of survivors in the "good recovery" range (Becker, Miller, Ward, Greenberg, Young, & Sakalas, 1977; Bowers & Marshall, 1980). Strategically located hospitals, specially equipped and staffed, should be designated as head-injury treatment centers—much as there are hospitals that serve as burn centers in many metropolitan areas. These hospitals should attempt to utilize standard procedures for gathering admission data, evaluating progression or remission of symptoms, and determining treatment outcome. In this way, epidemiologic, prognostic, and treatment-effectiveness data can be gathered in several centers for later pooling in the form of collaborative research studies within and between cities, states, and even countries.

Obviously, if all of us drove at a reasonable speed and wore our seat belts—or (for motorcyclists or bicyclists) crash helmets—the number of motor-vehicle-related head injuries would be reduced. Until such time as this becomes a reality, we will be forced to expend far more effort upon treatment than prevention. Rehabilitation of the head-injured patient begins with the first attempt to treat the acute effects of the trauma. It ends only when the patient has reached his or her maximum benefit from the best treatment techniques available. As providers of this treatment, we must strive to treat not only the tangible, mechanical effects of craniocerebral trauma but also the more subtle psychosocial and economic sequelae that often persist for a lifetime.

4. References

Adams, K. In search of Luria's battery: A false start. *Journal of Consulting and Clinical Psychology*, 1980, *48*, 511–516. (a)

Adams, K. An end of innocence for behavioral neurology? *Journal of Consulting and Clinical Psychology,* 1980, *48,* 522–524. (b)

Adams, K., Brown, G., & Jacisin, J. *Limits of computerized tomography in neuropsychology.* Paper presented at Eighth Annual Meeting of International Neuropsychology Society, San Francisco, California, January 1980.

Backer, T. *New Directions in rehabilitation outcome measurement.* Washington, D.C.: Institute for Research Utilization, 1977.

Beardsley, J., Matthews, C., Cleeland, C., & Harley, J. *Neuropsychological test battery: Adults 15 and older.* Unpublished manuscript, University of Wisconsin, 1972.

Beck, A., & Beck, R. Screening depressed patients in family practice. *Postgraduate Medicine,* 1972, *52,* 81–85.

Becker, D., Miller, D., Ward, J., Greenberg, R., Young, H., & Sakalas, R. The outcome from severe head injury with early diagnosis and intensive management. *Journal of Neurosurgery,* 1977, *47,* 491–502.

Benton, A. Motivational influence on performance in brain-damaged patients. *American Journal of Orthopsychiatry,* 1960, *30,* 315–321.

Benton, A. *Revised visual retention test* (4th ed.). New York: Psychological Corporation, 1974.

Benton, A., Hamsher, K., & Stone, F. *Visual retention test: Multiple choice I.* Iowa City, Iowa: Division of Behavioral Neurology, 1977.

Bigler, E. Neuropsychological assessment and brain scan results: A case study approach. *Clinical Neuropsychology,* 1980, *2,* 13–24.

Bond, M. Assessment of the psychosocial outcome after severe head injury. In *CIBA Foundation Symposium 34: Outcome of severe damage to the central nervous system.* Amsterdam: North Holland, 1975.

Bowers, S., & Marshall, L. Outcome of 200 consecutive cases of severe head injury treated in San Diego County: A prospective analysis. *Neurosurgery,* 1980, *6,* 237–242.

Bricolo, A., Turazzi, S., & Feriotti, G. Prolonged posttraumatic unconsciousness—Therapeutic assets and liabilities. *Journal of Neurosurgery,* 1980, *52,* 625–634.

Buschke, H., & Fuld, P. Evaluating storage, retention, and retrieval in disordered memory and learning. *Neurology,* 1974, *24,* 1019–1025.

Christensen, A.-L. *Luria's neuropsychological investigation: Text.* New York: Spectrum, 1975.

Chute, D. Phosphodiesterase inhibition and memory facilitation. *Clinical Neuropsychology,* 1980, *2,* 72–74.

Costa, L., Vaughn, H., Levita, E., & Farber, N. Purdue Pegboard as a predictor of the presence and laterality of cerebral lesions. *Journal of Consulting Psychology,* 1963, *27,* 133–137.

De Renzi, E., & Vignolo, L. The Token Test: A sensitive test to detect disturbances in aphasics. *Brain,* 1962, *85,* 665–678.

Derogatis, L., Lipman, R., & Covi, L. SCL-90: An outpatient psychiatric rating scale—Preliminary report. *Psychopharmacology Bulletin,* 1973, *9,* 13–28.

Diller, L., Ben-Yishay, Y., Gerstman, L., Goodkin, R., Gordon, W., & Weinberg, J. *Studies in cognition and rehabilitation in hemiplegia.* New York: Institute of Rehabilitation Medicine, 1974.

Dunn, L., & Markwardt, F. *Peabody individual achievement test manual.* Circle Pines, Minn.: American Guidance Service, 1970.

Dunn, M., Davis, J., & Webster, J. Voluntary control of muscle spasticity with EMG biofeedback in three SCI quadriplegic patients. *American Journal of Clinical Biofeedback,* 1980, *3,* 5–10.

Fauman, M. Treatment of the agitated patient with an organic brain disorder. *JAMA*, 1978, *240*, 380–382.

Feigenson, J., Polkow, L., Meikle, R., & Ferguson, W. Burke stroke time-oriented profile (BUSTOP): an overview of patient function. *Archives of Physical Medicine and Rehabilitation*, 1979, *60*, 508–511.

Gaitz, C., Varner, R., & Overall, J. Pharmacotherapy for organic brain syndrome in late life. *Archives of General Psychiatry*, 1977, *34*, 839–845.

Garwick, G. *Advanced topics in goal attainment scaling.* Minneapolis: Program Evaluation Resource Center, 1977.

Golden, C. J. *Diagnosis and rehabilitation in clinical neuropsychology.* Springfield, Ill.: Thomas, 1978.

Golden, C. J. In reply to Adams' "In search of Luria's battery: A false start." *Journal of Consulting and Clinical Psychology*, 1980, *48*, 517–521.

Golden, C., Hammeke, T., & Purisch, A. Diagnostic validity of a standardized neuropsychological battery derived from Luria's neuropsychological tests. *Journal of Consulting and Clinical Psychology*, 1978, *46*, 1258–1265.

Golden, C., Purisch, A., & Hammeke, T. *The Luria-Nebraska neuropsychological battery.* Lincoln, Neb.: University of Nebraska Press, 1979.

Goldman, R., Fristoe, M., & Woodcock, R. *G-F-W auditory memory tests.* Circle Pines, Minn.: American Guidance Service, 1974.

Goodglass, H., & Kaplan, E. *The assessment of aphasia and related disorders.* Philadelphia: Lea & Febiger, 1972.

Greenberg, R., Becker, D., Miller, J., & Mayer, D. Evaluation of brain function in severe human head trauma with multimodality evoked potentials: Part II. *Journal of Neurosurgery*, 1977, *47*, 163–177.

Greenberg, R., Mayer, D., Becker, D., & Miller, J. Evaluation of brain function in severe human head trauma with multimodality evoked potentials: Part I. *Journal of Neurosurgery*, 1977, *47*, 150–162.

Gudeman, H., & Craine, J. *Principles of neurotraining.* Unpublished manuscript. Kaneohe, Hawaii: Hawaii State Hospital, 1976.

Halstead, W. *Brain intelligence: A quantitative study of the frontal lobes.* Chicago: University of Chicago Press, 1947.

Hamsher, K., & Benton, A. Interactive effects of age and cerebral disease on cognitive performances. *Journal of Neurology*, 1978, *217*, 195–200.

Hayden, M., Kalisky, I., & Hess, A. *Use of Luria's neuropsychological methods on a rehabilitative service.* Paper presented at 8th Annual Meeting of International Neuropsychological Society, San Francisco, 1980.

Hendrie, H. Organic brain disorders: Classification, the "symptomatic" psychoses, misdiagnosis. *The Psychiatric Clinics of North America*, 1978, *1*, 3–19.

Jackson, D. *Personality research form manual.* Goshen, N.Y.: Research Psychologists Press, 1974.

Jastak, J., & Jastak, S. *The wide range achievement test manual of instructions* (rev. ed.). Wilmington, Del.: Jastak Associates, 1978.

Jennett, B. Scale, scope and philosophy of the clinical problem. In CIBA Foundation Symposium 34: *Outcome of severe damage to the central nervous system.* Amsterdam: North Holland, 1975.

Jennett, B. Prognosis after head injury. In P. Vinken & G. Bruyn (Eds.), *Handbook of clinical neurology* (Vol. 24). Amsterdam: North Holland, 1976.

Jennett, B., & Bond, M. Assessment of outcome after severe brain damage: A practical scale. *Lancet*, 1975, *1*, 480–487.

Jennett, B., & Teasdale, G. *Management of severe head injuries.* Philadelphia: Davis, 1981.

Jennett, B., Teasdale, G., & Knill-Jones, R. Prognosis after severe head injury. *CIBA Foundation Symposium 34: Outcome of severe damage to the central nervous system.* Amsterdam: North Holland, 1975.

Jennett, B., Teasdale, G., Galbraith, S., Pickard, J., Grant, H., Braakman, R., Avezaat, C., Maas, A., Minderhoud, J., Vecht, C. J., Heiden, J., Small, R., Caton, W., & Kurze, T. Severe head injuries in three countries. *Journal of Neurology, Neurosurgery, and Psychiatry,* 1977, *40*, 291–298.

John, E. *Neurometrics: Clinical applications of quantitative electrophysiology.* Hillsdale, N.J.: Lawrence Erlbaum Associates, 1977.

Kiresuk, T., & Sherman, R. Goal attainment scaling: A general method for evaluating comprehensive community mental health programs. *Community Mental Health Journal,* 1968, *4*, 443–453.

Knights, R. Problems of criteria in diagnosis: A profile similarity approach. *Annals of the New York Academy of Sciences,* 1973, *205*, 124–131.

Knights, R., & Watson, P. The use of computerized test profiles in neuropsychological assessment. *Journal of Learning Disabilities,* 1968, *1*, 696–709.

Levin, H., O'Donnell, V., & Grossman, R. The Galveston orientation and amnesia test: A practical scale to assess cognition after head injury. *The Journal of Nervous and Mental Disease,* 1979, *167*, 675–684.

Lewis, A. J. *Mechanisms of neurological disease.* Boston: Little, Brown, 1976.

Lezak, M. Living with the characterologically altered brain injured patient. *Journal of Clinical Psychiatry,* 1978, *39*, 592–598.

Luria, A. R. *Restoration of function after brain injury.* New York: Macmillan, 1963.

Luria, A. R., & Majovski, L. Basic approaches used in American and Soviet clinical neuropsychology. *American Psychologist,* 1977, *32*, 959–968.

Luria, A., Naydin, V., Tsvetkova, L., & Vinarskaya, E. Restoration of higher cortical function following local brain damage. In P. Vinkin & G. Bruyn (Eds.), *Handbook of Clinical Neurology* (Vol. 3). Amsterdam: North Holland, 1969.

Lynch, W., & Mauss, N. Brain injury rehabilitation: Standard problem lists. *Archives of Physical Medicine and Rehabilitation,* 1981, *62*, 223–227.

Mahoney, F., & Barthel, D. Functional evaluation: Barthel index. *Maryland State Medical Journal,* 1965, *14*, 61–65.

Martin, A. D. Aphasia testing: A second look at the Porch index of communicative ability. *Journal of Speech and Hearing Disorders,* 1977, *42*, 547–562.

Mauss-Clum, N., & Ryan, M. Brain injury and the family. *Journal of Neurosurgical Nursing,* 1981, *13*, 165–169.

Meldman, M., McFarland, G., & Johnson, E. *The problem-oriented psychiatric index and treatment plans.* St. Louis: Mosby, 1976.

Miller, L. S., & Miyamoto, A. T. Computed tomography: Its potential as a predictor of functional recovery following stroke. *Archives of Physical Medicine and Rehabilitation,* 1979, *60*, 108–109.

Moskowitz, E., & McCann, C. Classification of disability in the chronically ill and aging. *Journal of Chronic Diseases,* 1957, *5*, 342–346.

Oldendorf, W. The quest for an image of the brain: A brief historical and technical review of brain imaging techniques. *Neurology,* 1978, *28*, 517–533.

Osborn, A. Computed tomography in neurologic diagnosis. *Annual Review of Medicine,* 1979, *30*, 189–198.

Osborne, D., & Davis, L. Standard scores for Wechsler memory scale subtests. *Journal of Clinical Psychology,* 1978, *34*, 115–116.

Overall, J., & Gomez-Mont, F. The MMPI-168 for psychiatric screening. *Educational and Psychological Measurement*, 1974, *34*, 315–319.

Overall, J., & Gorham, D. The brief psychiatric rating scale. *Psychological Reports*, 1962, *10*, 799–812.

Peters, B., & Levin, H. Memory enhancement after physostigmine treatment in the amnesic syndrome. *Archives of Neurology*, 1977, *34*, 215–219.

Peters, B., & Levin, H. Effects of physostigmine and lecithin on memory in Alzheimer disease. *Annals of Neurology*, 1979, *6*, 219–221.

Peterson, G. C. Organic brain syndromes associated with brain trauma. In A. M. Freedman, H. I. Kaplan, & B. J. Sadlock (Eds.), *Comprehensive textbook of psychiatry* (2d ed., Vol. I). Baltimore: Williams & Wilkins, 1975.

Porch, B. *The Porch index of communicative ability* (Vol. 1.). Palo Alto, Calif.: Consulting Psychologists Press, 1967.

Porch, B. Multidimensional scoring in aphasia testing. *Journal of Speech and Hearing Research*, 1971, *14*, 776–792.

Porch, B., & Collins, M. *The rating of patient's independence (ROPI)*. Unpublished manuscript. Albuquerque, N.M.: VA Medical Center, 1974.

Porch, B., Collins, M., Wertz, R., & Friden, T. Statistical prediction of change in aphasia. *Journal of Speech and Hearing Research*, 1980, *23*, 312–321.

Rappaport, M., Hall, K., Hopkins, K., Belleza, T., & Cope, N. Disability rating scale for severe head trauma patients: Coma to community. *Archives of Physical Medicine and Rehabilitation* 1982, *63*, 118–123.

Reinstein, L. Problem-oriented medical record: Experience in 238 rehabilitation institutions. *Archives of Physical Medicine and Rehabilitation*, 1977, *58*, 398–401.

Reinstein, L., Staas, W., & Marquette, C. Rehabilitation evaluation system which complements problem-oriented medical record. *Archives of Physical Medicine and Rehabilitation*, 1975, *56*, 396–399.

Reitan, R. An investigation of the validity of Halstead's measures of biological intelligence. *Archives of Neurology and Psychiatry*, 1955, *73*, 28–35.

Reitan, R. A research program on the psychological effects of brain lesions in human beings. In Normal R. Ellis (Ed.) *International review of research in mental retardation* (Vol. 1). New York: Academic Press, 1966.

Reitan, R. M. Neuropsychology: The vulgarization Luria always wanted. *Contemporary Psychology*, 1976, *21*, 737–738.

Rey, A. L'examen clinique en psychologie. Paris: Presses Universitaires de France, 1964. Cited in Lezak, M. *Neuropsychological Assessment*. New York: Oxford, 1976.

Rohmer, F., & Buchheit, F. Clinical appraisal: Diagnostic tests and methods. In P. Vinkin & G. Bruyn (Eds.), *Handbook of clinical neurology*. Amsterdam: North Holland, 1975.

Russell, E. A multiple scoring method for the assessment of complex memory functions. *Journal of Consulting and Clinical Psychology*, 1975, *43*, 800–809.

Russell, E. *The chronicity effect*. Paper presented at the 7th annual meeting of the International Neuropsychological Society, New York, 1979.

Russell, E., Neuringer, C., & Goldstein, G. *Assessment of brain damage: A neuropsychological key approach*. New York: Wiley, 1970.

Sbordone, R., & Caldwell, A. The "OBD-168": Assessing the emotional adjustment to cognitive impairment and organic brain damage. *Clinical Neuropsychology*, 1979, *1*(4), 36–41.

Schuell, H. *The Minnesota test for the differential diagnosis of aphasia*. Minneapolis: University of Minnesota, 1965.

Smith, A. Objective indices of severity of chronic aphasia in stroke patients. *Journal of Speech and Hearing Disorders*, 1971, *36*, 167–207.

Stablein, D., Miller, J., Choi, S., & Becker, D. Statistical methods for determining prognosis in severe head injury. *Neurosurgery*, 1980, *6*, 243–248.

Starr, A. Sensory evoked potentials in clinical disorders of the nervous system. *Annual Review of Neuroscience*, 1978, *1*, 103–127.

Swiercinsky, D. *Manual for adult neuropsychological evaluation*. Springfield, Ill.: Thomas, 1978.

Taylor, R. *Taylor-Johnson temperament analysis manual*. Los Angeles: Psychological Publications, 1968.

Teasdale, G., & Jennett, B. Assessment of coma and impaired consciousness: A practical scale. *Lancet*, 1974, *2*, 81–84.

Teuber, H.-L. Recovery of function after brain injury in man. In *CIBA Foundation Symposium 34: Outcome of severe damage to the central nervous system*. Amsterdam: North Holland, 1975.

Tiffin, J. *Purdue pegboard examiner's manual*. Chicago: Science Research Associates, 1968.

Tsai, L., & Tsuang, M. Computerized tomography and skull x-rays: Relative efficacy in detecting intracranial disease. *American Journal of Psychiatry*, 1978, *135*, 1556–1557.

Tsushima, W., & Popper, J. Computerized tomography: A report of false negative errors. *Clinical Neuropsychology*, 1980, *2*, 130–133.

Wechsler, D. A standardized memory scale for clinical use. *Journal of Psychology*, 1945, *19*, 87–95.

Wells, C., & Duncan, G. *Neurology for psychiatrists*. Philadelphia: Davis, 1980.

Welsh, L., Welsh, J., & Healy, M. Central auditory testing and dyslexia. *Laryngoscope*, 1980, *90*, 972–984.

Willeford, J. Assessing central behavior in children. In R. Keith (Ed.), *Central auditory dysfunction*. New York: Grune & Stratton, 1977.

Yesavage, J., Tinklenberg, J., Hollister, L., & Berger, P. Vasodilators in senile dementias. *Archives of General Psychiatry*, 1979, *36*, 220–223.

Zung, W. A self-rating depression scale. *Archives of General Psychiatry*, 1965, *12*, 63–70.

10

An Elementary Cognitive Assessment and Treatment of the Craniocerebrally Injured Patient

Theodore Najenson, Levy Rahmani, Betty Elazar, and Sara Averbuch

1. Introduction

This chapter aims to present the ongoing work of the Occupational Therapy (OT) Department at the Loewenstein Rehabilitation Hospital and has largely grown out of our practical work with the patients there. Certainly, we have been inspired by the rich literature dealing with these topics. Since other chapters in this volume have amply reviewed available testing procedures (see the chapter by W. J. Lynch), reference is made only to work directly related to this presentation. Furthermore, the work performed by the OT staff is an integral part of the inter-disciplinary rehabilitative activity of this institution (Najenson, Mendelson, Schechler, David, Mintz, & Grosswasser, 1974; Najenson, Grosswasser, & Mendelson, 1980; Najenson, 1980). We thought to focus this paper on this fragment of our rehabilitative program.

Theodore Najenson, Levy Rahmani, Betty Elazar, and Sara Averbuch • Loewenstein Rehabilitation Hospital, Ra'anana, Israel, and University of Tel Aviv, Sackler School of Medicine, Tel Aviv, Israel.

2. Rationale

The cerebral dysfunctions caused by brain lesions, notably those due to head injuries, are expressed in intellectual and/or behavioral changes. These changes are demonstrated by a diminished capacity to carry out daily tasks. The management of the brain-damaged patient and the effort to restore his intellectual–cognitive abilities require their assessment. The study of brain–behavior relationships, in particular under pathological conditions, has been the concern of various disciplines and eventually evolved into a distinct discipline: neuropsychology.

A major task of neuropsychology has been that of developing methods for the measurement of cognitive deficits. Standardized batteries have been elaborated, primarily designed to determine the intellectual deficits produced by localized brain lesions. The tests have also endeavored to reach a differential diagnosis between organic and nonorganic disorders. The set of tests introduced by Halstead (1947) and further developed by Reitan (1974) represent the most elaborate battery to date for these purposes. However, the usefulness of these tests as a starting point for the training of impaired intellectual capacities is limited. Tests that may have proved reliable in making a differential diagnosis appear to be of little use in planning the rehabilitation training.

On the other hand, Luria's (1973) neuropsychological tests, integrated into a set by Christensen (1975) and recently developed into the Luria-Nebraska battery (Golden, 1980), were meant to serve as a guide for the training of the impaired intellectual functions in individual patients. Yet the training carried out by Luria was of a rather limited scope: (1) it was apparently aimed primordially at testing Luria's assumptions about the cerebral localization of intellectual functions; (2) it was reduced to a number of didactic procedures—indeed, masterfully used—to improve the patient's performance on a definitive task; (3) the training, at least as presented in Luria's writings, was not embedded in a comprehensive rehabilitation program; and (4) there was no systematic, periodic follow-up of the patient's performance in his daily duties.

Hence, the need has been acutely felt in our institution to work out a set of tests specifically and prevalently related to rehabilitation purposes. The goals of the multidisciplinary rehabilitation work performed here are (1) to improve the patient's functioning in areas in which his difficulties are rather a direct effect of neurophysiological handicaps; (2) to improve the patient's ability to cope with occupational tasks in terms of their perceptual, mnemonic, practical, and problem-solving demands; and (3) to enhance the patients understanding of his limitations, which is the first condition for accepting them and acting accordingly. It has been our experience that the patient's awareness of his condition in not a purely cognitive ability. It is contingent upon a number of factors, among which are environmental, familial, and employment circumstances. However, such awareness does require a certain level of intellectual ability, which should be attained through cognitive training.

The patient's intellectual abilities should be assessed with the above rehabilitation goals in mind. Thus, the assessment is meant (1) to indicate what the patient's abilities/disabilities are in the areas of perception, memory, language, problem/solving, and praxis; (2) to determine the patient's limits in these areas, so that these may be taken as starting points in the training; (3) to point at environmental and other factors that may have an impact on the level of the patient's intellectual performance; (4) to enable the formulation of specific and graded therapeutic goals; and (5) to enable the assessment of results of the therapy along a number of degrees of complexity until the patient reaches a plateau.

The purpose of this chapter is to present the process of cognitive evaluation and training performed at the basic level handled by the Occupational Therapy Department of our institution in collaboration with and under the supervision of the Psychology Department.

3. Assessment

The evaluation of the craniocerebrally injured (CCI) patient by the occupational therapists-serves a twofold purpose. First, it is meant to provide an initial picture of the intellectual abilities of the individual to whom a head trauma was inflicted and who had lost consciousness for some time. Second, the evaluation should serve as a screening test aimed at indicating the appropriate time for a patient to be referred to the examination carried out by psychologist. Thus, the occupational therapist evaluates the patient's ability to cope with an elementary set of tests as a measure of the intellectual functions thought to be a prerequisite for managing everyday encounters with the environment. A patient of a low premorbid capacity would not be referred to further neuropsychological assessment and training, while a patient of a higher premorbid intellectual capacity (a high school graduate) who passes the OT test is referred to further evaluation. A patient of the latter category who fails the basic test would not be referred to further neuropsychological evaluation and training before he reached the level of passing it.

The set of tests used for the evaluation of the CCI patient at the OT level—as well as the level of neuropsychology—has been chosen on a rather wide empirical basis and is still in the process of being refined. It is a rehabilitation-oriented test; that is to say, it is not primarily designed to differentiate between organic and nonorganic conditions. Neither is it aimed at the localization of cerebral regions, the impairment of which may be responsible for the patient's intellectual disabilities, although the test may suggest certain localization patterns. Its primary goal is to provide a functional picture of the patient's cognitive abilities.

The following is a description of the set tests, which cover nine areas of cognitive functioning.

3.1. The Orientation in Place and Time

The patient is asked whether he knows where he is: Is this a hospital, a school, etc.? He is then asked to grossly locate the institution in one of the major regions of the country mentioned to him. The patient is asked whether he is now at Golan Heights (in the north) or in the Sinai Desert (in the farthest southern area). Loewenstein Hospital is located in the central region of the country about 20 km from Tel-Aviv, so that its location by the patient in Tel-Aviv is accepted.

The patient is asked about how long he has been in the hospital: month, year, the nearest festival, past or forthcoming, etc.

3.2. Visual and Spatial Orientation

The perceptual abilities tested ranged from the identification of clear pictures of objects and their attributes to the identification of objects photographed from unusual angles, embedded and incomplete drawings of objects, identification of changing details in similar pictures, and recongition of spatial relations.

3.2.1. Identification of Objects

The patient is asked to identify a given object, a picture of which is presented to him, among four pictures of objects. This is a nonverbal matching test. The verbal instruction is restricted to a minimum and the patient's response is correct if he points at the picture identical to the target object. Four trials are being done to check for response consistency. In the first trial, the target object is a chair and the four choice objects are fish, tree, teapot, chair; in the second trial, the teapot is target and the choices are chair, teapot, tree, fish; in the third trial, glasses are target, and glasses, key, grapes, bucket, are choice objects; and in the fourth trial, key is target, and bucket, key, teapot, glasses are choice

Figure 1. Visual identification of objects.

objects. For illustration, see Figure 1. The same procedures is used with colors, sizes, and directions.

3.2.1.1. Color Trials. The four color trials are as follows:

1. Target black; choices: green, white, yellow, black
2. Target red; choices: orange, red, purple, white
3. Target orange; choices: orange, red, white, purple
4. Target blue; choices: yellow, black, blue, green

3.2.1.2. Shape Trials. The four shape trials run as follows:

1. Target square; choices; trapezoid, diamond, square, triangle
2. Target triangle; choices: triangle, square, trapezoid, diamond
3. Target circle; choices: hexagon, square, semicircle, circle
4. Target semicircle; choices: rectangle, semicircle, circle, triangle

In another shape trial, a large and a small wooden piece of the same shape are used as target objects; they have to be identified from among four wooden pieces of the same shape but other sizes from small to large.

3.2.1.3. Direction Trials. These tests assess the patient's identification of directions.

1. He is presented with a card showing a child holding a ball and is asked to identify this picture from among three other pictures showing respectively a child holding a ball in his left hand, over his head, and in his right hand.
2. He is presented with a picture showing a table under which there is a bag and is asked to identify this picture from among three other pictures showing respectively a table with a bag on it, a table with a bag at its left, and a table with a bag at its right, under it. See Figure 2.

Only four correct pointing responses for each category of stimuli get

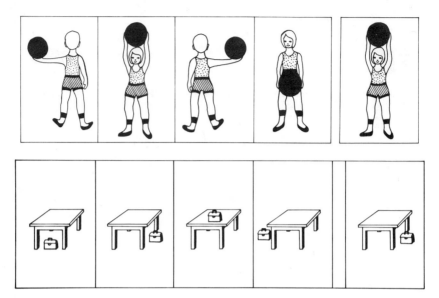

Figure 2. Visual identification of directions.

a 1 score, so that the scores for all identification tests range between 0 and 4. The following tests of visual perception are meant to assess the ability to identify objects when the pictorial information is not optimal; that is, the patients are not given the perceptual information on which the identification of these objects is usually based. The ability to recognize objects or drawings on the basis of partial information and to make inferences about their identity has been shown to be a major feature of normal cognitive functioning (Bruner & Potter, 1964).

Developmental studies have documented the gradual reduction of children's dependence on redundant sensory information for the identification of objects. On this basis, the inclusion of tests to assess the patient's capacity to use reduced visual information about objects for their identification was thought justified.

3.2.2. Identification of Photographs

The photographs used are taken from angles that do not bring into relief those features of objects that usually serve as cues for identification. The photos show a book, a fork, the back side of a car, and the back of a shoe. The response is scored 0 or 1, so that the score ranges between 0 and 4. Figure 3 illustrates the photos used.

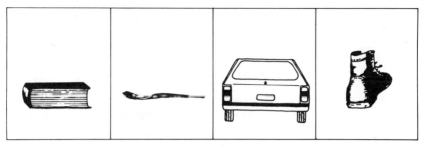

Figure 3. Identification of photos.

3.3. Retention Tests

After the patient's ability to identify things presented to him has been tested, his ability to retain mental representations of objects and their attributes is assessed through another group of tests. The materials used for identification tests are those used for testing patients nmemonic ability except for the size tests, which are inappropriate. The target stimulus—object, color, shape, and orientation—is presented for 5 seconds, then removed from the patient's sight for 30 seconds, during which he is not spoken to or given any task.

3.4. Tests of Linguistic Ability

The testing of the patient's linguistic abilities is restricted, as it is handled primarily by the Department of Communication Disorders. The patient is asked (1) to point to named pictures of objects, the identifica-

Figure 4. Identification of embedded drawings of objects.

tion and recall of which were tested previously, and (2) to name these items. The scoring for both (1) and (2) is identical to that for the identification of items.

The next group of tests assesses the patient's ability to relate a given item to other items associated with it in a relevant way. We have been impressed in our daily contact with patients by the poor mental connections among pieces of information—objects, people, events—when they have to retrieve them from memory. Thus several associations tests were included in the set to assess the ability to abstract common relevant attributes of different things.

3.5. Association Tests

The patient is presented with the picture of a given object and is asked to point at one of four pictures of objects related to it. Four trials are done, each involving a target object and four choice objects:

1. Target: broom; choice objects: dust pan, scissors, glasses, bed
2. Target: cow; choice objects: milk bottle, funnel, butterfly, dustpan
3. Target: paintbrush; choice objects: funel, chicken, scissors, cow
4. Target: chicken; choice objects: scissors, bed, eggs, milk

This test is illustrated in Figure 5.

3.6. Tests of Categorization

Categorization is tested in two trials, in each of which the patient is asked to classify objects into two groups.

Figure 5. Associations among objects.

1. The patient has to group a pile of pictures into pictures of clothes and food. The clothes are a woman's dress, a fur coat, a skirt, a shirt, a pair of pants, and a sweater. The food items are an eggplant, a bunch of grapes, an onion, some beans, a banana, and a lemon. Figure 6 illustrates this test.
2. The patient is asked to divide the food pictures and the clothing pictures into two subgroups. Figure 7 illustrates this test.

The large body of evidence about the difficulties encountered by some brain-damaged individuals in handling items presented sequentially or among which there is a sequential connection prompted us to include in tests a measure of this aspect of cognition. The patient is presented with a set of five pictures in the following sequence:

1. A man holding a ladder approaches an orange tree.
2. He climbs on the ladder, leaning on the tree.
3. He picks oranges and fills up a basket.
4. A girl approaches the tree and the man gets down the ladder.
5. The man gives the girl an orange.

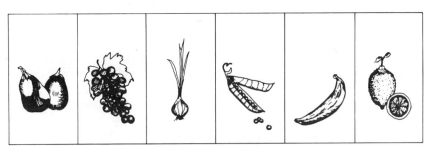

Figure 6. Categorization of objects into classes.

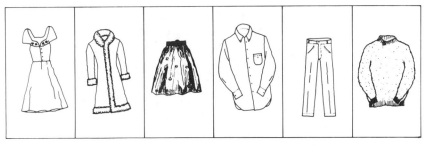

Figure 7. Categorization into subclasses.

Figure 8 illustrates this test.

3.7. Conservation Tests

Conversation tests are given to test logical thinking. (Although objections have recently been raised regarding Piaget's methodology in assessing children's thinking, the ability to make this type of judgment may be regarded as an indicator of elementary logical thinking.)

1. The patient is shown two glasses of the same height but with different circumferences and filled with water to the same level (halfway). He is asked which glass contains more water.
2. The patient is shown two similar containers filled with plasticine; from one we make a ball and from the other a roll. Question: Which has more theraplast?

Brain-damaged patients experience difficulties when faced with the task of copying visually identified forms, building designs using given patterns, and completing models on the basis of given schemes.

3.8. Visual Tests

Motor tests selected for our set evaluate the patient's abilities in some graded manner. The selected parameters are (1) number of dimensions—bidimensional and tridimensional designs, (2) degree of independent reproduction, (3) placing the pieces for the construction of the model on the design or separate from it, (4) use of cues—colored black–white constructional pieces.

Figure 8. Logical sequence of pictures.

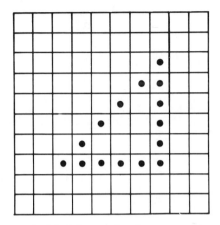

Figure 9. Model reproductions on pegboard.

The systematic assessment of these "praxis" abilities is intended to serve as a guide for training and orienting the patient toward a certain type of activity. Admittedly this systematization is still in need of refinement.

1. The patient is asked to copy four geometric shapes: a triangle, a circle, a square, and a diamond. The copying of the last shape is expected to be more difficult than that of the previous ones. A score of 7 is given for each successful copy, with allowance for inaccuracies due to weakness.

2. The patient has to form a compound geometric shape using plastic tokens which he places on the drawn model. The test consists of two items: (a) a compound form of six shapes: four rectangles and two semicircles; (b) a compound form of four shapes: two triangles, one square, and one circle. An accurate performance yields a score of 1.

3. A pegboard test is given to the patient. It consists of a 2 by 2 in board, the whole surface of which is made of equally spaced holes, a pile of pegs, and three successive cards of the same sizes as the board divided into squares, on which are drawn a cross, a triangle, and a diagonal. The patient is asked to reproduce the drawn designs with pegs on the board. A score of 1 is given for each accurate performance. The materials of the last two tests are part of the Developmental Learning Materials (7440 Natchez Avenue, Niles, IL 60648). Figure 9 illustrates the test.

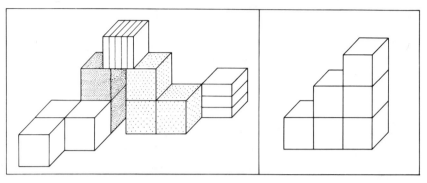

Figure 10. Reproductions of simple block designs.

4. The reproduction of simple block designs not involving perspective, on one plane, done in two variations: (a) colored designs; (b) black-white designs. The test is illustrated in Figure 10.
5. The reproduction of complex block designs require spatial representation as some blocks are partially hidden. This test is also performed in two variations, as was the previous test. The score ranges between 0 and 4. The test is illustrated in Figure 11.
6. The reproduction of a butterfly puzzle by placing the pieces on the model.
7. The patient is asked to draw a watch, a house, a flower, and a cube.

The results obtained with this set of tests on 76 CCI patients and on a group of patients after cerebrovascular accidents were analyzed using

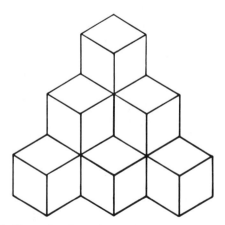

Figure 11. Reproduction of partially hidden block designs.

Figure 12. Reproduction of butterfly puzzle.

Guttman's Small Space Analysis (SSA) with the purpose of getting a picture of the correlations among these tests and attempting to differentiate between neuropsychological profiles. These types of analogies enabled the reduction of the rather large number of test items to a small number of dimensions.

The analysis had a twofold purpose: (1) to reveal in the SSA configuration of tests, a function-related dimensionality, and (2) to map the patients on the test configuration so that their location could differentially indicate impaired intellectual functions. The data analysis pointed at a first dimension clearly separating between tasks involving verbal communication (understanding and actively using the names of objects, colors, shapes, and directions) and perceptual-motor or praxis tasks (copying drawings, reproducing block designs, setting puzzles). A second, less distinct dimension was obtained by distinguishing between tests for intellectual processes (conversation, forming associations and categories of objects), and more complex perceptual or gnostic tasks (identifying objects from partial information) on the one hand and memory on the other.

The data analysis for the cerebrovascular patients pointed at a single dimension that corresponded to neurolinguistic findings on hemispheric preponderant involvement. The validation of the second dimension for the CCI patients is an open issue and more extensive testing of the intellectual ability of these patients is needed. The correlation matrix of items suggests a pattern of relationship between them in terms of "distance" and relative difficulty. This is being taken as a guide for the improvement of the set of tests. Furthermore, this type of analysis may pave the way for the location of each individual patient on the "map" of intellectual functions. As the testing procedures are developed and refined, more detailed statistical analysis will be required.

The available findings could be conceptualized under a number of propositions concerning the effects of brain damage on intellectual functioning. Brain damage reduces the ability to process information. This effect is felt in various degrees in different patients in the processes of recognizing drawings/pictures of objects, of sorting them on the basis of relevant criteria, and storing and retrieving amounts of past and incoming information. In the field of visual perception, patients fail to make inferences about the availability of objects in pictorial representations that supply only partial information, drawings of embedded objects, schematic drawings of objects, and so on. One may notice a certain gradient of the ability to "go beyond the information given" (Bruner, 1973), which seems to be related to the severity of the neurological condition.

In the domain of conceptualization, patients may group objects into broad, clearly distinct categories (e.g., food vs. clothes) but experience difficulties when asked to differentiate between subcategories (kinds of clothes), either because of failure to stick to the same criterion throughout the sorting act or because they get lost when dealing with a large number of items. Additional classification tests not included in the standard set described here have shown that patients may be able to sort things using an appropriate criterion when a small number of items are involved and become inconsistent with a larger number of items. They may take a given attribute as sorting criterion (e.g., shape) but fail to disregard a complementary attribute (e.g., color, pieces of the same shape are arranged in the same order according to their colors); pick up a criterion but fail to shift to another one; or fail to separate shape from size. Patients appear to have difficulties in approaching an object as belonging to more than one group, or, as Rosch (1978) put it, to assess the degree to which an object is prototypical for a given category as determined by the extent to which it bears a family resemblance to other members of that category.

The reduced ability of traumatically brain-damaged patients is expressed in a relatively low capacity to recall newly learned material. Specifically, this limitation is mirrored in (1) limited amount of information that can be stored/retrieved; (2) poor organization or the material to be recalled, an obvious feature particularly when verbal material is concerned (e.g., the recall of a story); (3) dependence on extensive cueing—patients need leading questions, pieces of information that they can associate with the information they unsuccessfully try to bring to the fore spontaneously; (4) a marked disturbing effect of events interfering between the registration of information and its retrieval.

The brain damage appears to weaken the formation of mental schemata, the structuring of information, its clustering into larger units. The previously acquired experienced is poorly crystallized into general models with which incoming stimuli can be compared so that adequate responses may be produced. This poor comparison of the incoming information with mental models results in a failure to gain a quick grasp of relevant features. The information is poorly assimilated as validation/invalidation of expectancies based on previous experiences. This may account for the slow performances of many of the tested patients.

4. Treatment

The general purpose of training the processes of perception, conceptualization, and memory has been to broaden the patients' capacity to handle information and transform it into purposeful actions (Rahmani, 1981a, 1981b). The training is expected to lead to a gradual transformation of the actual manipulation of objects into inner mental representations of these actions and of the properties of handled objects. Furthermore, it is expected to result in a subsequent generalization and abbreviation of the external, actual operations (Galperin, 1969). The training should lead to a more systematic search for information. The patients are assisted in generalizing adequately from their previous experience. They are trained to become less dependent on variations of objects that they are already familiar with and encouraged to focus on relevant information. In the course of training, the patients' acquaintance with the structure of things, with the relative roles held by their attributes, is enriched. Patients are encouraged to assess changes in pictorial representations of objects, to decide which of them are within the same category and which make the transition to a different category. The testing described above indicates the base on which the training is to be constructed.

The three levels described below and illustrated in the two cases are roughly landmarks in the training process—from elementary to complex, from concrete to more abstract, from less to more information to be handled. A level is characterized by a certain amount of information to be processed, by its being a prerequisite for training at the next level, by developing skills to handle more complex tasks. Thus, patients are trained to identify pictures by analyzing their features to prepare them to cope with the recognition of more complex pictorial material. They are trained to find similarities and differences between things to enable them to group them adequately. The impaired intellectual functions are trained according to the results of the tests. Three levels are being presented here for the sake of schematization.

4.1. Training of Visual Perception

4.1.1. Level I

The purpose of training is to attain the identification of concrete objects, isolated attributes of objects, and clear pictures of objects. Three procedures are used:

1. Various objects are presented, first separately and then together. (Touch is used as an additional source of information whenever necessary).
2. After the patient has become acquainted with the objects and is able to recognize them among others, he is trained to discern their relevant attributes—color, shape, size—and to identify toys or miniature models.
3. The patient is then trained to identify pictorial and schematic presentations of these objects. The major procedure is that of drawing the patient's attention toward the relevant and specific features of objects and their pictorial presentations. "Relevance" is assessed in terms of a feature's role for the specific functioning of an object. For instance, the patient's attention is oriented toward the relevance of "pointedness" and "elongation" of pencils and pens; an object or a picture which does not possess these features is unlikely to be a writing tool. The patient's familiarization with ways of identifying the perceptual world is tested on objects/pictures not used in the training.

4.1.2. Level II

The purpose of training at this level is to attain the identification of:

1. Pictures of various degrees of ambiguity
2. Photos of objects taken from angles that do not provide the information usually obtained from viewing these objects
3. Embedded drawings of objects
4. Objects on the basis of parts of them

The training uses the following procedures:

1. Identification of pictures of objects while lying in bed
2. Identification of pictures of objects rotated 45, 90, and 180 degrees
3. Identification of objects and of drawings partially hidden by other objects/drawings
4. Identification of objects on the basis of their most relevant features
5. Identification of pictures of varying degrees of ambiguity, the milder degrees of ambiguity serving as cues for the identification of more ambiguous variations of the same pictures

4.1.3. Level III

The purpose of perceptual training at this level is to enable subtle discrimination between objects. The following procedures are used:

1. Comparison of two pictures differing from each other in a single detail
2. Elimination of one exceptional picture from a set of four pictures
3. Matching pictures with a large number of variables

4.2. Training of Spatial Perception

4.2.1. Level I

The purpose of the training is that of the orientation in the personal space. The procedures used are:

1. Familiarization with body parts and their location
2. Making the patient aware of the body's middle line and the right–left position of body parts
3. Execution of commands demanding crossing of the middle line (e.g., instructing the patient: "point with your right hand to your left eye.")

4.2.2. Level II

The purpose of this level is the orientation in the extrapersonal space. Procedures: identification of the position of objects placed near–far from the patient, above–under, and at his left–right sides; for the identification of the left–right positions, pairs of objects are presented the right–left position of which is relevant (e.g., knife and fork; match and matchbox).

4.2.3. Level III

The purpose is that of recognition of spatial reversals. The main procedures are:

1. Identification of right–left parts on the body of the trainer facing the patient; in the course of training, the trainer points at his right and left arms while sitting behind the patient so that their location is identical; while sitting at the patient's right and left sides; and only subsequently facing him.
2. The patient is trained to differentiate between right–left sides of different objects from the observer's perspective: the right–left side of a bisected line; the right–left, outwards/inwards position of the point of a pencil placed before the trainer and trainee facing each other.

4.3. Training of Constructional Activities

4.3.1. Level I

The purpose of training at this level is that of enabling the patient to transfer simple perceptual models into motor acts; that is, the reproduce visual–perceptual designs. The following procedures are used:

1. Copying simple forms
2. Reproduction of simple designs compounded of clearly distinct parts which readily match the constructional pieces that have to be placed on the model itself

4.3.2. Level II

At this stage, the patient is trained for more demanding constructional activities in terms of components. The following procedures are used:

1. Reproduction of a model requiring counting (of dots) and accurate location of compounding parts
2. Reproduction of models outside them, first with pieces readily matching the parts of the model and then with pieces that have to be put together to obtain the compounding parts of the model

3. Copying of more complex forms such as a cube and reconstruction with cubes
4. Reproduction of block designs

4.3.3. Level III

Construction based on a given plan with pieces of Lego, Techno, Fisher, or Mechano.

4.4. Training of Thinking

4.4.1. Level I

The purpose of training at this level is to develop elementary logical thinking, basic classification skills, and understanding of simple logical sequences. Procedures:

1. Conservation tests of the kind known from Piaget's studies are used to develop the patient's ability to overcome perceptual appearances.
2. Patients are familiarized with a set of several pictures representing a simple sequence of events.
3. Training in the assignment of pictures of objects to a number of categories and subcategories (food—vegetables, fruit, clothes). The patient is trained to make distinctions between relevant and irrelevant features of objects, to shift from one criterion to another.

4.4.2. Level II

The purpose of training at this level is that of developing the logical operations of transitivity and the understanding of cause–effect relations. Procedures:

1. Solving logical problems involving three, four, five, or more interrelated compounding parts.
2. Matrices.
3. Verbal material is used consisting of questions and answers, excerpts of read stories, drawing conclusions, giving a title to stories and to excerpts read from them.
4. Serially ordered items are handled and the patient is trained to recognize these series, when they vary along one or another feature, to supply missing links.

4.4.3. Level III

The purpose of training at this level is that of improving the patient's ability to solve problems requiring the use of the conclusion drawn from one stage to the next.

4.5. Training of Topographic Memory

4.5.1. Level I

The purpose of training at this level is that of assisting the patient to orient himself in his immediate environment—that is, in the OT department. The procedures used are those of providing the patient with an instruction sheet and accompanying him while he is trying to find his way out.

4.5.2. Level II

At this level the patient is trained to find his way from one treatment department to another.

4.5.3. Level III

The patient's orientation is broadened to the environment of the hospital and the way home. At this stage the training develops topographic representations and concepts.

5. Case Histories

Patient A. M.

A. M., a 35-year-old economist, was married and had three children. Previously successful in a high executive position, he showed great organizational talent. He was injured in a road accident, remained unconscious for 2 weeks, and was markedly confused, restless, and aggressive for an additional 2 months. Gradually he improved and became more cooperative. The following deficits were revealed at his first examination:

Orientation. Severely disoriented in time and place. He was unaware of being in hospital and claimed to be at home. He did not know where he was—in his room, on the floor of his ward, in the nurse's room, or in the dining room. Time seemed to be a concept that he was not capable of relating to.

Short-Term Memory. A. M. was not capable of retaining the image of an object or of someone's physiognomy for even a few minutes. He would identify

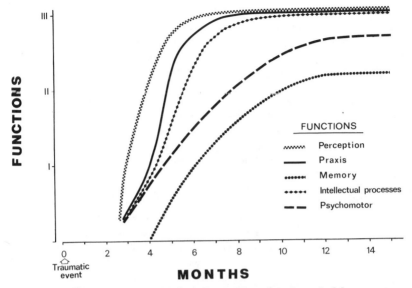

Figure 13. Course of improvement of patient A. M.

an object, but the moment he turned away from it, the thing was blocked out of his memory. He seemed puzzled by questions like "What did you see before?" He could not remember having seen something. He displayed the same behavior when faced with words, conversations, commands, or anything that is expected to be stored in one's memory for a short period of time. He recognized the close members of his family yet confused the names and ages of the children.

Long-Term Memory. He recalled events before the accident but was not capable of reporting them in an organized sequential manner. There were large areas that A. M. tended to fill in with confabulations.

Other Cognitive Functions. Visual perception, praxis abilities, and logical thinking as assessed by the OT set of tests were normal. As long as a task did not require the recall of stimulus material, the patient coped with it quite adequately.

Treatment. It was necessary at first to help the patient orient himself in the area of the hospital, to identify his room and the people looking after him. We worked with him on three parallel planes: by means of conversations, written instruction, and the systematic enrichment of his everyday experiences. The information about surroundings, routine daily events, and people was given to him bit by bit. New items were added as he mastered previous ones. The therapist helped him seek visual and verbal associations that could help him to remember. For example, his doctor was a fat man who used to smoke a pipe; the psychiatrist was a short bearded man; the name of the occupational therapist was like the name of the first mother in the Bible.

Each time A. M. tried to remember certain pieces of information at the therapist's request, he was prompted to use the association formed in the course of his training. The spatial cues were reinforced on every occasion. The same procedures were used for spatial orientation. Every picture on the wall in the corridors, every vase or window, served as a landmark on his way to physiotherapy, speech therapy, and so on. The training was prolonged and took place several times a day.

In the early stages of the training, the patient felt at a loss with the use of these memory cues. Gradually, he succeeded in managing with the reliance on associations without the therapist's prompting. Later on, he became progressively less dependent on clues. A. M. extensively wrote down things he had to remember in his notebook, guided by the therapist. He recorded the times of treatment, the names of the people treating him, and the names of visitors, and he even prepared summaries of what was happening. A heavy stress was placed on training the ability to classify various items as a means of strengthening the encoding of sorted materials in memory. Four cards for each of the categories were presented, such as animal and food. The patient had first to remember the category. He did this quite easily. Then he was asked to remember the items included in the categories. The number of items was gradually increased and the semantic distance between the groups of objects was reduced by using subcategories, such as milk products and meat products or male and female clothing.

At this stage of the treatment, we began to work on the recall of excerpts from newspapers and books that did not involve more than 10 to 15 simple, concrete, and clear informative items. The content analysis of the material and its division into meaningful parts, pointing at the logical sequence of events or ideas, was a major feature of this training. A. M. was guided in this process and prompted to use it as a memory technique. Thus, when he was asked about material read and failed to recall it, he was asked questions like: What kind of story was it? About people, animals? What sort of things happend, comic or otherwise? Was it funny? Was it about a man or a woman? A. M. indeed started employing this self-cueing method and reached the point when he was able to recall articles of newspapers and short chapters of books. The patient is now capable of remembering details of everyday life quite reliably. He still has to rely on his notebook to plan his daily work schedule.

Patient: S. L.

S. L., a 37-year-old doctor of psychology, was hospitalized with full right hemiplegia and aphasia. He cognitive difficulties were as follows:

Gnosis. He readily identified objects and their qualities (color, shape, size). However, he had a hard time when he attempted to identify pictures containing partial information or to discriminate between a number of details. He also had great difficulty in grasping rather complex scenic pictures.

Spatial Orientation. S. L. could identify body parts but was at a loss when asked to indicate directions (right/left and up/down) on the body of the examiner sitting opposite him and occasionally on his own body. He failed to cross the midline and he could not cope with tasks demanding orientation in extrapersonal space.

Praxic Functions.   S. L. was unable to dress himself, a difficulty that quite obviously stemmed from spatial problems and from deficits in motor planning. He was able to reproduce models of average difficulty but failed to grasp the models as gestalts and went about by reproducing them in a piecemeal manner. The reconstructional activities demanded great concentration; the moment he lost the thread of continuity, he made rather gross mistakes and had to begin the process anew.

Intellectual Processes.   There were blatant difficulties at the level of simple nonverbal categorization tasks such as sorting on the basis of a simple criterion (by color as opposed to shape or visa versa). It was hard for him to choose a criterion and stick to it.

Treatment.   Since S. L. was so widely impaired cognitively that a training plan was worked out with most basic functions for everyday management at the top of the list. We set improvement of spatial orientation as our first task.

We began by training S. L. to distinguish between parts of the left and right sides of his body. A number of procedures were used. Motor tasks were given that had to be performed in the midline, with the left hand helping the right. The left functional side was given preponderance both in feeling and handling things. Practice was given in dressing by emphasizing not only the dressing act as such but also making the patient aware of his body. We used a mirror as an additional aid.

S. L. was most cooperative and we were able to rely heavily throughout therapy on his most important intellectual asset: his ability to understand the therapist's instructions. His aphasic disorders were manifest only on presentation of more complex linguistic material. Every treatment was started with an explanation of its nature and aim, so that the patient became an active partner. As he became oriented to the left/right sides of his body, he attained almost full independence in his dressing. There was a smooth transfer to orientation in the extrapersonal space, including reversals (identification of right/left body parts) on the body of the therapist facing him. However, until quite recently, the planning and execution of tasks requiring spatial orientation remained slow.

Gnosis.   The purpose of training the identification process was that of broadening the identification range to include more complete pictorial materials. We took advantage of S. L.'s tendency to dismantle every complex task. Thus, we broke down the pictures to be identified into their detail and classified these details according to their relevance and information value. In the course of training, we also used pictures of identical objects differing from each other in one, two, or three small details so as to sharpen S. L.'s search for meaningful information. Differently phrased, we focused on the recognition of features that are common to varying examples of the same kind of object as opposed to features that vary between objects.

Intellectual Processes.   We worked on a variety of tasks involving the processing of verbal material. This was done in close cooperation with the speech therapist. The training proceeded on two planes. First, extensive work was done on grouping objects and identifying concepts both related to objects of common use and arbitrary combinations of attributes of abstract stimuli such as geometric

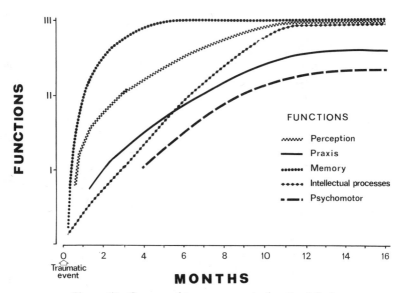

Figure 14. Course of improvement of patient S. L.

shapes of varying colors and sizes. We aimed to develop the ability to categorize in an appropriate and consistent manner. The number of items to be processed was gradually increased. The bases for classification were systematically varied. Following Rosch's (1978) suggestions, we trained S. L. to approach objects as belonging to various categories with varying degrees of representation and "family resemblance." In the process, we encouraged him to give verbal accounts of his conceptualization attempts and to speak out his hypotheses. Second, we concentrated on solving matrices, grasping series of items both pictorial and verbal in the form of logical sequence of events. We worked on the solution of logical problems. The ways in which the various types of tasks can be handled were analyzed. We endeavored to develop some general schemes that could serve S. L. as guidelines.

As we progressed, we included professional material in the training. S. L. read psychology texts and was asked to summarize short paragraphs orally or in writing. In the early stages of the training, this proved to be an overwhelming and frustrating task. He was stopped by sentences that he painfully failed to grasp. Quite understandably, S. L. often substituted for the meaning of these texts irrelevant terms and phrases drawn from his psychological vocabulary. We made extensive use of leading questions to help the patient organize the material. In this, we insisted upon getting answers strictly related to the questions, provided either orally or in writing. S. L. compliantly coped with this task, and after a while our efforts began to bear fruit. We could follow his steady improvement and the point was reached when he could prepare an accurate abstract of a rather lengthy paragraph. This point, at Level III, we reached after about 10 months. As yet, his work is slow, but he is definitely organized and systematic in his thinking.

Current Status. By now S. L. walks with the help of a cane. His right hand is not functional. S. L. has overcome most of his difficulties and performs at acceptable levels. Whenever he feels the need, he makes use of procedures that he acquired during training. In the performance of certain tasks he is slow and obsessive—there is some exacerbation of a premorbid personality trend—and he may be somewhat easily perturbed.

As a final stage of his training, S. L. was provided by psychologists on the hospital's staff with tests for analysis and report. He fulfilled this task in a very satisfactory manner. S. L. is now in the course of returning to work.

ACKNOWLEDGMENTS

The authors wish to thank Dorit Hafner and Yaffa Yardeni for their assistance in testing and training the patients, Batia Yedid-Levy for her contribution to preparing tasks used in training, and Amnon Ben-Zvi for the analysis of findings.

6. References

Bruner, J. S. *Beyond information given.* New York: Norton, 1973.

Bruner, J. S., & Potter, M. Interference in visual recognition. *Science,* 1964, *144,* 424–425.

Christensen, A. L. *Luria's neuropsychological investigation.* New York: Spectrum, 1975.

Galperin, P. J. Stages in the development of mental acts. In M. Cole & J. Maltzman (Eds.), *A handbook of contemporary Soviet psychology.* New York: Basic Books, 1969.

Golden, C. J. A standardized version of Luria's neuropsychological tests: A quantitative and qualitative approach to neuropsychological evaluation. In S. B. Filskov & T. J. Boll (Eds.), *Handbook of clinical neuropsychology.* New York: Wiley, 1980.

Halstead, W. C. *Brain and intelligence: A quantitative study of the frontal lobes.* Chicago: University of Chicago Press, 1947.

Luria, A. R. *The working brain.* London: Allen Lane. The Penguin Press, 1973.

Najenson, T., Mendelson, L., Schechter, I., David, C., Mintz, N., & Groswasser, Z.: Rehabilitation after severe head injury. *Scandinavian Journal Rehabilitation Medicine,* 1974, *6,* 5–14.

Najenson, T., Groswasser, Z., & Mendelson, L. Rehabilitation outcome of brain damaged patients after severe head injury. *International Rehabilitation Medicine,* 1980, *2,* 17–22.

Najenson, T. *Rehabilitation of severely brain injured patients.* Lecture at the 4th Annual Post-graduate Course on the Rehabilitation of the Traumatic Brain Injured Adult, Williamsburg, Virginia, 1980.

Rahmani, L. *Neuro-cognitive theory and the intellectual rehabilitation of brain-damaged patients.* Paper presented at the Workshop on Recovery from Brain Damage, Rotterdam, April 1981.

Rahmani, L. The intellectual rehabilitation of brain-damaged patients. *Clinical Neuropsychology.* In press.

Reitan, R. N. Methodological problems in clinical neuropsychology. In R. N. Reitan & L. A. Davison (Eds.), *Clinical neuropsychology: Current status and application.* Washington, D.C.: Winston, 1974.

Rosch, E. Principles of categorization. In E. Rosch & B. Lloyd (Eds.), *Cognition and categorization.* Hillsdale, N.J.: Erlbaum, 1978.

Index